Astrology and Cosmology in the World's Religions

Astrology and Cosmology in the World's Religions

Nicholas Campion

NEW YORK UNIVERSITY PRESS
New York and London

NEW YORK UNIVERSITY PRESS
New York and London
www.nyupress.org

References to Internet websites (URLs) were accurate at the time of writing. Neither the author nor New York University Press is responsible for URLs that may have expired or changed since the manuscript was prepared.

Library of Congress Cataloging-in-Publication Data
Campion, Nicholas.
Astrology and cosmology in the world›s religions / Nicholas Campion.
p. cm.a
Includes bibliographical references (p.   ) and index.
ISBN 978-0-8147-1713-4 (cl : alk. paper)
ISBN 978-0-8147-1714-1 (pb : alk. paper)
ISBN 978-0-8147-0842-2 (ebook)
ISBN 978-0-8147-4445-1 (ebook)
1. Astrology. 2. Cosmology. 3. Religions. . Religion. I. Title.
BF1729.R4C355 2012
202'.4 — dc23
2012008639

Manufactured in the United States of America
c 10 9 8 7 6 5 4 3 2 1
p 10 9 8 7 6 5 4 3 2 1

To my parents

Contents

Acknowledgments

I thank Ben Adams, Bruce Masse, David Pankenier, Keith Snedegar, and Ivan Sprajc for their very helpful comments on early drafts.

Cosmology and Religion

Measurement and Meaning

It has long been known that the first systems of representation that man made of the world and of himself were of religious origin. There is no religion that is not both a cosmology and a speculation about the divine.[1]

We are a way for the cosmos to know itself. We are creatures of the cosmos and always hunger to know our origins, to understand our connection with the universe.[2]

There is no human society that does not somehow, in some way, relate its fears, concerns, hopes, and wishes to the sky, and to the organizing principle behind it, the cosmos. Neither is there any society that does not express at least some fascination with the sky and its mysteries. This is as true of modern culture as of ancient culture—witness the media attention given to recent revelations, via the Hubble and Herschel telescopes, of strange and wonderful visions of far-distant parts of the universe, millions of light-years from our own planet. It is still the case that "Like every earlier culture, we need to know our place in the universe. Where we are in time, space, and size is part of situating ourselves in the epic of cosmic evolution."[3] And note the rise, in tandem with 20th-century cosmology, of beliefs in alien visitation and abduction, and of contact with spiritually superior beings from other worlds. For many modern cosmologists, cosmology itself remains a human study, we ourselves lying at the heart of it.

This book considers cosmology as a meaning-system, examining its relationship with religion. It focuses on astrology, which is the practical implementation of cosmological ideas in order to understand the past, manage the present, and forecast the future, in a range of cultures, past and present. It deals with mythic narratives, ways of seeing the sky, and the manner in which human beings locate themselves in space and time. It looks at magic, ritual, and the actions that people take to negotiate destiny and find meaning in the stars. Among the themes covered are the use of celestial myth and story to provide insight and meaning, the role of sky and stellar deities as organizing principles in both social and political organization, as well as in sacred texts and calendars, and the understanding of stars as offering a path to salvation.

This book opens new territory that will be of use for the study of comparative religion, especially addressing such issues as origin myths, sacred calendars, and time and destiny, as well as the question of astrology as an application of, and aid to, religious behavior. It will also be of great interest to astronomers, who are concerned with the history of their subject, its wider relevance, and such areas as "ethnoastronomy" and "cultural astronomy."

Astronomical theory fed through into the political and religious thought of the ancient world, when the sun, the king of heaven, was the celestial counterpart of the emperor on earth.[4] The connection of the stars to politics is no less insistent in the modern world. Notions of the celestial emperor were challenged in the 18th century when radicals seized on Isaac Newton's demonstration that the entire universe was governed by one natural law, gravity, in order to argue the consequence—that all human society, being an integral part of the cosmos, must also be governed by one law, kings included. By the end of the century Newtonians, flushed by the discovery that planetary orbits could be explained by mathematics alone, with no need for divine intervention, began to promote scientific arguments for atheism. And so, the notions of the rule of law, taken for granted in Western-style democracy, and of a world without a supernatural creator, can be seen, in part, as functions of astronomical-political theory. More recently, Einsteinian relativity—from which it can be argued that there is no fixed center to the universe, only an infinite series of observers trapped forever in their own reference points—has encouraged the onward march of cultural relativity, the ultra-liberal belief that, as no one culture is "central," all cultural perspectives and practices must be respected on their own terms. All such views are versions of what I term the Cosmic State, the application of cosmological theory to political ideology and the management of society.

We might call such political opinions cosmic, or cosmological, a description endowing them with a power which that other classical word, "universe," completely lacks; if we describe something as universal we know it is everywhere, but if we describe it as cosmological it has depth. *Universus* is the primary Latin word that replaced the Greek *Kosmos* for Latin writers. *Unus verto* means literally "changing into one" and is closer in meaning to the Greek *panta*—everything—than to "cosmos." Given Latin's legalistic nature (it was the language of law and civic matters) as opposed to Greek's continued use as the language of philosophy, *universus* represents the Roman view of the world—as a unified collection of people subject to Roman law. Universe, we might say, is a matter of quantity, but cosmos is concerned with quality.

The questions this text poses of cosmology are, first, How does it tell stories? Second, How does it assign meaning? And third, How is such meaning manifested in the detailed activities that are its primary functions, such as managing time, understanding the self, pursuing salvation, or predicting the future, all of which can be gathered together under the heading of astrology? Each chapter covers a different region and religious worldview and has a different emphasis. Some, particularly those that concern the Mediterranean and Near Eastern worlds and their intellectual descendants, contain obvious overlaps. Some have more of a historical emphasis, some modern, and, in others, the distinction is irrelevant. All, though, offer common ways of seeing the cosmos as an integrated, interdependent whole in which the sky and the earth are reflections of each other and the movements of the heavenly bodies function simultaneously as a demonstration of universal order and constant variety, indicating a dialectical and symbiotic relationship between repetitive constancy and endless change, and revealing messages and meaning to those who care to look and listen. Order and permanence, variety and change are, as Seneca wrote, at odds. His view, common among many cultures that value social order, was that change undermines order: "Deviation by nature from her established order in the world," he argued, "suffices for the destruction of the race."[5]

Most cultures share the notion of the sky as a theatrical device, a stage on which celestial dramas are played out. In China, "the sky was like the setting of a stage on which all kinds of events were happening."[6] For the Maya, meanwhile, "The sky is a great pageant that replays creation in the pattern of its yearly movements."[7] Many cultures also assume the relativity of time and space. For the Aztecs, it has been said, "time and space were naturally juxtaposed."[8] They moved in step with each other and were inseparable—one could not be understood or perceived without the other.

But what, exactly, is cosmology? This book is concerned with cultures from around the world, but the discussion of what cosmology is happens to be mainly a concern of Western scholars. In one sense, cosmology is "the science, theory or study of the universe as an orderly system, and of the laws that govern it; in particular, a branch of astronomy that deals with the structure and evolution of the universe."[9] This, of course, is a modern view, emphasizing the *logos* of cosmology as a study, as the detached, scientific investigation of the cosmos. In a different context the *logos* might be the word, which is how it is translated in the famous opening passage of John's Gospel, suggesting that the cosmos is an entity which speaks to us. This is the standard premodern perspective, in which the study of the cosmos aids understanding of the nature of existence. In Islam, cosmos can therefore be understood as the vehicle by which one obtains knowledge of the external world (*al-ʿalam al-khaariji*), as opposed to the inner world within each person (*al-ʿalam al-daakhili*). In this sense, the cosmos, by which we mean everything other than God, is therefore a means for God to speak to humanity.

"Cosmos" is a word of Greek origin that translates roughly as "beautiful order," a meaning probably used first by one of the 5th- and 6th-century BCE philosophers Parmenides or Pythagoras. In the Greek conception, as expressed through such influential schools of thought as the Platonic and Stoic, the cosmos is, simply, beautiful. It may be an "order," but is also an "adornment." The Romans converted "cosmos" into their word *Mundus*, which for us means mundane, or worldly. As Pliny (23/4–79 CE) wrote:

> The Greeks have designated the world by a word that means "ornament," and we have given it the name of mundus, because of its perfect finish and grace. For what could be more beautiful than the heavens which contain all beautiful things? Their very names make this clear: Caelum (heavens) by naming that which is beautifully carved; and Mundus (world), purity and elegance.[10]

Hans Jonas summed up one version of the classical approach in his study of the Gnostics, whose cosmology he described as follows:

> By a long tradition this term ["cosmos"] had to the Greek mind become invested with the highest religious dignity. The very word by its literal meaning expresses a positive evaluation of the object—any object—to which it is accorded as a descriptive term. For *cosmos* means "order" in general, whether of the world or a household, of a commonwealth, of a life: it is a term of praise and even admiration.[11]

In some religions, such as classical Gnosticism, the cosmos itself can become an object of veneration. One might even identify in some forms of religious cosmology a species of what Festugière called cosmic piety, a reverence for cosmic order almost as divine in itself.[12] And, against the pietists and cosmophiles, who believe that the cosmos is essentially good, we might pose the cosmophobes, for whom it is essentially threatening and something to be escaped (as in the case of the most pessimistic Gnostics) or dominated (as by those well-funded modern scientists who depend on research grants to avert the threat of future collision with rogue asteroids or comets). The cosmophobes, meanwhile, are represented by Blaise Pascal's often-quoted infinite dread of the endless, silent eternity of the universe.

Some classicists actually use "world" as a translation for Greek *kosmos*.[13] The leap from "heavens" into "world" is a useful one, challenging the general modern distinction between what is down here and what is up there. Cosmology is therefore a matter not just of exploring the far reaches of the universe but of recognizing that we are an integral part of it and that our environments, our houses, feelings, families, communities, towns, and cities are part of the cosmos as much as are the sky and stars. This is why, in premodern cultures, kinship structures could have correlates with the heavens:

> It has been proposed that kinship itself constructs social systems according to cultural rules. Different Kinship systems may transform notions of personhood, gender, the transmission of ancestral substance to offspring, metaphysics and cosmology.[14]

Great cities, such as Baghdad, might have been founded when the planets were in an auspicious alignment and designed in accordance with the principles that, it was thought, underlay the cosmic order, but nothing in traditional cosmology is ever permanent. Among the North American Lakota people, "Far from being a static entity, cosmology is dynamic, changing and moving through time as ritual moves through space."[15] The most immediate exemplars of cosmic power are heat from the sun and light from both the sun and moon, but also wind, rain, and the change of weather through the day and the seasons. In pre-modern cultures we may even use "nature" as a convenient synonym for "cosmos."[16]

A cosmology is also a conception of the cosmos, a thought that takes us back to the notion of cosmos not of something that encompasses us but as an idea that we create. We can identify different cosmologies, many of which may have common features but that are all the products of their own cultures. The ecologist Freya Mathews's words are appropriate here. She considered that

Cosmologies . . . are conditioned by many and various historical, environmental, technological, psychological and social factors. A flourishing community is likely to evolve a bright, self-affirming cosmology, and a languishing community is likely to see the world in darker shades. . . . A good cosmology . . . is good for its adherents.[17]

She added that, having been constructed, a cosmology achieves a life of its own, like any other ideology, becoming an active force. As an example, we might point to millenarian beliefs that the cosmos is heading toward cataclysmic destruction—and perhaps rebirth; such beliefs have long been a force in revolutionary politics, as well as an inspiration in more harmless activities such as radical art movements.[18]

If we adopt a broad understanding of cosmology, the difference between traditional and modern cosmologies disappears. The historian Steve McCluskey is persuasive on the matter. Writing of Native American cosmologies, he argued that they

display those general characteristics of "traditional" understandings of nature: conservatism, resistance to change and a close interconnectness with society, myth, and ritual. This should not be taken as a defining characteristic, however[,] for in this regard they differ only in degree from modern scientific cosmologies. Like modern cosmologies they are tied to empirical observations of celestial phenomena, to theoretical models that render those observations intelligible, and to general explanatory themata that guide a whole range of a culture's intellectual, political, and artistic endeavors, including those theoretical models themselves.[19]

For pre-modern cultures, the cosmos was interior as much as exterior; it was inside us as much as outside us. The implications of such a view are considerable for what it is to be human and take us toward those cosmogonies (theories about the origin of the universe) in which the gods and goddesses—or God—made people in their own image; humanity is then reflective of the creative force from which the cosmos is engendered. The individual, both in mind and body, becomes a replica of the cosmos, expressing hopes, fears, desires, and expectations that follow an order evident in the motion of the celestial bodies. In China, "state and the body were so interdependent that they are best considered a single complex."[20] In this sense the body itself becomes an expression of cosmology, or even, as in traditional African philosophy, a cosmology in itself.[21] Cosmogonies themselves may be classed either as chaotic on the one hand, emanating in unplanned steps from an original formless state that is simultaneously something and nothing or, on the other hand, as cosmic, created as a deliberate act by a creator God.[22] Such schemes may pose emanation of the cosmos out of matter (as in Babylon, where it emerged out of water), or consciousness (as in classical Platonic thought). We find chaotic cosmogonies in China, Polynesia, and ancient Egypt, while Judaism, Christianity, and Islam include the most important examples of cosmic cosmogonies.

One of the great issues in comparative cosmology is universalism, which is now out of fashion but pervades the literature of the 1960s and earlier and argues that people in geographically diverse cultures share certain fundamental, universally valid conceptions of the cosmos. One who followed this line was the anthropologist and structuralist Claude Lévi-Strauss. He viewed calendar rituals and star stories as containing encoded information about such matters as fertility, both of the land and of people, and sexual relationships, both on earth and in the sky, and as revealing of common ways of thinking in multiple cultures.[23] Yet, there is a simple problem with Lévi-Strauss's work. His attempt to identify underlying hidden patterns in myths relied on the unproven notion that they correspond to a structure that is both universal and can be expressed through mathematical formulae. He could achieve such precision only by incorporating anomalies and contradictions as mathematically precise "reversals," adjusting the facts to fit his theory.[24] Another popular version of what we call "essentialism," the notion that there is an underlying essential reality, is the psychologist C. G. Jung's theory of archetypes, innate ideas that inhabit the universal collective unconscious.[25] In the final analysis, essentialism is only a useful model: The existence of an underlying reality can no more be proved than can that other favorite of the modern scientific cosmologist, the parallel universe. Current scholarship tends to emphasize localism, focusing on the distinctive characteristics of different cosmologies. The attempt to avoid the generalizations inherent in universalism, though, bring their own misconceptions, often obscuring the genuine similarities between different cultures.

Modern cosmology is not confined to scientific views—at least, not if we include as modern everything that exists in the modern world. Contemporary cosmology can include divine intervention; obviously Christian cosmologists, for example, must reserve a place for God in their thinking. A notable example is the physicist John Polkinghorne, for whom there is no difficulty in imagining a Christian God who allows His creation to operate via the laws of physics.[26] From a non-Christian perspective, Joel Primack, distinguished as one of the team responsible for the recent idea of "cold dark matter," sees a reciprocity between physics and the intuitive and symbolic characteristics of religious thought. In his view,

> There is no way to describe scientifically the origin of the universe without treading upon territory held for millennia to be sacred. Beliefs about the origin of the universe are at the root of our consciousness as human beings. This is a place where science, willingly or unwillingly, encounters concerns traditionally associated with a spiritual dimension.[27]

This discussion leads us somewhat neatly to the difficult question of what exactly is a religion. Impossible it may be to define, in a context in which scholars such as Jonathan Z. Smith have questioned whether, as a specific idea, it can be understood in isolation of the rest of human activity, it is a fabrication of Western scholars, but one cannot write a book on religion without some idea of what we mean.[28] The popular understanding of the term, as J. G. Frazer, one of the founders of comparative religion, put it, is "a propitiation or conciliation of powers superior to man which are believed to direct and control the course of nature and of human life."[29] Such a view, while it still has considerable currency, is out of favor with those scholars in the field who acknowledge the variety of religious traditions in the world. Some turn to sociological definitions, defining religion by its social functions, derived from Emile Durkheim's opinion that "Religious beliefs proper are always shared by a definite group that professes them and that practices the corresponding rites. Not only are they individually accepted by all members of that group, but they also belong to the group and unify it."[30] However, to insist that religion is only a matter of social relationships ignores the profound sense of engagement with the cosmos, and the divine, that lies at the heart of religious experience. Exclusively supernatural definitions, though, ignore the debate as to whether a religion requires a divine being. The question often focuses on Buddhism, which is usually defined as a religion even though many of its Western adherents insist that it is a "philosophy" or "way of life." Some scholars have even spoken of Marxism, which denies the existence of the supernatural altogether, as a religion. The only reasonable modern response is to take a balanced view, and I am happy to follow J. Milton Yinger, undoubtedly one of the most influential figures in the debate. He concluded that we find religion wherever

> one finds awareness of an interest in the continuing, recurrent, "permanent" problems of human existence—the human condition itself, as con-

trasted with specific problems; where one finds rites and shared beliefs relevant to that awareness which define the strategy of an ultimate victory; and where one has groups organized to heighten that awareness and to teach and maintain those rites and beliefs.[31]

Yinger relies on inclusivity (he regarded atheist Marxism as a religion)—any ritual approach to the problem of human existence can be religious. Ninian Smart's seven dimensions of religion—or of "worldviews," the term he preferred for its neutrality and lack of historical baggage—flesh out Yinger's broad-based approach. Smart identified the following components that are more or less present in all religions: the ritual or practical, including "worship, meditation, pilgrimage, sacrifice, sacramental rites and healing activities"; the doctrinal or philosophical; the mythic or narrative; the experiential or emotional; the ethical or legal; the organizational or social; and the material or artistic.[32] Smart's is really the best solution to the problem of definition of religion so far, allowing for diversity, rather than a single formula. In particular he allows for an understanding of religion not just as orthodoxy, understood as correct belief, but as orthopraxy, or correct action, which is how most religious behavior may be understood. Religion then becomes a matter not of what we believe but of what we do. I have not labored to relate Smart's seven dimensions in every chapter in this text, but they remain a guiding framework for the content I have selected and can be applied in various ways to different cultures.

Ultimately, attempts to define religion disintegrate to the point where we need to find an alternative. One solution is to abandon the word altogether in favor of the secular-sounding "worldview," which finds support in certain quarters; at Bath Spa University in England, where once I was privileged to be a part of the Study of Religions Department, regular public seminars were arranged under the general auspices of the "World View Society." There, as in other similar fora, the term was designed to signify inclusivity and to send a message that the still-widespread Western assumption that religions are defined by Christianity, Judaism, and Islam (all sharing the worship of a God) is a bar to understanding the phenomenon of religion as a whole. The term "worldview" finds its origin in the German *Weltanschauung*, as in Malinowski's statement that "what really interests me . . . is the [native's] outlook on things, his *Weltanschauung*"; "[E]very human culture," he continued "gives its members a definite vision of the world."[33] The fundamental statement of the nature of a "worldview" was made by the theologian Robert Redfield in 1951. A "worldview," he wrote, is that outlook upon the universe that is characteristic of a people . . . which allows us to describe a way of life and to compare ways of life with one another. . . . World view differs from culture, ethos, mode of thought, and national character. It is the picture the members of a society have of the properties and characters upon their stage of action. Worldview attends especially to the way a man in a particular society sees himself in relation to all else. It is the properties of existence as distinguished from and related to the self. It is[,] in short, a man's idea of the universe. It is that organization of ideas which answers to a man the questions: Where am I? Among what do I move? What are my relations to these things?[34]

Redfield, then, offers the simple and, for this book, very useful statement that a worldview is "the way a people characteristically look outward upon the universe."[35] For our present purposes, Redfield's question "Where am I?" is answered by a location in time and space. In terms of this book, the question "Among what do I move?" is answered by "the stars," and the supplementary question "What is my relation to these things?" concerns the steps that one can take to interact with them, whether through mental processes, behavioral changes, magical acts, ritual participation, or initiatory processes. A cosmological worldview, simply, is that set of ideas about the cosmos which reinforces, explains, or motivates cultural forms or processes.

Narrowly understood, cosmology is the scientific study of outer space. Broadly defined, it deals with the ways in which human beings locate themselves in relation to the cosmos, seen as the totality of everything. It has huge significance for almost every aspect of human behavior. This book is the first to take a global perspective on the relationship between religion and cosmology. It is also the first to consider the uses of astrology across cultures and time periods as a means of enacting cosmic principles in everyday existence.

Following the next chapter, which introduces astrology in a fuller way, the chapters in this book trace the various understandings, practices, and experiences related to beliefs about the heavens in religions ranging from ancient Egyptian, Chinese, and Indian traditions to the Maya and Aztecs to Judaism, Christianity, and Islam to New Age traditions today. Beliefs about the cosmos go to the heart of most religious traditions; by more fully understanding how the adherents of various religious traditions related the heavenly bodies to their lives and events on earth, we gain a deeper understanding of each tradition's core worldview.

Astrology

The Celestial Mirror

Whatever is born or done at this particular moment of time has the quality of this moment of time.[1]

Astrology assumes that there is a significant relationship between the stars or planets and affairs on earth. From this simple principle have developed all the many forms of astrology practiced or studied across the world. The word is derived from the Greek *astron* (star) and *logos*. *Logos* is simply translated as "word," so astrology is, then, the "word" of the stars: The stars "speak." However, in the context of classical thought, we may also consider that the stars possess reason, or a kind of logic, that can provide important information. Until the 17th century the word was frequently interchangeable with "astronomy," the "regulation" or "law" of the stars. In *King Lear*, Shakespeare had Edgar refer to his brother Edmund, who had been posing as an astrologer, as a "sectary astronomical." Other terms Shakespeare might have used include "mathematician" (the astronomer Johannes Kepler studied astrology as part of his duties as "Imperial Mathematician") or "Chaldean" (both astrology and astronomy were commonly traced to Chaldea, or Mesopotamia). Neither do most non-Western countries employ different words to distinguish traditional astronomy from astrology. In India both are *jyotish*, the "science of light." In Japan they are *onmyōdō*, the "yin-yang way"; and in China astrology is *tian wen*, or "sky patterns." When I use the words "astronomy" and "astrology" in this book, for simplicity, I apply "astronomy" to the measurement of the positions of the celestial bodies and "astrology" to the assumption that the stars and planets possess, or impart, meaning. A note on terminology is necessary here: "Astrology" always includes the sun and the moon as planets, which is not how modern astronomy classifies them.

Narrowly, astrology has often been defined as a peculiarly Hellenistic practice combining the use of horoscopes (mathematical diagrams intended to represent the heavens and used to gain insight into the past, present, and future) with an Aristotelian theory of celestial influence. This view, which pervades the historiography on the topic, is only now being abandoned by younger scholars on the grounds that it rules out some varieties of practice (such as an astrology based on signs—omens revealed in celestial patterns) and denies the practice of astrology to any culture other than the Greek or its intellectual heirs: It's not the mechanics that define astrology, but the practice.

Certain of the assumptions that underpin astrology are universal and can be reduced to the notion that either the entire cosmos is alive, or all its parts are interdependent, or both. Sky and earth are therefore related, and the fortunes of one can be read in the other. One useful phrase that comes to mind is "life-world," a term popular among phenomenologists which suggests that nothing can be experienced in our world except as lived. Modern science may tell us that certain things are alive and others are not, but we actually experience the whole world as alive.[2]

Astrology exists in most cultures at different levels of complexity and develops, like all other human activities, over time. However, in various forms it assumes one or more of the following: (1) the celestial bodies are divine, (2) the stars and planets send messages (Latin omen, or warning) on behalf of gods and goddesses, or God, (3) all things in the cosmos are interdependent, (4) the cosmos unfolds according to a strict mathematical or geometrical order, and (5) different times have different qualities.

Thus astrology works either because the messages dispatched by the divinities are reliable or because the movements of the stars and planets are guides to terrestrial affairs. The Greek philosopher Aristotle added other explanatory models, including a theory of celestial influence, with which we shall deal in chapter 13. Broadly there are always three stages to the process of working with astrology, stages that are common to all cultures. First the sky is observed; this is now included in astronomy. Second, celestial patterns are interpreted. And, third, action is advised. This last consideration is vital, for astrology is invariably a guide to action.

There are few reliable scholarly books on astrology, as most discussions of the subject are distorted by either an overly hostile or uncritically sympathetic perspective, and most deal only with the Western tradition; Roy Willis and Patrick Curry's *Astrology, Science and Culture* is a rare attempt to consider modern astrology from an anthropological and philosophical perspective.[3] My own *Astrology and Popular Religion in the Modern West* is the only sociological analysis of modern astrology, considering whether it may be classed as a vernacular religion.[4] Lynn Thorndike's eight-volume *History of Magic and Experimental Science* remains the starting point for histories of Western astrology from the late classical period to the 17th century, and my own two-volume *History of Western Astrology* extends the story back to prehistoric origins and forward to the present day.[5]

This book is not concerned with astrology's detailed technical procedures. However, there is an abundance of primary material from which the technical fabric and interpretative processes of both Western and Indian astrology can be learned. Margaret Hone's *Modern Text Book of Astrology* is a sound guide to the basic calculation and reading of birth charts in the modern Western style and a good basis for going on to explore other applications of astrology, as well as traditional practices.[6] There is no single equivalent for Indian astrology, although B. V. Raman's collected works could provide a similar function. Derek Walters's *Chinese Astrology* is the only general introduction to the Chinese art in English translation. The Mexican astrology of the Maya and Aztecs is awaiting a suitable treatment, as are the many astrologies of the so-called indigenous peoples of Australia, Polynesia, and Africa.[7]

The best-known language of modern astrology is that of the twelve zodiacsigns derived from ancient Babylon: Aries, Taurus, Gemini, Cancer, Leo, Virgo, Libra, Scorpio, Sagittarius, Capricorn, Aquarius, and Pisces. Each sign has a "personality," a set of meanings that can be applied to detailed questions and individual circumstances through examing its location at an exact time of day, and in relation to the planets and other celestial bodies. As we shall see, though, different cultures developed their own systems of zodiac-signs or constellatons that are entirely unrelated to the familiar Western scheme.

The fundamental premise of astrology is reflective: that the earth is a mirror of heaven, in the sense of the celestial realms, and vice versa. This is also a core tenet of cosmology across the ancient and medieval worlds. As the historian Xiaochun Sun put it in China, "The universe was conceived not as an object independent of man, but as a counterpart of and mirror of human society."[8] Native North American cosmology has been described as depending upon a "patterned mirroring" between sky and earth.[9] The classic statement of this interdependence is found in the Islamic text known as the *Tabula Smaragdina*, or *Emerald Tablet*, which was probably written in the Middle East about the year 800 and contains sentiments that would be as familiar in China as much as in India, Europe, Africa, and the Americas. The *Tablet*'s opening words, "That which is above is from that which is below, and that which is below is from that which is above, working the miracles of one, as all things were from one," are cited to this day as a rationale for astrology in the simplified form "as above, so below"—as in the sky so on earth.[10] A popular series of astrology books published in the United States in the 1970s was even marketed under this description.[11]

The notion of reflection, though, is only part of the story. Equally important is the concept of relationship—that the cosmos is alive and that everything in it exists in a series of relationships with all other things. Just as people relate to one another, so planets relate to people, and people to planets, indeed to everything. Most ancient cultures appear to have a view of the cosmos in which all things in the universe are connected in a web of personal relationships. The astrology that emerges from this proposition tends to be pragmatic and flexible. The stars and planets have no fixed meanings, and if one celestial pattern does not fulfill a particular function then another may do just as well. Such astrology is "chaotic," in a sense derived from Mircea Eliade's view of some cosmogonies as chaotic—unplanned and spontaneous.[12]

A complex, highly codified astrology, with both well-defined meanings ascribed to particular stars, planets, or sections of the sky and a requirement for precision in timing and location in space, emerged in three regions: Mesoamerica, China, and the Near East/Babylon. It was a fusion of Babylonian astrology, Egyptian religion, and Greek philosophy in Hellenistic Egypt in the last two centuries B C E that produced the complicated astrology which became the foundation of the discipline still practiced in India and the modern West. This highly codified astrology is "cosmic" in the sense derived from Eliade's identification of "cosmic" cosmogonies, based in a deliberate creation and characterized by order.

The notion of relationship was systematized and codified in the cosmic astrologies of the classical world. The Greek Stoics developed a system of interlocking "correspondences," in which the essence of everything we can see, touch, or imagine is connected by a web of "correspondences," or "sympathies," a scheme named, by the historian Arthur Lovejoy, the Great Chain of Being.[13] We should think of the constituent parts of the Chain as having agency, which is to say that they can function as agents of change: A stone, a flower, or a cloud can have agency, as much as can a person. The Chain of sympathies then becomes the basis of astrological magic, in which objects are created or words spoken that have "sympathy" with particular stars, planets, or zodiac signs.

Most pre-modern societies recognize two kinds of astronomical phenomena. First is the ordered and predictable as observed in the periodicities of the sun, moon, and stars and expressed through calendars and their attendant rituals and the form of astrology that developed in Mexico, China, and the Hellenistic world, the last of which became the basis of both Indian and

Western astrology. Second is the exceptional and unpredictable as manifest in the changing appearance of the sky and celestial bodies (such as whether the moon is surrounded by a halo), shooting stars, and thunder and lightning (which occur in the sky and so were included as celestial omens in many societies). Other types of phenomena, such as eclipses and planetary motions, were originally thought to be random but, in many societies, were later found to be ordered and predictable. The distinction between the predictable and the exceptional, the ordered and the chaotic, remains fundamental to astrology's dual nature: In Babylon, for example, the regular cycles of the sun and the moon punctuated the year with its sacred festivals, but their visual appearances could never be foreseen. In many cultures order was evidence of the cosmos's benevolent nature, and close attention to calendar rituals was required in order to maintain the protection bequeathed by this order through the benign flow of the seasons and hence guarantee society's survival. Disorder, by contrast, was seen as evidence of supernatural threats, against which astrological prediction, magic, and prophylactic rituals might be employed. In Greek astrology, and in its Indian and Western descendants, unpredictability was gradually removed from the astrological canon, and no modern Western astrologer pays any attention to meteor showers or whether the moon is surrounded by a halo: Order and predictability of astronomical data are essential.

The general recognition of two kinds of astronomical phenomena relates to other ways in which astrologers work. Historically, astrological meanings have been constructed in two ways. In the first, empirical data is collected. As soon as a celestial event coincides with a terrestrial occurrence, the correlation is noted and can become the basis for a future prediction. In the second, a theoretical framework is imposed on the heavens, such as a zodiac or set of personalities for the planets, that then allows for the construction of a kind of biography of human life, or the planning of future actions.

The varieties of astrology in the classical world give us some idea of astrology's diversity.[14] Astrology could be rationalized through theories of celestial influence, divine warnings (omens), sympathies or correspondences, or correlations, in which terrestrial and celestial events were connected purely because they occurred at the same time, what C. G. Jung was to term acausal synchronicity.[15] The concept of astrology as a matter of influences or effects in which object "a" affects object "b" as an independent agent was unknown until the 20th century, and it remains a minority view. We can conclude that, at least in most of its forms, astrology does not conform to a modern scientific paradigm that may require statistical samples and repeatable experiments. The codified astrology of China, India, and the West is science in the traditional meaning of the word, in the same sense that divination is a science—as a discipline with its own rules. The astrological cosmos may be better seen as "imaginal," a term popularized by the philosopher Henry Corbin in order to distinguish products or characteristics of consciousness that are "real" from those that are "imaginative," in which qualities of the mind have no reality. The word also has other associations, such as of the religious "image" as an icon, or embodiment of numinous reality, or of the whole world itself as an "image" of heaven.[16]

One useful distinction among types of astrology in the West is that between natural and judicial. Natural astrology places the emphasis on the natural world, making generalized statements on the basis of celestial influences or planetary cycles. Some modern astrologers claim that the sunspot cycle (an eleven-year cycle in solar radiation) should be classed as natural astrology. Judicial astrology, on the other hand, as the name implies, requires that the astrologer make a judgment, usually using a horoscope, a highly codified diagram of the heavens for a precise time and place. The scope of judicial astrology's functions was defined in the classical period, and medieval Europeans understood judicial astrology, which rested in the use of horoscopes to reach judgments, as divided into four categories: Interrogations were horoscopes cast for the moment that a question was asked, genethlialogy was the interpretation of horoscopes set for birth, revolutions dealt with political and general worldly affairs, and elections were used to choose the most auspicious time to arrange important events. Not included in this typology were uses of astrology for magic, such as the casting of talismans (objects having astrological significance and intended to manipulate the psychic and physical environment) and the diagnosis and treatment of disease. Astrology might be used to analyze personal destiny, assess the soul's chances of salvation, cast spells, apply celestial myths to everyday problems, shed new light on history, find lost objects, predict the outcome of a battle, find the most auspicious time to launch a new enterprise, perform a ritual act, or construct a sacred calendar. It could be more or less deterministic, but it invariably required active human participation. If the sky is a dramatic stage set for telling stories about human affairs and the passage of the year, then the cosmos requires active participation by human beings as actors in the drama, an expression of the anthropologist Lucien Lévy-Bruhl's *participation mystique,* the sense of being at one with the cosmos.[17]

Every form of astrology begins by posing a level of fatedness, in which human beings assume a lack of control over their lives but then set out to create choice, negotiate with nature, and enter into a dialogue with time.

Such negotiation may take the form of magic, prayer, ritual, or, in the modern world, counseling or therapy in order to achieve the ancient classical goal of self-awareness. Typically, choice in astrology exists within a context of purpose and an acceptance that the world is providentially organized.

From the inclusive perspective, there is no culture which does not have an astrology. The name itself, though, is often a problem, encumbered as it is by the anti-astrology rhetoric of the scientific Enlightenment. Various solutions have been proposed to this problem. One is that we replace the word "astrology" with either "Star Talk" or "Star Study."[18] We might also use the astronomer Ed Krupp's term, "Sky Tales."[19] I have suggested Star Stories, which can include the stories that stars tell about humanity as much as the ones that people tell about the stars: If we exclude any question of an external objective reality—the measurement of planetary cycles or celestial influences—astrology can be seen as fundamentally a narrative, a discourse. It has its believers in the literal truth, and in the absolute objectivity of its truth-claims, but it may still function as a conversation, its participants being people (astrologers and their clients) and the cosmos (time, eternity, pattern, rhythm, and fate in its many forms).

As a language, astrology speaks in symbols. It relies on metonymy, using one word to mean another, so that when modern Western astrologers utter the word "Mars," their colleagues hear the words "anger," "danger," and "energy." When astrology says "Venus," it is code for love, peace, and desire or, in Aztec and Maya culture, war and violence. Some of astrology's modern adherents claim its language is universal, which it clearly isn't: In the Greek tradition the moon is the symbol of womanhood; in the Babylonian the Moon-god, Sin, was a man, as was the Egyptian Thoth. Its symbols are, though, like any other, polysemic: They have multiple meanings and require interpretation. From a symbolic perspective, then, the logic that leads a Western astrologer to interpret Venus as peace and an Aztec to look at it as war does not deny the existence of a universal symbol. Of course, if we reject the notion of universally valid symbols, the problem of cultural distinctions between different astrologies remains. For example, it is well known that the Aborigines perceived a radically different set of constellations from those that were seen in China, Babylon, and Mesoamerica, evidence in itself that there are no universals in the way the sky is perceived and used. The physical appearance of the celestial bodies and the mathematical measurement of their apparent movement is not negotiable, but, apart from the measurable solar and lunar influences, all other aspects of astrology are local and culture-specific. A substantial number of modern Western astrologers agree with this view. Perhaps the most influential was Dane Rudhyar, one of the most respected American astrologers of the 20th century. He wrote that

> Astrology of itself has no more meaning than algebra. It measures relationships between symbols whose concreteness is entirely a matter of convention, and does not really enter into the problems involved—just as the symbols of algebra, *x, y, n,* are mere conventions. . . . In other words, the astrological realm of moving celestial bodies is like the realm of logical propositions. Neither one nor the other has any real content. Both are purely formal, symbolical, and conventional.[20]

Rudhyar was no cultural relativist, though, and he believed that, while the rules of astrological interpretation are cultural conveniences, the spiritual truths they reveal are absolutes. As Claude Lévi-Strauss considered, astrological classifications are totemic. Their logic, he argued, "works rather like a kaleidescope, an instrument which also contains bits and pieces by means of which structural patterns are realized."[21] Lévi-Strauss's structuralism would probably have made sense in Rudhyar's Platonic world, with its concept of geometrically defined archetypes, even if he might have rebelled against structuralism's excessive rigidity. The psychologist C. G. Jung, who described astrological symbols as "mythological motifs," "categories of the imagination," or "primordial thoughts," might also have disapproved of Lévi-Strauss's mathematics but not his quest for underlying patterns.[22] Jung was himself an enthusiastic astrologer for whom astrology worked because time itself was an organizing principle, controlling the mutually satisfying relationship between celestial symbols and human psyche, a theme that will recur throughout this book. "Whatever is born or done at this particular moment of time," Jung wrote, "has the quality of this moment of time."[23] And here we come to another of astrology's characteristics, at least in cultures that develop a highly codified form of the discipline—the deification of time. The Persian Zoroastrians actually imagined time as the lion-headed deity Zurvan. Most cultures have not gone this far, but, implicitly, time is often regarded as having agency, as being an active participant in the cosmos.

Why some societies should develop such complex systems is not clear; the archaeoastronomer Anthony Aveni's comment about the Maya ("Why [they] became such ardent astrophiles is a problem not yet resolved"[24]) may equally well apply to the ancient Babylonians or Chinese. One obvious answer is that societies with complex socioeconomic and political systems develop technically complex cosmologies as an aid to management of society and the state. What all three cultures shared was a sense of precision, that the merest details of life could be timed to correspond exactly to the flow of celestial time. One persistent argument holds that the appeal of astrology, like that of religion, rests in its ability to provide security for insecure people. However, the argument has been challenged on the grounds that it is an anachronistic projection into the past of modern skeptical critiques of astrology.[25] It may be more productive to consider the reasons for star stories. Do they encode information about the world?[26] Is the power the motive? Possibly: Stephen McCluskey concluded that "Astronomical observation and knowledge were, for the Aztecs, signs of sacred power and status."[27] Were ancient people looking for patterns that might make better the management of the world? Perhaps. Among the Maya, we read "The paramount goal of the astronomically and mathematically knowledgeable scribes was to use what they saw in the sky to pattern time."[28] Aboriginal astronomy, meanwhile, locates the stars in social context and value systems: "Like the Newtonian-based system of Western science, it represented an attempt to construct a view of the universe as an ordered and internally consistent system, and hence to obtain some sense of control over the natural world."[29] Further,

> Their careful astronomical observations were motivated not by inherent curiosity but by their belief that the stars had an intimate pragmatic and relational role in their culture. One role was economic: the need to establish predictive correlations between the position of the constellations and other natural events important to the survival of the community such as the availability of particular foods or the onset of particular weather conditions. A second function, equally necessary to preserve the group's identity, was a socio-moral one: the association of the various constellations with a complex system of moral guidance and education in tribal lore. Thirdly, the Aborigines regarded the stars as an integral part of both the physical landscape and a philosophic system, each element of which helped to explain, reinforce and legitimate the others and guarantee their continuity.[30]

Such a description may be equally applied to Chinese, Indian, Mesoamerican, and Western astrology. Keith Thomas considered whether Western astrology had a function in the development of historical thought. He concluded that it did, adding that the sociological worldview has at least partial roots in the astrological. In his words,

During the Italian Renaissance astrological doctrines about the recurrence of planetary conjunctions had helped to form the concept of a historical "period." . . . In their [the astrologers'] confident assumption that the principles of human society were capable of human explanation, we can detect the germ of modern sociology.[31]

Perhaps ancient star myths and modern astrology are also both means of transmitting culture.[32] Elsewhere Inca astrologers are referred to as "folk-astronomers," suggesting that their function was to convey astronomically derived social, political, and agricultural information to the population at large.[33] This might ring true of the ancient world and oral cultures, but does the modern astrological consultation, with its use of archaic symbolism, bind both practitioner and client into an otherwise forgotten world of magic and shamanism? That is a question I don't think we are yet equipped to answer. Are astrologers better described as "calendar priests," as has been said of Mayan practitioners?[34] Are their modern descendants the equivalent of the Peruvian "calendrical shamans" who traveled from village to village with their books of prognostications tucked under their arms?[35] It is certainly possible. Talking of astrology's increasing popularity in the 1980s, Liz Greene and Howard Sasportas, pioneers of the integration of depth psychology and astrology, wrote:

> The astrological consultant has, willingly or not, been usurping what was once the role of the priest, the physician, and the psychiatrist. . . . And with due respect to those readers who may be members of the clergy or of psychiatry, [the] client with psychological problems may often fail to find the tolerance or depth of understanding that the clergy might justifiably be expected to provide, receiving meaningless aphorisms instead; or may fail to obtain the insight into symptoms and the openness to discuss them without clinical labeling which the orthodox medical establishment sometimes finds rather difficult to offer.[36]

Does this mean that astrology itself is a religion? Here again, the answers are mixed. The question can become meaningless in those cultures that make no distinction between religion and any other aspect of life: There is no point in asking whether astrology is a religion in India, or among Australian Aborigines, or indigenous Polynesians. Some historians assume that astrology was a religion once, when it was an accessory to the worship of celestial deities, but may not be now. The historian of science Bartel van der Waerden was following the consensus when he argued that "Babylonian astrology depended on astral religion. . . . The guiding concept of astrology, that the gods of the sky rule our lives, was a religious concept. Very right were the Fathers of the Church to condemn astrology!"[37] The German philosopher Bernulf Kanitscheider thinks astrology still is a religion: "Astrology," he wrote, "must be seen in its origins as a religion based on the stars."[38] For the sinologist Joseph Needham, astronomy itself was derived from religion, or, perhaps better to say, it was an application of religion. In his opinion, "[A] stronomy was a science of cardinal importance for the Chinese since it arose naturally out of that cosmic 'religion', that sense of unity and even 'ethical solidarity' of the universe."[39] Modern critics of astrology likewise tend to argue that it must be a religion on the very grounds that its claims are false.[40] Some astrologers accuse their fellows of using it as a religion in that it becomes an answer to every problem, from grand questions of human existence to the best time to make a phone call. A few Western astrologers, though, do regard astrology's role as religion as a good thing. In 1927 Julius Bennett, writing in *Astrology*, the journal of the Astrological Lodge of the Theosophical Society, claimed that the "combined science and religion of the New Age" would be astrology.[41] Some modern astrologers agree. Pam Crane, a well-known British astrologer and minister in the theosophically inclined Liberal Catholic church, concludes:

> With the discovery of the Outer Planets, we men and women have taken a lot of spiritual power for ourselves. Nowadays it is unfashionable—even in some quarters unacceptable—to conceive of ourselves as truly children of an almighty being we call God, that this being is a person, and that He sent his Son into incarnation to teach us how to love, and to die for love of us. At this time in our history when hubris has rendered us desperately vulnerable to self-created disaster, is it not time we reconsidered? Look at all I have shown you here. Is not Christ coming to us over and over again, in every conceivable way, as he always promised?[42]

Is Crane putting God at the center of the cosmos, or is she placing humanity there? Certainly some forms of astrology are focused on the individual—"person-centered" in the modern jargon. Astrology's characteristic earth-centered cosmos has been described as not so much "Geocentric [as,] more embracingly, egocentric."[43] What exactly is it that astrology says about the nature of personhood? This is the question asked by Stephen Kemper in his study of Sinhalese astrology.[44] There is indeed something egotistical about astrology, as many modern astrologers will agree: The birth chart, the map of the heavens for the moment of birth, is calculated with the infant at the center of the entire universe. In this sense, if the complex interpretative astrologies of Babylon, India, China, the Islamic world, Europe, and Mesoamerica have anything in common, it is that the focus of all creation, the sum total of space and time, is placed on the individual as the act of astrological interpretation proceeds. The center is not where God is, or the Goddess, or the gods: If astrology has a religion, perhaps it is humanism. An entirely separate question is whether astrology has religious uses. The answer to this, obviously, is yes, for there is no area of human activity to which it cannot be applied.

To return to the question, then: Is astrology a religion? Not if we require a narrow definition of religion as requiring the worship of a supreme being and a set of dogma located in a sacred text. In part the answer depends on how broad or narrow is our definition of religion. Elsewhere I have concluded that we may consider astrology to be a "vernacular religion" in the general sense that it is part of the prevailing worldview of the modern West.[45] For Emile Durkheim, astrology was more magical than religious, for the precise reason that it lacks a congregation and institutional framework and instead relies on an individual practitioner's performing a service for a single client.[46] Durkheim's distinction between magic and religion is no longer tenable, though, for it denies the extent to which formal religious practice relies on magical acts, transubstantiation in the Catholic Mass being a prime example.

J. G. Frazer's view of religion as based on the propitiation of superior powers certainly has relevance in some contexts but fails to account for those areas of astrology that require action and assert humanity's role as a co-creator.[47] J. Milton Yinger's inclusive definition of religion, based as it is on a collective attempt to deal with the problems of human existence, can certainly include astrology at its broadest (the construction and celebration of sacred calendars) but is so all-encompassing that there is little left that is not a religion.[48] Only Ninian Smart's seven dimensions of religion offer a sufficiently rich framework within which to consider not whether astrology is a religion but whether it is a religion in certain contexts. In the text that follows, though, I tend to emphasize astrology's relationship with religion, which, for these purposes, I define cautiously as the worship of supernatural beings. I then pose such questions as how the cosmos came into existence and what is the stars' role in the construction of sacred calendars or the salvation of the soul. Smart's seven dimensions then provide a framework for whether astrology is a religion in particular instances. I have also emphasized those applications of astrology that may be religious in a broad sense so that we may ask, if astrology is a religion, what are its rituals, philosophies, narratives, experiential content, and social context. This does not, it must be stressed, mean that all astrology is a religion. The use of astrology by modern business analysts or psychologists, working in a secular context, is clearly not religious. The statement "Astrology is a religion" is simply wrong. In particular instances, though, it may have religious qualities and functions, and it is these with which we are concerned in this book.

As we have seen, astrology is marked by diversity, causing some modern commentators to refer to "astrologies" in the plural on the grounds that the use of the single term "astrology" too easily leads to the suggestion that there is a monolithic system and single dogma to which all astrologers subscribe. Astrology may treat the stars as signs, causes, or influences, while the stars may act on terrestrial affairs, correlate with them, or simply indicate them. And, even when they are causes or influences, they may not have any power in themselves but be acting on behalf of some superior force, creator, or god. In this chapter I have suggested some useful distinctions between different kinds of astrology: Chaotic astrology is flexible, spontaneous, and pragmatic; cosmic astrology is codified, highly structured and complex; natural astrology deals with general influences or patterns, while judicial astrology requires the presence of an astrologer to make a judgment. It makes more sense to look at what astrologers actually claim and do, and imposed categories such as "divination," "science," "magic," and, of course, "religion" are invariably misleading and fail to account for the diversity of practice across the globe, let alone the contested meanings of these words. In this book we take a broad and eclectic view of astrology, encompassing as wide a range as possible of applications of the stars for religious purposes or to provide meaning. In the following chapters, for the first time, we examine a range of practices and beliefs from around the world, some that have been challenged by forces such as colonialism, while others are living traditions. There will inevitably be many points of comparison and evidence of differences as well as similarities, both of which will help us answer questions about how human beings use the sky as a theatrical backdrop for their myths, rituals, religions, and personal engagement with the cosmos.

Australia

The Dreaming

Moon makes baby come. . . . When the moon is full the woman knows her time is near.[1]

The ancient culture of Australia presents us with a living picture of a religious cosmology that may date back tens of thousands of years in a continuous tradition. It has been said that the aboriginal Australians were arguably the world's first astronomers, a view proposed by Roslyn Haynes.[2] Actually, however, it's more likely that the first astronomers were Africans, for Africa is where all the current evidence indicates human life began. That said, the Aborigines certainly have a sky-based culture of considerable antiquity. There is some datable, material evidence for this claim in the form of artifacts such as a diprotodon (giant wombat) tooth dated to around 18,000 BCE that is carved with twenty-eight notches, perhaps representing the days of the lunar month.[3] There are also intriguing instances of rock art and some examples of other notched bones that are frequently interpreted as lunar counters. To quote Haynes, the Aborigines' "complex systems of knowledge and beliefs about the heavenly bodies evolved as an integral part of a culture which has been transmitted through song, dance and ritual over more than 40,000 years."[4] Now, while this statement could also be true of any other culture, the distinctive feature of aboriginal astronomy—and cosmology— is its continuity. What we see now, we suspect, we might have seen 40,000 years ago. At least, that is our working assumption. On the other hand, just as there are local variations in aboriginal cosmology, so we should be alive to the possibility of evolution and adaptation through time.

Australian cosmology, like that of many ancient peoples, is "chaotic" in the sense that it postulates that the world emerged through a sequence of steps, not as an orderly creation but as a gradual emergence of living things. Its overwhelming characteristic is relational: People are related to stars, stars are related to animals, animals are related to the land, and all are related to the invisible beings who are everywhere and who "sang" creation into existence. Two distinctive qualities of the aboriginal view of the cosmos require attention. One is the "Dreaming," or "Dreamtime," with which we shall deal below. This is an eternal dimension that finds parallels in other cultures. It is similar to the concept of unchanging "Being," which we find in Platonic cosmology, and may be described by the term "Imaginal," in which things that exist in the imagination are as real as anything in the physical world. The other, which is perhaps unique to Australia, is the concept of Songlines, traces left in the landscape by the creatures that sang the world into existence. This concept is the cue for a form of solitary pilgrimage that becomes a means for contacting the Dreaming. All these notions, though, are contested, and subject to competing interpretations by those few Western scholars who have investigated them.

We face significant problems in our attempt to understand traditional Australian cosmology. The collapse of aboriginal culture exemplified in the shrinking of social and language groups from between 350 and 750 in 1770 to fewer than 150 in 2000 is the most obvious. In addition, until recently the convention among most educated white Australians was to hold that the Aborigines either had no astronomy or were simply not interested in the sky. The situation has been partially rectified as a result of the efforts of some scholars, but there is still immense scope for scholarly work, especially for ethnographic accounts of the use and meaning of astronomical information. There are now a number of sound accounts of aboriginal cosmology.[5] However, a new issue has emerged. As aboriginal culture has suddenly become fashionable among sections of the white population, a tendency has emerged to reconstruct aboriginal astronomy. There have always been feedback loops, a familiar problem in anthropology, in which people provide researchers with material adopted from either them or previous visitors. This is a problem if we are interested in authenticity, in genuinely recovering aboriginal worldviews. On the other hand, the adaptation of indigenous astronomies from around the world under the impact of the globalizing tendencies of New Age culture is a legitimate topic of religious study.

The sources for aboriginal cosmology are as limited as they are in any other oral culture, a problem that is compounded by the initiatory nature of much traditional knowledge and a consequent reluctance to disclose it to outsiders; disclosure would, of course, destroy its value. Isobel White has pointed out that, in an initiatory context, it may not be the actual knowledge that matters, but what one is permitted to know.[6] Such knowledge possesses value only according to who knows it, and, as value is everything, it has no power if it is disseminated among the uninitiated. It will, in effect, cease to be knowledge.

This is precisely what has been found in interviews with aboriginal artists about the distinctive feature of the Aboriginal cosmology the "Dreaming," or "Dreamtime." According to a report on one interviewee,

> We asked her how she differentiated ordinary night dreams from these kind of dreams, and she said that first they had to be explained to an elder. Then she added the remark "It's gotta be sung," which we had only heard from one person. At this point in the conversation, the curator clearly became worried. And she seemed to retreat from her previous statements, saying outright that her paintings did *not* come from dreams.[7]

Our available texts therefore consist of ethnographic reports by anthropologists who, inevitably, have their own agendas and interpretations and may be talking to Aborigines whose ideas may, in turn, have been influenced by contact with other Westerners, especially missionaries and, sometimes, other anthropologists. On the other hand, some evidence emerging from anthropologists in recent years suggests that some aboriginal elders would rather trust academics with their knowledge than their own youngsters, on the grounds that the former are sometimes now more respectful than the latter. The Aboriginal Australian Astronomy research group based at MacQuarie University, for example, works with Aborigine advisers.

The difficulties of distinguishing Australian astronomy that has been influenced by colonial ideas from that which has not are evident in our understanding of the "Dreamtime." The term was coined by Francis Gillen, promoted by Walter Baldwin Spencer in 1896, and publicized in 1899 in their major study of aboriginal culture, *The Native Tribes of Central Australia*, and is a translation from the Arrernte word *alcheringa*. "Dreamtime" is often used as a synonym for "Dreaming," which is frequently preferred on the grounds that it is more suggestive of a general process than a defined past period, which is implied by the use of the suffix "time."

The standard view of the Dreaming, as commonly accepted, holds that it contains the originals of everything that exists in the physical world. We may describe these ideas as "souls" in the sense that they constitute a life force that both manifests in matter and animates material objects. At the creation of the physical world, some of these souls became stones, others plants and animals and the rest human. The Dreaming then establishes order for everything in humanity's experiential, phenomenological world—social order, moral order, and natural order—and can be accessed and experienced through creative engagement with the environment, including song, dance, story, and visual images. In the creation, the ancestors, however they are conceived—whether as human, or animal, or fantastic—moved across a formless land creating the hills, valleys, plains, and forests that are, in different ways, sacred or significant. As they moved they created the Songlines, paths in the sky and land. If walked, the Songlines will connect the traveler with the Dreaming, with the underlying creative, living power. As the novelist Bruce Chatwin put it, "legendary totemic beings . . . wandered over the continent in the Dreamtime, singing out the name of everything that crossed their path—birds, animals, plants, rocks, waterholes . . . so singing the world into existence."[8]

Dreamtime stories come in a huge variety of forms, as might be expected on a continent that contained hundreds of languages. They have been told, acted, sung, painted, walked, and chanted for tens of thousands of years, and they have been overlaid on other stories, creating a rich and deep tapestry of thoughts, images, and impressions. Popular Songline creators that feature in these stories include snakes, whose movement is echoed in the serpentine form of valleys, caverns, and weathered rock faces; and birds, whose flight paths become Songlines in the air.

However, and this is a very big "however," the entire concept of Dreaming has become entangled in the obsession with categorization that afflicts so much Western academic discourse. Does Dreaming, anthropologists ask, relate to a time in the past or is it ever-present—and, if the latter, does it reveal itself in ordinary dreams?[9] To this we may respond, Why can't it be all these things, and why do so many scholars attempt to categorize human experience out of existence? Then there is the claim by radical academics that Dreaming is nothing more than an anthropological construct, a Western ideology that Aborigines accept because they are unaware that they are being subjected to a form of philosophical neocolonialism.[10] The problem here is really over-intellectualization on the part of those anthropologists who remain perpetual outsiders, unable or unwilling to actually experience the mindset of the people they study. The way to experience the Dreaming is to live outside, under the sky, moving through the land, letting modernity slip away, enjoying whatever meditative, ritual, or ecstatic practices, induced perhaps by song or dance, allow one to actually experience what, in the modern West, is often called an "alternative reality."

The earliest substantial accounts of aboriginal astronomy were published in the late 19th century but were largely restricted to terminology. The amateur astronomer Peter MacPherson gave his report to the Royal Society of New South Wales in 1881. Relating Western constellations to varieties of their aboriginal equivalents, he pointed out that the Northern Crown is a Boomerang, part of Leo an Eagle's Claw, the Crow a Kangaroo, the Coalsack Nebula (actually a dark cloud rather than a group of stars), an Emu. MacPherson also summarized the information provided by W. E. Stanbridge in 1857. Stanbridge's concern was with stars as season markers and, in MacPherson's version, Stanbridge reported that

> The Pleiades (*Larnankurrh*) are a group of young females playing to a corroboree [a ritual assembly] party of young men (*Kulkunbulla*) represented by the belt and dirk of Orion. The red star Aldebaran, *Gellarlec*, or rose-crested Cockatoo, is an old man keeping time to the dancers. This as a summer group corresponds well with the beautiful moonlight nights of November and December, when the air is balmy, and the signs in the heavens are the resplendent groups of Orion and the Pleiades, with such individual bright stars as Sirius and Aldebaran.[11]

This is a rather fine description and brings alive the notion of the sky as theater—a dramatic setting for the living spirits of the Dreaming. As seasonal markers, stars enabled the Aborigines to navigate their life-world. We should not imagine, though, that a seasonal marker merely marks the passage of the seasons for functional reasons. True, when Arcturus appears in the eastern sky at sunrise, the Aborigines of Arnhem Land harvest the *rakia*, a spike rush valuable for making baskets and fish traps, while, in Victoria, when the star was in the north in the evening, it indicated that it was time to find and eat *bittur*, the pupa of the wood ant and an excellent source of protein.[12] Yet in marking the seasons, the stars reveal the Dreaming as experienced in the rhythms of life. Seasonal rituals might be determined by the seasons of the sun, the monthly patterns of the moon, or the regular appearance and disappearance of Venus. In Arnhem Land, in the north, the Venusian "morning star ceremony" is an important feature of the ritual for the dead. During the ritual, Venus, *Barrumbir*, is represented by a cluster of white feathers or down, and long strings with other feathers attached at the ends represent, it is said, rays, on top of a totem stick.[13] Feathers, though, may represent flight as much as light, and it is invariably a mistake to imagine that a symbol has only one meaning.

In the Northern Territory, Yolngu cosmogony has a celestial element.[14] The spirit that flew across the land from the east to the west, bringing the first people to the land and creating plants, animals and landscape, was Barnumbirr, a being associated with Venus. In Western Australia, the Boorong people believed that the sun, Gnowee, was made by Pupperimbul, one of the old spirits that were removed to the sky before ordinary humans populated the earth. According to this belief, the sun was actually created when Pupperimbul threw an emu egg into the sky, the egg burst, the sky was flooded with light, and the sun was born. As the celestial bodies were created, so they formed genealogical relationships, constituting a heavenly clan to watch over earthly families. Among the Boorong, Venus, or Chargee Gnowee, is the sun's sister and is married to Jupiter, Ginabongbearp. Not all celestial relationships were friendly, and one of the common heavenly motifs, a popular one for modern aboriginal "dot" painters (in which images are built up through a series of dots), is the perpetual pursuit by Orion of the Pleiades, the seven sisters.[15] This story occurs in many cultures in Europe and the Americas and appears to be one of the archaic, Paleolithic star tales whose origins precede the dispersal of humanity. Astronomically, the myth personalizes the fact that the stars of Orion's belt follow those of the Pleiades across the sky. Socially, it has been interpreted as a motif of pursuit, rape, and sexual fear or fantasy. Yet, if astronomically Orion can never catch the Pleiades, does this provide reassurance that he will never reach the end of his chase? In some versions of the story one of the Pleiades is caught and raped while on earth, but in the sky the pursuit is perpetual, its quarry never caught: The starry realm offers safety in its regularity and order. Another point we should draw attention to is the fluidity of astronomical relationships in societies that have not developed a highly codified astrology. It appears that Orion's role as pursuer might be taken by the moon, or the bright stars Castor and Pollux (the Geminian twins in the Greek zodiac), Aldebaran, or Canopus.[16]

The aboriginal cosmos was gendered, and, generally, the sun was male and the moon female.[17] This seems to have been a widespread assumption in an environment that could encompass a host of local variations. Although we find as many regional differences in the physical structure of the cosmos as we do in the nature of the Dreaming, the model developed by the Tiwi people, who occupy the Bathurst and Melville islands, some 50 to 60 kilometers north of Arnhem Land, itself the far north coast, is typical.[18] The Tiwi hold that the earth, *kaluwartu*, is a flat disc, surrounded by water and covered by a solid dome, *juwuku*. So prevalent is this scheme, prior to the development in the first millennium BCE of classical notions of a spherical earth suspended in space, that we may assume it developed as soon as human beings were able to conceptualize and visualize their wider environment. There was also a world beyond the *juwuku*. Some imagined it as a place where the dead lived on, appearing as stars as they shone through holes in the dome, and surrounded by flowers that were always in bloom and never wilted. Communication between the *juwuku* and earth could be two-way and take place via a rope, spear, tree, or rainbow, and a person who reached the sky might become a star or constellation. The dome itself is supported by wooden posts in some versions, or by a tree in others, or by star people or, in one constellation version, by two guardians of the circumcision ceremony who live in the equivalent of the Greek stars of Scorpius, and are responsible for moving the sky. Below the earth, meanwhile, was an underworld—*Yilaru* to the Tiwi—through which the sun traveled at night and that, for some people in the south, was home to the spirits of unborn children.

Some star myths preserve the memory of possible celestial cataclysms, again a genre of myth that is shared with most cultures and is usually read as representing a distant memory of ancient meteor collisions.[19] For example, the giant crater at Gosse Bluff, west of Alice Springs, is said to have been formed when the baby of one of the ancestral women fell to earth. The story tells that the ancestral woman put her baby down while she danced in the Milky Way, so it contains a clear double meaning. On the one hand it explains an astronomical event of great magnitude and, on the other, it warns new mothers to take care where they put their children. The explanation is at once scientific and social.

We have evidence of the use of a general astrology by the Aborigines, in their devotion to the ritual harmonization of their lives with the stars, but we have only the slightest glimpse in the surviving evidence of an astrology in the sense of the interpretation of the meaning of celestial signs, and consequent action. The moon, we understand, is more mysterious than the sun, and hence more dangerous, and it serves as a warning against immoral action. The obvious association between the lunar and menstrual cycles resulted in a link between the moon and fertility and a warning to young girls not to look at the moon unless they wished to become pregnant. If one falls pregnant, though, the moon will provide a celestial timekeeper. The Tiwi, who live on Melville Island, off the north coast, believe that "As soon as a woman knows she is pregnant, she starts to 'follow moon.'" "Moon makes baby come"... "When the moon is full the woman knows her time is near."[20]

That physical formations on the surface of the earth were an integral part of the living cosmos gives added significance to the rock art that constitutes a secondary source of information about aboriginal cosmology; to create rock art is to engage with the spirits that created the forms of the earth during the Dreaming. Certain carvings north of Sydney are dated to between 4,500 and 6,000 years old and are said to represent a series of prominent star groups equivalent to the Pleiades, the classical constellations Scorpius and Orion, and the modern constellation the Southern Cross.[21] It would be entirely consistent with what we know of such representations in other cultures that these images are more than symbols; they are also the same as the thing that is being represented and can, in a magic sense, invoke the power and protection of that thing. The problem with rock art, though, is the extensive and often speculative interpretation it requires; and the claims made about it are often unverifiable. We are left with the general proposition that aboriginal rock art is ceremonial, ritual, and cosmological and likely to contain astronomical referents, but, of the details there is little we can say with any degree of certainty.

The evidence we have now gathered suggests that the Aborigines made no more distinction between land and sky than did any other pre-modern people, and that the sky (and the land) constituted a stage set within which, and against the background of which, they lived. This analogy, in turn, makes sense only if we imagine the earth and the sky as also living—as alive as are human beings. Aboriginal cosmology was rich, complex, and an integral part of the life-world, an aid to survival, and expressed through every facet of daily and ritual life.

Australian aboriginal cosmology was chaotic, based on an emanation of the world from an original formless state. The concept of the Dreaming, by which the creative powers that formed the world may be contacted, is egalitarian. In other words, although there might be complex kinship relationships and taboos concerning the knowledge that different people might hold, there was no inherent distinction between different parts of the world in terms of their innate power. A piece of rock, or rock art, for example, might acquire power through its role in the Dreaming or by virtue of being decorated. We may never recover the full details of the diverse range of traditional Australian constellations, although we do know that they were radically different from those in other systems. Astrology was important as a means of providing information on appropriate times for different actions, but our knowledge of it is fragmentary. We have no evidence of complex, codified systems, so we assume that Australian aboriginal cosmology was pragmatic, flexible, and designed to serve human needs rather than to subject individuals to a greater cosmic scheme. Above all, it was concerned with the stars, planets, people, and everything on the earth as a single, living community. Finally, Australian religion was concerned with the propitiation of higher powers, but it also accorded an important role to human beings. Walking the Songlines, for example, helped maintain the health of the cosmic ecosystem. In this sense we can describe Australian cosmic religion as co-creative. People did not bring the world into existence but, once it existed, their task was to maintain it.

Oceania

Navigating the Sky

Here am I on the peak of day, on the peak of night.
The spaces of air,
The blue sky I will make, a heaven.[1]

Oceania is a vast geographical region consisting primarily of ocean populated by (mainly) very small islands that extends over the Pacific in a vast triangle from Hawaii at the apex to New Zealand and Easter Island at the southwestern–southeastern extremes respectively, an area of around 25 million square kilometers. Within this area are identified the three zones of Polynesia; the majority of the region, Micronesia, to the west; and Melanesia, the smallest in terms of overall area, reaching from New Guinea in the west to Fiji in the east. The entire region was settled by migrants from Asia, with two main periods of expansion across the Pacific. The first wave of migrants set out from New Guinea around 1500 BCE, reached Tonga and Samoa in the west a thousand years later, and spread over the whole Pacific island region by 800–1000 CE; New Zealand, the final destination, was settled between around 800 and 1000 CE.[2] Contact was even made with the coast of Chile by 1300 CE. Although the Polynesians speak around thirty-six languages, Oceania is a single cultural zone, with a shared cosmology. As applied to the stars, most scholars are in agreement on this matter. For example, David Lewis claimed that "Astronomy . . . is practically the same in Polynesia as in Micronesia, every significant concept being, in some degree, duplicated."[3] This duplication is evident in the consistency of naming: The Pleiades were revered as Matariki by Easter Islanders and New Zealanders, Matali on Hawaii, and Matarii by the Tahitians.

The inhabitants of the region paid as much attention to the sky as we would expect of any people who not only lived under the stars but made astonishing ocean voyages guided by them.[4] The sacred and the functional were often intertwined, as they must be in any culture in which the natural world is inseparable from the divine.[5] Everything in Polynesian life could be related to the stars, from seafaring to farming, religious ritual and the rise and fall of dynasties.[6]

The cosmology of the Pacific islands shares much with those of other cultures: The cosmos emerges from a formless void and human beings inhabit a world imbued with life, and with meaning. One of society's main priorities, if not the main priority, was to live in harmony with the stars in order to grow crops, to sail the oceans and revere the gods and goddesses, and to observe the messages these deities sent in order to be forewarned of trouble to come. Yet it was the environment as a whole that was alive, so the stars were just a part of a living cosmos that also included the wind, the forests, birds, and beaches—everything that could be seen, touched, or experienced.

Among the major works on Polynesian cosmology and astronomy are Robert Williamson's encyclopedic *Religious and Cosmic Beliefs of Central Polynesia*, Maud Makemson's *The Morning Star Rises*, and *Na Inoa Hoku* by Rubellite Kawena Johnson and John Mahelona.[7] Margaret Beckwith's *Hawaiian Mythology* covers the field of myth in suitable detail; and the volume by W. Bruce Masse, Rubellite Kawena Johnson, and H. David Tuggle—*Islands in the Sky: Traditional Astronomy and the Role of Celestial Phenomena in Hawaiian Myth, Language, Religion and Chiefly Power*—includes the latest information and recent research.[8] The most substantive study of Maori astronomy is Elsdon Best's *The Astronomical Knowledge of the Maori*, written in 1922 at a time when the author could already bemoan the disappearance of most Maori star lore and the impossibility of ever recovering the mass of lost information.[9] Similarly, across the region, ideas and traditions that were passed down orally, from one generation to the next, have been forgotten or, if they were written down, were recorded by indigenous scholars who had benefited from a Western schooling. For all its virtues, such an education encouraged them to see local religion through a framework in which all beliefs were judged against the "truth" of Christianity and found wanting. The texts with which the 21st-century scholar has to work therefore consist of information that can be extracted from colonial-era records going back through the 19th century, together with recent archeoastronomical investigations of shrines and stone monuments.

The interpretation of folklore presents us with various problems. For example, when the Hawaiian cosmogony tells of the first man's breaking of the law, for which his punishment is expulsion from a garden, is its similarity to the Biblical story of the eviction from the Garden of Eden evidence of the Christianization of an indigenous story?[10] Or is it genuine and the result either of a common Paleolithic ancestry or of humanity's tendency to create myths that have a common pattern? A further alternative, recently suggested from the natural sciences, is that many widespread myths, including those with Christian themes, are derived from the common observation of natural phenomena and events.[11] Finally we have the problem of the break in transmission of indigenous ideas as they confronted that difficult combination of Christianity and colonial power. When Elsdon Best, the author of the only dedicated account of Maori astronomy/astrology, was able to record the names of only 12 out of 2,500 stars that are visible to the naked eye, we have two solutions: Either the Maori didn't give him the information, or they didn't care. The latter is unlikely.

We do have fairly good accounts of Polynesian cosmogony, though. In the central Carolines the creator was a goddess, Lukelong, and in the Gilbert Islands, now part of the republic of Kiribati, the male creator, Naruau, or Na Reau, collaborated with his daughter, Kobine. Generally, all creation originates in *po*, the dark, preexistent cause, eternity, the beginning of all things. *Po* had a counterpart, *ao*, or *aiu*, that was light, brilliant, and virtuous. From *po* and *ao* emerges the divine trinity of Kane (who was associated with the sun and sky), Ku (the god of war), and Lono (representing fertility, agriculture, rainfall, and music). The three may be regarded as either separate entities or different aspects of a single being. As recorded by Margaret Beckwith, "The three gods Kane, Ku, [and] Lono come out of the night (*po*) and create three heavens to dwell in, the uppermost for Kane, the next below for Ku, and the lowest for Lono."[12] The normal sequence of creation moves from *po* via the Sky Father and Earth Mother through the creation of generations of deities; the material cosmos, including the celestial bodies; and finally humanity. The first people were made out of mud taken from the four quarters and so themselves incorporated the structure of the cosmos in their being.

In the version compiled by the Christian convert Kepelino, rather than three creator gods, Kane exists as a triad—Kane, Ku, and Lono—and exists alone in the dark night. As creation begins, he brings into existence, in a sequence, first light, then the heavens, followed by the earth, ocean, and then the sun, moon, and stars. As Kane creates, he chants the following words:

> Here am I on the peak of day, on the peak of night.
> The spaces of air,
> The blue sky I will make, a heaven,

A heaven for Ku, for Lono,
A heaven for me, for Kane,
Three heavens, a heaven. Behold the heavens!
There is the heaven,
The great heaven,
Here am I in heaven, the heaven is mine.[13]

A standard interpretation of the Polynesian creation has Kane accompanying himself with a chant while he creates. Perhaps, though, as in some cultures (such as Egypt's), the chanting itself was the creative act, and it summoned the world into existence The three heavens are spatial in that they are hierarchical but conceptual in that they are qualitative, defined by the deities that inhabit them or correspond to them. Physically, the Hawaiian cosmos was a dome, or bowl, a model familiar from many cultures that could be compared to a calabash, or gourd, with the astronomical reference points inscribed on it. *Aiu*, Light and Sky, exists above the Kaingu (land, the surface of the earth) and *Po*, darkness, exists below it. Kaingu, also perceived as the Womb of the Earth, therefore becomes the means for communication between *Aiu*, the world in which humanity exists, and *Po*, the source of creation. Sacred places are therefore liminal zones that facilitate communication between creator and creation.

The chief celestial bodies, as elsewhere, were the sun and the moon, the latter the basis of a lunar calendar.[14] About 700 other stars and constellations were named, of which the mightiest, perhaps, was the Shark, which occupied the Milky Way and points to the importance of the oceans in Polynesian civilization. In the Gilbert Islands the sun and the moon were the children of the first man and the first woman, an unusual inversion of the normal sequence of creation, in which the sun and the moon precede humanity. In a tale that carries clear warnings against disobedience yet suggests that punishment can be avoided if there is a sufficiently persuasive explanation, Na Reau, the male creator, threatened to beat his human children to death for defying his order that they have no children of their own. The primeval man and woman then appealed to Na Reau's good sense by pointing out that both the sun and the moon are useful: The sun enabled them to see by day and, when he is resting, the moon gives enough light to allow them to fish at night. In terms of cosmic politics this piece of astronomical myth also provides a model for good governance: Even when people break the law they may be able to give a reasonable account of their behavior, to which the wise ruler will pay attention. Invariably the universe was described as alive and dramatic. Sometimes the sun and the moon were a pair of eyes, as in the Cook Islands, conveying a feeling of being spied on, stared at, or perhaps watched over protectively. In the Celebes, the sun, moon, and stars were the body of a girl who was thrown into the sky. Some stories explain the origin of day, others the origin of night. In the Banks Islands, in northern Vanuatu, the story is told that, in the distant past, the day was endless. The creator, Qat, received complaints about this monotonous, endless day from his brothers and so, taking a pig as barter, set off to find Night, and buy nighttime. When he returned home, nighttime slipped into the sky and the sun slid down over the horizon, inaugurating the first night; Qat even taught his brothers how to sleep, thoughtfully providing roosters to wake them at dawn.

In all societies astronomy serves a navigational purpose, but for the island dwellers of Oceania, its application by travelers was of supreme importance. To sail hundreds of miles between islands that may be barely visible on the horizon only when relatively close is an astonishing achievement, and the means by which this was accomplished has only recently been understood by Westerners.[15] However, the question is whether the meticulous observation of the stars necessary for an ocean-going voyage was reflected in other aspects of daily or ritual life. The calendar seems to have generally begun with the first appearance of the Pleiades in the eastern sky at sunset, followed by, typically, twelve thirty-day months. But of the precise calendrical markers and seasonal rituals that were in some other cultures marked by astronomically aligned sites, we are only now establishing evidence, after some false starts resulting from over-enthusiasm and lack of rigor.[16] We also need to consider the relationship between astronomical and topographical features. In a study of a group of temples—*heiau*—on the island of Maui, it has been found that those which were north-facing were dedicated to Ku but aligned to the coastline rather than the stars, east-facing sites were dedicated to Kane but were not exactly aligned to any particular east point, while another group, dedicated to Lono, faced the rising position of the Pleiades.[17] Polynesian *marae*, sacred platforms, might be aligned to a variety of directions, including the summer solstice, the Pleiades, the cardinal directions, or, apparently nothing.[18] Alignments to Aiu (the sky) and Kaingu (the land) were therefore dictated by local requirements at different times. It seems, then, that the Hawaiian temple builders might have prioritized any feature of the terrestrial or celestial cosmos, with one part being inherently more important than any other.

As with the astronomical alignment of sacred sites, astrology in the sense of the use of stars and planets to derive meaning or anticipate the future is only now being recovered.[19] As soon as the celestial bodies functioned as superintending deities, as they did across the region, a relationship developed that has to be described as astrological. Of this we have simple examples. In parts of Fiji, the god of hell, a one-toothed man who devours the dead, flies through the sky as a meteor—so both here and in other places, such as the Torres Straits Islands, meteors were often evil omens. Meteors might not always be malicious, but, if they weren't, they were, at least, frequently both powerful and implicitly threatening. In Tahiti, the god Tane could be a meteor, and in New Zealand, the god Rongo-mai came to earth like a ball of fire, suggesting that the shooting star either embodied him or acted as his agent.[20] Comets, which are sometimes difficult to distinguish from meteors in ethnographic accounts, might also be doom-laden portents. In New Zealand Tunui-a-te-ika, a comet, seems to have been less a star for the Maori than a demon and presages death and violence.[21] What little has survived of Maori star knowledge and practice was designated by Elsdon Best as "natural astrology," its remit being the general significance of celestial phenomena. Atmospheric events, we should also remember, are sky phenomena and therefore potentially astrological. In New Zealand, Raki, heaven, sheds tears of love for Papa, earth, which fall as dew, while Papa's sighs of love for Raki rise toward him as mist. There may be no stars involved in this account of meaning in the cosmos, but it portrays the cosmos as infused with romantic love better than any stellar story.

The relationship between planets and human activities, such as the oversight of women's work by Hina, the Polynesian moon, also points in an astrological direction. Even in navigational matters, sailors would consult the stars to find the most auspicious times to sail, just as fishermen might seek advice on the best time to fish, farmers to sow their crops, and soldiers to go to war.[22] The details, though, await further research, assuming they can be recovered. It has been suggested that the appearance of a bright supernova caused the Polynesians to take to their boats and migrate, a theory somewhat reminiscent of the Magi's pursuit of the Christmas Star; in any case, it cannot be proved.[23]

The astrologers tended to be divided into two groups: the sky watchers, whose task was to watch for omens, keep the calendar, and arrange rituals and festivals; and the wayfinders, who presided over the knowledge necessary for navigation. In New Zealand, the Maori developed a class of experts in the entire range of celestial lore, including the measurement of celestial positions and evaluation of their significance. We can infer their actions and the value attributed to them from secondary accounts. These were men of high rank, and they were known as *tohunga kokorangi*. We read of the thoughts of one famous old wise man of the 19th century who spent long nights watching the stars from the summit of a hillock near his hut.[24] At such moments, the venerable sage would have dwelt in the past, communing with his ancestors and the voyage they took to reach New Zealand, perhaps even turning to the beginning of the world and reciting one of the songs of creation, such as Kane's chant at the birth of the world. A night under a starry sky, though, could have had other functions. The *tohunga kokorangi* could have been watching for omens—messages from the stars—purging his soul or communing with celestial deities. He may even have been actively engaging with the sky, acting as a co-creator, for there was a belief that certain men, with sufficient power, could cause a solar halo to appear at will.[25] If the *tohunga kokorangi* saw a dangerous sign, such as a comet, he would recite ritual formulae to defuse the threat and protect his people.[26] The wise man would have known that a lunar occultation—when the moon passes directly in front of a certain star—is a potentially difficult military omen: If the star reappears when the moon has passed, it was said, a fort will be captured. One informant reported that "the star knows all about the coming trouble. . . . Just before the battle of Orakau we saw this sign. . . . As we were a war party of course our warriors made much of this omen."[27]

Best also noted what he described as the sentimental tone of Maori astronomy. The women, he reported, would greet important stars such as Canopus or the Pleaides with "song, lamentation and possibly," he cautiously added, "with posture dancing."[28] We have surviving examples of such chants in the late 19th century. One incantation to the mythical hero Ta-Whaki is typical:

> Climb, ascend, O Ta-whaki!
> To the first heaven.
> Soar to the second heaven,
> Where sacred powers reside,
> And sacrifices are made,
> And offerings are given.[29]

Other astrological signs had agricultural significance, but no distinction was made between celestial omens and seasonal markers—all were signs that required a correct response, whether lifting a crop or reciting a sacred chant.

Canopus, the Pleiades, and the three stars of Orion's Belt, for example, regulated the harvesting of the *kumara*—sweet potato—crop.

There has been a tendency to reduce Oceanic astronomy to the purely functional in the form of navigation, as if the stars can be measuring points devoid of meaning. It is now increasingly accepted that the sky functioned both as a source of order according to which important religious, political, and social events should be organized and as a theatrical medium through which celestial deities could transmit meaning to humanity. Whether the full extent of Oceanic astral religion, divination, and astrology of various kinds can ever be recovered, though, is doubtful.

Polynesian cosmology is part of that family of world cosmologies we know as emergent and chaotic, in that the world originates in a formless, original nothing/something that gradually gives rise to creator divinities, the flow of time through day and night, and, eventually, human beings. A great emphasis was placed across the region on cooperation between society and the wider environment, in which stars were one component along with the ocean, mountains, and all forms of natural phenomena. So much Polynesian sky lore has been lost, and we have little or no evidence of the development of a highly codified astrology. Instead, the sky was seen as a tableau across which living beings moved, sending messages concerning the regular unfolding of time (as in the cycles of the sun and the moon) or unexpected events (such as comets) that warn of coming drama. The Polynesian cosmos was, above all, theatrical. Yet it was an essential ally, for without the predictable motions of the stars, navigation between islands would have been impossible and the unity of the entire culture would have been no more. Polynesian religion is based in nature, in the expression of the cosmos through the sun, moon, winds, and ocean currents. It is greatly concerned with higher powers, but these are friends as much as to be feared: Without the movement of the oceans and seasonal changes in the weather, and without the signs of these alterations in the stars, Polynesian culture would have come to an end.

North America

The Great Spirit

We are the stars which sing,
We make a road for spirits,
For the spirits to pass over.[1]

In the traditional societies of pre-colonial North America, the sky and earth are a single part of the same life-world, containing all visible and invisible things. The stars, as much as people, are part of the natural world, full of life and endowed with meaning, and the natural world is indistinguishable from the supernatural.

The study of Native American cosmology, as with the study of all things Native American, is beset by political problems. While there is an abundance of literature, much of it intelligent and sympathetic, most of it is by Westerners who, perhaps inevitably, cannot possess an insider's understanding of Native American beliefs and tend to fall into camps for the best of intentions. First, there are those who attempt to particularize Native American cosmology, making it special by rendering it unique and different from, for example, European thought. Second are those who attempt to normalize Native American ideas by drawing out similarities to European concepts.[2] All accounts of Native American cosmology should therefore be treated with moderate skepticism, for Western scholars cannot, however hard they try, completely abandon their own educations.

The scholarly study of traditional North American cosmology dates back to the mid- to late 19th century, but it is only since the 1970s that the subject has attracted a dedicated group of academics. Anthony Aveni's *Native American Astronomy*, Von Del Chamberlain's *When Stars Came Down to Earth*, Jerry Gill's *Native American Worldviews*, Trudy Griffin-Pierce's *Earth Is My Mother, Sky Is My Father*, Dennis and Barbara Tedlock's *Teachings from the American Earth: Indian Religion and Philosophy*, and Ray A. Williamson's

Living the Sky and (with Claire Farrer) *Earth and Sky: Visions of the Cosmos in Native American Folklore* are all highly recommended.[3] Kim Malville's *Guide to Prehistoric Astronomy in the Southwest* is an excellent introduction to the incorporation of celestial significance into architecture and rock art.[4]

The geographical boundaries of American cultural zones are not precise. Most writers take the modern arbitrary boundary between the United States and Mexico as indicative of a pre-Columbian reality, and so, with a few notable exceptions, we tend to see books either on the Maya and Aztecs on the one hand, or the Native Americans of the modern United States and Canada on the other. However, the recognizable cultural zone represented by major features of Mesoamerican culture, such as monument construction, extended well north of the modern Mexican border, while an insistence on the importance of aspects of horizon astronomy—especially the rising and setting of the sun at particular moments of the year—appears to be universal. Additionally, of course, the people of North America were themselves diverse and might be either settled or nomadic and inhabit the Floridian swamps or the Arctic ice sheets. While I have therefore taken the culture of North America as a whole, we need to remember its diversity. I agree wholeheartedly with Steve McCluskey, who said, quite rightly, that "[i]t would be a gross oversimplification to speak of a single Native American cosmology."[5] It is, nevertheless, possible to draw out certain themes while at the same time being aware of the significant achievements and points of view of particular cultures. Similarities can tell us as much as differences.[6]

To begin with, we need to address the problems of evidence. First, the origins of human occupation in the Americas are difficult to date and subject to the constantly shifting discoveries of archaeologists. If we wish to identify pre-colonial cosmology we also have to identify and filter out possible Western imports. For example, could the Skidi Pawnee belief that the good are transported to the stars after death while the bad are turned to stone be an adaptation from Christian missionaries? Alice Fletcher thought so, although precisely why is not clear: There is no Christian dogma that evil people are turned to stone, unless there is a confusion with their presumed descent to a subterranean Hell, or with the story of Lot's wife.[7] There is also a certain confusion in the transcription of names, let alone their translation, as linguists have struggled to communicate subtle concepts in European languages, using the best approximation to Native American words.

Our knowledge of Native American cosmology is fragmentary, partly because of the widespread destruction of material during the period of colonization, but there are other culture-specific problems await the researcher.

The First Nations of North America were systematically uprooted from their lands, brutalized, and humiliated. The consequence is a resistance to outside investigators, fueled by resentment in some quarters at recent New Age adaptation of Native American lore, which is making research into, for example, archeoastronomical remains extremely difficult. Even a casual tourist question concerning, for example, the activities that might occur in a *kiva*, the building within which religious-shamanic activities take place, can be met by hostility. Understandable as such attitudes may be, and even though there are many exceptions, even the most welcome of Western scholars frequently find that they are not trusted with the knowledge considered to be available only to insiders. To be fair, such secrecy is also borne of the belief, shared with so many traditions, that the sacred must be protected by discretion, a point of view summed up in the Jewish reluctance to write the name of God and the Islamic prohibition on representing Him. This is especially true of initiatory knowledge, which, as we have seen, loses its power and value if disseminated to the non-initiated.

There may be no single cosmological dogma across the entire continent, but there are recognizable, widespread assumptions that we may identify as follows: The cosmos is an essential unity bound together sometimes by its origin in a single creator, but always by the interlocking relationships of all living beings among whom we must include not only animals, birds, and fish but also water, plants, meteorological phenomena (such as clouds, winds, and thunder), and the invisible beings of whose existence one is aware of only through dreams and the imagination. The sun, moon, and stars form an important component of this living cosmos, engaged as they are in a symbiotic relationship with humanity. The repetitive patterns evident in the motions of the celestial bodies point to a world governed by a cyclical law of birth, decay, and regeneration. This living, breathing, thinking world is then described through myth and managed through ritual. Finally, there is a tension between the predictable order of events such as solar and lunar cycles and the nightly rising and setting of the stars, on the one hand, and the alarming incidence of unpredictable events, such as eclipses and the appearance of comets, on the other.[8] The purpose of calendrical rituals managed by (at least among the Pueblo, specialist "sun-watchers") was to actively ensure the continued smooth operation of the entire cosmos.

The ethnographic evidence suggests that the most antique item of star lore in North America, one that is strongly suggestive of a shared legacy with northern Europe and Asia dating back to the Paleolithic, before human beings migrated over the Bering land bridge, relates to the Great Bear. This constellation, Ursa Major in its conventional Latin form, is one of the largest in the sky and is recognized as a bear both in northern Europe and among certain North American peoples.[9] Aside from its status as one of the largest of the constellations, the Great Bear's principal astronomical feature points to its potential religious significance; from the point of view of any observer in the northern hemisphere, it never dips below the horizon. Instead—and this is a simple experiment that anyone with the energy to spend a sleepless night outdoors can conduct—it rotates around a central point in the night sky (now occupied by the pole star). This point therefore tends to become representative of stillness and symbolic of an absence of movement through either time or space. This is certainly how the Egyptians, for example, saw it when they described the stars that orbit it as immortal, free from the patterns of birth and death that pervaded the universe. It has been argued that this point of stillness was the upper part of the pillar on which the world rotates, and the focus of the ancient shamanic bear cult for which evidence may be found in modern folklore.[10] The constellation was known sometimes as the Seven Brothers—over an area that ran north–south from Saskatchewan to Oklahoma—but more often as the Bear. In some stories the two motifs overlap. For example, one version that is told among the Blackfoot, Wichita, and Crow involves seven brothers and two sisters, one of whom becomes a bear and chases the others, who then take refuge as the stars of the constellation; the sky, in this sense, offers safety and reassurance.[11] The notion of seven siblings suggests an exchange of motifs with the equally ancient star group the Pleiades, whose standard myths involve a chase involving seven sisters, while the theme of a Magic Flight, in which fugitives place a series of obstacles in the path of their pursuers and find refuge among the stars, or as stars, is reminiscent of a wide body of celestial journey stories in which safety or salvation is found in the sky.

The possibility that Paleolithic links between the northern areas of Europe, Asia, and America are evident in astronomical tales was first proposed by the folklorist Charles G. Leland, who traveled among the Algonquin Indians, collecting stories, poems, and songs that he published in 1884.[12] One is a beautiful evocation of the shamanic relationship between the Algonquin and the sky.

> We are the stars which sing,
> We sing with our light;
> We are the birds of fire,

We fly over the sky.
Our light is a voice.
We make a road for spirits,
For the spirits to pass over.
Among us are three hunters
Who chase a bear;
There never was a time
When they were not hunting.
We look down on the mountains.
This is the Song of the Stars.[13]

William Gibbon, who is responsible for significant cross-cultural com-
parisons among European, Asiatic, and American astronomy, pointed out
that the Milky Way, the "stars that sing," was identified as a path for flights
of birds among the Algonquins of Quebec and Ontario, as well as among
Finns, Estonians, and certain tribes of Turco-Tatar stock.[14] The question,
which is ultimately unanswerable, is whether the bird–Milky Way analogy
is the legacy of some shared story told by homo sapiens tens of thousands
of years ago in central Asia and preserved only by selected groups, including the Finns and Algonquin, or whether there is a coincidence and that,
sooner or later, two peoples in different parts of the world were bound
to come up with the connection independently. In the final analysis, the
widespread occurrence of the Bear is convincing and there is no theoretical
objection to a shared origin. This is in spite of the fact that there are sugges-
tions that a Bear constellation may have been located elsewhere. Von Del
Chamberlain suggested that, for the Skidi Pawnee, the Bear might actually
have corresponded to Sagittarius, a constellation entirely unrelated to the
stars of Ursa Major.[15] The argument is tenuous but is enough to remind us
of the caution required when one is reliant on second-hand ethnographic
evidence.

The most common and near-universal theme of American religious
astronomy is the worship of the sun. Here, we do not need to worry about
the transmission of ideas, for reverence for the sun is a feature of virtually
all religious traditions. The native peoples of North America tend to accept
the existence of a primeval Great Spirit, a monotheistic creator, who is
sometimes equated with the sun. First, though, a word of caution. The word
"monotheism," loaded as it is with Judeo-Christian preconceptions, may be
used in such a way as to shape Native American ideas so that they are seen as

equal in value to Western ideas, a tendency to which both Native Americans and Western scholars may be susceptible; on the other hand, neither should we rule out the possibility that there is a genuine similarity.[16]

The Skidi Pawnee creator, a version of the ubiquitous Great Spirit, was Atius Tirakittako, a name that may be translated as "Father Highest-Power Sitting Above." That the spirit is Wakan Tanka in Lakota, Ababinili among the Chicksaw, and Gitchi Manitou in Algonquian points immediately to possible differences of detail within the overall conception; to the Blackfoot he is the Old Man while the Hopi Spirit, Spider Woman, is female. Among the Inuit the Spirit is Torngasoak, the most powerful of all spirits, although not all-powerful. Some prefer the term Great Mystery to Great Spirit, on the grounds that the term "Mystery" defuses anthropomorphic associations inherent in the word "Spirit." The truth seems to be that the North American supreme deity fulfills the functions that tend to have been separated among different varieties of creator elsewhere. He or She, or It if we prefer, is at once the impersonal force that holds the world together, permeating the entire cosmos, and the personal, supernatural parent who provides a protective role, teaching the first humans the skills and secrets of survival and guiding those who observe the harmonies of the natural world. He or She is both a single entity and a composite of all that exists.

The variety of cosmogonies among the Native Americans is as great as that which we find on any other continent. The creation of the world often begins in the sky, but rarely, if ever, suggests creation *ex nihilo*. In some cosmogonies, the process begins with an original supreme creator, imagined not as a personal god but as an original form of creation. The Hopi story is particularly poetic, beginning with nothing but infinite space:

> In the beginning there was only Tokpella, Endless Space. . . Only Tawa, the Sun Spirit existed, along with some lower gods. Tawa . . . gathered the elements of Endless Space and put some of his own substance into then, and in this way he created he First World.[17]

Among the Iroquois and Hurons, the chief deities were those who embodied the power of nature, Wind and Thunder and Echo. Thunder, the highest god, lived above the clouds in the space occupied by the sun, moon, and stars. Generally all the peoples of the Americas, in common with much of the rest of humanity, believed in an upper world, the home of the heavenly powers; a lower world populated by the dead; and the middle world, inhabited by people, animals, plants, and spirits.

The notion of order in the cosmos frequently functioned as an organizational justification for social and political affairs, what we might call a "patterned mirroring" between sky and earth.[18] On this, all anthropologists agree. It is only the details that are a matter of uncertainty and disagreement, partly because Westerners have too often jumped to conclusions, but also because their modern informants are themselves often unsure of the origin of their own sky traditions.

The cosmological organization of the Skidi—or Skiri—Pawnee, who were originally settled along the Missouri River before being ejected by white settlers, is a case in point. Aspects of Skiri-Pawnee cosmology, including the Morning Star sacrifice, were noted as early as the 1820s, and, in the 1980s, more than a century-and-a-half's worth of observations were used in order to reconstruct a systematic account of Skiri-Pawnee religious astronomy.[19] Even given the uncertainty in the evidence, which makes any precise account of Pawnee astronomy highly speculative, it is apparent that their cosmology emerged from general cosmogonic principles into a very precise astrology: The term "astronomy" is anachronistic in this sense because it is clear from the earliest systematic work, published in the 1900s by Alice Fletcher, that the Pawnee were concerned with actively living in a meaningful and harmonious relationship with a universe governed by obvious and repetitive celestial laws.[20]

The Zuni, a Pueblo people (the Pueblo being the characteristic settlement of much of what is now the southwestern United States), were typical. The movements of the celestial bodies and conceptions of the structure of the universe provided a paradigm by which the Zuni organized all aspects of their lives, the most dramatic evidence being in their rituals and rock art.[21] The Zuni had two seasons, one of which began at the winter solstice, the other at the summer, and each consisted of six months conceived of in two pairs: Each month in one season bore the same name as one in the other. The duality of night/day and winter/summer and the two war gods (the morning and evening stars) was expanded into a fourfold cosmos when both rising and setting points of the winter and summer solstice suns were taken into account, and a six-fold scheme when the zenith and nadir—the highest and lowest points of the sky—were added. Their sacred and calendrical rituals were focused on six *kivas* that represented not just six directions but six colors, rain-hearing winds, water-bringing birds, and rain priests.

Despite our best efforts, there is still doubt about the identity or location of many of the Native American constellations. I have already noted that the Skiri-Pawnee constellation of the Bear has been equated with Sagittarius, which is distant from and entirely unrelated to the conventional Great Bear constellation, but the identification is highly speculative. Even if we wanted to, we cannot reconstruct a precise religious cosmology in the Native American sky. Far more significant, it seems, is the numinous power of the stars, with whom one's personal relationship was more important than questions of mathematical precision.

After the sun and moon, the most important of the celestial bodies was Venus, a significant planet in all cosmologies because of its periodic brilliance either in the western evening sky after dusk or the eastern morning sky before sunrise. However, while some designations are obvious, others are not. It may be apparent that a star described as "a great warrior, painted red, carrying a club in his folded arms, and having on his head a downy feather" is Mars.[22] However, the identity of the morning star is entirely uncertain, and its identification as Venus is a consequence of the simplifying instincts of the first Westerners to encounter the Pawnee.[23] The morning star may well be Venus on occasion. But it could equally be Mars, or it might, some think, be Jupiter.

We can face this problem from a number of directions. One is that the Pawneee priests deliberately obfuscated, refusing to reveal secret knowledge to outsiders. In a context in which the name of the celestial father, Tirakittako, was spoken only in hushed tones, even among insiders, such discretion is plausible. Another solution identifies 19th-century Pawnee astronomy as the fossilized remnant of a tradition that might date back to the 14th century or earlier and that was no longer understood. A third possibility is that the Pawnee, unlike their Western interrogators, were simply concerned not with precision but with meaning. They were speaking in a language of symbols— yellow star, black star, morning star, and so on—symbols that were multivalent. Not only might such symbols have multiple meanings, but they might be shared by different celestial bodies. A well-understood analogy from the Near East is the relationship between the sun and Saturn, in which the latter was called the "star" of the former, and in which a single deity might have multiple celestial affiliations.[24]

Native American astrology was intended to harmonize human life with celestial powers and was largely collective, expressed through the ritual pattern of life. However, as stars and people were both alive, the relationship between them could be individual and dynamic. We are told that if a Skiri-Pawnee child is born at night then the stars are observed, but the only interpretive factor mentioned in the surviving accounts is the weather: A calm night followed by a clear morning signified a healthy, problem-free life, but violent weather indicated the opposite. The relationship continues into adult life. According to one Pawnee informant, "[I]t often happens that when a person goes out on the hills at night to fast and to pray to the powers above, he will, as he is praying, become conscious that a particular star is looking at him."[25] The consequence of being singled out by an individual star in such a manner would invariably be a vision followed by the requirement to implement whatever instructions the star sends. The results were not always desirable. Fletcher's informant told her of one incident in which a star made a boy crazy. That this was a familiar problem is suggested by the immediacy with which a healing ritual was conducted. The shaman or priest took the boy outside and waited for the guilty star to rise. When it did so, the boy was painted black, covered in white spots, wrapped in a fawn skin, and a star was painted on his forehead; the treatment was successful as long as the star remained on his forehead, but when it wore off he went mad again.

Concepts of linear temporal progression do not seem to occur among the peoples of North America, for whom time may be seen as atemporal, or ahistorical, in the sense that the passage of time does not require any kind of evolution or qualitative change. Instead it is repetitive, cyclical, and seasonal.[26] We shouldn't imagine that time doesn't matter, for observation of the calendar festivals is crucial. Nevertheless, space is as important as a guide for one's relationship with the cosmos as is time. This is, as it often is, when the focus of one's engagement with the sky is through the horizon. As the rising (or setting) sun shifts its position between midwinter and midsummer, it carves an arc along the horizon, encoding time in the landscape: At the summer solstice it is at its northerly extreme, at midwinter at its southerly. From a particular vantage point the daily sequence of risings and settings can become its own epic drama, now appearing over a distant mountaintop, now a valley. The primary referent on the horizon, and the one that enables the division of space into quadrants, is the location of the solstice points, the locations on the horizon at which the sun rises on the shortest day of the year, and the longest. The additional points—at which the sun sets—are often, if not always, as important, and are directly opposite the rising points. This solar grid formed the basis of a fourfold division of space which contrasts with the four cardinal points—north, south, east, and west—that commonly divide time and space into four in Europe and Asia.

The typical division of time and space into four, which appears to be an (almost) universal feature of human culture, occurs across the Americas. From the north of what are now the states of North Dakota and South Dakota, the Lakota, according to Tyon, one of their wise men, recorded in the early 20th century, grouped all their activities by fours. "This," the sage continued, "was because they recognized four directions: the west, the north, the east, and the south; four divisions of time: the day, the night, the moon and the year."[27] The list continued to include every feature of the natural or supernatural world imaginable: the four parts of a plant (root, stem, leaf, fruit), kinds of things that breathe (those that crawl, fly, walk on two legs, and walk on four legs), ages of human life (infancy, childhood, adulthood, old age), things above the world (sun, moon, sky, and stars), and the kinds of god (the great, their associates, the gods below them, and the spirits). The Navajo surrounded their world with four sacred mountains, each associated with colors and stones and kinship clans. East, for example, was the color white, a white shell, and the Leaf Clan.[28]

The living, moving structure of the cosmos was enacted in rituals designed, as in all religious cultures, to harmonize with and pay respect to the greater life-field of which humans are a part. The ritual enactment of the fourfold cosmos was observed in the 1920s, among the Hopi of First Mesa.[29] The Hopi celebrated a series of three winter festivals: First the Wöwöchim, then the Soyala, celebrated at the winter solstice, the shortest day; and, finally, the Powamu. All three festivals feature corn, a staple of the Hopi diet. The Wöwöchim was significant as the occasion for the initiation of boys into manhood, but our description of the Powamu contains more astronomical detail. The official observations were conducted by a "Sun chief or watcher," which may have been a position that was hereditary and, while being exercised, took the observer outside of the usual clan structure.[30] The Sun watcher then entered into the same kind of universal, timeless, shamanistic condition occupied by many priests at significant moments. The Powamu commenced with the first appearance, which would have been in the early evening shortly after sunset, of the new moon in late January or early February, corresponding to the Greco-Babylonian sign Aquarius. The anthropologist Julian Steward recorded in his diary:

> January 22. On this day the new moon appeared. Kachina chief looked for it, but was unable to see it on account of clouds. He must actually see it.
> January 23. The Kachina chief looked again for the moon and was successful in seeing it. This day is not counted as part of the ceremony. The following day is the first day.[31]

Already, at the previous full moon the Kachina chief had planted a box of corn. The seedlings were then distributed in the early days of the ceremony, their healthy sprouting being a good omen for the coming year. A Kachina is a spirit being, a reminder that the astronomy of the situation requires both ritual enactment and co-operation with invisible intelligences.

Once the moon had been seen, the "raising up of the sun" ritual could be performed. One participant took the part of Ahül, the Sun kachina, beginning with nightfall and then welcoming the rising sun, before visiting significant *kivas*, houses, and natural locations, observing the four directions, spreading corn paste, buying prayer sticks, and so on. The ceremony then proceeded for seventeen days of events, sometimes serious, at other times playful, often contemplative, but also festive, until the power of the life-world had been restored.

The use of stars to time rituals is apparent in some cultures, as in the case of the Mescalero Apache female puberty ritual. According to the anthropologist Claire Farrer,

> It's all in the stars. . . . Arcturus sets approximately one hour before timing begins with the Big Dipper. Alkaid ticks off hours by degrees [and] by the time that Capella is first visible . . . all the night's songs should be finished and a rest break called . . . as the stars fade and the sun once more fulfils the promise of the Creator, the girls will be painted [with solar symbols] the crowd will be blessed [and] the girls will complete the last of their runs to the east and around the ceremonial basket.[32]

The astrology operating here is one of signs, involving an active dialogue between sky and earth. The human act cannot actually start until the time is right, and this information must be revealed by the moon. While it is clear, then, that there is a notion that time unfolds in rhythms and patterns, understanding their meaning requires an act of communication between moon and human: Human sees moon and moon sends information to human.

If cosmology was enacted in ritual, it was also embodied in the built environment, and many, if not "most," Native Americans orient their dwellings to face the rising sun.[33] One might imagine that this tendency is purely natural in origin: What better way to wake up than with the first rays of light? On the other hand, there is no need to face the sun in order to either experience morning light or wake up; it is circadian (daily) rhythms in body chemistry and physiology that cause human beings to make that crucial shift from sleep to wakefulness, and no direct exposure to the sun is necessary for the resulting hormonal event to take place. Besides, it is also perfectly natural to pitch one's dwelling with a view of the most inspiring landscape feature or, if the sun is the crucial factor, to the south, in order to enjoy the maximum benefits of the sun's heat and light—an important consideration for northerners. A fixation with the east is, then, a religious imperative. It results from an understanding that the quality of time varies throughout the day, and at dawn one partakes of the source of the life itself. Celestial relationships could also be much more elaborate. The Skiri-Pawnee, for example, who, as we have seen, had a sophisticated system of constellations, embodied stellar patterns in the layout of their villages.[34] Domestic architecture, as well as religious and social, incorporated cosmological principles (such as the use of four supporting posts to represent the fourfold structure of time and space), even though preferences varied between both circular and square forms. Of a purely ritual/astronomical nature are the so-called medicine wheels, the surviving examples of which are found mainly along the foothills and plains to the west of the northern range of the Rockies, with most in the Canadian province of Alberta, suggesting the phenomenon is strongly regional. The best-known example is the Big Horn Medicine Wheel in Wyoming, which consists of a central cairn of around four meters in diameter, surrounded by twenty-eight spokes, consisting of stones, extending about twelve meters to an outer circle that contains, or is surrounded by, six other stone cairns. These can be used to measure both sunrise and sunset on the summer solstice as well as the rising of three bright stars—Aldebaran, Rigel, and the brightest of all the fixed stars, Sirius.[35] The medicine wheels in general are difficult, if not impossible, to date, but they would have functioned as timers for the ritual year particularly, perhaps, for the Sun Dance ceremony, which, for some tribes, marked the summer solstice. Unfortunately, many of the medicine wheels have been interfered with and so we cannot be entirely sure of their original layout.

On a more massive scale, the cosmological monument-building practices of Mexican civilization are evident in the extensive structures of the Puebloan culture in the southwestern United States, of which the best known are the ruins at Chaco Canyon in New Mexico, which were constructed between around 850 and 1150 CE.[36] Key structures, such as Casa Rinconada, the Great Kiva at Chaco Canyon, were a model of the creation, of the unity of time and space; and the rituals performed at critical points of the year, such as the solar solstices, reenacted the birth of humanity, as well as of the world as a whole, in a moment that enabled the process of life to continue.

From Alaska to Florida and from Labrador to California, Native American cosmology was based on an essential unity between all things, and its astrology operated on the premise that humanity was a willing participant in a dialogue with the stars, a partner in the endlessly repeating patterns of the sun and moon and the wandering paths of the planets. In certain fundamental respects, the Native American schemes share significant features with those in other regions, including the widespread reverence for a supreme creator, near-universal worship of the sun, a belief that terrestrial society should be harmonized with the passage of time as revealed in the passage of the celestial bodies, and the division of space and time into four. The existence of a creator locates North American cosmology on the boundary of the "chaotic" and "cosmic" cosmogonies, although the creator is hardly a personal God in the Jewish or Christian sense and is more akin to an impersonal, original, creative power. Native American astrology was, in terms of classical typology, "electional" and designed to identify auspicious moments for conducting the rituals that tied their societies to the heavens. It was also magical, in the sense that structures which incorporate celestial principles function as talismans, protecting humanity by calling heaven down to earth. The Native American religion, or worldview, was based on communication—talking to the spirits, conversing with the sky—in order that they could play as full a part in the life-world as possible. In this sense for the Native Americans, to live meant to act.

South and Central America

Salvation and Sacrifice

And since until noon the sun was rising, they heightened their voices, and after noon they slowly softened them, always in step with the movement of the sun.[1]

The best-known cultures of Mesoamerica, those of the Maya and Aztecs, and, in the Andes, that of the Inca, are well known for the attention they paid to the harmonization of their societies with the celestial realms. The civilizations of Central and South America were prime examples of "cosmic states," in which political and astronomical matters were intended to match each other in meticulous detail. Their cosmogonies were "chaotic" in that the universe came into being through a series of ad hoc, unplanned stages. Whatever interpretative, predictive astrology may have been practiced by the Inca has disappeared, but the astrology of Central America, which has survived from the Maya and Aztecs, was "cosmic" in that it was intricate, highly codified, and mathematically precise, at least at the official level. Perhaps the most important single feature of religious cosmology throughout the region's empires was reverence for the sun as a supreme deity and ruler of time. We know there were also unofficial local astrologers—sometimes we also know them as folk astronomers or calendar shamans. The only major technique used by them that has survived, though, is the Maya divinatory calendar, with which we shall deal below. Elsewhere, away from the great urban centers, in countries such as Colombia and Brazil, we still find evidence of astrological practices that are more spontaneous and "chaotic," in the sense that codification and precise interpretations are less important than a spontaneous engagement with the stars.

Most of the surviving evidence concerning the astrology of the Andean and Mesoamerican cultures relates to its official functions in relation to political matters; historical periodization and dynastic power; and war, peace, and ritual observance of the religious-agricultural calendar. The possible style and quality of unofficial vernacular or "folk" astrology may be understood from recent ethnographic work in Central and South America. The literature on Andean and Mesoamerican cosmology is not extensive, but there are sufficient studies to present a rich picture of societies that paid intense attention to the sky as a guide for ritual, social and agricultural affairs, and engagement with the divine.

The leading works include Anthony Aveni's *Skywatchers of Ancient Mexico* and his edited collections, *Native American Astronomy* and *The Sky in Mayan Literature*; while his *Empires of Time: Calendars, Clocks, and Cultures* contains up-to-date and useful summaries of Maya, Aztec, and Inca calendar systems. Anthony Aveni and Gary Urton's *Ethnoastronomy and Archeoastronomy in the American Tropics* is an early and useful collection of papers in the field. David Friedel, Linda Schele, and Joy Parker's *Maya Cosmos: Three Thousand Years on the Shaman's Path* is an excellent and comprehensive account of Maya cosmology, complemented by the astronomical details in Susan Milbrath's *Star Gods of the Maya*. Don McCaskill's *Amerindian Cosmology* contains papers on North, South, and Central America. The literature on the Inca is sparse, but Brian Bauer and David Dearbon's *Astronomy and Empire in the Ancient Andes* is a fine summary, and Gary Urton's *At the Crossroads of the Earth and the Sky: An Andean Cosmology* is also recommended. Gerardo Reichel-Dolmatoff's *Amazonian Cosmos: The Sexual and Religious Symbolism of the Tukano Indians* is a rare study of non-Andean, South American cosmology.[2]

Our understanding of the history of pre-Columbian South and Central America is constantly shifting as archaeologists make new discoveries and palaeographers work with (Mesoamerican) textual sources. The recent discovery of monumental remains in the Amazon, on the Brazilian-Bolivian border, dating to around 200–1283 CE and capable of supporting 60,000 people, has cast serious doubt on fond notions of the Amazonian forest as "virgin."[3] In addition, recent work at a site at Monte Verde in southern Chile has produced an apparent dating of 20,000 BCE, 10,000 years earlier than the date that was once given for the migration from Siberia to Alaska across the Bering land bridge. Carbon 14 dates of about 20,000 BCE of human remains were also obtained decades ago at Tlapacoya, Mexico, and in Pikimacahy Cave near Ayacucho, Peru, but were not universally accepted. Whatever is stated about American prehistory—that, for example, agriculture may have appeared in Central America by 5000 BCE but in North America around 2000 BCE—must therefore come with the major qualification "according to current archaeological evidence." The same caveat applies to our understanding of American religious practices, cosmology, and astronomy.

The source problems are also considerable. It is a small consolation that, although the peoples of South and Central America were systematically brutalized by their conquerors, and their culture devalued and destroyed, we do have the advantage of some written sources in the form of monumental inscriptions, and surviving texts known respectively as the Dresden, Madrid, Paris, and the (possibly inauthentic) Grolier Codices, named after the locations of the archives that now house them, as well as scores of other postcolonial texts that provide accounts of earlier cosmology. Such work has contributed much of value to our understanding of Mesoamerican culture since the major breakthrough in the translation of the Maya script took place in the 1970s, as a result of a concerted effort building on earlier successes; by 1989, about 800 hieroglyphs had been identified.[4] Possibly around 70 to 80 percent of the Maya script has now been deciphered. This has allowed a valuable reconstruction of the major features of pre-Columbian cosmic religion, but there is still considerable work to be done. Everything else, along with the notebooks we know that the astrologers carried, has been lost. When we move to Peru, the situation is worse, because of the Inca habit of keeping records on thin, golden sheets that were melted by the conquistadores, for whom cash was of far greater importance than knowledge. This leaves us with little more than visual clues: We have just one precious drawing of a wall in the Coricancha, the main temple in the capital, Cuzco, dedicated to, among other deities, the sun, moon, and stars. But, as to the meaning of the Coricancha's portrayal of the Inca cosmos, there is little certainty. However, to our list of "texts" we can add two important sources. The first are the monumental buildings and sculptures, of which the richest examples survive from the Mesoamerican cultures, which either contain celestial iconography or are aligned with significant celestial patterns. The other, which has proved fruitful in our understanding of Maya cosmology, is the testimony of modern Indians and the anthropologists who have lived with them. Even so, all our understanding of pre-Columbian cosmology is provisional and dependent on fragmentary sources, archaeological interpretation, colonial-era texts that may be filtered through Christian eyes, and anthropological accounts that are, inevitably to some extent, corrupted by their assumptions and preconceptions.

We have a good account of the origins of the Maya cosmos itself, which came into being as a gradual emergence of order, of something from nothing. The opening lines of the great creation epic the *Popul Vuh* expresses the still beauty of a calm morning, the dawn of everything:

Now it ripples, now it still murmurs, ripples, still it sighs, still hums
and it is empty under the sky.
Here follows the first words, the first eloquence:
There is not one person, one animal, bird, fish, crab, tree, rock, hollow,
canyon, meadow, forest. Only the sky alone is there; the face of the
earth is not clear. Only the sea alone is pooled under all the sky;
there is nothing whatever gathered together. It is at rest; not a single
thing stirs. It is held back, kept at rest under the sky.
Whatever there is that might be is simply not there: only the pooled
water, only the same sea.[5]

And then, the text continues, deep within the dark, the Plumed Serpent,
the Aztec Quetzalcoatl, the Maker and Modeler of all, stirs and speaks with
the Heart of Sky, also known as Hurricane, and the creation begins. The cosmos of the great Mesoamerican and Andean civilizations was alive. Its structure was that of a living body. In this sense it is not necessary to ask what
something is made of, or how it moves, but what one's relationship with it is.

Some descriptions of the Aztec cosmos talk of "nine heavens" inhabited by Tonatiuh, the sun; Meztli, the moon; and Tlahuizcalpantecuhtli,
the dawn. The Mesoamerican universe was envisaged as revolving around
a world tree, also a common motif in Europe and Asia; and, like the Native
Americans to the north and the Europeans to the east, the Mesoamericans
venerated the number four as a means of dividing time and space. The tree
stood at the center of the four cardinal directions, although in some versions
there might be a tree for each direction. Fourness, though, is not necessarily defined spatially by north, south, east, and west but may also be marked
by the four points at which the sun rises and sets at dawn and dusk on the
winter and summer solstices.[6] In a sense, the four quarters were themselves
divine, as the locations of four of the chief deities: Tezcatlipoca, who inhabited the north; Huitzilopchtli, who dwelt in the south; Tonatiuh, the sun, who
occupied the east; and Quetzalcoatl, who presided over the west. This belief
in fourness as the basic structure of time and space extended to the Andes,
where the Inca envisaged four heavens, with the greatest god in the highest
heaven. Fourness as a fundamental property is also evident in the *Popul Vuh*,
which records the "lighting of the sky-earth" in which by "halving the cord
(and) stretching the cord," the maker of the world undertook "the fourfold
siding, fourfold cornering, measuring, fourfold staking . . . in the sky, on the
earth [of] the four sides [and] the four corners."[7] Although the world is laid
out in a fourfold pattern, fourness is not created in the process of construc-

tion, but construction proceeds in a fourfold manner because fourness is written into the fabric of existence.

In a parallel with schemes found in Greece, Mesopotamia, and India, the fourfold division of space was also generally extended into notions of time. The Maya envisaged four successive worlds, named respectively in order, Jaguar Quitze, Jaguar Night, Mahucutah, and True Jaguar. The Aztecs, coming later in time than the Maya, added a fifth world: their own. The four Aztec worlds, or suns, all lasted for multiples of fifty-two years and were destroyed by catastrophes related to the sun's name. The first sun, 4 Jaguar, was destroyed by wild animals; the second, 4 Wind, by wind; the third, 4 Rain, by a rain of fire; and the fourth, 4 Water, by a deluge. The Aztecs believed that they were living in a fifth age, 4 Movement.

Such repetitive cosmogonies incorporate a dialetical relationship between chaos and order, with attendant hopes and fears—hope for order and fear of chaos. The Aztec version includes the creation of the fifth sun—and the moon—brought into existence by the deliberate self-immolation of the gods Nanahuatzin (or Nanahuatl) and Tecuciztecatl. The tale contains a combination of features from the profound to the mundane. The latter is represented in a simple explanation for a typical item of observational astronomy: After Tecuciztecatl initially refused to jump into the great fire prepared by the other gods, one of them hit him in the face with a rabbit, explaining through an event of almost slapstick triviality the resemblance of the blemishes on the moon's surface to a rabbit. The story, though, also contains motifs of messianic resurrection and salvation; it is through Nanahuatzin's noble sacrifice that humanity survives: The god dies and human beings are saved. In recognition of his willingness to offer his own life so that others may live, Nanahuatzin is transformed into the sun, Tonatiuh. When, then, solar rituals were enacted and solar alignments written into sacred monuments, the Aztecs were engaged in a deeply respectful acknowledgment of the great sacrifice made on their behalf. In observing the ebb and flow of the sun's life as he moved this way and that along the horizon, between the solstices, they were observing a drama that, through its repetitive nature, held echoes of the great calamity and renaissance to which they owed their existence.

Like many polytheistic systems, in which the relationship with monotheism is fluid and uncertain, the Mesoamerican may be portrayed as a scheme in which many deities emerge out of the one. The Maya, for example, clearly envisaged a Great Spirit, not unlike the Native American model. In the *Popul Vuh*, this being is described as the

Maker Modeler,
mother-father of life, of humankind,
giver of breath, giver of heart,
bearer, upbringer in the light that lasts
of those born in the light, begotten in the light;
worrier, knower of everything, whatever there is:
sky-earth, lake-sea.[8]

The Great Spirit, if we can apply that North American term to the Maya deity, is, then, the world and whatever is in it, the creator and the creation, life and the source of life. He was also known as Hunab Ku (the one god), and, as elsewhere, solar and universal deities are often coincident, the universal being expressed through the particular. In some stories Itzamna, the legendary founder of Maya culture and the supreme deity and creator, was a savior and a civilizing hero who, among his other skills, was able to return the dead to life. The colonial sources are far from precise and may be misleading, but Itzamna himself can also be associated with Hunab Ku or the sun; celestial and divine identities may both be polysymbolic.

The details of the Maya constellations are better understood now than they were a few decades ago, but the identification of Maya stars with their Western equivalents are less important than the use of the sky as a huge stage set for imaginal engagement between humanity and the cosmos, a means to engage not just with the creation but with the act of creation.[9] The gods and goddesses of the Mesoamerican pantheon were personifications of everything considered important in the phenomenological world and included a range of celestial deities. The Aztec sun god was known under various names depending on how he was best invoked in different rituals. In his main form he was Tonatiuh, the leader of heaven. As Tezcatlipoca (or Smoking Mirror—a reference to the use of obsidian mirrors for divination), he ripened the harvest, but he might also have inflicted drought and threatened starvation. It is difficult to unravel myths after centuries of syncretism and cross-cultural transmission, but, in an early form, Tezcatlipoca was the Heart of the Sky who initiated the creation with Quetzalcoatl in the *Popul Vuh*. The two creators, though, were also sworn enemies, expressing the motif of struggle between two gods familiar from Persia, Egypt, and Christian mythology.

The worship of the snake-bird, the Plumed Serpent, is attested under a variety of names across the region since the Preclassic period, probably in the late first millennium BCE, and was clearly associated with the planet Venus, which achieved the same profound significance for the Maya and Aztecs as it did for other pre-modern cultures, by the classical period, from around 300 CE.[10] No astronomical logic dictates why Venus should be at war with the sun, so the enmity between the two gods may be a legacy of the Aztec conquest of the Toltecs, who had revered Quetzalcoatl as the creator, lord of the winds, and master of life. He was a civilizer, a creator and inventor, responsible for art, crafts, knowledge, and technology, and he was connected with merchants, was related to the dawn and the gods of the wind, and was a patron of the priesthood. Like many other conquerers (the Romans and Assyrians come to mind), the Aztecs were syncretizers who adopted the gods and goddesses of the people they subjugated, along with their land and wealth, and deities could be added to the pantheon with no concern for precise consistency. The Aztecs also had a goddess, Tlazolteotl, who had a relationship, albeit a marginal one, with Venus and was connected with, among other things, love and sex (she was the patronness of adulterers).

Quetzalcoatl may have been a creator, but his affairs were, above all, tied to the cycles of the planet Venus, and to its regular periods of invisibility; when it moved too close to the sun to be seen, it was personified, as in Mesopotamian stories of Inanna's descent to the underworld, to a classic motif of death and resurrection. Anthony Aveni takes up the story:

> [A]t the time when the planet was visible in the sky (as evening star) Quetzalcoatl died. And when Quetzalcoatl was dead he was not seen for 4 days; they say that he dwelt in the underworld, and for 4 more days he was bone (that is, he was emaciated, he was weak); not until 8 days had passed did the great star appear; that is, as the morning star. They said that then Quetzalcoatl ascended the throne as god.[11]

Such resurrection themes also occurred in Inca religious iconography, for solar mythology generally features the imaginative accounts of the sun's daily disappearance into the darkness and rebirth into the light. The Inca celestial trinity consisted of Inti, the sun; his wife and sister Mama Quilla, the moon; and Chasca, his page, the god of Venus and the dawn.

The meanings of the Inca constellations appear to have no central patterning and so may be based on the gradual accretion of regional ideas over centuries, rather than a single invention. Their correspondences with terrestrial phenomena appear to be primarily animal and botanical. The Pleiades, one of the most familiar of all seasonal markers, were related to maize production, as they still are by the Incas' modern descendants.[12] In Mesoamerica, the Pleiades were also venerated for their protection of cereals, which could be the result of a shared ancient tradition or, equally, the simple observation of a common natural cycle. However, most of the Inca astronomical referents are still uncertain, especially the constellation of the Llama, one of the most important of celestial animals on account of its terrestrial equivalent's critical importance: Its body may actually be a dark cloud in the Milky Way, its eyes the stars Alpha and Beta Centauri.[13] Similar uncertainties afflict our understanding of the constellation of the Snake (where was it, and was it a dark space instead of a star group?), as well as Inca observations of Venus: We know they watched the planet closely, but we have little or no idea how they attributed significance to it. Neither do we have any evidence of notions of time among the Inca comparable to the complexity of calendrical counting among the Mesoamericans. However, modern ethnography may give a better picture of popular astrology in the lands ruled by the Inca, or adjoining them, of which the anthropologist Gerardo Reichel-Dolmatoff's work among the Desana Indians of the Colombian-Brazilian border remains the principal exemplar. Such astrology includes moral tales (the sun repents his unwitting act of incest with his daughter, Venus), warnings of chaos as a result of moral collapse (solar eclipses), and important information for food collection (the nights of the full moon are bad for fishing; the constellation of the shrimp heralds the rainy season). Reichel-Dolmatoff was particularly alert to the notion of astrological theory as a celestial projection of social codes. Describing Desana cosmology, he explained how

[a] relationship also exists between the moon and the conditions of health and sickness. When there is a full moon, people observe in which zone the spots are most outstanding, east, west, south or north and fro[m] their position the direction from which the sickness come is deduced. Because these spots, according to myth, represent the menstrual blood of the Daughter of the Sun [Venus?], we observe again an association between sexual physiology and the concept of imminent danger.[14]

The details may not be exactly those of Andean popular astrology under the Inca, but the spirit, most likely, is. Later work extended this research into other Colombian peoples, demonstrating an astrology very similar to that familiar in North America, including very careful attention to the sun, moon, and calendars; a ritual approach to daily life expressed, for example, in the incorporation of cosmic principles (such as the universal division of space into gender—male and female—or by the number four); and a participatory attitude to the cosmos as a whole, recognizing that human action is required to ensure the cosmos's continued harmonious functioning.[15] Following the example of Lévy-Bruhl and the structuralists, it is often easier to identify native star stories as containing an underlying social message rather than a prognostic function. For example, when the Barasana, who live on the Colombian-Brazilian border, tell of the conception of the solitary hero as a result of the moon's impregnation of his younger sister, they are both accounting for blemishes on the moon's surface and warning against incest.[16] Such an astrology is fluid in its relation to the actual positions of the stars and planets, and, if one celestial pattern fails to announce the right time to perform a ritual, another one may suffice. This is what we term "chaotic" astrology—spontaneous, flexible, and pragmatic.

The official astrology of the Aztecs and Maya, on the other hand, was "cosmic," highly codified, and concerned with precision. The accuracy of Mesoamerican astronomy points to the concept of the world as precisely regulated by mathematically definable patterns—the cosmic ticking clock. The Maya of the classical period could forecast the dawn appearance of Venus or a total eclipse to within a day, a century in advance.

The purpose of astronomy was to forecast the future and manage the present, two functions that are symbiotic. As the historian Stephen McCluskey puts it, "To the extent that in the high cultures of Mesoamerica cosmologies are tied to a predictive astronomy, these astronomies are arithmetical rather than geometrical and they are concerned with the prediction of the dates of astronomically and astrologically significant events. . . ."[17] For the influential archaeastronomer Anthony Aveni, who was equally strong in his opinion, the Mayan astronomical texts were "purely astrological" in their function and intent.[18]

The surviving evidence points to the private, sacred nature of the astrological documents, at least at an elite level, and their use primarily by a wealthy, literate elite. The name for a Maya priest was Ah Kin, or Ah Kin Mai, which means "He of the Sun," suggesting "a close connection with the calendar and astronomy" in the fulfilling of sacred functions.[19] These officials were actually the equivalent of similar state functionaries across the world—of whom we might cite as examples the hour-watchers in Egypt and the temple-scribes in Babylon. They were highly educated and responsible for maintaining the calendar, arranging and conducting official rituals, and providing to the political elite advice and answers to their questions, all activities that required mathematical and astronomical skill and a sophisticated awareness of the intricate meaning of each phase of the unfolding patterns of time and space.[20] However, Anthony Aveni also writes of the Maya "calendrical shamans . . . [who] travelled from village to village with their books of prognos-tications tucked under their arms."[21] In the Inca realm such people were the *yanca*, or *yanac*, a term translated by the Spanish as "astrologer," and they might be found advising the urban elite as much as rural villagers. Even if the Maya calendrical shamans'—or astrologers'—preferred customer was the wealthy landowner, there is a clear inference that astrologers could be acces-sible to anyone.

The surviving almanacs from the post-conquest period give a flavor of the reasons for precise prediction in order to warn of future danger, a cus-tom that continued until the Conquistadores arrived. Both the Inca and the Aztecs observed dire omens that presaged or coincided with their conquest by the Spanish. The Aztecs witnessed a column of fire that burned dread-fully in the air for a year in 1517, four years before the Conquistadores' final victory. The subsequent account reported how "when this sign and portent was first seen, the natives were overcome with terror," aware that a calamity was approaching but unsure of its nature.[22] We also have earlier examples, such as the following: "Woe to the turtle [drought?]: woe to the warrior and pregnant female; his sacrifice, his divine punishment is set; evil excessive sun; the misery of the maize seed."[23] The threat is clear: Drought leads to a poor harvest and a poor harvest to possible starvation. Again, a multitude of examples from the Old World suggests the means that might be taken to stave off such a disaster, from the natural (reinforce the water storage and irrigation systems) to the supernatural (appeal to the gods via prophylactic rituals) and a mixture of the two (manage the environment by manipulating magical sympathies). At any rate, we see in operation here one of astrology's prime functions: to maintain the ecological harmony between humanity and the environment.

We can identify three other major characteristics of Mesoamerican astrol-ogy. First, it was concerned with the individual's duty to engage with the cosmos and preoccupied with "the appropriate course of human action to keep the civilized world running on sacred time."[24] Second, functionally, the primary collective activity in which most people would have been engaged was participation in rituals designed to maintain the annual cycle of plant-ing and harvesting. Third, such manipulation of time on a daily human scale should be seen as a microcosmic drama that took place within the macro-cosmic concern with the long-term cycles of the creation and destruction of the world, the birth of the gods, and the origins of humanity. As Aveni put it, "[T]he main business of the Maya codices was to keep track of cycle upon cycle of time."[25] We can say exactly the same of Inca astronomy, wherein the notion of the cosmic state was acted through time via, on different occasions, sequences of lunar and solar months, with their attendant rituals.[26]

The unique feature of the Mesoamerican calendar was the Tzolkin (Tonalpohualli to the Aztecs), the "day-count" of 260 days, composed of 20 named days and 13 numbers, which occurs in the *Dresden Codex*.[27] The scheme is constructed from 20 named days and 13 numbers, with 260 permutations, one day at a time. The Tzolkin's origin is uncertain; it was probably developed in the late formative or early classical periods, perhaps between 300 BCE and 300 CE, spread to all Mesoamerican cultures, and is still in use.[28] It is certainly divinatory in purpose, as it cannot be used to time the seasons, and each day has a range of iconic images that varied among different cultures and can be interpreted symbolically. For example, the first of the 20 day signs, Imix, was a water lily to the Maya and a caiman (Cipactli) to the Aztecs. It represented the surface of the earth and was bad for leaders.[29] In this case Imix is therefore a day on which every leader knows that risk should be avoided and caution exercised. This prognostic system still survives in unchanged form among some isolated folk in southern Mexico and the Maya highlands, under the care of calendar priests, and it has also performed an easy and popular leap into Western New Age culture.[30]

The 260-year count ran simultaneously with the 365-day Haab, known as a "Vague Year" to modern historians and approximating to the solar year, which extended the total number of combinations to a "Calendar Round" of 18,980 days, or 52 years. The current "Long Count," which began on 11 August 3114 BCE, is measured in a series of units, a *uinal* of 20 kins (days), a *tun* of 360 days, a *katun* of 20 tuns, and a *baktun* of 20 *katuns*, or 144,000 days. The thirteenth *baktun* was seen to come to an end on ad 21 December 2012 (the Maya date 13.0.0.0.0) and became the focus of a great deal of New Age apocalyptic excitement as well as *2012*, a classic Hollywood "disaster" movie, largely thanks to Jose Arguelles's imaginative reconstruction of the Mayan original.[31] The apocalyptic prophecies supposedly based on the Maya calendar, though, seem to be a combination of a series of misunderstandings of the original material and distortions caused by its incorporation into a Western New Age, millenarian framework.[32] The sequence can be extended into multiples of *baktuns*, potentially, as in Indian chronology, adding up to billions of years: More interesting than the Mayas' supposed millennial concerns is the notion that they could peer infinite distances into both the past and present.

Also of crucial significance was Venus's average 584-day synodic period— the time between its conjunctions with the sun. The real gap between Sun–Venus conjunctions varies from 580 to 587 days, but the average, over five complete conjunctions, is 584 days. Without getting too involved in numbers, the significance is that every eight years, almost to the day, the sun, moon, and Venus all returned to the same place in the sky. That three great cycles of cosmic time had simultaneously come to an end and were beginning again appeared to be a dramatic indication of the infinite possibilities of creation. The mere description of this event does not do justice to its potentially awe-inspiring appearance when, for example, the first appearance of a new crescent moon in a clear evening sky coincides with Venus's brightest phase and the two celestial bodies occupy the sky in a vivid display of numinous power. Any cycle involving Venus was reminiscent of Quetzalcoatl and so concerned with war and violence.[33] Yet bloodletting in Mesoamerican culture was a necessary means of repaying the debt owed to the gods for the blood they shed during the creation and for securing fertility and maintaining the cosmic order: Prisoners of war were sacrificed in this cause, although the figure of up to 20,000 that has fueled popular images of the Aztecs is demonstrably an exaggeration based on tendentious early Spanish reports.

The Maya, Aztecs, and Inca all managed time through an elaborate series of rituals whose timing was defined by astronomical patterns, chiefly the phases of the sun and moon, throughout the year, and were intended to maintain the equilibrium of the seasonal cycle, preventing extremes of drought or flood, a purpose achieved through the careful propitiation of the relevant deities.[34] The ceremonies, though, were conducted with elaborate attention to detail, including the wholesale sacrifice of prisoners of war. Every year, for example, just one prisoner, whose looks were suitably powerful, was chosen to impersonate Tezcatlipoca, one of the creators. For most of the following year he was treated with deep reverence and lived in great luxury, waited on by eight devoted servants. He was a living god in human form. Twenty days before he was sacrificed, the intended victim took four wives, representing goddesses who embodied the female aspect of the division of space-time, initiating a series of festivals. On the day of his blood sacrifice the solar man-god was led to the top of the temple, where his beating heart was ripped out and offered to the sun god.

The great Inca calendar rituals were as magnificent as anything in Mesoamerica. We have a colorful description of a solar harvest-festival ritual that took place in Cuzco in 1535, witnessed by the Spaniard Bartolomé de Segovia, presided over by the Inca—the emperor—and attended by 600 magnificently dressed nobles:

They stood in two rows, each of which was made up of over three hundred lords. It was like a procession, some on one side and the others on the other, and they stood very silent, waiting for sunrise. When the sun had not yet fully risen, they began slowly and in great order and harmony to intone a chant; and as they sang they each moved forward . . . and as the [sun] went in rising, so their song intensified . . . and so they sang from the time when the sun rose until it had completely set. And since until noon the sun was rising, they heightened their voices, and after noon they slowly softened them, always in step with the movement of the sun.[35]

As in many solar states, the Inca, in his person, embodied the sun on earth. He stood at the fulcrum of the system of ritual action, architecture, and astronomy that preserved harmony on earth. It is often said the cosmic political systems of Mesoamerica and the Andes were designed to maintain the power of the elites. This is misleading. The Mesoamerican and Andean rulers were quite capable of abusing their positions, but they were also expected to express the general quality whose equivalent was known in Medieval Europe as "virtue," according to which they were as much servants of their people as masters, obliged to care for their subjects rather than exploit them. The emperor was an embodiment of the sun and could be associated with other celestal bodies, including Venus, and was a link with the divine and a magician, a living talisman, channeling the power of the heavens for the benefit of his people.

Time, in the form of Venus's motions, as well as those of the other cosmic cycles, was embodied in a series of sacred buildings in the Mesoamerican realms. Typical was the so-called Palace of the Governor, a richly decorated structure in Uxmal, the capital of a Mayan state that appears to have flourished between around 500 and 1200 CE. The building itself was probably completed in the early 10th century and is a long, low structure built over a platform with a long façade containing a series of openings and covered in around 350 Venus-related glyphs. These images suggest that the entire building has a celestial function, perhaps to maintain harmony between Venus's earthly responsibilities and its heavenly motions. The first evidence suggested that the building's central doorway was aligned with the center of a double-headed jaguar throne in the courtyard, and from there to a pyramid-like structure on the southeastern horizon that approximated to Venus's southernmost rise, a point it reaches every eight years and that marks the culmination of a phase of Venusian time. This view has been challenged on the grounds that the difference between the alignment and the southernmost rising point of Venus as morning star is almost three degrees, or five diameters of the sun, and no firm conclusion can be drawn from such loose measurements.[36] The palace's orientation, however, agrees perfectly with the northerly extremes of the evening star (Venus in the evening sky), which always occur from April to May and thus announce the beginning of the rainy season; the Venus glyphs on the façade of the building are placed in the cheeks of the rain god Chac. The issue, then, is not whether there is a celestial relationship but of its details.

The construction of sacred space using both natural features and monumental architecture was a profoundly important matter for the civilizations of the Andes and Mesoamerica, and the latter are especially known for their building of pyramids.[37] These, probably more frequently than their Egyptian equivalents, often possess precise astronomical identities. Some commentators claim that Mesoamerican cities are "cosmograms"—designed to embody the cosmos in their layout and structure.[38] Such sacred buildings as the Mesoamerican pyramids are talismans, providing a medium for the harmonization of a potentially disordered society with the permanently ordered patterns of the cosmos, whether through their structure, their astronomical orientations and the ceremonies performed on them, or a combination of all three. They also, in that the stellar and calendrical patterns they incorporate are divine, are themselves divine.

Some of the best-known examples are located in one of the greatest of all astronomical cities in the world—a true cosmopolis, the city of Teotihuacan, the "place of the gods."[39] From perhaps around 200 CE, or a little earlier, until the 7th century, Teotihuacan was the most powerful and sacred city in ancient Mexico, home to around 200,000 inhabitants. Even in the 14th century its reputation was such that the Aztecs still buried their rulers there. Teotihuacan's pyramids rivaled those of ancient Egypt, and the greatest, the Pyramid of the Sun, rose 230 feet from a base the same size as the Great Pyramid of Giza. The smaller Pyramid of the Moon was 150 feet high, but built on higher ground so that its summit matched that of the Sun Pyramid. The third pyramid, dedicated to Quetzalcoatl, was located at the southern end of the main boulevard, the Avenue of the Dead, which ran precisely 15½° east of due north. The three pyramids are also aligned with the surrounding mountains, suggesting that the entire city was seen as the focus of terrestrial and celestial forces. The key to the astronomical code lies in the 260-day calendar and the regularity of the dry and rainy seasons that governed maize production. The Pyramid of the Sun, for example, is aligned with sunrise on 11 February (start of agricultural season, clearing of the fields), sunset on 30 April (the onset of the rainy season and the time for planting) and 13 August (the ripening of the first corn cobs), and sunrise on 29 October, the end of the rainy season. The Maya then moved through a cosmic web in which the formula star = god = rain = maize varied throughout the year depending on time, and the religious-cosmic structure of the state as expressed through architecture, sacrifice, and ritual was designed to keep the *machina mundi* in operation.

The relationship between the sky and the landscape in the Inca realm was less spectacular than that in Mesoamerica but ingenious and unparalleled in any other culture. One unusual feature was the system of pillars on the horizon outside the Inca capital, Cuzco, which could be used to track the daily movement of the sunrise point backward and forward across the horizon between the summer and winter solstices.[40] The pillars have largely been destroyed, so we have no idea how many there were, only that they existed as one of the most extensive public astronomical measuring devices ever conceived on a par, in their own way, with the Great Pyramid. Also unique were the *ceques*, lines that radiated out from Cuzco, dividing the region into quadrants, and containing shrines known as *huacas*.[41] The role of the *ceques* together with the *huacas* was calendrical, astronomical, ritual, and sacrifical, and they were designed, through the manner in which they were constructed in the landscape, to bring sky and living earth together in harmony.

The great civilizations of South and Central America were driven by a profound sense of the intricate and intimate relationship among divinity, earth, and stars. Within the overall region we can identify differences among the official cosmologies of the great empires, with their precise calendars or devotion to the sun, and those of the indigenous native peoples, in which a spontaneous engagement with the whole environment, both earth and sky, was the guiding principle. We can also identify different astrologies, from the highly structured "cosmic" versions designed to serve the Aztec and Maya states to the flexible "chaotic" forms evident among the forest dwellers of Colombia and Brazil. Each may suggest different attitudes toward fate, which unfolded with mathematical precision in the cities of Mexico but could be a matter of more fluid negotiation for mountain and forest dwellers. In all cultures, though, divinities, stars, and food—usually corn—are combined in such a way that the overwhelming goal is clearly submission to a greater order in order to ensure a single priority: survival. If we can generalize at all about the religion of this diverse region, it was heavily concerned with the natural world, for which evidence is found in the central importance attached to the iconography of corn, or maize. But for the Inca, Aztec, and Maya it was also based in a profound view of the need to navigate one's way, and society's path, though the changing qualities of time and space as indicated by the passage of the constellations and the rising and setting points of the sun, moon, and significant stars.

Sub-Saharan Africa

Heaven on Earth

Oh, if there were a place in heaven for me!
That I would have wings to fly there![1]

Traditional African cosmology accords a huge importance to the belief that the entire cosmos is alive, populated by invisible living beings, including spirits and ancestors, and animated by soul. Among many peoples, even the individual has a "double," who may animate him or her but is separate and may also walk away.[2] For these reasons, while engagement with the entire cosmos is vibrant, astrology is "chaotic" in the sense that, while the sun, moon, and stars may be important as calendar markers or sources of meaning, there is little indication of codified systems of astral divination except in areas heavily influenced by Islam.

The division of Africa into regions is problematic and is best done in terms of linguistic groups: Afro-Asiatic, Nilo-Saharian, Nilo-Saharian, Niger-Kordofanian (Bantu), Khoisan, and Malayo-Polynesian (Austronesian). However, for general purposes a division into two—the north and the sub-Saharan—is logical on the simple historical grounds that the entire region along the southern Mediterranean fringe was subject to intense influences from the Near East—chiefly the Phoenicians—and Greeks, along with occupation by Rome, conversion to Christianity, and invasion by the armies of Islam. In general, much of the area to the south of the Sahara was untouched by such cultural forces until the colonial period, although there were exceptions, notably the extension of Islam as far south as northern Nigeria in the west and the coastal area of modern Mozambique. The Mozambiquan coast was also previously in range of Roman and, later, Chinese traders; the latter, or their intermediaries, penetrating inward to the political and financial hub at Great Zimbabwe, which flourished for 300 years, from the 13th to the 15th century; during the heyday of Great Zimbabwe, there may have been between 1,000 and 2,000 Muslims engaged in diplomatic and commercial activities in the Zimbabwean uplands. Africa was both a source of cosmological ideas and a participant in the long-range relationships that connected Europe to Asia in the ancient world.

No cultural boundaries are watertight, and in the far northeast of the continent, the ancient Egyptian civilization, which requires a separate chapter, was in constant communication not only with its Mediterranean and Near Eastern neighbors but also with people to the south and was also subject to at least one dynasty of Nubian pharaohs. In addition, since the early centuries CE, Ethiopia has been Christian, while in the 1980s the presence of African Jews in the country became worldwide news. In the west, a network of medieval kingdoms extending down to the coasts of modern states such as Ghana profited from trade with the north. The most celebrated of all cities in the region was Timbuktu, a remarkable cultural center that flourished from the 11th century until Moroccan occupation in 1591 initiated a decline in both trade and scholarship.[3]

Our knowledge of African cosmology, astronomy, and astrology has suffered from a range of methodological problems. Those scholars who have paid attention to African culture, and they are not many, have generally been ignorant of celestial matters. Or, rather, if they have dealt with cosmology, it has been in terms of social hierarchies and kinship relations, with little attention paid to the sky or celestial deities. Only terrestrial cosmology seems to be of general interest to anthropologists, and the astronomical dimension is largely ignored. Therefore, while the practice of divination is ubiquitous, evidence for astrology itself is sparse, except where part and parcel of Islam. A much higher value appears to have been placed on divinatory methods that communicated with the immediate environment rather than the distant, with local spirits rather than celestial deities. In this sense, heaven, as a source of wisdom, is here on earth.

In addition, if we wish to engage with African cosmology prior to Western colonization, we confront significant problems associated with Western influence, a key example of which is the Dogon controversy, which we will turn to below. The historian Keith Snedegar summed up the problem, in his excellent introduction to the area, thus: "[A]ll scholarship from the field," he wrote, "must be handled with care."[4] Africans themselves can experience personal difficulties; when confronted with Christianity or science, they struggle to either reject or salvage their traditional learning.[5] The South African astronomer Thebe Medupe, for example, talks of the way in which his scientific education has created a gulf between his own self-identity and his roots in the 2008 film *Cosmic Africa*.

An additional problem, of course, is the reliance on oral traditions and the general absence of written sources, which always creates such problems for anthropologists; African religion does not have sacred texts and its cosmology is not described in encyclopedias. Then there are the political agendas. For example, we may encounter ethnocentrism, in which theories that have developed in Western contexts are then countered by an equally misleading reaction in which non-Western astronomies are seen as complex, unique, and defined by their difference from Western ideas.[6] These are ideological positions that can prevent a good understanding of the evidence. On the positive side, we can point to the recent initiatives of the physicist and anthropologist Jarita Holbrook, who has done her best to put African astronomy on the academic radar by bringing scholars in the field together. Her efforts resulted in a conference in Ghana held to coincide with the total solar eclipse of 26 March 2006, and a resulting publication, *African Cultural Astronomy*.[7] The proceedings of a previous conference, the African Astronomical History Symposium, held in Cape Town in November 2005, were published in the journal *African Skies*, and are available online.[8] Dominique Zahan's *The Religion, Spirituality and Thought of Traditional Africa* is a comprehensive introduction to the subject area, while John S. Mbiti has dealt well with general African cosmology in his *African Religions and Philosophy*.[9] A number of scholars, though, have raised problems. For example, many anthropologists, being concerned with the collection of regular information, tend to "ignore ephemeral phenomena, especially irregular ones, such as comets, regarding their infrequency as a sign of irrelevance."[10] This could perhaps account for the overwhelming emphasis on earth-based ritual, religion, and divination in most ethnographies. The African anthroplogist Maxwell Owusu went further. Speaking of Western ethnographies of African culture, he wrote, "[F]requently it is not clear whether the accounts so brilliantly presented are about native realities at all, or whether they are about informants, about scientific models and imaginative speculations, or about the anthropologists themselves and their fantasies."[11] Such skepticism is well advised.

All the current evidence suggests that human beings evolved in Africa and migrated to the rest of the world in successive waves. The implication is that, once these early people had developed sufficient awareness of the world around them, and when they had evolved into storytelling beings, they would have had invented tales about the stars. They would then have taken these stories to Asia and Europe as they moved from one place to another. Astronomy, therefore, began in Africa. The archaeologist Jacquetta Hawkes reasoned that it must have been back in East Africa, where the fossil record shows that the earliest humans were walking on two legs and making tools around 3 million years ago, that they began to notice the sun as a separate, powerful force in their lives.

> Now at last mind was dawning [she wrote], raised between sun and earth. . . . In that dawn of mind, sunrise and sunset, if not the sun itself, seem likely to have been among the first things to have been named by the first men. Even such a being as Oldoway Man [Olduvai man, from the Olduvai Gorge in Kenya], one of the earliest known hominids . . . must always have been very much aware of the passage of the sun across the gorge where he lived. He may conceivably even have [expressed] its coming and going. If so, then here already was a step in creation through *logos*—the separation of day and night.[12]

Hawkes, as she freely admits, was engaging in imaginative speculation. The material evidence dates from millions of years later, when Africans were marking lunar calendars on animal bones; a baboon's thigh bone, discovered in the Lebembo mountains bordering Swaziland and dated to 35,000 BCE, contains twenty-nine notches, suggesting, plausibly, that it may have been a counter for the synodic month (from new moon to new moon) of 29.53 days.[13]

African religion contains distinctive features such as shamanic practices, the transmigration of souls, and veneration of ancestors, but in this chapter we focus only on its celestial components. African cosmology is as subtle, nuanced, and varied as that of any other continent.[14] If we can generalize, and so risk misrepresenting the variety in African cosmology, then we can point to the following major characteristics: The universe is broadly divided into three zones (sky/heaven, earth, and an underworld); there is often a single creator, but with myriad other deities and spirits, who are often the souls of the dead; the entire world is alive; magic, in the sense of manipulation of the world through engagement with visible and invisible forces, is taken for granted; the sun and moon are venerated as vital to human existence; the sky is a dramatic stage-set for telling stories about human affairs; and the passage of the year and the cosmos requires active participation by human beings, an expression of Lucien Lévy-Bruhl's *participation mystique*.[15] All these characteristics, of course, are standard features of pre-modern culture. What we don't find in Africa, except under Islamic influence, is the absolute devotion to the exact, precise motions of time and the directions of space that was a feature of those societies that developed technically complex "cosmic" astrologies. We could argue, then, that African cosmology allows more room for the human than the celestial, and we might, therefore, with caution, describe it as humanist.

The African approach to time is active and participatory, which is, in itself, a fairly uncontroversial statement. African timekeeping is also generally (although not universally) experiential and defined by seasonal events and their attendant rituals. We can also consider the traditional African approach to time through a comparison based on modes of economic production. Whereas in the modern West we might see time as a preexisting commodity that can only be utilized, bought, and sold, in Africa it has to be created or produced. In Africa, Mbiti writes, "Man is not a slave of time; instead he 'makes as much time as he wants.'"[16] As a vivid comparison, when foreigners such as Europeans and Americans observe the local people apparently sitting around doing nothing, they are not "wasting" their time but are actually making it in preparation for the next round of action. The day, for example, is based not on the precise stations of the sun but on human activities. Again, although

> the rising of the sun is an event which is recognised by the whole community. It does not matter . . . whether the sun rises at 5 am or 7 am, so long as it rises. When a person says that he will meet another at sunrise, it does not matter whether the meeting takes place at 5 am or 7 am, so long as it is in the general period of sunrise.[17]

The cosmological focus is therefore on lived experience on earth rather than on abstract measures of time. The day, then, is related to terrestrial events and actions so that, for example, milking may take place at 6 a.m. not because it is 6 a.m. but because the milking has to take place. Actually, this is also a general, pre-modern, pastoral view of time that we might have found until recently in Europe and certainly still can find in any peasant culture. Other qualitative aspects of African timekeeping are also alive and well in modern Western culture. For example, the Luo people of Kenya refer to times past by the memory of general disasters.[18] Similarly, for most Europeans of a certain age, the periods "before" and "after" the "war" still have a profound resonance, while for those known as the Baby Boomers, the "summer of love" has an enduring, iconic mystique. It's not clear, then, in what way a supposedly distinctive African view of time is actually distinctive. Rather, it should be seen as a rich example of a once-pervasive worldview. In addition, we should avoid the trap of imagining that African time is entirely subjective and anthropocentric. No timekeeping system can ignore the fact that the regular cycles of the sun and the moon continue no matter what human beings do. In addition to their use of qualitative, experiential time, the Luo still require a sense of abstract time in order to fulfill specific tasks, a framework within which one can be early or late, fast or slow.[19]

Our knowledge of African calendars is, like our understanding of African timekeeping, fragmentary and subject to instances of over-interpretation. One theory is that the thirteen-month moon-based calendar was near-universal and that, where twelve-month calendars occur, they are the result of cultural transfer, which, in most of the continent before the colonial period, means they are Islamic origin.[20] Calendars, then, are generally lunar and named according to the changing agricultural, herding, or meteorological qualities of the year, given that it is in the nature of moon calendars to slip out of synchrony with the solar year, and hence with farming and the weather, by eleven or twelve days every year. The Latuka people of the Sudan, for example, have months with precise natural names such as "Give your uncle water," "Let them dig," and "Grain in the ear" but that would cease to have any relevance under a purely lunar system, in which the months slip out of synchrony with the seasons. Societies for which precise timekeeping is a religious necessity often deal with this problem by periodically including extra, intercalary months. We should not forget the the terrestrial, rather than celestial, basis of timekeeping, in which case we should consider the "hunting month": "It does not matter whether the 'hunting month' lasts 25 or 35 days: the event of hunting is what matters."[21] Similarly, whether a year lasts 350 or 390 days is less important than that nature's benevolent rhythms continue. However, most Africans seem as happy to use abstract, ordered systems as experiential ones, and the Yoruba of Nigeria appear to have used a divinatory calendar that was based on fixed number values, including such notions as the rectangular division of the earth into quadrants.[22]

As an example of the problems of understanding African calendrical systems and the way they have been reported, the story of research into the Borana people of Ethiopia is instructive. Information about the Borana calendar attracted attention in the 1930s and was first published in the 1940s. The Borana have a calendrical system based on such periods as the *gada*, in which successive generations of men are linked to a forty-year cycle that dominates their political system. The Borana scheme appears to be based entirely on astronomically determined cycles and therefore challenges the convention that African calendars are experiential. The system was studied in the 1960s by Asmaron Legresse, who reported that the *ayyantu*, the Borana calendar-making, timekeeping experts, can tell the day and time either from memory or, if a guide is needed, from the moon's relationship to the stars, in a system that was comparable in its complexity to those developed, say, by the Maya or Chinese.[23] There was considerable discussion concerning the precise details and a certain excitement that the inhabitants of Kenya might be using a calendar that might use megaliths (at the site at Namoratanga II, by Lake Turkana), such as a marker to set the moon against the background of the stars (like the Islamic calendar) and, moreover, could have been calibrated in 300 BCE.[24] It has been claimed that nineteen basalt pillars, together with a grave marked by other stones, may incorporate significant sight lines for the rising of a number of important stars around 300 BCE, including Sirius, the Pleiades, and Aldebaran, all stars that tend to be significant in most cultures because of their prominence. On the other hand, the anthropological advocates of Kenyan calendrical complexity were accused of willfully exaggerating the intricacy of the system in order to over-compensate for all their academic predecessors who had variously regarded Africans as savage or primitive, and the entire debate ended, inconclusively, in an issue of *Current Anthropology*, with no fewer than thirteen contributors arguing for different positions.[25]

The Borana question, though difficult, has attracted nothing like the Dogon problem, which has overshadowed all other major controversy in African astronomy. The Dogon, who live in Mali, were studied by the French anthropologist Marcel Griaule for various periods over twenty-five years, from 1931 to 1956. In 1946 Griaule was told that Sirius, the brightest of the fixed stars, has two companion stars, which is the case, even though the two additional stars are invisible to the naked eye and hence would be unknown to the Dogon. Griaule and his partner, Germaine Dieterlen, also claimed that the Dogon knew of Jupiter's moons and Saturn's rings, all of which are visible only with the aid of a telescope. The Dogon's supposed, inexplicable astronomical knowledge remained largely unnoticed until the publication in 1976 of Robert Temple's *The Sirius Mystery*, which interpreted their apparent awareness of a triple star as the legacy of extraterrestrial contacts with the ancient Egyptians.[26] Griaule's Dogon mystery turns out not to be a mystery at all, and it appears that the Dogon had previously had sufficient contact with Westerners for there to be no puzzle as to the source of their knowledge of Jupiter and Saturn, while Sirius's two stellar companions appear to be the result of Griaule's own enthusiastic over-interpretation of his informant's accounts.[27] Nevertheless, the Dogon have become an important feature of modern UFO-religion, propagated by Temple's ongoing publicity machine.

In the far south, in the Free State (former Orange Free State) in South Africa, there is another intriguing site, active between the 14th and 18th centuries, an Iron Age settlement known as Nstuanatstatsi, which, in the Sesotho language, means "sunrise." The monument marks the spot where Bafokeng chiefs held their councils and where their ancestors had first risen from the earth, and it is oriented to the east, meeting the rays of the rising sun. Rituals held here enacted and reenacted the creation, renewing the cosmos and maintaining the rhythms of life on their endlessly repetitive journey. The rainmakers of Bunda Mountain, among the Chewa people in Malawi, performed a rite in which the focus was the lighting of a fire, reinventing fire itself in the process, in order to mirror the primeval conflagration. According to one account,

> On the appointed day in August he walks to the shrine, a small round hut at the foot of the mountain with walls of poles and branches, a roof of dry thatch and four doors opening to the north, south, east and west.[28]

Eventually, after about a week, the whole mountainside is scorched; creation, earth, and heaven are reborn; and life can continue.

There are some indications of a certain casual "chaotic" attitude toward the coordination of communal activities with celestial events. The !Kung Bushmen, or San, people of southwest Africa, who conduct healing dances for the sick, "almost invariably dance at least once during the full moon" and believe there is a "special potency" if a dance is performed at dawn.[29] If a similar custom had existed in China, every detail, including whether, when, and where the dance was to be performed, would be prescribed by tradition, rules, and divination. For the San, though, human intentionality and action seems to be more important than precision in timing. That said, ritual times every individual's journey through life. For example, the performance aspect of Nigerian Igbo (or Ibo) cosmology has been summed up as follows:

> The universe is seen as the regulator of human events and human cycles that are divided into various cultural activities denoting the passage of time and events. . . . [T]he various rites of passage are sanctioned and were related to the cosmological worldview which involved various ceremonies right from birth, naming of a child, initiation to boyhood/girlhood, marriage and finally death.[30]

In some versions, the traditional African cosmos is structured as a state in which power relations on earth were reflected in the sky, and vice versa, although the anthropologist R. J. McIntosh has challenged too easy an application of an astral-hierarchy model.[31] Nevertheless, the sun, typically, represented the power of the ruler, who in turn possessed the power of the sun, a sympathetic link between terrestrial and celestial monarchs that is almost universal, not just in Africa, but in every human society. Often the universe is gendered with a male sun and a female moon, sometimes partnered as a married couple.[32] While division of the world into quadrants occurs widely, as it does in other cultures, it is also often round: The Yoruba of west Africa have a round earth and a four-day week.[33] The Igbo structure the cosmos with a lower realm, the earth, and a higher, *Igwe*, sky or heaven, which is sometimes deified as *Igwe Ka ala*, who, having been endowed with personality, can be consulted on everyday matters.[34]

A belief in a single, sometimes sky-based, creator is also ubiquitous although sometimes, as in other traditions, in association with deities who may be identified either as separate or as forms of each other. The Yoruba, for example, are said to worship a supreme sky-based god, Olorun or Orunmila, from Orun-ni-o mo eni-ma-la, translated as "only heaven knows the secret to salvation and survival."[35] However, like all deities, African divinities have multiple forms, a matter of great confusion to both Western scholars on the one hand, and, on the other, indigenous people who have the thankless task of representing their beliefs to Westerners, who are intent on establishing precise categories and correspondences in an area that may be best comprehended through imagination and metaphor. The situation may be understood if we imagine the reverse of the normal research context and consider a hypothetical example in which a series of pre-colonial African anthropologists embark on fieldwork in Europe and attempt to describe Jesus: Is he a man, a god, a third of a god, a carpenter, a king, dead, alive, a bringer of good luck, a savior of the poor, or a guarantor of military victory? If one attempted to define him as any of these, one would be missing the point. Yet this is precisely the way in which Westerners have approached African religion.

There has been no consistent and comprehensive study of African star names and stories, which is a somewhat astonishing lapse in scholarship. However, we do have good information on the Bushmen, now properly known as the San.[36] This is supported by other, scattered information such as the following brief account of the astronomy of the San people of the Nyae Nyae region of southwest Africa (modern Namibia):

The Nyae Nyae !Kung have various beliefs and lore about the sun and moon, Canopus, the Pleiades and other stars, and they have the well-known myth of the moon and the hare; but they do not attribute active divinity to the heavenly bodies, which are "just stars," they say, in effect, and we did not find that they either fear them or seek to gain beneficent influence from them. As far as we know, they do not pray to them for food as the Cape Bushmen are said once to have done, or for rain as the Naron and Auen and !O !Kung do.[37]

This passage is rich in information. Notably, stories of the hare and the moon occur from China to Mesoamerica, suggesting that either there is something deeply archetypal in the connection that storytellers the world over recognize or that the origin predates the human migration out of Africa. We may find another archaic theme in the identification of the stars Canopus and Capella as the horns of *tshxum*, possibly a magical rain-bull and perhaps connected with the Pleiades, part of the Babylonian constellation of the Bull. Other stories are told that relate the stars to human action in a playful manner.[38] One myth tells of a girl who threw ashes from her campfire into sky, where the sparks became stars. Another tells of the sun chasing the moon across the sky, biting pieces out of it until it shrinks and disappears into the new moon. Such stories reflect, above all, a love of storytelling as a means of transforming the cosmos from a huge, dark, and dangerous night sky into a friendly and domesticated place.

The African cosmos was also articulated through, and in, the built environment, a practice of which there are different kinds of evidence, including two much-studied examples of megalithic sites. The earliest is the stone circle in the Egyptian desert, at Nabta Playa, on what was once the shore of a lake to the west of the Nile and that appears to have marked the rising summer solstice sun around 4000 BCE.[39] The sun is, in these terms, a crucial calendar marker, but it's also entirely consistent with later Pharonic cosmology to regard it as a symbol of resurrection.

The vernacular architecture of west Africa also shows evidence of symbolic as well as functional purposes.[40] For example, the Mamprusi people of northern Ghana construct the doors of their houses facing the west so that the elders can sit in the rays of the setting sun: As the sun sets at the end of a day spent accumulating experience and wisdom, so do the elders. There are pragmatic, functional reasons for such alignments as well, for the sun's evening light falls on a wall that functions as a calendar. But then, of course, as soon as we make a distinction between the symbolic and the functional we are imposing Western categories that do not make sense in the Mamprusi's cosmos.

Events of general significance that in the Western tradition are characterized as natural astrology were often recognized. For example, among the Nigerian Igbo, a red sunset is a sign of death, dark clouds indicate rain, and a full moon exacerbates mental problems.[41] The Sandawe of Tanzania believe that the moon exercises an influence on the gender of their unborn children.[42] Some omens have multiple, sometimes contradictory, meanings. For the Igbo, a rainbow, for example, may indicate the end of rain but, if it appears suddenly, great sorrow, while a shooting star may presage either good fortune or the death of an important person. We must suspect, although we do not know, that the difference in meaning may depend on the precise context in which the phenomenon is observed. Alternatively, it may depend entirely on the judgment of the observer; both options are consistent with astrological practice. There were other regional variations; meteors, like comets, were generally bad omens, but the Tswana of Botswana, the San, and the Masai in Kenya and Tanzania, as well as certain groups in Morocco, regarded them as benign.[43]

Celestial timing could also be used in the manufacture of magical or ritual objects, what would be called in the Western tradition astral magic. The Igbo, for example, make "certain entities or *ogwu* . . . when the Moon is waning, some when it is waxing and some when the Moon has gone in," the last of these a reference to the dark nights of the new moon.[44] We also find instances wherein personal identity is linked to periods of time, whether days or seasons. Among the Luo people in western Kenya, people tend to be named after the time of day when they were born. Girls born during midday (*odiechieng'*), when the sun (*chieng'*) is at its highest—around 11:00 a.m. to 3:00 p.m. in Western reckoning—will be called *Achieng'* while boys born at the same time are known as *Ochieng'*.[45]

Such practices coexist in large parts of the continent with the Babylonian-Greek-Indian version of horoscopic astrology, which spread wherever Islam took root (and latterly, where European influence is strong, as in South Africa). We know, for example, that the *Kitab al-falak* (*Book of the Planets*), written by the Moroccan astrologer 'Abd al-Haqq, was read throughout west Africa in the 16th and 17th centuries.[46] A Near Eastern system of astrological geomancy, which relies on number and symbol rather than on the planets, was adopted by the Yoruba in Nigeria, and may also have reached the island of Madagascar, on the other side of the continent.[47] Madagascar is also home to a complex system of astrology that is based on a lunar calendar and appears to contain Arabic, South Asian, and Indonesian influences, as well as its own distinctive features in which "Each astrological month or day in place determines in which capacity or with what quality or destiny places, things or activities are generated and take shape."[48] Arabic influence extended as far south and inland as Botswana, where it is evident in constellational symbolism (Cancer and the fixed star Spica) and may occur in the common, so-called four-tablet divination system.[49] To the north, Arabic astrology is apparent in Somalia, where the seven-day week, together with Arabic months and lunar mansions, provides a framework for counting time and assigning significance, as they do in west Africa and the Swahili-speaking regions, from Kenya down to Mozambique. Prognostication in Somali astrology begins with the days of the week, each of which has its own quality. Friday is auspicious but Thursday (contrary to the Islamic tradition) inauspicious, and, if a year begins on a Thursday, the entire period is difficult. One rule claims that "the plants shriveled by the drought of the Thursday year may be revived by the rains of the Friday year and the youths who thirsted will regain their strength and go wooing."[50] A child born when the moon is in the lunar mansion Dirir, which contains the benevolent star Spica, is thought to posesss *buruud*, the ability to inspire respect, and will have good fortune in the ownership of camels and horses, an indication of wealth.[51] Other celestial omens are purely transient. For example, the *Mood*, an indication of prolonged dry weather, occurs when the setting sun sends dark radiating lines into the sky. Others are regular and seasonal; the constellation *Hal-Toddobaaddo*, the "seven-in-one" (the Great Bear), predicts rain, and, if the rain has not started by the time it reaches its significant position, sinking below the horizon, it is a warning to prepare for drought.[52]

The identity between individual and star could also be represented via bodily markings; in Mozambique it is the custom of some women to incise circular marks, usually on their foreheads, to represent the moon, while solar marks are also known. Lines representing meteors have been observed on forearms, and in some southern Sudanese tribes, some women ornament their lower lips with pieces of polished quartz, representing stars that have fallen to earth.[53] In this sense, the body itself becomes an expression of cosmology or, even, a cosmology in itself.[54]

The invasion of Africa by Western ideas in the colonial era had had a significant impact on traditional cosmology, and anthropologists encounter many individuals who have become Christian and are ashamed of former practices. There has, of course, been a counter-movement, mainly through the wholesale export of African culture to the Americas, with profound consequences for American religious practices.[55] In the past, though, African culture was systematically belittled by Western scholars. It is not so long ago, for example, that it was assumed that Great Zimbabwe was built by Arabs on the grounds that Africans were incapable of such a feat. However, there is also now a counter-tendency: to promote African culture as possessing unique features, such as a particular attitude toward time. However, where African cosmology is intriguing is in its presentation of a matrix of active, ritual, and participatory practices that, heavily codified, underpin the astrological systems of China, Mexico, and the Western-Islamic-Indian tradition and that are currently thriving in New Age culture with its channeling of disincarnate entities, use of crystals and distance-healing, and the rest of the paraphernalia of a magical, meaningful cosmos. It is, perhaps, not that Africa is like the rest of the world but the rest of the world is like Africa.

The core feature of traditional African culture is the integration of sky and earth, and the lack of any defined boundary between all living things. Both cosmology and astrology are "chaotic" in the sense that the cosmos generally comes into being through a series of unplanned steps, and what we can see as African astrology is not highly codified. Astrology exists in African culture in the broad sense, as a general emphasis on the alignment of life with the heavens although, as we have seen, there is no evidence of a belief that human affairs should be precisely and exactly choreographed with the stars in the sense we observe in the great "cosmic" astrological cultures, such as those of China, India, and Mexico. African divination, even in its celestial varieties, undoubtedly requires a heavy degree of human participation on the part of both diviner and client. Further, such human engagement involves the ancestors, souls, and "doubles."[56] As in many other cultures, cosmology can be expressed through music, poetry, song ritual, and dance. The strictly "astral" practice of astrology is therefore limited outside areas that have experienced heavy Islamic influence, and tends to be subsumed in a worldview in which the entire life-world can be approached and managed through ritualized activity. It is almost impossible to generalize about African religion, but we can take one feature as particularly important—the belief that all things are alive and therefore able to communicate with one another. The sun, moon, and stars therefore have to compete for attention with other parts of the environment, such as forests, mountains, and rivers. It may then genuinely make less sense to talk of an African "cosmos" and more to speak of an African "life-world."

Egypt

The Solar Society

May the sun in heaven be favourable to thee.[1]

Egyptian cosmology is significant both as a study in itself and in view of its significant impact on later Western worldviews, especially in relation to its notions of a cosmos struggle between light and darkness, and elaborate views on the soul's ascent to the stars, including a judgment of the dead.[2] Merged with Babylonian astral divination and Greek philosophy, Egyptian spirituality gave rise to the Western-Islamic-Indian tradition of astrology. If there is a single theme that lies at the heart of Egyptian spiritual astronomy, it is of the sun in its splendor as an image of monarchy and, in its nocturnal descent to the darkness and rebirth at dawn, as a model both for the repetitive nature of existence and the hope of resurrection after death. It is for these reasons that we may describe ancient Egypt as a "solar society."

The antecedents of Egyptian civilization in the Nile Valley are evident in the so-called Gerzean culture of around 3200–2850 BCE, when the country's characteristic monumental architecture and hieroglyphic writing begin to appear. The most dramatic periods from a cosmological point of view are the fourth dynasty of the Old Kingdom (c. 2613–2589), whose Pahoraohs constructed the pyramids at Giza, and the creation of the New Kingdom in around 1570 BCE, which coincided with the first surviving evidence of interest in the planets. Finally, conquest by Alexander the Great in 332 brought Greek domination but also a remarkable period in which the new city of Alexandria became the creative hub of Hellenistic culture, fusing Greek, Babylonian, and Egyptian cosmology into the system that survives as the technical and ideological foundation of all modern Western and Indian astrology.

The reliable sources on Egyptian cosmology are few but nevertheless provide sufficient basis for a satisfactory account. I deliberately distinguish reliable from unreliable sources because the latter, which are numerous, are based on speculation and wishful thinking and a curious desire for Egypt to have been a center of wisdom, magic, and technology beyond anything we can establish in the historical record.

Most of the available textual sources on Egyptian cosmology are readily available. Parker's volume of primary sources, *Egyptian Astronomical Texts*, compiled with Otto Neugebauer, is an essential work.[3] The other crucial primary sources are *The Book of the Dead*, of which there are two main versions, by E. A. Wallis Budge and O. R. Faulkner, together with a collection of documents by Thomas Urban, Faulkner's three volumes of *The Ancient Egyptian Coffin Texts*, and Samuel Mercer's *The Pyramid Texts*.[4] As the titles imply, these works consist of the collected accounts of texts associated with cosmological matters, including funerary rites and the journey to the stars, primarily from pyramids, tombs, and coffin lids. Marshall Clagett's *Ancient Egyptian Science: A Sourcebook*, also contains much of relevance to astronomy, calendars, and timekeeping.[5]

The most authoritative scholarly works on Egyptian astronomy are R. A. Parker's articles on "Egyptian Astronomy, Astrology and Calendrical Reckoning" and "Ancient Egyptian Astronomy."[6] There are additional articles by Otto Neugebauer, Gregg de Young, Kurt Locher, and Ronald Wells.[7] The recent volume edited by Juan Antonio Belmonte is, though, a major addition to the field.[8] Together, Jan Assmann's *The Mind of Egypt: History and Meaning in the Time of the Pharaohs*, Siegfred Morenz's *Egyptian Religion*, Stephen Quirke's *The Cult of Ra: Sun-worship in Ancient Egypt*, Byron Shafer's *Religion in Ancient Egypt*, and Louis Žabkar's *A Study of the Ba Concept in Ancient Egyptian Texts* give excellent accounts of Egyptian spiritual cosmology.[9] Jeremy Naydler's work is also recommended.[10]

The Egyptians' religious system is best described as cosmotheism, a term which suggests that the cosmos itself is the object of worship.[11] Even though there was a multitude of deities in the Egyptian system, each had a function and a place in the cosmic order, so much so that it was the cosmos itself—the spinning of the stars, the daily movement of the sun, the monthly changes of the moon, and the annual shift of the seasons—that was the ultimate focus of religious ritual. We should be aware, though, of certain limitations in our knowledge. First, in 3,000 years of recorded history we must expect that the meanings of stories and objects could change, develop, and evolve. Second, the modern interpretation of Egyptian hieroglyphics must be necessarily uncertain and provisional: We can neither grasp the nuances nor be certain of any use of metaphor or simile. Third, there is a huge amount of source material, much of it contradictory, so we should resist the tendency to assume a single coherent system of thought and belief, even when it is necessary to generalize. Fourth, most texts contain extracts from stories rather than the full version, and the fullest accounts are often late in the period. It is therefore difficult to construct a complete picture of Egyptian religious literature and myth. As an example, the stories of Osiris and Isis, the archetypal heavenly king and queen, survive only in Greek from the 1st century CE.[12] Last, the cosmology, religion, and pantheons of Pharaonic Egypt developed as the synthesis of dozens of local cosmologies as the state was created in the late fourth millennium BCE. We should therefore not expect to find single origins.

A number of cities contributed local variations to Egyptian cosmology, Khnum (the Greek Hermopolis, or Hermes' city), Iwnw or On (the Greek Heliopolis, or Sun's city), and Memphis, to which we can add Busiris and, later, Thebes, the New Kingdom capital.[13] As the city-states of the Nile became kingdoms, and the kingdoms united, so each city's cosmology was adopted, the result being a proliferation of deities with overlapping characters and functions. We may, though, identify four major male creator gods: Thoth (linked with the moon), Ra (a solar deity), Ptah (the "Eternal Mind," also associated with the underworld), and Osiris (connected to the three stars of Orion's Belt). Thebes contributed its chief god, Amun. Such male creator gods could also be gathered together, as they were in the temples constructed by Rameses II at Abu Simbel in the 1240s BCE. There was also a powerful feminine element evident in such goddesses as Nut (the sky) and Isis (the archetypal queen), who was associated with Sirius, the brightest of the fixed stars.

In spite of the diversity, though, we can identify certain key themes: The entire cosmos was alive, ensouled, and endowed with personality; human beings possessed an immortal soul that might travel to the stars, the stars and (from the mid–second millennium) the planets were either divine or controlled or represented by deities; and the heavenly bodies moved in an unchanging order that was the basis of the sacred calendar and the timing of religious ritual through the day, month, and year. To the foregoing we need add an important qualification. There is considerable uncertainty as to the precise nature of the Egyptian conception of the soul—whether it was, for example, coincident with the whole human being or separate from it. That it was divided into different constituent features doesn't help. So, while we know that the king could travel to the stars, there is doubt as to whether ordinary people might also make this journey. Scholars are coming to accept that they could.[14] The concept of the soul's ascent to the stars was, according to Herodotus, borrowed by the Greeks.[15] It then became a central feature of Hellenistic astrology and ultimately encouraged Christian belief in a journey to a celestial paradise.

Although there was great diversity in the detail of various cosmogonies, they generally tend to assume one of two possibilities: either the emergence of order out of a primeval chaos or creation as deliberate, a physical act. In Mircea Eliade's terms the origin of the cosmos could therefore be either chaotic or cosmic.[16] In one version of the cosmogony popular at Khnum, the original existence was Nun, the Primeval Waters or Primordial Ocean, dark, deep, endless, and infinite. Sometimes called "Father of the Gods," Nun had neither temples nor worshippers and manifested in eight original deities, representing his four qualities, subdivided in turn into male and female forms. In another variant, a lotus flower grew out of the Primeval Waters. When its petals, which had been closed in the primeval darkness, opened, the creator of the world sprang from its heart in the form of a beautiful child. This was the infant sun, who immediately spread his rays of light throughout the world; at dusk, darkness falls as the lotus petals enclose the sun, while at dawn they open and light floods out. In a third version the creator god, Neb-er-Djer ("the Universal Lord"), created the deities from his sweat and humanity from his tears (*remeyt* = tears, *romet* = men).

Nun also seems to have been revered at Iwnw, but Atum (probably meaning the "Complete One") was the effective creator. In earlier versions Atum emerged out of Nun as a hill (like an island forming in the middle of the Nile?), or in that he was a form of the sun, associated with Ra, as the sunrise, and was either a child of Nun or self-created. He was originally alone, and then creation began out of his being, after an act of masturbation in which spit and expectorate are euphemisms for semen. Pyramid Text Spell 600, which dates to around 2400 BCE, reads

> O Atum-Koprer, thou becamest high in the height. Thou did rise up as the *benben* stone in the Mansion (i.e., Temple) of the Bennus Bird (Phoenix) in Heliopolis. Thou didst spit out Shu. Thou didst expectorate Tefenet (or Tefnut), and thou didst set thy arms about them as the arms of a ka-symbol that they essence might be in them.[17]

The structure of the cosmos was similar to that in many ancient cultures. The sky was usually a canopy supported at four corners by pillars or mountains, but it could also be a celestial ocean (suggested by its blue color). If so, it provided a mechanism for the sun to travel—in a boat (the remains of a great solar boat have been discovered at Giza and are exhibited next to the Sphinx). Naturally, the center of the created world was the Nile, surrounded by the "black land," the alluvial plain around the river, and the "red land," the desert. Earth itself was divided into two river banks (the Egyptians never found the source of the Nile, at which the banks would have disappeared), one (our west) the land where the sun set, the other (our east) the land where the sun rose. More distant places such as Ethiopia and Syria were the "mountainous countries" that ringed Egypt. The physical structure, though, was contained within the notion of cosmos as a giant, ticking, participatory *machina mundi*, a huge clock whose mechanism was maintained partly by human activity. Plumley summed up the priorities of Egyptian cosmology succinctly and effectively—it was based, he wrote, on the belief that the maintenance of the original creation and resistance to all threats to its stability was, for the benefit of all, a collaborative venture among gods, goddesses, men, and women.[18]

Ma'at, the cosmic order itself, was personified as a goddess but may also be seen as an abstraction, a force, a power, as well as the ethical behavior and devotion to truth and justice required for men and women to collaborate with the gods and goddesses in the maintenance of order. She also represented the ethics that recognize the need to act in all circumstances for the upholding of the universal order. It was Ma'at's symbol, the feather of truth, that was placed in one pan of the balance used for the weighing of the hearts of the dead in their judgment by Osiris in his role as the god of the dead.

All Egyptian religion can therefore be seen as an expression of the need to maintain Ma'at, and all ritual was devoted to the need to renew creation, and order, every day without fail. Although this renewal was the work of the gods, priests, and the reigning pharaoh—in theory the high priest of every temple—and the gods' representative on earth, the Egyptians were obliged to assist by uttering the required incantations and making the correct sacrifices at the appropriate times. It was primarily for this work that the temples existed, and their function was to assist the defense of the state against hostile forces; they were not houses of prayer to which people might resort to seek comfort for their souls. If the preservation of order, though, was the goal of religion, the means was harmonization with time, and this prime necessity was the rationale for all measuring systems and the resulting rituals, from the daily welcome given to the rising sun to the major calendar festivals.

The pre-dynastic calendar was probably lunar, or "luni-stellar," measuring the moon's passage, or the movement of Thoth, against the background of the stars, or Nut.[19] It relied on the appearance of the crescent new moon in order to time the month and the annual rising of Sirius, which coincided with the annual flooding of the Nile in July, and our earliest written record if it is from the Fourth Dynasty, that of the Great Pyramid builders.[20] The year was divided into three seasons based on natural cycles rather than celestial, a reminder that sky and earth are inseparable. *Akhet*, "Flood" or "Inundation," coincided with the rise and flood of the river and was followed by *Peret*, "Emergence," which saw the water subside and the land reemerge, and finally *Shomu*, "Low Water" or "Harvest," saw the height of agricultural activity.

The solar year itself was tied to observation not only of the sun but also of the stars, particularly Sirius, the star of the goddess Isis. For a certain period of time every year Sirius was so close to the sun, as seen from the earth, that it was invisible, and its reappearance as a bright evening star on the eastern horizon in late summer coincided with the annual Nile flood, which restored fertility to the land and signified the new year, reviving the eternal cycle of solar time. The observation of this coincidence can be traced back to the First Dynasty, perhaps as early as 3000 BCE.[21] Equally impressive, though less frequently mentioned, would have been the rising of the stars of Orion earlier in the year. The period of invisibility was seventy days, and there might just be a connection with the seventy-two accomplices who assisted Osiris's murder by his evil brother, Set.[22] There is certainly a connection with the entire notion of divinity either journeying to the underworld (as the sun did every night) or being subject to a cycle of death and resurrection. In the case of Isis, though, it was her husband Osiris who died and her tears of grief that caused the annual inundation of the Nile, which, in turn, restored fertility to the land.

The twelve months were each named after an important celestial festival, usually lunar. The first month was named after the *Tekhy* feast, the third from the feats of the goddess Hathor, and the eighth from the festival of Ernutet, the goddess of the coming harvest. The twelfth month was named after the heliacal rising of Sirius, known as *Wep-renpet* ("Opener of the Year") or later *Peret-Sepdet* ("the Coming Forth of Sirius"). However, new moons happen on a different day of the solar year every year while the rising of Sirius stays constant. A simple rule was therefore applied that whenever Sirius was seen to rise heliacally (before dawn, immediately prior to sunrise) for the first time, in the last eleven days of the twelfth month an additional, thirteenth, month was added, named after Thoth, the lunar god. The extra month was added every three or, occasionally, two years and had the effect of guaranteeing that the next year Sirius would still rise on the twelfth month. Now, we might see such rules as the mere meaningless tinkering with dates and times with which we might regard the addition of a day every four years to give a leap year in the modern calendar. The truth is very different. For the Egyptians such adjustments were part of the absolutely essential attempt to maintain Ma'at and preserve order in a system that was permanently on the edge of disorder: They were actively participating in an attempt to keep the entire cosmos in harmony.

There were five primary celestial deities: the sky itself, the goddess Nut, the sun, the moon, and Sirius and the stars of Orion's belt. Although the primary substance of the Egyptian cosmos can be perceived in nonpersonal terms as "order" or "time," once the cosmos achieved three-dimensional form it was alive, physical, and sexualized, and its different constituents held the same relationship to one another as do humans. Nut, for example, was a beautiful mother goddess, and the lover of her brother Geb, the earth. The two were separated by their father, Shu, the air, son of Atum, but it was the act of copulation between them that was responsible for all the generative processes in nature—the birth, nourishment, and growth of all things. The celestial bodies moved across, or through, Nut's body, and she, in turn, protected them.

The most powerful of all heavenly bodies was the sun, with which Old Kingdom monarchs increasingly identified themselves, the first signs of a tradition that was eventually bequeathed to the Roman emperors. Spell 15 in *The Book of the Dead* contains a hymn specified for the "Worship of Re when he rises in the eastern horizon of the sky, when those who are in his following are joyful":

Hail to you, O Re, at your rising, O Atum-Horakhty! Your beauty is worshipped in my eyes when the sun-shine comes into being over my breast. You proceed at your pleasure in your Night-bark, your heart is joyful with a fair wind in the Day-bark, being happy at crossing the sky with the blessed ones. All your foes are overthrown, the Unwearying Stars acclaim you, the Imperishable Stars [i.e., the circumpolar stars] worship you when in the horizon of Manu, being happy at all times, and living and enduring as my lord. . . . How beautiful are your rising and your shining on the back of your mother Nut, you having appeared as King of the Gods.[23]

The Imperishable Stars are usually thought to be those in the north that, in the northern hemisphere, never set and so are considered to be immortal: They were therefore the "indestructibles," "those who know no tiredness" or "no destruction," perfect symbols of immortality.[24] By associating with them, the sun may then share in their freedom from death. In reality, though, the sun engages in a struggle with mortality every night when he descends below the earth, facing a struggle with Set, the brother of Osiris, and son of Nut and Geb. The sun presided undisputed over the day and his daily journey was a permanent reminder of the eternal struggle between light and dark and perhaps the central feature of the religious cosmology. In one myth Re impregnates his mother, Nut, each day, while in another he enters her mouth and travels though her body during the hours of darkness, and in both he is reborn at dawn, a matter for the greatest rejoicing.

The moon was only slightly less important than the sun. Represented in the celestial kingdom by Thoth, who was pictured either as an ibis-headed man surmounted by a crescent moon or as a dog-headed ape, perhaps representing the union of two more archaic traditions, he was an ally of Isis and Horus in the struggle against Set, became Osiris's chief minister, and was charged with measuring time, much like the Babylonian god Sin, and his importance was recognized when the first month of the year, Thoth, was named in his honour. A host of other talents were the natural consequence of Thoth's ability to count and measure; he was the clerk, herald, and arbiter of the gods, resolving disputes between them and announcing Osiris's verdict on the dead. He kept a complete inventory of all natural resources and property, and he invented every one of the arts and sciences including surveying, medicine, and music. He also invented writing, and hence magic. The reason why the one implied the creation of the other is simple: Words contain the power of the beings, ideas, or objects they represent, which is why the texts we find on the inside of tombs are interpreted less as pleas to the gods to accept the soul of the deceased than as a form of magical technology designed to facilitate the soul's journey to the *duat*.[25]

The planets do not appear to have been important in early Egyptian cosmology and never achieved a pivotal role in the divine kingdom until the introduction of a complex judicial astrology in the 3rd century BCE. Our earliest known portrayal of the planets (excluding Mars) is found in a painting in the tomb of Senmut, a high official in Queen Hatshepsut's court at Thebes around 1473 BCE. The Egyptians knew the planets as "stars that know no rest" and identified three (if not all) of them—Mars, Saturn, and Jupiter—with Horus.[26] Jupiter was "Horus who bounds the two lands" or "Horus who illuminates the two lands" and, later, "Horus Who Opens Mystery"; Saturn was "Horus-Bull-of-the-Sky" or just "Horus the Bull." Mars was "Horus of the Horizon" or "Horus-the-Red," and while the last name is obviously purely descriptive, the first two suggest religious significance, and all three suggest that they were aspects of the sun god—or, perhaps it's truest to say the universal god manifested in the sun. Currently, though, we have no clear evidence to substantiate what might otherwise be an obvious conclusion—that from around 1500 B C E onward, the planets assumed a divinatory function.

We suffer from a similar lack of knowledge concerning the constellations. As far as we can tell, about twenty-five star groups were recognized and represented by animal and human figures in an abundance of sacred texts, but we have little sense of their meaning, and, although the various scholars disagree, we can identify the location of perhaps no more than three with any certainty.[27] In addition, there were thirty-six constellations, generally known to us by the Greek word *decan*, although they were known to early Egyptologists as diagonal calendars or, more properly, as "star clocks."[28] These were used to record the time, a critical process if nocturnal religious rituals were to be conducted at the divinely sanctioned moments, and made their appearance in drawings and texts on twelve coffin lids surviving from the Tenth Dynasty onward, before 2100 B C E, perhaps by 2400 B C E.

The earliest known complete catalogue of the universe, compiled around 1100 B C E by Amenope, a scribe of sacred books in the House of Life, was intended to comprise everything made up of "heaven with its affairs, earth and what is in it" but adds little: Five constellations were listed, only two of which can be identified.[29] The most important constellation we can identify with any certainty is in fact a single star, Sirius, sacred to Isis and one of the *decans*, which appears to be part of a stellar grouping pictured as a recumbent cow.

Our lack of knowledge, though, does not lessen our awareness of the immense effort that was put into the attempt to preserve the balance between sky and earth, Ma'at and human life. In this respect, the incorporation of cosmic mathematics and symbolism into monumental architecture is probably the most famous feature of Egyptian culture. The three pyramids at Giza are the best-known examples and, of these, it's the Great Pyramid, built by the pharaoh Khufu (Cheops) around 2480 B C E, that has the clearest celestial engagement. The pyramid faces almost exactly due north and the match is astonishing: the north side's deviation from true north is out by only two minutes and twenty-eight seconds.[30] The pyramid therefore faced the eternal, never-setting northern stars, the immortal pharaoh's celestial kingdom; the Pyramid Text 269 reads, "He [Atum] assigns the king to those gods who are clever and wise, the Indestructible stars."[31] It appears that there are also stellar alignments from the four hitherto unexplained shafts that run in an upward diagonal fashion from the center of the pyramid, to Orion's belt and, perhaps, Sirius, representing Osiris and Isis, the celestial king and queen.

Two each start at the king's chamber and the queen's chamber, one pointing north, the other south. The southern king's shaft pointed to the stars of Orion's belt around 2500 BCE, suggesting that at the appropriate moment the Khufu's soul would be able to travel to Orion, to be welcomed by the great king and judge Osiris.[32] Pyramid Text 508 reads, "I have trodden those thy rays as a ramp under my feet whereon I mount up to that my mother, the living Uraeus on the brow of Re," and Utterance 523 tells us, "May the sky make the sunlight strong for you, may you rise up to the sky as the Eye of Re."[33] The point was to journey to a physical, not an ethereal, life, in the *duat*, and the pyramids were the means by which this might be accomplished.[34] The soul, the *ba*, might travel either to the sun's rising or to Orion and achieve precisely the same result: immortality.[35] This was no otherworldly religion, though. The physical world existed in partnership with the other world, the *duat*, and Khufu's "agenda was nothing less than the stability and continuity of the world, and he exerted celestial power to fulfil it."[36]

The Egyptian temple was a liminal zone, connecting this world with the other, time with space, humanity with divinity, light with darkness, and creation with creator.[37] The astronomical practice was complex and temples were aligned with the solar cycle, the two bright stars Sirius and Canopus, the cardinal points and, in the Nile valley, with the river itself, to which they tended to be perpendicular.[38] To face the east, the rising sun, was suggestive of life, and to look to the west, the setting sun, was indicative of death.

Our evidence suggests that, for most of the history of ancient Egypt, astrology in the broadest sense fulfilled the same function as in, say India until the early centuries CE, in that its primary function was timing—to gain foreknowledge of the auspicious moments for the enactment of crucial rituals. There was certainly a class of priest known as the *imy-wnwt*, variously translated as "hour-watcher," observer, or "astronomer." One Eighteenth Dynasty (1550–1295 BCE) tomb, famous for its decorative scenes of daily life, belonged to a man called Nahkt whose titles included an "Hour Watching Priest of Amun."[39] The only detailed description of an hour-watcher's duties date from the 2nd or 3rd centuries BCE—and include timekeeping, calendar collation, the holding of purification rituals, and "announcing all (the) wonders" of the star Sirius.[40]

The current evidence indicates that an elaborate interpretative astrology, including the twelve-sign zodiac, was first imported from Babylon in the Persian era, probably in the 6th or 5th centuries BCE.[41] The substantial creative period, though, took place in the 3rd and 2nd centuries BCE after

Alexander the Great's conquests laid the foundation for Hellenistic culture, that fusion of classical, Near Eastern, and Egyptian thought that, carried by the Greek language, was eventually to spread east to India and—under the Romans—west to Morocco, Spain, and Britain. The earliest surviving Babylonian zodiac in Egypt is a monumental carving dating to some time before 30 BCE. Now in the Louvre but originally from the roof of the East Osiris Chapel in the temple of Hathor at Dendera, "Dendera E" incorporates ancient Egyptian constellations such as the Ox leg and the Hippopotamus as well as Orion and Sothis, suggesting that there was an attempt to merge the two systems rather than replace one with the other.[42]

Two genres of astrological literature were created. The first was primarily passive and interpretative and dealt mainly with establishing the nature of the soul's current incarnation as well as predicting the future. The second was active and, again, falls into two varieties. One, which we may describe as magical, dealt with the use of talismans or spells in order to manipulate the future. The other, to adapt a term that came into philosophical use in the 3rd century, was theurgic (theurgy is "god-work," as opposed to theology, or "god-knowledge") and dealt with the soul's desire to return, via the stars, to the creator. The original texts of Hellenistic interpretative astrology are lost, although sufficient material survives from the 1st to the 5th centuries CE. Theurgic astrology was represented in a group of texts ascribed to Hermes Trismegistus (literally Hermes thrice-great, or "the greatest") and known to us collectively as the *Corpus Hermeticum*. These works assumed a single creator, envisaged in a divine, supreme consciousness, a physical cosmos that was essentially evil and a path to salvation through the planetary spheres.[43]

True, some astrology appeared to be completely deterministic. We can pick an example from one of the eclipse omens that were adapted from a Babylonian to an Egyptian context, perhaps in the 6th century BCE: "If [the moon be eclipsed in II Shimu, (since) the month belongs to Egypt] it [means]: The chief of the land named shall be captured. The army shall fall to [battle]-weapo[ns]."[44] Such astrology, though, existed only within a context in which it was understood that the future could be negotiated, which is where the magical literature came in. One Hellenistic-era text advises on the role of talismans or magical rituals conducted when the moon is in different signs: "Moon in Virgo: anything is rendered obtainable. In Libra necromancy. In Scorpio anything evil. In Sagittarius: an invocation or incantations to the sun and moon" and so on.[45] The principle behind magic was the ancient doctrine of *Hike*, the active power that came into existence as the world was created. As *Hike* pervaded the cosmos, it provided a link between all things—including speech and objects.[46] The basis of magic, including astral magic, is therefore that by uttering or writing a word, one actively invokes the thing that the word represents. So, by speaking the name of Venus or inscribing a symbol representing her, one invokes the planetary deity, but perhaps as force, an essential component of the fabric of the cosmos, rather than as an anthropomorphized goddess. The act of horoscope interpretation itself in Hellenistic Egypt, therefore, borders on the magical in the sense that supernatural forces—powers beyond the material and physical—are being invoked. In the wider scheme of Egyptian history, astrology is best seen as a harmonizing system, a means of maintaining the smooth functioning of Ma'at by using sacred architecture, religious ritual, and management of the calendar to ensure that order was never overwhelmed by chaos. It wasn't religion, but it was religious, a statement that makes sense only in a context in which religion and daily life are interdependent and inextricably intertwined.

The Egyptian cosmogony was generally "chaotic," assuming the emanation of the world from a formless state. At the heart of the Egyptian worldview lay the proposition that the entire cosmos which emerged from this primeval condition was alive. That simple statement sums up some of its most important features—the attribution of personality and gender to objects such as stars, which in the modern world would be considered dead; the power of words to conjure miraculous events; and the existence of power relations in which the sun exerted a monarchical role over the earth. The primary human attitude to the sky, indeed to the entire environment, was one of relationship. People had relationships not just with one another but also with planets, animals, birds, fish, stones, plants, and the gods and goddesses, the powers who animated them. While cosmogony broadly remained chaotic, positing the spontaneous emergence of the universe from an original "nothing," and while there seems to have been little interest in a codified, structured astrology until very late, the attitude toward time seems to have always been very ordered from the beginning of the dynastic era. The exact observation of the calendar and the day through carefully timed rituals was vital to the ongoing survival of the world: The Egyptians were not passive observers but active participants in the cosmic cycle. When complex astrology did arrive in Egypt from Babylon, it fused with Egyptian spirituality and Greek logic to produce the particular form of the discipline that survives today in India and across the Western world. Wherever modern New Agers talk of the cosmic evolution of the soul or their spiritual conection to the stars, they are paying homage to a religious cosmology that once thrived in the Nile valley.

China

The Celestial Offices

To explore the boundaries between Heaven and Man.[1]

China, as we have noted, was the focus of one of the three major technically complex and philosophically sophisticated systems of astrology, along with the Near Eastern form that spread across Europe, North Africa, and India, and the Meso-American. All three share a fundamental similarity—that celestial patterns can, often in great detail, record the future and hence assist in management of the present. Chinese astrology, which is still practiced in an unbroken tradition (even if interrupted on the mainland by the communist regime) going back for several thousand years, possesses a number of core qualities. First, it has distinct, perhaps unique, technical features, such as the sixty-year cycle, although its rationale and philosophy are similar to those (albeit with different terminology) found in other astrological systems.[2] Second, the most complex astrology was "official" and an arm of the state. Third, personal astrology (*xing ming*) might have only a tenuous connection with the "real sky," being a subset of what was called Fate-Calculation, which was generally based on numerology and one's date of birth.[3]

Astrology's managerial function was assisted by ritual and architecture, both of which were connected by a shared emphasis on the exact alignment of human society with the heavens, as well as with features of terrestrial space, such as mountains. The Chinese placed as much importance on precision in such matters as did the masters of the other ancient cosmic states—the Inca, the Aztecs, the Maya, the Egyptians, the Babylonians, and the Indians. In some respects, they seem to place an even higher value on exactitude. To use a familiar metaphor, if earth was the mirror of heaven, then the duty of all individuals in the astrologically aware society was to ensure that their movements were matched with the motions of the heavenly bodies. This they did by harmonizing with the energies that flowed all around them, as applied through a whole series of practices, including both *feng shui*, the art of arranging the human environment in conformity with *chi*, the energy that pervaded space, and medicine, including acupuncture:

> [M]acrocosm and microcosms became a single manifold, a set of mutu-
> ally resonant systems of which the emperor was indispensable mediator.
> This was true even of medicine. . . . Cosmology was not a mere reflection
> of politics. Cosmos, body, and state were shaped in a single process, as a
> result of changing circumstances that the new ideas in turn shaped.[4]

The complex system of astrology practiced in China since the first millennium BCE was a state activity, prohibited to the ordinary people for security reasons; to know the future carried serious political implications that the government could not ignore. The majority made do with systematic fortune-telling systems that were time-based but not astral. Such Fate-Calculation might rely on the hour, day, month, and year together with a hexagram from the oracular text the *I Ching*, cast for the moment of inquiry.[5] So important was the matrix of ideas embodied in both official astrology and popular Fate-Calculation that when the Mongol conqueror Kublai Khan sought to legitimize his rule, he undertook a reform of the calendar: To manipulate time could be as important as to mobilize armies.[6]

Culturally, the focus of attention in this chapter is China; without belittling the cosmologies of its neighboring cultures, those of Korea, Japan, and the Chinese-influenced areas of Southeast Asia, they owe much of their cosmology to Chinese inventions and innovations, even if adapted to local conditions.[7] (The major differences between Chinese and Japanese astral religion is the importance of the latter's veneration for the sun goddess, Amaterasu, the chief deity of Shinto.) In Southeast Asia, Chinese influences overlap with those of that other cultural giant, India, especially in Thailand and Cambodia; southern Vietnam was for many years occupied by the Indian-oriented Khmer culture while, in the northern part of the country, Vietnamese court officials were trained according to Chinese Confucian precepts, which included the oracular text the *I Ching*, complete with its sophisticated notions of the changing qualities of time.[8] In 21st-century Vietnam, the government is currently promoting a trinity of Confucianism, Taoism, and Buddhism as ethical replacements for communism, on the pragmatic grounds that all three share (at least in the general understanding) notions of the cosmos as based on an essential order to which, in the ideal republic, the wise individual should conform. In modern Thailand, Chinese and Indian astrology coexist in popular culture, increasingly with their Western cousin as expressed in newspaper and magazine horoscopes. The rituals and practices of Chinese cosmology were also introduced into Malaya, where they coexist with Indian and Christian systems, as well as with native Malay customs.

The scholarly literature on Chinese cosmology was originally written by Westerners, of whom the greatest and most influential was Joseph Needham, although the situation is now changing. The up-to-date, standard text is now David Pankenier's *Bringing Heaven Down to Earth in Ancient China*. The available primary texts include the *Shu jing* (*Book of Documents*), which dates from the 5th century BCE or later; and the *Shi Ji* (*Historical Records*), composed by the Han astronomer Sima Qian around 90 BCE, which is available in English translation.[9] The most important astrological works were gathered together in 1742 in the thirty-six-volume *Ting Hsieh Chih Pien Fang Shu* (*The Book of Harmonizing Dividers and Distinguishing Directions*), and a modern edition is overdue. "The Treatise on the Patterns of Heaven," an invaluable summary of the cosmogony, astronomy, and astrology of the Han period (206 BCE–220 CE), is now available in a modern English version.[10] On a more accessible level, Derek Walters's *Chinese Astrology* is an excellent handbook of the accumulated traditions of Chinese astrology.[11]

We should also mention the great and unique oracle of time, the *I Ching*, or *Book of Changes*, which is perhaps the most accessible and instant tool for engaging with the practical application of Chinese cosmology to daily affairs. We also have various writings on the structure of the cosmos, such as the *Ling Hsien* (*Spiritual Constitution of the Universe*), composed by the 1st-century CE astronomer Chang Heng. The writings of the sages Confucius and Lao Tzu also provide rich insight into cosmological theory, and we should not forget "texts" such as those expressed through ritual or written into the landscape through gardens, temples, monuments, and the principles of *feng shui*. Any visit to a temple that is purposefully aligned with, say, a distant mountain peak, and in which one can obtain a divinatory reading from the throwing of inscribed pieces of wood will reveal to the interested scholar the living inheritance of an ancient tradition in which active engagement was required with a cosmos that was imagined in its terrestrial form as much as its celestial. Studying such divination can inform us about the participatory and reflective nature of Chinese cosmology.[12]

There are a number of pitfalls for the unwary, non-Chinese speaker. One, of course is the conversion of Chinese words to English, a process that involves both translation and transliteration. The 1st-century BCE astrological text the *Shi Ji* may be translated as the *Historical Records* and ascribed to Sima Qian, or written as the *Shih Chi*, translated as *Records of the Grand Astrologer-Historian* and attributed to Ssuma Chien, or Ssu Ma Ch'ien.[13] Then there are scholarly agendas. Sinologists, for example, as with all specialists, may try to represent their field as unique, while Westerners, among whom we may number the Jesuits who visited China in strength from the 17th century onward, brought much knowledge but also their own brand of misunderstanding. Scholars in general also fall prey to the typical tendency to downplay astrology. Needham, for example, having noted the central importance of astrology to Chinese cosmology, devoted 291 pages to the measurement of celestial positions, but none to their meaning. Such neglect is a boon for modern scholars in the area, for the work awaiting them is immense.

One influential account of the origin of the Chinese cosmos is set out in the "Questions of Heaven," chapter 3 of the *Songs of Ch'u*. The narrative has no creator but instead posits the gradual emergence of order from chaos, of a defined Something from a formless Nothing.[14] The primeval element, misty vapor, emerges spontaneously and is structured as a set of binary forces, yin and yang, embodying upper and lower, darkness and light. The resulting dialetical process then produces the celestial bodies, the vaulted sky with nine layers and nine gates, supported by eight pillars resting on the earth. The structure of the cosmos was envisaged both physically and metaphysically. There was a variety of physical models: the *kai thien* theory, in which the sky was envisaged as a hemispherical dome over a flat earth; the *hun thien* school, which envisaged the cosmos as spherical and which may date to around the 5th century BCE (when similar schemes were also developing in Greece); and the *hsüan yeh* teaching, which is attested from the late Han period (probably 1st or 2nd centuries CE) and envisaged the stars and planets as floating in infinite, empty space.[15] The 13th-century astronomer Têng Mu described space in the following modern terms:

> Heaven and Earth are large, yet in the whole of empty space (*hsü khung*) they are but as a small grain of rice. . . . It is as if the whole of empty space were a tree and heaven and earth were one of its fruits. Empty space is like a kingdom and heaven and earth no more than a single individual person in that kingdom. Upon one tree there are many fruits, and in one kingdom many people. How unreasonable it would be to suppose that besides the heaven and earth which we can see, there are no other heavens and no other earths.[16]

Speaking of the celestial bodies, Chang Heng grappled with notions of infinity and the impossibility of limits and wrote that "these things can all be calculated, but what is beyond [the celestial sphere] no one knows. And it is called the 'cosmos' (*yü chou*). This has no end (*wu chi*) and knows no bounds (*wu chhiung*)."[17]

The metaphysical structure was vertical, with heaven above and earth below, the two locked in a value-laden power relationship in which heaven is exalted, honored, and powerful while earth is lesser and lower. The way of heaven (above) was round, the way of earth (below) square, *chi* passed between them, and the task of the ruler, living in the square, was to grasp the round—to understand heaven—in order to benefit the square.[18] As the opening section of the *I Ching* puts it, "Heaven is high, the earth is low."[19] From this duality emerges the polarity of two states of existence, yin and yang. Pure yin, which is associated with earth, is tranquil, calm, cool, watery, feminine, dark, nocturnal, receptive, and yielding, while yang is associated with heaven and is active, creative, hot, dry, fiery, and light. Yin-yang then, in turn, gives rise to the *wu-xing*, or *Wu Hsing*, the system of Five Phases, commonly known in the West as five elements. The *wu-xing*, which can be traced to the 3rd to 4th centuries BCE, explained every terrestrial phenomenon from natural processes and seasonal cycles to the rise and fall of imperial dynasties.[20] In order, the energizing elements were wood (spring), fire (summer), earth (late summer), metal (autumn), and water (winter), and it was assumed that they flowed into one another just as did the seasons. The system was dynamic and constantly changing, and as the five phases ebbed and flowed, so life on earth changed.

The identifiable mechanics of yin-yang and the Five Phases were themselves contained within the ineffable paradoxes of Taoism. The opening lines of Lao Tzu's *Tao Te Ching* convey the tone, even if something of its spirit is inevitably lost in translation:

> The way [tao] that can be spoken of
> Is not the constant way;
> The name that can be named is not the constant name.
> The nameless was the beginning of heaven and earth;
> The named was the mother of myriad creatures.
> Hence always rid yourself of desires in order to observe its secrets;
> But always allow yourself to have desires in order to observe its
>   manifestations.
> These two are the same
> But diverge in name as they issue forth.
> Being the same they are called mysteries,

Mystery upon mystery—
The gateway of the manifold secrets.[21]

Any impression that the intricate logic of Taoist language suggests that Chinese cosmology was otherworldly should be dispelled by Confucianism's insistence that the entire cosmos is embedded in nature, and humanity's role is therefore to cultivate the cosmos by acting in accord with divine precepts and natural forces.[22] The very existence of the Tao necessitates human action, and the fact that desires are difficult requires that they be experienced.

Chinese religion is quite distinctive among the major world systems. Its major recognized forms, Confucianism, Taoism, and Buddhism, share a rational view of the cosmos as organized according to the principles found in any well-ordered society, but they are simultaneously contemplative and worldly in the sense that there is a focus on the here and now rather than on future salvation. Even heaven was organized in a structured form familiar to any imperial bureaucrat. The supreme deity, Ti, or Di (also known as *Tian huang shang ti*, the August Supreme Emperor of Heaven), was the first god (or one of the first of the gods). Celestially, Di was associated with the celestial north pole, the still point around which the entire sky revolves. God, in the Chinese conception, is therefore the central point where there is no motion and hence no change and, effectively, no time. As earthly representative of the pole, and the earthly partner of the supreme Lord Di, the emperor, imagined as Son of Heaven, fulfilled a role that would appear to have distant shamanic origins, in that he functioned as a bridge between the two realms. The emperor's function could also be considered messianic, not in the sense that he would engineer a future apocalypse but in that every ritual act he performed was soteriological, ensuring salvation through protection from harm. These, of course, are consistent features of monarchy the world over.

The other major celestial deities were the sun and moon, who were the focus of official cults but had few temples dedicated to them. The sun was the subject of only two major festivals, one at the new year, whereas the moon was the subject of more festivities, of which the most important was the lunar celebration at the spring equinox. This was especially a moment for women and children, who made a sacrifice consisting chiefly of fruit, preferably when the moon had clearly risen, so it was looking down on his human subjects.

The purpose of astronomy, according to the Han astronomer Sima Qian, was "to explore the boundaries between Heaven and Man, to comprehend changes old and new, and finally to form a total perspective" on the cosmos.[23]

For Needham, astronomy itself was derived from religion or, perhaps better to say, it was an application of religion. In his opinion, "[A]stronomy was a science of cardinal importance for the Chinese since it arose naturally out of that cosmic 'religion,' that sense of unity and even 'ethical solidarity' of the universe."[24] The observation and measurement of celestial phenomena were inseparable from their application to human affairs, which, in turn, was divided into two, *li*, or *li fa*, calendar systems, and *tian wen*, or sky patterns, which we would now know by the Greek word "astrology."

The earliest indications of a concern with astronomical orientation in China can be traced to the fifth millennium BCE, when archaeological evidence indicates a tendency to align buildings and burials—the homes of the living and the dead, respectively—with daily and seasonal variations in the sun's position.[25] Perhaps by the 24th century BCE (the dating is controversial), stars marking the seasons were recorded in the *Book of Documents*, or *Shu jing*. *Niao* (Bird, approximately the Greek constellation Hydra) marked mid-spring; *huo* (Fire, approximately Scorpius), mid-summer; *xü* (Void, corresponding to Aquarius) signified mid-autumn; and *mao* (Hair, the Pleiades).[26]

The earliest surviving records of observation of astronomical events are divinatory oracle bones that can be traced to the 14th century BCE, under the Shang dynasty. Originally turtle shells or cattle scapulae, the oracle bones were heated with a poker in order to produce cracks that would then be read by a diviner, who might be the king himself. The first ever known observation of a nova—a new star (*xin xing*), later "guest star" (*ke xing*)—is actually found on an inscription from an oracle bone of around 1300 BCE. Along with attention to new stars and other phenomena, such as eclipses, the oracle bones refer to the planets, but mainly as a group. Among the planets, only Jupiter is referred to by name in the earliest records, an indication, perhaps, of its early importance. The chief concern was with establishing auspicious times, at which successful action should be undertaken, and inauspicious ones, at which it should be avoided. A typical inscription reads: "On the day *guise*, the king divining: 'This ten-day week will be without calamity.' The King prognosticated, 'Auspicious.'"[27]

The insistence on ever-increasing accuracy in order to manage the state in more meticulous detail was the driver behind the development of Chinese astronomy. So extensive are the surviving records that they are almost the only ones available to modern historians in any culture from the 5th century BCE to the 10th century CE. The Chinese recorded events that other people ignored, including the supernova of 1054, and the even more impressive one in 1006, dramatic events that were almost completely—and inexplicably—ignored in Europe.

A significant systematization of the sky appears to have taken place by the middle Zhou dynasty—around the 5th century BCE, when the *hsiu*, or *xiu* (known in the West as lunar mansions), twenty-eight sections of the sky in effect constituting a lunar zodiac, were introduced.[28] An account of the *hsiu* is given in the *Chhi Yao Hsing Chhen Pieh Hsing Fa* (*The Different Influences of the Seven Luminaries and the Constellations*) dated most likely to the 8th century CE. This text, though, is very late and clearly influenced by non-Chinese ideas. The complete system of *xiu* is archaeologically confirmed by 433 BCE and their dimensions identified in texts by the 4th century BCE. The *hsiu* have strong similarities to other Asiatic systems—the Indian *nakshatra*, the Arabic *al-manāzil*, and the Jewish *mazzaloth*, suggesting the exchange of ideas between China and the West, although their origin is still a matter of scholarly dispute. Needham talks of the *hsiu* as analagous to roadside teahouses, providing resting places as they journey through the sky.

Regarding contacts with western Asia and the Mediterranean, Needham is skeptical of the story that the major encyclopedia of Greek astronomy, Claudius Ptolemy's *Syntaxis*, or *Almagest*, reached China in the 2nd century, but we do know that his astrological work, the *Tetrabiblos*, had reached Japan by the 8th century. Hellenistic, Persian, and Indian astrology would have been carried to China by the Indian Buddhist astronomers, calendar-makers, and astrologers who were resident in Beijing under the Tang dynasty (618–907 CE), which Needham records as a particularly creative one for the celestial sciences. Persian astrologers also visited China in the 8th century, and there seems to have been a line of communication through central Asia to Syria and Egypt, with Nestorian Christians and Manicheans involved in the translation of astrological texts.[29] Connections with the West had been strengthened following the Arab conquest of Persia in 651 CE, when the entire Sassanian court, together with much of the nobility, sought refuge with the Tang emperor, carrying their cosmology with them.[30] The earliest evidence for a personal horoscope in China occurs in a text dated to around the year 710 CE and is assumed to be the product of Indian contacts, although the major extant examples date from the 14th century onward, including some 40 dated to between 1312 and 1376.[31] It seems possible that that Chinese may have established the custom of drawing horoscopes as a square diagrams and then exported it back along the silk road to India, Persia, and Europe.[32]

Earlier evidence of systematization dates to the mid–second millenium BCE, when a luni-solar calendar was in use in which, similar to the modern Western calendar, twelve months consisted of either twenty-nine or thirty days, with the shortfall made up of an extra, intercalary month, approximately every three years. It was a time of conflict, the Warring States period of 481–221 BCE, which saw a creative period of calendar construction. Altogether more than a hundred examples survive from the Warring States period or later, of which fifty were issued officially.[33] The key anchor of all calendar systems, though, is the beginning of the year, which is greeted with great celebration at the point corresponding to the new moon in the Western zodiac sign Aquarius. The Chinese New Year, exported to the Chinatowns that have been created in order to market Chinese wares and cuisine in the great cities of the Western world, from London to San Francisco, has become a feature of the late-modern commodification of Chinese culture. The animal-astrological year-rulers (rabbit, ox, snake, and so on) are central to Chinese expectations of the year ahead and form part of the casual news fare of Western media.

The crucial concept in astrology, *tian wen* (celestial, or sky, patterns), was *xiang*, translated as image, or symbol.[34] Celestial phenomena were therefore *tian xiang*, celestial images. A star or planet might constitute a *xiang*, an image, symbol, or analogue of some phenomenon on earth, and the astrologer was therefore required to act as an interpreter, reading the heavenly signs. However, this was no random divinatory exercise, and the system worked only because of the interdependence of all parts of a cosmos in a constant state of motion in accord with immutable laws. The rationale behind astrology as a system based on universal order was set out clearly in the opening passage of the *I Ching*, in which the relationship between heaven, superior and creative, and earth, inferior and receptive, was elaborated. As heaven and earth relate to each other through the interplay of yin and yang, so the *I Ching*'s opening passage declares,

> Events follow definite trends, each according to its nature. Things are distinguished from one another in definite classes. In this way good fortune and misfortune come about. In the heavens phenomena take form; on earth shapes take form. In this way change and transformation become manifest.[35]

The distinguished sinologist Richard Wilhelm saw these changes as a matter of law (as his translation of the *I Ching* states, "movement and rest have their definite laws"[36]), although the word *fa* in this context is better translated as pattern. In either case, whether law or pattern, the accurate calculation of celestial positions can lead to the effective management of the whole array of social and political activities on earth from sowing and harvesting to warfare and imperial ritual. In its official guise astrology was, above all, political. Celestial omen reading (*tianwen*) was practiced as a matter of course, and it was taken for granted that the correct attention to ritual might avert threatened dangers and enhance benign indications. The Chinese cosmos, like the imperial government, was bureaucratic, and the celestial bodies were the court officials of the cosmic state. The heavens became a series of offices in which the celestial deities were also officers. The astrologers themselves might be called in by government officials to comment on celestial events as and when they occurred and could then be moved around the empire to perform specific tasks required by the heavenly administrators. One text, the "government commission" of the 7th or 8th century B C E, records how the emperor Yao ordered two brothers, Hsi and Ho,

> [i]n reverent accordance with the august heavens to compute and delineate the sun, moon and stars, and the celestial markers, and so to deliver respectively the seasons observed by the people. He [Yao] particularly ordered the younger brother Hsi to reside among the Yü barbarians [at] Yang-Ku and to receive as a guest the rising sun, in order to regulate the labours of the east [the spring].[37]

The story is not quite what it seems, for Hsi-Ho was actually the name of the being who is sometimes the mother, and sometimes the chariot-driver, of the sun, and was also applied to the four (not two) astrologers whose task was to direct the sun at the four crucial parts of its journey, the solstices and equinoxes. That there is a mythical quality to this story does not weaken the proposition that from early times astrologers were dispatched to distant parts of the empire to ensure that calendars were observed, prognostications made, and astral rituals performed in order to maintain political cohesion. Nevertheless, astrology was also a routine, functional, and technical activity, evidence for which is found in the Diviner's Plate, a complex instrument with moving discs, not unlike an astrolabe, inscribed with celestial symbols, which functioned as a cosmos in miniature and could be manipulated to secure information about any situation.[38]

One example of a typical incident in the life of an official astrologer dates from the 14th century C E—probably around 1360—and occurs in an autobiographical account by Yang Yü, whose official title was Co-signatory Observer in the Bureau of Astronomy. Yang Yü was called in by a Senior Observer, a Mr. Chang, in order to give an opinion on the appearance of an auspicious omen in the form of a *Ching Hsing*, or "Resplendent Orb" (or "Orb of Virtue"), a glowing disc that, it was said, appears in a calm night sky.[39] Mr. Li, a Commisioner who was present at the meeting, clearly wanted Yang Yü to validate the *Ching Hsing's* benevolent signification for propaganda purposes—to indicate heaven's blessing on the emperor. However, Yang Yü refused Mr. Li's request on the grounds that, in complete contrast with the omen, the times were actually inauspicious (epidemics and rebellions were rife) and it was therefore unlikely that the currently unfortunate Tao of Earth was being contradicted by fortunate indications in the Tao of Heaven. Besides, Yang Yü argued, only six observers had seen the *Ching Hsing*, so it could hardly be called a definite omen. Mr. Li agreed to wait to see if the *Ching Hsing* appeared the following night. It didn't, Mr. Li backed down, and Yang Yü was vindicated.

The earliest extant comprehensive description of the celestial bureaucracy, Sima Qian's *Tianguan shu* (*Treatise on Celestial Officials*) of the 1st century BCE, described about ninety constellations, including the twenty-eight *hsiu*. The whole system was envisaged as orbiting the *beiji*, or celestial north pole, the visual embodiment of Di, the supreme being and heavenly counterpart of the earthly emperor.[40] Around the pole were positioned the stars of the heavenly imperial palace. Four other palaces built around the four seasonal marker stars then represented the cardinal directions and the four seasons. The theme of fourness was extended into a four-fold division of the twenty-eight *hsiu* into groups of seven, and the whole system allowed the official astrologers to plot the empire, its regions, and passage through the year in the sky. The emperor, as Son of Heaven, was the earthly pole, the still point of eternity around whom all the world turned, the embodiment of cosmic kingship.[41] The authority of Confucius was enrolled in order to confirm the importance of this scheme: "[T]o conduct government by virtue," Confucius stated, "may be compared to the Northern Asterism: it occupies its place, while the myriad stars revolve around it."[42] The evidence indicates that, by the second millennium BCE, it was customary to embody these celestial truths in the built environment. The great buildings of state should be seen as ceremonial and designed to provide a set for ritual life to the extent that even inhabitants occupied in perfectly routine activities were, at the same time, engaged in harmonization with heaven. Palaces and royal tombs were typically constructed in a rectangular format, aligned with the cardinal points, with the main access from the south and the inner sanctum close to the north.[43] By the 11th century it had become customary to locate the cosmic heart of the empire in the *Mingtang*, the Hall of Numinous Brightness, a feature of all future capital cities, which was aligned with the cardinal points (north, south, east, and west), provided the main venue for imperial ritual, and allowed for observations of the sky to take place.[44] Capital cities, such as Beijing, centered on the Forbidden City, were constructed as ceremonial shrines according to a system in which the entire country was mapped out with celestial correspondences. This system, known as *fen ye*, or Field Allocation, or Field Division, was combined with the principles of *feng shui*.[45] The Yellow River, for example, was the Milky Way and, all things in heaven and earth being reciprocal, vice versa.

The main constellational system, aside from the 28 *hsiu*, was entirely indigenous and unaffected by contacts with Babylonian, Persian, and Indian astrology. The Chinese had such constellations as *Chih nü*, the Weaving (sometimes mistranslated as "Spinning") Girl, which it has become the custom to invoke on flags hung outside Taoist temples. The use of character names for stars, such as the "quarrelling brothers" for Antares and the stars of Orion, or the "Herd-Boy" and the "Weaving Girl" for Altair and Vega, allowed for the telling of sky stories as a means of dramatizing the heavens. However, although certain fundamental star groups were universally recognized, such as *beidou*, the Big Dipper or Ursa Major, all-important on the grounds that it orbits the north pole, there was change and variety over the centuries. There were three main schools of astrology in the Han period, and, in the 2nd century CE, Chen Zhuo noted that, among them, they recognized 283 constellations containing 1,464 stars. There seems to have been a constant, slow process of evolution, with constellations occasionally invented or replaced.[46] The planets were all connected with the yin-yang and Five Phase models. The sun was preeminently yang and the moon the very essence of yin. The planets were known under various terms such as *Wu Wei* (translated by Needham as the Five Wefts, a weft being a thread that runs through a length of cloth or a loom; the *jing/ching* or "warp" are the hour circles across which the planets move) or *Wu Pu* (the Five Walkers).[47] Other names reflect their function as officials in the celestial bureaucracy, such as the Supreme Lord Di's "Five Minister Regulators" (*wu chen zheng*), which is how they appear on the Shang oracle bones; "Five Ducal Ministers" (*wu gong chen*); and the "Five Counsellors."[48] The planets were incorporated into the five-fold structure of the cosmos as shown in the table on p. 106.

Attention was paid to all features of a planet's cycle, from its rising before the sun and setting after the sun to its retrograde (apparent backward) motion, speed, and periodic disappearance from the night sky. Major conjunctions of the planets were considered especially portent; the alignment on 1st–2nd May 205 BCE, when the moon, Mercury, Venus, Jupiter, and Saturn

Jupiter	Sui hsing	(the Year-star)	Wood	East	Spring	Blue-green	Dragon
Mars	Ying huo	(Fitful glitterer)	Fire	South	Summer	Red	Bird
Saturn	Chen hsing	(the Exorcist)	East	Centre	Late Summer	Yellow	Man
Venus	Thai pai	(the Great White One)	Metal	West	Autumn	White	Tiger
Mercury	Chhen hsing	(the Hour-star)	Water	North	Winter	Black	Tortoise

were all in the Western zodiac sign Gemini, was employed as a sign that the rule of the first Han emperor, Liu Bang, was sanctified by heaven.

The standard interpretations of planetary patterns, surviving from the last centuries BCE, adopt the standard "if-then" ("protasis-apodosis") formula familiar from the general Asiatic practice, from Babylon to Beijing. The statement begins with the comment that "if" or "when" a particular event occurs, there may "then" be a particular consequence. For example, from the *Shi Ji*, we find the following political reading of a conjunction of Mercury and Venus, rising just before the sun:

> When Mercury appears in company with Venus to the east, and when they are both red and shoot forth rays, then foreign kingdoms will be vanquished and the soldiers of China will be victorious.[49]

There are a number of comments to make about this omen. First, it is very likely based on empirical evidence (the observation that a previous victory coincided with the rising of Mercury and Venus). Second, while the planetary conjunction is predictable in the sense that the two planets have cycles that were well understood by the 1st century BCE, the precise details—their red color—relate to atmospheric conditions and are therefore transient and unpredictable. Astrological readings can therefore be based partly on calculations of planetary positions projected into the future but may also rely on a direct observation of the sky, which was the only way that a *Ching-hsing*, for example, might be spotted. There are other surviving examples of an astrology dependent on local weather conditions. For example, in 491 BCE "a cloud like a flock of red crows was seen flying around the sun," a reference to a solar halo, which would typically appear when the atmosphere was moist or dusty.[50] The interpretations of such phenomena also often reveal a clear logic. The *Shi Ji* records, for example, that when the planets appear larger than usual, great events should be expected, and that when they are small, only minor occurrences.[51] Similarly, if the pole star was faint, the emperor would be weak, while if the number of stars in the *guansuo* constellation, which ruled prisons, increased, many people would be jailed.[52]

The same observational conditions applied to other astrological phenomena, such as nova. In an 8th-century text on Venus, the *Thai Pai Yin Ching* (*Manual of the White and Gloomy Planet of War*), a nova is regarded as of great military significance, so we assume that the bone of 1300 BCE was used in order to obtain detailed information about the new star's political and military significance.[53] We have another example from 1054, when the supernova of that year was used for propaganda purposes. That the supernova did not infringe upon lunar mansion Net, the official astrologers announced, was a certain indication of the power, virtue, and benevolence of the emperor.

There are three organizational frameworks that have a direct astrological application, the first of which is the system of the 28 lunar *hsiu*. The second organizational scheme, now the most well-known feature of Chinese astrology worldwide, is the 12-phase Jupiter cycle, which has become associated with 12 animal signs; each of the 12 phases, or "branches," is a *tzhu*, and the whole cycle a *chi*. The system's origins are unknown, although Needham suggested an ancient recognition of the equivalence between the approximate 12 years (actually 11.86 years) of one complete Jupiter revolution and the 12.37 moon cycles in one year.[54] At any rate, the system occurs perhaps as early as the 6th century BCE. Later, possibly under Turkic influence, the 12 corresponding animal symbols were introduced; rat, ox, tiger, rabbit, dragon, snake, horse, sheep, monkey, cock, dog, and pig. Initially the system was designed to indicate auspicious periods, ruled by combinations of compatible animals. Latterly—we are not sure exactly when—every animal has been given a rich personality description that is then bequeathed to the year in the sequence it represents, and to every infant born in that year. Thus the rat is charming, so it may possess fine social skills but make a poor business partner, while the pig is domestic and industrious, so it may not be exciting company but can be an excellent professional colleague. Linking the 12 animal-years to the five Phases then produces 60 combinations, which adds a little more variety to the scheme. The advantage of this system is its ease of use for modern popular astrology. Anybody can understand statements such as "when the Serpent meets the Hare, it means supreme happiness" or "the Ox and Tiger quarrel ever."[55] The 12 animal-years were exported to the West via the annual New Year festivities that have become a tourist attraction in the Chinatowns of Western cities. They entered the popular literature of the West after 1979, following the publication of Theodora Lau's *The Handbook of Chinese Horoscopes,* which self-consciously adapted the personal style of the existing Western sun-sign guides, offering guidance on work, home life, and marriage to those people caught up in the wider reaches of New Age culture, in a clear example of the triumph of religious globalization.[56]

Not dissimilar to the *tzhu,* although not, so far, exported to the West, are the twenty-four fortnightly periods, each of which has a meteorological or seasonal character and can serve as a mnemonic for the farming year. The first of these, *chhi,* Li Chuun, or Beginning of Spring, runs from 5 to 19 February, and the last, Ta Han, or Greater Cold, begins on 21 January and concludes as Li Chuun begins.[57] Another system took the five phases, wood, fire, metal, earth and water, each of which has a yin day and a yang day, and produced ten variations which then provided a guide for auspicious actions—action on a yang-fire day, for example, passivity on a yin-water day, and all shades in between on the other days.

The third framework was provided by the personal horoscope, divided fundamentally into twelve sections and containing meanings that contain traces of its Indian and Persian origins; both the sixth "sphere of influence" and the Indian sixth "house," for example, represent servants and service.[58] The horoscope's value was located in its mathematical structure, which provided a map for the individual life that could then be matched against the ebb and flow of cosmic law. While the structure of a Chinese horoscope was identifiably the same as, or similar to, that of India and the Islamic world, the language indicates the use of Chinese assumptions. In one example, dated to 1325 CE, the location of the Wood planet (Jupiter) in the Basket (the 7th *hsiu*) offered a warning to beware of Saturnine men, while *Chi Tu,* the moon's south node and "Evil Aura of Saturn," can be interchanged with the comet, the "Evil Aura of Mercury," an exchange of location that, in Indian astrology, would probably defuse the danger emanating from both.[59] Horoscopic astrology is currently undergoing a revival in Taiwan and is spreading to Hong Kong, its appeal perhaps reinforced by its general similarity to the Western system now familiar from popular horoscope columns in newspapers.

Chinese cosmology depended on a concept of unity and interdependence of all things, tangible and intangible, existing within a matrix of meaning, purpose, pattern, and order. It survived the suppression of communism thanks to the size and vigor of the communities of "overseas" Chinese. Notions of kinship and the veneration of ancestors (the interdependence of all family members, alive and dead, as a model of the interdependence of all things in the cosmos) and of ritual means of engaging with the environment such as *feng shui* are credited for the commercial success that distinguishes Chinese communities in Southeast Asia and North America. The adoption of physical and medical applications of Chinese cosmology, such as acupuncture, herbalism, and various martial arts in the West, testifies to the wider appeal of such holistic concepts. The study of the origins of Chinese cosmology is therefore very much concerned with understanding the present, especially as the post-Maoist regime has moved progressively toward an encouragement of traditional learning to provide an ethical replacement for Marxism, while in the overseas communities traditional practices have always been central.

Traditional Chinese cosmogony was "chaotic," based on the belief that the world emanated from an original formless state. However, the Chinese worldview was far from spontaneous, and its astrology was "cosmic": At the official level it was highly codified, and even the popular "Fate-Calculation" practiced by the masses worked on the basis of precise formulae and an understanding that time moved in precise patterns. The orientation of sacred and imperial buildings and the practice of *feng shui* indicate a highly developed sense of terrestrial cosmology in which engagement with the celestial heaven requires exactly regulated forms of behavior on earth. Yet, although the system required great precision, it was far from rigid, and it depended on the dynamic relationship of yin and yang and the constant motion of the five phases, or "elements." Chinese religion was designed to propitiate higher powers, yet it was also contemplative, meditative, and concerned with the harmonization of earthly and heavenly life. We may even consider the cosmos itself to be an object of veneration and apply the epithet "cosmotheism" to Chinese religion.

India

Ancient Traditions and Modern Practice

The moon was born from his mind; from his eye the sun was born.[1]

India is home to a living tradition of technical astrology that extends back in an unbroken lineage for around 2,000 years, has roots that may be traced to the first or second millennia BCE, and is firmly based in Hindu religion. Traditionally, astronomy and astrology are known together as *jyotish*, or *jyotisha*, translated as the "science of light," and constitute one of the six *vedangas*, the topics necessary for the correct understanding and application of the *Vedas*, the sacred texts. In Vedic learning, *jyotish* is primarily concerned with the selection of auspicious dates and moments for sacrifice and ritual. Technical horoscopic astrology was introduced from the Hellenistic world in the first few centuries CE, but there had been a long tradition of reciprocal contacts with the West prior to this; it is a short journey from India to Mesopotamia, and there is evidence of the spread of Babylonian astrology to India in the first millennium BCE, if not earlier, and of intense communication between India and Greece, which manifests in similarities (such as a belief in reincarnation) between certain aspects of classical philosophy and Indian teachings.[2] Considering astrology's importance in Indian culture, the extent to which it is ignored by academics is surprising, especially in view of its sacred role as one of the pillars of Indian religion and its secular function in the arrangement of marriages and prediction of almost every aspect of life, from career and financial prospects to wealth, health, and death.

There is no shortage of instructional books on Indian astrology, but the scholarly books, whether on astrology in specific or on cosmology in general, are scarce. *Issues in Vedic Astronomy and Astrology* by Pandya, Dikshit, and Kansara is a thorough investigation of the cosmogony, astronomy, and astrology in the sacred texts, the *Vedas*.[3] There are also excellent histories of astronomy by Richard Thompson, and Sen and Shukla, and a volume by Lishk that covers the first millennium BCE to the early centuries CE.[4] Hari Prasad's collection of essays on time is essential, and R. F. Gombrich's article on Indian cosmology is still a sound introduction to the topic, even though written more than forty years ago, while Kuiper's work on cosmogony is comprehensive.[5] The authoritative guide to astronomical alignments in Indian temples and cities is Rana Singh's *Cosmic Order and Cultural Astronomy: Sacred Cities of India*.[6] David Pingree, meanwhile, is the only Western historian to have addressed the early history of Indian astrology, mainly through his book *From Astral Omens to Astrology*, together with a series of papers spread across scholarly journals.[7] On modern astrology there is astonishingly little. Stephen Kemper's discussion of astrology in Sri Lanka contains a discussion of time as an organizing principle for astrological signs and the concept of the individual, while Martin Gansten's work on *nadi jyotish*, or "palm-leaf astrology," remains extremely rare as an example of a doctoral thesis that examines contemporary practice.[8]

There is, though, a wealth of primary source material in English translation. The earliest extant astrological text is the *Vedanga Jyotisha* of Lagadha, which is dated to anywhere between the late second or first millennium BCE. The text is primarily calendrical and concerned with ascertaining the correct date and time for appropriate actions, mainly on the basis of solar and lunar positions.[9] The classic text is *The Yavanajataka of Sphujidhvaja*, a 3rd-century version of a 2nd-century work probably written in Alexandria and translated by Yavanesvara, or "Lord of the Greeks."[10] The 6th-century textbook the *Brhat Samhita* by Varahamihira is still in use by present-day astrologers, while there is a mass of modern introductory material available both by Indian popularizers such as B. V. Raman, author of a major series of textbooks, and Komilla Sutton, and Western practitioners such as Ronnie Dreyer and David Frawley.[11] For space reasons, but also because they have a far less intimate relationship with astrology than does Hinduism, this chapter does not deal with Jain and Sikh cosmologies.

The religious culture of India is marked by complexity, subtlety, and pluralism. The term "Hinduism," in the sense that an "ism" signifies a single set of beliefs, is a product of 19th-century Western scholarship and the assumption that, like Christianity, Indian religion must consist around defined sets of dogma and ritual.[12] We have to use the term "Hindu," for it has become common currency, but it is better to see Hinduism as a set of networks based on shifting and overlapping allegiances to a multitude of gurus, gods, and goddesses. In effect Hinduism is defined negatively: A Hindu is generally a person of Indian origin who does not practice either one of the imported Abrahamic faiths (Islam, Christianity, or Judaism) or the indigenous non-Vedic religions, Jainism, Sikhism, and Buddhism. There are, though, commonalities that are shared by most of the varieties of Hinduism.[13] If we could draw out a single thread, Hinduism would consist of a series of principles or laws.

The Hindu cosmos is governed by *samsara*, translated as "continuous flow," the process by which individual souls pass through successive incarnation. *Dharma*, translated as "that which supports," or loosely as "way" or "law," is not unlike the Greek *heimarmene* or the Chinese *tao*, in that it presents a path that, paradoxically, we can both choose to follow and that we must follow; it is the totality of one's submission to ethical values, life circumstances, spiritual condition, and purpose. *Karma* is, then, the totality of one's past and present actions, which are lived out through *dharma* and *samsara*. The entire system is bound up with a notion of cause and effect that is not linear or mechanical but in which all things in the universe, both material and nonmaterial, are bound together in webs of what are known in classical Stoic thought as sympathy and correspondence. The pantheon is neither polytheistic nor monotheistic, categories that do not apply to a system in which complexity exists within unity and, therefore, many deities can be seen as aspects of the One. These are the principles on which Indian astrology is based, then: a combination of a cosmos that is essentially spiritual in nature, driven by laws that can be understood through the observation of astronomical patterns, and in which divinities and spirits speak through the stars, planets, and periods of time that they either rule or to which they correspond.

The earliest known Indian civilization, at least according to current archaeological knowledge, flourished in the Indus Valley—modern Pakistan—from around 3300 to 1300 BCE. However, our knowledge of the Indus Valley script is still so uncertain that there is little or nothing we can say about the civilization's cosmology with any certainty. The earliest literary sources for Indian cosmology are the *Vedas*, the sacred texts that, in their written form, appear to date from the late second millennium, perhaps around 1200 BCE (although we have no way of knowing how old any prior oral tradition may have been), and contain rules for the timing of sacred rituals.[14] Such rules are, though, often opaque to the outsider. The Vedic hymns are concerned more with reverence for the sun, and fascination with the numbers seven and twelve, planets and months respectively, and with 360—the number of days in an ideal year—and 720, than with astronomical detail or astrological rules. In the *Rig*

Veda, we read, "Seven horses draw the seven who ride on the seven wheeled chariot," while the "twelve-spoked wheel of Order rolls around the sky and never ages."[15] There is no practical, interpretative astrology in the *Vedas*, with the exception of reference to the 27 Nakshatras, the lunar mansions, a kind of zodiac based on the lunar month.[16] However, since the 1980s, American practitioners of Indian astrology have branded it as "Vedic" in order to locate it in a spiritual tradition rather than a people or a country.[17]

In general, the creation of the universe is couched in nonpersonal terms, as a series of natural processes, but described poetically. The *Rig Veda*, the oldest of the *Vedas*, describes how in the state of existence and nonexistence, heat and water interact, and desire gives rise to mind:

> There was neither non-existence nor existence then; there was neither the realm of space nor the sky which is beyond. . . . Darkness was hidden by darkness . . . with no distinguishing sign, all this was water. The life force that was covered with emptiness, that one arose through the power of heat. Desire came upon that one in the beginning; that was the first seed of mind.[18]

Heat, in turn, produces order and truth, the foundations of a harmonious and ethical life, as well as the ocean, which then gives rise to the year and days and nights—time as its passing is experienced.[19] As to whether there was a creator, this remains an open question: "Perhaps it formed itself," the *Rig Veda* says of the cosmos, but, then, "perhaps it did not."[20]

Important for the notion of cosmology and astrology as relational, in which all parts of the world may be understood by their relationships with all other parts, is the concept of the cosmos as an archetypal man, the cosmic giant Purusha, who "has a thousand eyes, a thousand feet [and] pervaded the earth on all sides and extended beyond it as far as ten fingers."[21] The text continues in a cosmological vein:

> The moon was born from his mind; from his eye the sun was born. . . .
> From his navel the middle realm of space arose; from his head the sky evolved. From his two feet came the earth, and the quarters of the sky from his ear. Thus they [the gods] set the world in order.[22]

Purusha, in his dismemberment by the gods, became the man whose sacrifice enabled the creation of the world and the being to whom, ultimately, all sacrifice is offered.

Indian cosmology, like Indian religion, is essentially syncretic. The core position of both is not that theories need to be true but that they can be pointers to the truth, whether as metaphorical statements, models for the structure of rituals, or organizing frameworks for thought. Paradoxes, inconsistencies, and contradictions do not pose the same problems as they do within the positivist context of modern science or the dogmatic schemes of the Abrahamic faiths. This is not to say that there is no systematization but that it proceeds by "aggregation and encapsulation," sometimes by locating different cosmologies either within one another, a "smaller" one inside a "larger" one, or as successive phases.[23] For example, in the *Rig Veda* the cosmos may either be dual in nature, consisting of heaven and earth, or tripartite, consisting of earth, air, and heaven, while both the two and the three levels may consist of either two or three strata each, leading to a total of either six or nine in total. Time and space were also both structured according to the division by four that is a near-universal feature of pre-modern culture. As the *Atharva Veda*, which probably dates to between the 12th and 10th centuries BCE, put it, "Four directions has the heaven, and also four the earth: [from these] the gods created the embryo. May they open her that he will bring forth!"[24]

The division of cosmic-historical periods according to sexagesimal mathematics—multiples of the number six—is documented in the epic poem *Mahabharata*, which reached its final form around the 4th century CE. The basic sequence of four *yugas*, or ages, existed within a sequence of decline from an original era of perfection, the *Krita Yuga*, through the periods of *Treta Yuga* and *Dwapara Yuga*, to the present-day period of corruption, violence, and immorality, the *Kali Yuga*.[25] The duration of each period was calculated according to multiples of six (4,800, 3,600, 2,400, and 1,200 years, respectively) but was extended by a factor of 360—one year in the life of the gods and the number of days in one ideal solar year.[26] Multiplied by 360, the four *yugas* combined into a *Maha Yuga* of 4,320,000 years, which began when Brahma opened his eyes and the universe emerged out of the navel of Vishnu, who was asleep, dreaming the cosmos into existence. Two thousand *Maha Yugas* form a *Kalpa*, a Day and Night of Brahma, which lasts 8,640 billion years. Infinity, for the Hindus, has no starting point, and they can probe as far back into the past, or into the future, as their sacred mathematics allows. The cosmos is created and destroyed, but in an endless sequence, in which destruction is conceived of as renewal, rather than an ending: The key concept on the macrocosmic level is eternity, with no limit to time, space, or consciousness.

Cosmology was embedded in the social system through the four castes. The scheme's origins are unknown, although they may be a particularly firm codification of hereditary principles, reinforced by conquest, but envisaged as a means of ensuring that society adequately mirrors the cosmos, in the form of Purusha, the cosmic man, the human figure who represents and embodies the entire universe.[27] The four castes (*Brahmins*, priests and teachers; *Kshatriyas*, kings, aristocrats, and soldiers; *Vaishyas*, mechants and farmers; and *Shudras*, laborers) were known as *Varnas*, which translates from Sanskrit as appearance, form, or color, suggesting that the order of human life was the apparent form of some deeper existence.

It was also common for significant sacred sites to be aligned with the cardinal points (north, south, east, and west), one of the most impressive examples being the orientation of the hundreds of temples in the complex at Angkor in Cambodia to a north-south-east-west grid. The astronomical alignment of sacred sites, temple construction, and city plans was a common characteristic of Indian architecture, the purpose of which was summarized by the archeoastronomer Kim Malville:

> By their respective geometries, each of these places establishes an interior cosmos with order and meaning. Geometries utilizing lines, triangles, rectangles, and circles were used to couple interior spaces with those of the larger cosmos. The geometric connection between microcosm and macrocosm that has always been easiest to construct and to interpret is cardinal orthogonality. Space within the city was designed to mimic the geometry of the larger cosmos by constructing a grid work of mutually perpendicular lines aligned to true north.[28]

The principle is extended to domestic architecture in a practice known as *vaastu*, an equivalent of the Chinese *feng shui*, in which the structure and orientation of one's home becomes a means of ensuring stability and harmony.[29]

The physical structure of astronomically aligned and symbolic architecture was the manifest form in space of the temporal progression of the calendar. There are many traditional variants on the calendar, but by the mid- to late first millennium BCE the year was divided into 12 months, seven-day weeks, and other variants such as *tithis*, or lunar days, of which there were 30 in each lunar month.[30] The calendar then becomes the basis for a series of festivals, of which the most famous is now *Divali*, or *Diwali*, the festival of lights (including the "inner" light, we should remember), a five-day post-harvest, pre–winter solstice celebration that coincides with the new moon in the sidereal zodiac sign Libra. Other festivals are based on a planetary calendar. The greatest of these is the *Khumba Mela*, which is timed according to the cycles of Jupiter and the sun and is held every 12 years, with smaller, intermediate festivals and occasional, much larger ones.[31] The last *Maha* (great) *Kumbha Mela*, which is held every 144 years, or 12 Jupiter cycles, was celebrated in 2001 and reputedly attended by 60 million people, all of whom purified themselves by ritually bathing in the Yamuna River. Such events, in essence pilgrimages, are the most dramatic, primary, collective expression of astrology as a need to actively celebrate and harmonize with the cosmos and moments determined by astronomical patterns.

Horoscopic astrology brings such immense cosmic patterns into the mundane details of personal life. It flourishes in India today in very much the form in which it was imported from the Hellenistic world in the early centuries of the Christian era. It retains both the technical astrology of the classical world and its overtly religious and magical qualities, and it occupies a central and unquestioned part of Indian life, most publicly in its use in arranged marriages, from providing an additional (although rarely the only) factor for assessing compatibility to arranging the date for weddings.[32] It also lacks the hostility that Western astrology has experienced for hundreds of years from religious groups and, more recently, from scientists. Even though a tiny group of skeptical scientists speaks out against the practice, a colleague in a physics department in an American university once told me that all his Indian students have their horoscopes cast and would not consider this at all strange. The only sustained skeptical objection to astrology focused on opposition to the announcement by the University Grants Commission in February 2001, that it was intending to launch astrology departments in various universities.[33]

The Indian zodiac, it is important to say, increasingly diverges from the Western zodiac, being based on the locations of the fixed stars, whereas the Western ("tropical") version is tied to the seasons. Being based on the stars, the Indian zodiac is known as sidereal, from the Latin *sidus* or star. The difference between the two zodiacs, the *ayanamsa*, is currently around 25^0, which means that, while the sun always enters Aries at the spring equinox—usually 21 March—in the Western zodiac, on the same day in the Indian zodiac it is at 5^0—6^0 Pisces. This is a technical point with no relevance to any understanding of astrology's character or function, but it is important to astrology's critics, who regard it as evidence of what they believe to be astrology's inconsistent technical foundations.

The structural framework of the horoscope is fundamentally that worked out in the Hellenistic Near East in the last centuries BCE. A horoscope can be cast for any moment or purpose, whether for a birth, a question, or an event. In *Prasna Shastra*, for example, a horoscope is cast for the moment that a question is asked (the Sanskrit *prasna* translates as "question"), the answer being contained within the relationships between the planets at that moment. The seven traditional planets—in order, the moon (Chandruma or Soma), Mercury (Buddha), Venus (Shukra), the sun (Surya), Mars (Kartika, Mangala, or Kuja), Jupiter (Brihaspati or Guru), and Saturn (Shani)—are known as *grahas* in Sanskrit. The moon's nodes, Raha and Ketu (the two points at which the moon's path in the sky crosses the sun's path), are also regarded as planets, so there are nine *graha* altogether. *Navagraha* (nine planet) temples are well known and occur wherever Hinduism has spread, often unnoticed: I and a party of my students were once invited to attend planetary rituals designed to mitigate the effect of dangerous planetary alignments at a discreetly placed *navagraha* temple on the Archway Road, a busy thoroughfare in north London. *Navagraha* rituals appear to be growing in popularity; there is also a large *navagraha* temple in Washington, D.C.; and temples in southern India are now catering for expatriates on their visits home. We have one recent acount of a *navagraha* ritual in Sri Lanka.[34] The ritual begins with a prepubescent girl preparing a string of nine strands, one for each planet, which then protects the client against malignant planetary influence or signification. The priest then uses the string to conduct the ceremony while Buddhist monks chant protective verses, which reinforce the auspicious power of the girl and the planets as embodied in the string. *Graha* can be translated as seizing, laying hold of, or holding and can imply a kind of possession, the point being that the planets exist inside each individual as well as in the sky.

The interpretation of the horoscope on the basis of which such problems are solved proceeds via an examination of the planets' relationships with one another and their location in the *rashis*, or zodiac signs, and the twelve *bhavas* (division), equivalent to "houses" in Western astrology. The religious significance of these divisions is always present in their names. The zodiac is known as *kalapurusha*, "the eternal time which has no beginning and no end," while, in the *Vedas*, the ecliptic (on which the zodiac is based) is termed the *Sudarshan chakra*, the wheel (*chakra*) in the hand of *Lord Vishnu*, creator of the universe.[35] A horoscope cast for the time, date, and place of birth is then known as a *bhava chakra* or *rishi chakra*. The *Nakshatras*, or twenty-seven lunar mansions, are also used to provide additional information. *Gochara* (transits—actual planetary movements from day to day) and *dashas* (time phases ruled by particular planets) are then relied on for prediction, to establish periods that are either favorable or difficult for particular kinds of action. The birth chart, or any horoscope for that matter, can then be divided by any number from 2 to 16 to produce a *varga* (part or division), a complete new horoscope mathematically derived from the original. The most common of these is the *navamsha* chart, in which each sign of the zodiac is divided into nine. The first nine sections of Aries are then Aries to Sagittarius. The nine sections of Taurus then begin with Capricorn, Aquarius, and Pisces until the sequence begins again with Aries.[36] The consequence is that each planet moves into a different zodiac sign, and an entirely new horoscope is created, emerging from the original chart but conveying much more specific information. The reason for the *navamsha* chart lies in the information it reveals about a particular topic, and its appeal to modern practitioners is clear: concerns "marriage and the partner . . . relationship in general . . . our ability to share our inner or spiritual values in relationship."[37] Such personal matters are frequently of greatest interest to the astrologers' clients.

The implications of the *vargas* for an understanding of time are really quite intriguing, and the closest analogy may be the modern notion of complexity and fractals, in which the same pattern repeats itself in ever decreasing—or ever increasing—sequences. The horoscope, itself set for a measurable moment of time and point in space, then divides itself in orderly stages, each of which produces a new chart that represents a "reality," but no longer the reality that was originally based on measurable celestial positions. The cosmos can fold in on itself, yielding different kinds of truth as it does so. As the astrologer performs mathematical tricks, so fresh information becomes available that, in the case of the *navamsha*, is the likely marriage partner.

The *gunas* (literally "strands") give a further insight into the religious nature of Indian astrology. These derive from the creation that occurred when Purusha, the male principle, the cosmic man, encountered Prakriti, the female principle, and together they gave rise to *ahankara* or individual ego and intellect.[38] The three *gunas* themselves are aspects of universal consciousness: *Sattva* is truth and purity, *rajas* is the cause of action, and *tamas* is darkness and ignorance. These necessarily shift out of balance at birth, and by examining the powers of *Purushi* (represented by the sun), *Prakriti* (embodied in the moon), and *ahankara* (symbolized by Mercury) in the birth chart, the astrologer can locate the individual's spirituality in relation to the forces of primeval cosmic creation. The cosmos may be unbearably huge—infinite, in fact—but each man and each woman has his or her own significant place within it.

The paradoxes of time and the spiritual nature of reality are brought into sharp relief in *nadi* astrology, which relies on palm-leaf horoscopes (so called because they are written on palm leaves).[39] There are a number of collections of these horoscopes that anyone can visit to obtain his or her birth chart and an account of his or her life. The curious feature of these horoscopes, though, is that the visitor finds that his or her personal *nadi* birth chart has already been prepared before the individual's arrival, unannounced. Not only that, but it was prepared at some time in the remote past. One might object that it is beyond the powers of anyone to prepare horoscopes for everyone who will ever live. The answer, which takes us back to the kind of paradox inherent in the simultaneity of existence and nonexistence before the creation, is that *nadi* horoscopes were written only for the people who were destined to collect them. There's a rigid, hard determinism at work here, yet one that one can reflect on and enjoy: The personal testimony I have received from individuals who have collected their *nadi* horoscopes is that the very fact of their apparent accuracy evokes a sense of wonder and belonging in the cosmos.

The classic astrological texts are composed in terms that appear to be rigid and unbending, as if the interpretation of horoscopes is a purely mechanical exercise, and such is the power of an unavoidable *karma* that spans multiple lifetimes extending into the infinite past and the eternal future that the only response is passivity. Sections from the *Yavanajataka* give the flavor:

> If, at the time of death, [all] the benefic planets are in their own vargas in the signs of their exaltation and cardines, or if the lord of the eighth place is a benefic and is in this yoga, it provides the way to the abode of the Sun (Suryaloka). . . . If (the planets) are in their own houses, their friends' navamsas or their base-triplicities in the seventh of eight places, or the navansas of the signs in those places, and if they are not overcome, they cause rebirth to occur in the world of men; the direction and the region (where the birth takes place) is determined by the birth-sign (and its lord).[40]

The astrologer needs to know that the benefic planets are Venus and Jupiter, the signs in which they are exalted are Pisces and Cancer respectively, and that the cardines are the first, fourth, seventh, and tenth *bhavas*, or houses, together with all the other required technical information. The consequence, if we require all these separate technical features to coincide, is that the relevant factors can occur only at certain precise times of day in two separate periods of around twenty-five days, every twenty-nine or thirty years. Time unfolds in mathematically precise periods into which each individual is placed, like a small cog in a giant machine of fate. However, if we alter our perspective and view the cosmos as a living organism, planets as living beings with likes and dislikes, and time itself as a "person," then the *machina mundi* may still be subject to what are, in effect, laws of physics, but it is a machine with which one may have a personal relationship, exactly as with a member of one's family.

Indian astrology's interpretive functions are just one phase in a process in which, as human beings are creations of the cosmos, but not separate from it, they are therefore active participants in it. Passivity may be a part of the astrological mindset, but so, equally, is action. There is therefore a second stage to the astrological process, which is to engage with whatever information the astrologer has imparted. True, one can simply accept that life is going to take a particular course and accept one's fate. However, the omens of future difficulties dispatched by astrological configurations can be dealt with by rituals designed to avert a future problem, of the kind I attended at the *navagraha* temple in London, or by prayer, meditation, ritual, *pujas* (purifications), and talismans. In the 1980s I observed just such acts at the Shwedagon pagoda in Rangoon, one of the most magnificent, if not the most magnificent, of all Buddhist temples. Around the base of the central 321-foot high gilded *stupa* are located eight shrines to the planetary rulers of the days of the week; the sun (Sunday), the moon (Monday), Mars (Tuesday), Mercury (Wednesday before noon), Rahu (Wednesday after noon), Jupiter (Thursday), Venus (Friday), and Saturn (Saturday). Dispatched by their astrologers, local people engage quietly with one of the planetary shrines, meditating in front of it, contemplating its beauty, making offerings of flowers and pouring water or milk over it, and lighting incense to carry prayers to heaven. The principle is quite simple: If one is suffering from an excess of Mars—a fever perhaps, or violent threats, or spiritual agitation—one may counter this by performing the appropriate ritual at the shrine of Venus, whose nature is calm and peaceful. On another occasion, perhaps, the solution might be to attend to the Mars shrine precisely in order to persuade the Martian principle in the cosmos to call off its threats. A similar situation was observed by Peter Holt in his travels through India. He describes a visit to a temple in the 1980s with a guide, Santi Lal:

> We stopped by a large marble image of Lord Shiva's bull, the means by which, according to legend, he travels through the heavens. The flower garlands wrapped around his horns gave off a perfume. Santi Lal touched the statue. He kissed the head and mouthed a prayer. . . . (He) whispered to me "All knowledge comes from Shiva and his wife Parvati, including the knowledge of astrology. Any predictions are made for them."[41]

Astrologers may be found in the temples, where a knowledge of the art can be a part of priestly duties, but they also exist in a secular context, on the street, or in their offices. But one point they agree on is that, if astrology is divine knowledge, the astrologer should be in a fit state to receive it. The *Brhat Samhita* makes this clear:

> The predictions made by an astrologer who has mastered both the theory and practice of the science of astrology, and astronomy, as if it were spread before his eyes in the world, inscribed in his intellect and firmly implanted in his heart, will never go wrong.[42]

That is, astrology is infallible, but the astrologer's ability to comprehend its truths, communicate them to others, and recommend appropriate action is dependent on a suitable combination of wisdom and compassion. There is, then, an inevitable tension between those who practice astrology for money and those who do not. This problem was addressed by the guru Sri Yoganada (1893–1952), who claimed that

> [c]harlatans have brought the ancient stellar science to its present disrepute. Astrology is too vast, both mathematically and philosophically, to be rightly grasped except by men of profound understanding. If ignoramuses misread the heavens, and see there a scrawl instead of a script, that is to be expected in this imperfect world. One should not dismiss the "wisdom" with the wise.[43]

A brief word about Buddhism: As a product of a reforming branch of Hinduism, Buddhist texts have little to say about astrology but can be slightly antagonistic to it, partly because it smacks of that elaborate imagery and ritual in Hinduism which can be seen as a distraction from the simplicity of cosmic truth and the purity of the path to enlightenment. I have discussed this with educated Buddhists in Sri Lanka, where astrology is an instrument of state (the moment at which the republic was proclaimed—12:43 p.m. on 22 May 1972—was chosen by astrologers who were actually Buddhist monks), who were bemused that anyone would practice astrology. However, I suspect the influence of Western skepticism in such attitudes. In Burma I was told a different story by a Buddhist astrologer (not a monk) who explained how Buddhism permitted astrology but restricted its remit. According to my informant, the Buddha ordered all the four books on astrology to be burned, but the birds, fearing that such wisdom would be lost, then gathered the ashes and reassembled them. When the task was complete, only one book was missing, and that was the one that contained the rules for prediction. Astrology is therefore permitted for self-knowledge and the selection of auspicious moments for action, but not for knowledge of the future. The reason is simple: The future is no longer fixed, for an individual who gains enlightenment changes the future. Time, for a Buddhist, is therefore not set in stone but is fluid and malleable. With this in mind, astrology is an integral part of popular Buddhist culture, notably in Tibet, if not sanctioned by scripture.

Ultimately, the study of Indian astrology suggests that the key principle in Hinduism is not the character of the gods, the worship of individual deities, or the elaborate rituals that allow individuals to engage with the cosmos, but deified time. If we stripped away everything else in the cosmos, we would be left with time. Even people exist only because they are made, live, and die in time. Here is how the *Atharva Veda* describes Kala, or time personified as a primordial power:

> With seven wheels does this Time ride, seven naves has he, immortality is his axle. He carries hither all these beings (worlds). Time the first god, now hastens onwards . . . him, verily we see existing in many forms. . . . Time begot yonder heaven. He surely did bring hither all the beings (worlds), he surely did encompass all the beings (worlds). Being their father he became their son; there is, verily, no force higher than he.[44]

The eternal and the individual are inextricably linked. There is no distance between a remote period of time and a distant part of the cosmos, and the details of the here and now of individual affairs. The continuing notion in modern India that the divine is manifest in the mundane is evident in the widespread use of astrology for almost every aspect of life. Time is a matter both of the infinite and the here and now. In late 2010 the *Washington Post* reported on a typical marital problem, and the solution astrology offers:

> Ruchira Varmaa's marriage was already in trouble when she found out she was pregnant. She didn't know what to do, so, as with most life decisions, she consulted her astrologer. Ms. Varmaa and her child would be fine, the astrologer said, as long as the baby was born on one of three *mahurats*, or auspicious days, near her due date. She then did what doctors say an increasing number of middle-class Indians are doing these days: She scheduled a caesarean section in order to nail that good-luck date. The

perfectly timed birth not only gave her a wonderful daughter, Ms. Varmaa says, but also got her own life back on track. Her career and health have improved and her brief, arranged marriage has ended in an amicable divorce. "I didn't want my bad luck to affect the child," says Ms. Varmaa, 34 years old, a director for a clothing exporter in Mumbai. "If the position of the sun and moon are right, then the baby has a good life and even the mother's life improves."[45]

Indian cosmology is chaotic, based on a belief that the world emerged from an original, undefined state. Its focus is on eternity and the function of astrology, which is complex, highly codified, and therefore "cosmic," is to intervene in the world of humans, trapped in an illusion of change, and to help them manage daily affairs by reconnecting them with the permanence of cosmic existence. The desirable consequence of this activity is then an imposition of order, so that the inevitable ups and downs of a life lived in a physical incarnation stay as close as possible to the patterns of the celestial bodies, and crisis and catastrophe are avoided. This may not always be possible. Indeed, disaster may be part of the cosmically ordained sequence of events. But the hope is invariably otherwise. Indian religion accords a central place to astrology. Indeed, it is impossible to understand or engage with the daily functioning of religious life without a knowledge of the techniques, assumptions, and requirements of judicial astrology. From the reverence accorded to planetary deities to the significance attached to the individual moment of birth, and the timing of major events in life, such as marriage, astrology plays a key role in the management of human destiny, connecting past lives to this one and all future existence.

Babylon

Signs in the Sky

> Signs on earth just as those in the sky give us signals. Sky and earth both produce portents though appearing separately, they are not separate (because) sky and earth are related.[1]

Mesopotamia, equating roughly to present-day Iraq, was once revered as the "cradle of civilization." As archaeological discoveries have progressed, though, the origins of art, agriculture, and astronomy have been pushed back by many thousands of years and located in other areas. However, the civilization that emerged in Sumer, to the south of the country, in the third millennium BCE was remarkable in its sophistication. Thanks to its invention of writing, we also know more about the minds of early Mesopotamians than about any other people of the time, with the possible exception of the Egyptians. The Mesopotamians' cosmogony influenced Greek notions on the origins of the universe, and the Mesopotamian calendar is still used by the Jews. The particular style of astrology that developed in Mesopotamia, and of which the earliest textual indications emerge in the late third millennium, is the ancestor of the systems of modern India and the West. The reader of horoscope columns in London, the New Age astrologer in Los Angeles, and the priest conducting a planetary ritual in a Hindu temple all share a legacy that can be traced over 4,000 years to the temples of the great city-states of ancient Sumer. More than 130 generations connect an astrologer advising a modern Indian politician to one consulted by Gudea, Lord of Lagash, around the year 2000 BCE.

Mesopotamian astrology was initially conducted almost entirely by an elite group of scribes and priests on behalf of the king, allowing him to receive instructions or guidance from the gods and goddesses who presided over the cosmos. It was originally chaotic in the sense that it depended on direct observation of the sky, with no prediction of planetary positions and very little codification. However, there seems to have been a constant tendency toward the identification of consistent meanings, so that the next time a particular alignment occurred, the astrologers could be ready with their advice. Astrological meanings appear to have been developed in two ways. One was the exploration of theoretical possibilities, theorizing what might happen, for example, if an eclipse occurred on the wrong day—which was a bad omen. The other was the accumulation of empirical data, based on the recording of events that coincided with particular celestial patterns. It was assumed that a repetition of a celestial event would indicate a similar repetition in terrestrial affairs. Both approaches, though, the theoretical and the empirical, were designed to establish divine intentions, so that the state might harmonize with the cycles of time and pay due respect to the presiding gods and goddesses. Sometime before 500 BCE a cultural revolution took place that consisted of two main developments. First was the organization of the sky into the 12 zodiac signs. Second was the emergence of the birth chart, the use of astrology to establish individual destinies, based on the date of birth. Both developments point to a massive increase in the importance attached to the individual's place in the cosmos. For the first time, ordinary people had a direct and personal relationship with individual planets.

The general scholarly sources on Mesopotamian cosmology, mainly by Henri Frankfort and Thorkild Jacobsen, are excellent and accessible introductions to the subject. However, they are regarded with some suspicion by current specialists on the grounds that they tend to speculate on the basis of material that, in the past forty years, has been reviewed and revised.[2] Samuel Kramer's work on Mesopotamian mythology also remains a sound and authoritative account.[3] Although the vast majority of cuneiform clay tablets have yet to be transcribed, and even most of those we know to be astrological have not yet been translated, there are some valuable collections of letters and reports by Assyrian astrologers of the 7th and 8th centuries, together with omens from the *Enuma Anu Enlil*, a major collection compiled in the Assyrian period.[4] The closest to a sacred cosmological text is the *Enuma Elish*, the creation epic, which tells the story of the origins of the gods and their creation of humanity.[5] There is also now a number of excellent scholarly commentaries on, or histories of, Mesopotamian astrology, edited or written by David Brown, Herman Hunger, David Pingree, Francesca Rochberg, and Erica Reiner.[6] Michael Baigent's *From the Omens of Babylon* is a fine general account.[7]

Political and social organization in third-millennium BCE Mesopotamia was based on the region's fertility and, hence, prosperity, which allowed the development of food surpluses and settled communities based on temples, the emergence of larger city-states, and, encouraged by the demands of trade and accounting, the development of writing, the original language being Sumerian. By 2360 to 2180 BCE, the first recognizable "empire" emerged, conquered by the Akkadian Sargon the Great, from which the earliest surviving fragments of astrological texts have come down to us.

The first Babylonian Empire witnessed another peak of centralization and cultural patronage under the emperor Hammurabi, who ruled from around 1728 to 1686, as well as the first complete surviving astrological text, the "Venus Tablet of Ammisaduqa." The rise of the Assyrians, based in the north, began after 1400 BCE, and, after a number of periods of advance and retreat, the Assyrian state entered a period of supremacy that lasted from the 9th to late 7th centuries, included the brief occupation of Egypt, and has left us our most substantial evidence for the nature and use of astrology at the highest levels of politics in the form of letters and reports, covering a relatively brief period, dispatched from the astrologer to the king. The Assyrians were replaced in turn by the second, or neo-Babylonian, Empire, and, in 539, the city of Babylon itself was conquered by the Persians. The Persian Empire extended across a vast expanse of Asia, from Afghanistan and the Indian frontier to the east to Egypt and the borders of Greece to the west, becoming the catalyst for a rapid exchange of cosmological ideas between the subcontinent at one extreme, and the Mediterranean at the other.

All political authority in the Mesopotamian cosmos was vested in the gods and goddesses who, the *Enuma Elish*, the creation myth (named after the entire epic's opening lines, "when above"), tells us, had molded the first humans out of clay as their servants.[8] The original substance of the cosmos was water, out of which the world emerged not as the result of divine creation but as a form of natural evolution. Gradually, matter, the water of life, evolved into the first gods and goddesses and progressed through their relationships, rivalries, marriages, and offspring. In the beginning, we are told, the universe consisted of three entities, Mummu, Apsû (fresh water), and Tiâmat (salt water), or "she who gave birth to them all." The passage begins in enigmatic style:

> When above the heavens had not (yet) been named,
> (And) below the earth had not (yet) been called by a name . . .
> (At that time) were the gods created within them.[9]

The Mesopotamian creation was chaotic ("destinies had not [yet] been fixed"[10]), and order developed gradually from a disorganized state with no overseeing divine presence. Rather than creationist, the Mesopotamian model was emanationist, but unlike some other schemes (such as the Platonic), emanation proceeded out of matter, not consciousness.

The process of reproduction resulted in the creation of the first generation of gods, including Anu, the sky, and Ea (Sumerian Enki), the god of the subterranean fresh water. Inevitably, generational tensions developed as children fell out with their parents. These culminated in a cosmic struggle that was won by the younger generation. The subsequent birth of Marduk, who was to be chief god of Babylon, together with a further series of gods and goddesses resulted in yet more generational conflicts, which were resolved after a final apocalyptic battle. Tiamat, the original goddess, who had by then been demonized into a terrifying monster, was vanquished, and Marduk's eternal rule was established.

Physically, the Sumerian universe was made up of *an-ki*, heaven and earth; the Sumerian *an.ki.nigin.na* translates as "the entire universe," and the equivalent in the Akkadian language was *kippat šamê u erseti*, "the totality of heaven and earth."[11] Cosmos was, therefore, sinply "everything." The earth itself was flat, and heaven was conceived of as being enclosed top and bottom by a solid vault, arranged in different layers, made of stone, of which the lowest, made of jasper, had the stars drawn on it.[12] Separating heaven and earth, holding them apart, was *lil*, air, out of which the stars and planets were created. So far this is a naturalistic cosmology. The system was structured in three layers: the air and heaven above and the earth in the middle, floating on a gigantic ocean.

Having emerged out of water, the gods and goddesses then became creators of everything in the world; people, animals, plants, stones. And, in return, their grateful children, human beings, worshipped them. The gods and goddesses operated democratically, taking decisions through their divine assembly, where they met to discuss their plans for the future. Considerable attention was paid to the cosmos as a medium for communication. The movement of the stars was understood as *šitir šamê*, the "writing of heaven," a means for the divine powers that emerged at the creative intersection of salt and fresh water, to send warnings, messages, and orders to the earthly creation.[13] The official diviners identified their heavenly parents' intentions through messages, often warnings (*omina* in Latin) that could be transmitted through a variety of methods. Messages might be sent via the natural environment—thunder, lightning, or the flight of birds—or through dreams or the examination of animal entrails (an expensive option for most people could hardly afford to sacrifice their animals at will), or via almost any suitable ritual practice or chance occurrence.

The *Enuma Elish* records how order was finally imposed by Marduk, who, although specifically associated with the planet Jupiter, was to become the presiding sky-god and cosmic king in Babylon after 1800 BCE. It was Marduk who created the structure of the heavens, the boundaries of the constellations, and the divisions of the year, all of which made it possible for a sacred calendar to be constructed and divine wishes to be ascertained. The sky was initially divided into three zones, with three groups of twelve stars arranged in three paths across the sky, one based on the celestial equator, one north of it, and the other south.[14] The central zone was ruled by Anu (heaven/the stars), the northern by Enlil (lord of the air), and the southern by Ea (earth/water), and the location of astronomical phenomena, such as eclipses, in each zone could indicate the general location of future events. At some point, probably in the mid- to late second millennium, a lunar zodiac was added to the three celestial zones, consisting of the eighteen constellations "which stood in the path of the moon":[15]

Mul.Mul The Stars (i.e., the Pleiades)
Mul GALENA The Bull of heaven (Taurus)
Mul SIPA.ZI.AN.NA The True Shepherd of Anu (Orion)
Mul SU.GI The Old Man (Perseus)
Mul GAM The Crook (Auriga)
Mul MAS.TAB.BAGAL.GAL The Great Twins (Gemini)
Mul AL.LUL The Crab (Cancer)
Mul UR.GU.LA The Lion (Leo)
Mul AB.SIN The Furrow (Virgo)
Mul Zi-ba-ni-tu The Scales (Libra)
Mul GIR.TAB The Scorpion (Scorpio)
Mul Pa-bil-sag The god Pabilsag (Sagittarius)
Mul SUHUR.MAS The Goat-Fish (Capricorn)
Mul GU-LA The Great One (Aquarius)
Mul KUN mes The Tails (Pisces)
Mul SIM.MAH The Swallow (SW Pisces)
Mul A-nu-ni-tu The goddess Anunitu
Mul HUN-GA The Hired Man (Aries)

The twelve-sign solar zodiac, of which the origins can be identified in the lunar constellations, is first recorded in a tablet dating to 475 BCE, after which it was transferred to Greece and, from there, to India and the Roman world.

The calendar was based on the moon's cycle—from new moon to new moon. Each month began with the rising of the crescent moon, and, if all was in order, the new moon's first appearance after the spring equinox (21 March) marked the beginning of the first month, Nisan. The rising of the crescent moon in Nisan also signified the beginning of the greatest of the calendar festivals, the Akitu, or Zagmug, the prototype of the Christian Easter, which included, over the space of twelve days, a ritual recital of the *Enuma Elish*, weeping over Marduk's tragic death, celebration over his subsequent resurrection, and the reading of the destinies for the coming year. The great calendar festivals were rituals in which the entire society participated in the unfolding life of the cosmic state. The entire community was enrolled in the attempt to work with the divine will, as expressed at a particular time and place, such as the temple at the new moon, to ensure that a menace was averted, a promise was fulfilled, and peace, stability, and order were maintained. The Akitu and *Enuma Elish*, the ritual and the myth respectively, established the great cosmological theological motifs of Western religion: apocalyptic battles followed by everlasting kingdoms; the divine descent to the underworld accompanied by repentance and followed by forgiveness, resurrection, and salvation; and all associated with the spring equinox. The recitation of the Epic of Creation, of the transformation of chaos into cosmos, was a magical act, providing a context for humanity's repetitive participation in the ordering of the universe.

During the festival, death was vanquished, chaos defeated, order restored, and kingship renewed, and failure to observe the appropriate rituals in the correct form at the required time might result in the withdrawal of divine favor and the threat of national decline or destruction.[16] The religious imperative in Mesopotamian astrology was persistent and profound, in the sense that superior powers had to be propitiated, and rituals and prayers could be addressed to any divinity who possessed stellar associations, often at the new or full moons. A poetic appeal to divine assistance, the *Prayer to the Gods of the Night*, survives from the Assyrian period. In this text, as they prayed for inspiration, hands raised to the sky, the astrologers would have asked:

> Stand by me, O Gods of the Night!
> Heed my words, O Gods of destinies,
> Anu, Enlil, Ea, and all the great gods!
> I call to you, Delebat [i.e. Venus], Lady of battles (or Lady of the silence [of the night]),

I call to you, O Night, bride (veiled by?) Anu.
Pleiades, stand on my right, Kidney-star, stand on my left![17]

The structure of the cosmos as both ordered and divine leads to multiple rationales for astrology as a means of employing the stars to derive information about human affairs. The notion of an unfolding order that links heaven to earth, and expressed in the regular patterns of sun and moon, is basic to Mesopotamian cosmology. However, the order of celestial motions is not just measured—it speaks, it sends messages. In the words of the so-called *Diviners Manual*, an Assyrian text, the "signs on earth just as those in the sky give us signals. Sky and earth both produce portents though appearing separately, they are not separate (because) sky and earth are related." [18]

As the origin of divine messages were the changing moods of the divine pantheon, the future could be negotiated, perhaps through magical ritual. An example is found in one letter to an Assyrian king that reads, "as for the messengers who the king, my lord, sent to Guzana, who would listen to the disparaging remarks of Tarasi and his wife? His wife, Zaza, and Tarasi himself are not to be spared. . . . Their women would bring down the moon from heaven." [19] Alterations in divine intent might also be achieved through *namburbi*, rituals intended to ward off evil. One mid-second-millennium BCE Hittite text serves as an example, providing instructions on the necessary action in the case of an evil omen from the moon, and success depends on the moon god's accepting a substitute: If the substitute was killed, then the king would be saved.

The king goes up the sanctuary [and speaks as follows: "That] omen which thou gavest, I Moon-god—if thou foundest fault with me [and] wishedst to behold with thine own eyes [the sinner's] *abasement*, [see, I the king,] have come in person [to thy *sanctuary*] and have [given] thee these substitutes. Consider the [substitu]tion! Let these die! But let them die!" [20]

Timing was crucial and, if a *namburbi* was performed on an inauspicious day, it might be ineffective. As one astrologer insisted,

Concerning the apotropaic ritual against evil of any kind, about which the king write[s] to me "Perform it tomorrow—the day is not propitious. We shall prepare it on the 25th and perform it on the 26th." [21]

There's an inference here that time is the organizing principle. The Mesopotamian scribes don't explicitly say that this is what they thought, but it is certainly one plausible reading of the text.

The planets themselves were distinguished from the other stars by their erratic movements and were known in Sumerian as the *udu.idim.mes,* or wild sheep—*bibbu* in Akkadian. The three most important were the sun, the moon, and Venus, the last of which was sacred to Inanna, or Ishtar, the Queen of Heaven. In the cosmic hierarchy, when Inanna spoke, the king obeyed. The priestesses of Ishtar were, as we may expect, important. We know of one, Enheduanna, who seems to have been a high priestess of Nanna, or Suen, the moon god, as well as daughter of Sargon, the great king of Akkad from perhaps 2270 to 2215 BC. Enheduanna was the author of forty-two extant hymns to Inanna that survive only from the Old Babylonian period, around 500 years after her death.[22] We can get a flavor of the devotion with which the goddess was regarded from a hymn that was written to venerate the goddess when Venus appeared after sunset as herald of night:

> At the end of the day, the Radiant Star, the Great Light that fills the sky,
> The Lady of the Evening appears in the heavens.
> The people in all the lands lift their eyes to her.
> The men purify themselves; the women cleanse themselves.

The core drama in Inanna's life was her love affair with Dumuzi, the shepherd-king, his betrayal and death, and her descent through the seven gates of the underworld to rescue him, shedding an item of jewelry or clothing at every one, with all its agony and passion.[23] It was precisely this motif of sacrifice, death, despair, and redemption/resurrection that became central to the Akitu, the spring equinox festival.

The moon god was originally Nanna or Suen, a name later contracted to Sin, by which the moon is generally known in the cuneiform texts. One Sumerian hymn praised Nanna as "you, who, perfect in lordliness, wear a right crown, awesome visage, noble brow, pure shape full of loveliness! Your grandeur lies imposed on all lands! Your glory falls over the clear skies! Your great nimbus is fraught with holy dread."[24] The sun was known in Sumerian as Utu, meaning "bright," in Akkadian as Shamash. Both are the names of solar deities, but the two words could mean either the visible body or the hidden power within it—the god. Utu has been described as the "power in light, the foe of darkness and deeds of darkness," a god who dispensed justice across the natural and supernatural realms.[25] None of the other planets seem to have commanded nearly the same attention in astrological omens as the sun, the moon, and Venus. That is even the case for Jupiter, the planet sacred to the god Marduk, whose status as cosmocrator—ruler of the cosmos—was made clear in the *Enuma Elish*. Mars was associated with Nergal, a god of the underworld, forest fires, fever, plague, and war. Mercury was usually identified as the planet of Nabu, the scribe, responsible for announcing destiny, while Saturn was linked to the god Ninurta and appeared to have little astrological significance.

It was with the development of the birth charts—astrological prognostications cast for the moment of birth—that we get the first indication of consistent interpretations of the meaning of planets in zodiac signs of a kind that are familiar today.[26] It seems that each of the planets was given a personality and a relationship to the zodiac. It is clear that the planets possessed an intimate relationship with the moment of birth, which therefore becomes a signifier of character and the quality of life.

The crucial readings are these:[27]

> the child born under Jupiter will have a "regular (life) . . . will become rich (and) will grow old.
> the child born "when Venus has come forth" will be have a life which is "exceptionally calm (and) favourable" and marked by longevity.
> the child born with Mars may have a hot temper.
> the child born when Saturn has come forth will live a life which is "dark, obscure, sick and constrained."

These planetary personalities have survived largely unscathed down to modern times, illustrating a remarkable consistency over two-and-a-half millennia: They are evident in Margaret Hone's *Modern Text Book of Astrology*, which was published in 1951 and became the standard British and English-language textbook on the subject until the 1970s. Influenced indirectly by the Nativity Omens, Hone recorded Venus as "harmonious, peace-loving [and] placid," Jupiter as "fortunate, generous and optimistic," Mars in its negative form as "aggressive, angry [and] impatient," and Saturn also in its negative form as "depressive, dull, limited [and] mean."[28] The continuity is striking and demonstration, if any were needed, of the survival of Near Eastern cosmology in the modern world.

Quite why the 5th-century revolution took place is not well understood. One theory, proposed by Bartel van der Waerden but not in favor with current scholars, holds that the story of Mesopotamian astral theology is of the gradual, though uneven, march from divine pluralism, from the many gods and goddesses, to the supremacy of the one.[29] And, van der Waerden argued, as religion gradually progressed from localized polytheism to universal monotheism, so the cosmos shifted its attention from the collective to the individual. The era of the self had arrived. Van der Waerden's speculative model is altogether too neat, relies on discredited theories of religious evolution, and lacks direct evidence. However, alterations in astrology do occur as it encounters different worldviews—witness the all-encompassing deterministic gloss it acquired from the Greek Stoics, or the emphasis on free choice in the 20th century. Something happened in Mesopotamian culture to trigger such a dramatic increase in the importance of the individual, but we don't know what. Quite plausibly, though, in one of the major developments in Near Eastern religious history, a rising concern with personal salvation was responsible for a dramatic shift in astrology's focus.

Easier to track, though, are the details of astrology's external history. With the victories of Alexander the Great, who entered Babylon in 332, Mesopotamian culture finally entered its terminal decline, though its astrology, mathematical astronomy, and cosmic religion survived in the Greek world, whence it became a part of the heritage of Western culture. Babylon remained a hub for astrologers, and the last surviving cuneiform astronomical almanacs, listing the information necessary to compute birth charts, date from between 31/32 and 74/75 CE.[30] The last Babylonian temples appear to have remained active until the 3rd century CE, by which time vital features of its cosmology had been absorbed into classical astronomy and astrology, and Christian theology.

Mesopotamian cosmology and astrology included certain key characteristics. The prevailing cosmogony was chaotic and emanationist. The cosmos emerged from water, a natural substance, and the Mesopotamians seem to have been happier in this physical world and less concerned with escaping it than, say, the Egyptians. That water was anthropomorphized as Apsû and Tiâmat does not mean that the creators were conventional deities but that water, as a material substance, was seen as having agency. People were made from earth and subject to the gods and goddesses, who can be understood partly as life forces, causing the wind to blow and water to flow, but also as capricious individuals who were offended if they were not worshipped with due respect. Astrology then functioned as a tool by which the divinities' intentions and wishes could be identified. It was "divination" in the classic sense—a conversation with divinity—but was also a science in the traditional sense: a discipline with its own rules and internal logic. The Mesopotamians employed a wide range of means of divining their deities' intentions, and astrology gradually assumed an increasing role, culminating in the revolution of the 5th century BCE. Running through the Mesopotamian worldview, though, is a paradox that scholars have not yet addressed, let alone solved. On the one hand the gods and goddesses were able to take free and independent choices. On the other, we know from evidence relating to the planet Venus and dating to around 1600 BCE, divine intentions were tied to the patterns of time as revealed in planetary patterns. There is no evidence that this paradox troubled the Mesopotamians, but in it we may identify the seeds of the modern tension between protagonists of religion and advocates of science.

12

Judaism

Myth, Magic, and Transcendence

The heavens declare the glory of God, the sky proclaims His handiwork.[1]

Jewish religion emerged as a result of a remarkable combination of circumstances and events, most of which are focused on the first millennium B C E, and few of which, if any, are well understood. The only point we can make with any certainty is that the consequences have been utterly profound for the history of human thought over much of the world, both directly through the creative impact of Jewish thought down to the present day, and indirectly through its derivatives, Christianity and Islam. With the exception of physical cosmology—the flat earth envisaged in the Torah—the rest of scriptural cosmology remains current, transmitted to the modern world by the ancient sacred texts.

We shouldn't imagine that Jewish cosmology can be simply understood as single set of teachings. First, we have to consider the historical question. The orthodox model assumes the historicity of such epic narratives as Abraham's journey from Ur to the Holy Land and the Exodus. The ultra-revisionist view envisages Jewish religion and pre-history as a product of the exile in Babylon and the post-exilic reconstruction, even doubting the existence of David, Solomon, and the first temple.[2] The middle way accepts the reality of the Jewish kingdom from the turn of the first and second millennia, while acknowledging that pre-kingdom history (as well as history up to the Roman era) is heavily overlaid with mythic and cyclic themes of oppression and redemption, of a repetitive moving away from God's law, and a period of alienation and punishment, followed by regret, return, and forgiveness.[3]

In spite of the diversity that we find over the development of Jewish cosmology, there is a central consensus based on the once-only creation of a single cosmos by a patriarchal God. That the creation possesses an internal order is evident in the repetitive cycles of the sun and the moon, and it was this concern with order that leads to an overwhelming emphasis on the repetition of themes in Jewish history (typically the alternation between alienation from God and oppression by foreign forces on the one hand, and reconciliation with God and political independence on the other) and the need to observe the Sabbath and the calendar festivals. Possibly more than any other culture, except that of the Chinese, Judaism stresses the observation of patterns in time as a prerequisite for divine favor.

The literary tradition represented in the scriptures, and commentaries on them, also presents us with other difficulties. First, although these texts exhibit certain attitudes to cosmology, they both evolved over time and are subject to competing interpretations. Second, we should pay attention to the lived tradition, the Jews' actual religious practice for much of the first millennium BCE, as opposed to the demands of the prophets, which have become the canonical version of Jewish history. The distinction between the prophetic and vernacular traditions is often forgotten, but it is made clear in the historical books of Kings and Chronicles, in which the prophets, for example, condemn planet worship, but large numbers of people, including most of the kings, were clearly practicing it.

The primary literary sources for Jewish cosmology are extensive. Obviously the foundational text is the Bible, the *Tanakh*, which is divided into three sections: the *Torah* (the first five books—*Pentateuch* in Greek—attributed to Moses and containing the Law, including the rules for the timing of the calendar festivals), the *Nevi'im* (the actions, sayings, and writings of the prophets), and the *Ketuvim* (the writings, such as Psalms and Proverbs).[4] This was supplemented after the 1st century CE by the *Talmud* (interpretation of the Law) and *Midrash* (commentaries on selected passages). The authoritative English-language versions of the *Pseudepigrapha* and *Apocrypha*, texts excluded from the official versions, are by Charlesworth and Sparks, respectively, although neither is above criticism, and there are a number of translations of the Dead Sea Scrolls, including a recent volume by Martinez.[5] The secondary literature on Hebrew cosmology and astrology is not extensive. Roger Beckwith's work on the calendar is reliable; Edward Wright's *The Early History of Heaven* is the best, comprehensive discussion; J. W. McKay's *Religion in Judah under the Assyrians* contains an account of astral religion in the first millennium; and Lester Ness's *Written in the Stars: Ancient Zodiac Mosaics* deals with a fascinating but little-known phenomenon, the construction of mosaic zodiacs in synagogues in the early Byzantine period, mainly the 4th to 6th centuries CE.[6] The other unique Jewish system we need to consider is

Kabbalah. For primary sources for Kabbalah see Gershom Scholem's translation of the *Zohar* and Ariel Kaplan's version of the *Sefer Yetzirah*; for secondary sources, see Scholem's *On the Kabbalah and Its Symbolism* and *Origins of the Kabbalah*.[7] There is also now a growing interest in the divinatory and magical practices, and mythological narratives, in the ancient and medieval worlds, which constitute the vernacular practices of Jewish cosmology.[8]

Pre-modern Jewish history is divided into distinct phases. The two key events in the second millennium, Abraham's journey and the Exodus, whether we regard them as mythical or not, are usually dated to around 1700–1600 and 1400–1300 BCE respectively. A more reliable historical narrative runs from the rule of the Judges around 1200 BCE, through the kingdom of Saul, David, and Solomon, from c. 1020 to 922 BCE; the split into the two states of Israel (the north) and Judah (the south); and the conquest of the former by Assyria in 732–722 and the latter by Babylon in 586, initiating the "Babylonian captivity." Persian occupation in 539 allowed the return to Jerusalem and the construction of the Second Temple, but Macedonian conquest in 322 was followed by Greek domination and incorporation into the Hellenistic world. A century of independence was won in the Maccabean revolt of 168–165 and came to an end when in 63 BCE Roman conquest converted the kingdom of Judaea into a client state under Herod the Great (37–34). The first rebellion against Rome in 66–70 CE culminated in defeat and destruction of the Temple in 70 CE, and the rupture between Judaism and Christianity. The failure of the second rebellion in 132–135 resulted in a bar on Jews entering Jerusalem more than once a year and the beginning of the diaspora. Priestly and scholarly endeavor then turned to the compilation of the Talmud and Midrash; and, around the year 1000 CE, the Kabbalah made its appearance in the sacred literature.

Each of these stages in Jewish history involved an exchange of ideas with surrounding cultures which means that identifying a "pure" cosmology is no more possible with the Jews than with any other culture, as Louis Jacobs so eloquently pointed out.[9] The early phase tells of the direct relationship between a simple people who alternate between devout fidelity and corrupt failure and the need to live according to the laws of time revealed in celestial order and established by their sky-god. The royal phase continues the theme of devotion versus fall and particularizes it in the dispute between the kings and the many people who practice astral worship, and the prophets, who claim popular support and assert the sole dominance of God. Judicial astrology was introduced following the Babylonian conquest, and especially under Greek rule, and centuries of engagement with Neoplatonic thought

and magical traditions eventually resulted in the mystical and contemplative practices of medieval Judaism, mainly Kabbalah, which were intended to
draw the individual into close contact with the divine.

The creation of the cosmos is set out in chapter 1 of Genesis, the first book
of the Torah. The complexities of this passage are often overlooked, as are the
questions arising from it: Did God create the universe *ex nihilo*; were there
many gods rather than one; were there multiple creations; was there a goddess, or female form of God?[10] In terms of later Jewish history, though, such
problems of origin can be ignored, for what matters from the late centuries
BCE onward is the consensus established in the Torah that there was only
one supreme, all-powerful, masculine God who created the cosmos out of
nothing. This single God was transcendent rather than immanent: outside of
and above the creation rather than inside and part of it. God was the ultimate
political authority: He was above the stars; as Isaiah 66.1 reports, "Heaven is
my throne and the earth is my footstool," and religious observation is a matter of paying respect to him and reflecting on the nature of his creation and
humanity's place within it.

There is no direct equivalent in the Bible for the Latin "universe" or the
Greek "cosmos." *Olam*, which means "world" or "universe" in Rabbinic literature, is better understood as "eternity" in the Tanakh. The cosmos is therefore all that there is, or can be, from the beginning of time to the end. By the
Rabbinic period, up to c. 500 CE, God is spoken of as *melekh ha-olam*, "King
of the Universe." He may have been the creator, but he possessed human
qualities—humanity having been made in his image: he could be violent, and
to offend him was to court punishment, as Psalms 18:13–14 makes clear:

> The Lord also thundered in the heavens,
> And the Most High uttered his voice,
> Hailstones and coals of fire.
> And he sent out his arrows, and scattered them;
> He flashed forth lightnings and routed them . . .

According to the clues we can glean from the Torah, physically the
earth was flat, either a disc or, perhaps, square, resting on pillars. The sky,
shamayim ("heaven") or *rakia* ("firmament"), was solid, and the sun, moon,
and stars are positioned in or just below it and move across it while, below
the earth is *sheol*, the abode of the dead. There are waters above the firmament as well as below it, where they are connected to *Tehom*, the great deep.
Above the waters and above the firmament is the "heaven of heavens," the

abode of God; according to Amos 9.5–6, "The Lord, God of hosts . . . builds his upper chambers in the heavens." God's order is revealed to humanity via the regular cycles of the sun and moon, which then form the basis of the ritual calendar (Psalms 19.1: "The heavens declare the glory of God, the sky proclaims His handiwork"), and his intentions are revealed via omens, including celestial warnings.

The agenda of the Jewish scriptures is both collective (right organization of society) and individual (the struggle for perfection). The Law, which allows the goals to be achieved, is partly tied to the flow of time, and extreme importance is attached to the celebration of the festivals of the Hebrew calendar at the specified times, measured by the sun–moon cycle from new moon to new moon, and the sun (the day begins at sunset). The fundamental rule of Hebrew cultic life is set out in the fourth commandment, in which observation of every seventh day, the Sabbath, became the supreme injunction, representing a reenactment of the day of rest following the six days of creation (Exodus 8.20). Indeed, the six days of labor during the week themselves represented the six days of creation, with man toiling for six days to manage what Yahweh had created in six. Each week, then, represented a complete cycle of experience from birth to maturity.

The calendar of twelve months was borrowed from Babylon, and, broadly, the names retained: Nisan (or Abib), Iyyar (or Ziv), Sivan, Tammuz, Ab, Elul, Tishri (or Ethanim), Marcheshvan (or Bul), Chislev, Tebeth, Shebat, Adar. Nisan, beginning at the new moon after the spring equinox, was fixed as the first month; Exodus 12.1 proclaimed that "This month shall be for you the beginning of months; it shall be the first month of the year for you." The astronomical rules for the calendar festivals were precise and were clearly set out in Exodus 12 and Leviticus 23.[11] It was laid down that Pesach, or Passover, commenced as the full moon rose over the eastern horizon on the fourteenth day of the first month, corresponding to Nisan in the Babylonian calendar, and, if by any chance any believer was unable to observe Passover at the required time, he or she was obliged to begin the commemoration at the moment at which the full moon rose above the eastern horizon on the fourteenth of the second month.[12] The New Year, Rosh Hashanah, is celebrated on the first two days of Tishri, the seventh month, when the crescent moon rises in the Babylonian zodiac sign Libra. Each festival represented a ritual return to the beginning of time, a conscious and cyclical return to the primeval order, before history became disrupted by disorder.[13] The re-creation of the cosmos is commemorated on a the short scale on the Sabbath, or Shabbat, the seventh day, following the six days of creation. While reverence for

God is the most apparent feature of these festivals, the key to their practical significance is active participation in the continued health of the earth.

In general, observation of the ritual calendar was the direct alternative to astral religion: "You shall make for yourselves no idols and erect no graven image or pillar, and you shall not set up a figured stone in your land, to bow down to them; for I am the Lord your God. You shall keep my Sabbaths and reverence my sanctuary: I am the Lord" (Leviticus 26 1–2). In the final centuries BCE the writers of the Dead Sea Scrolls were under no illusion as to the sacred power of the lunar and solar cycles. One scroll, the so-called Community Rule, records that blessings are due "at the entry of the (monthly) seasons on the days of the new moon, and also at the end when they succeed to one another. Their renewal is a great day for the Holy of Holies."[14]

If the specified rituals were correctly observed, the survival of the state would be guaranteed for another year. Yahweh, it was hoped, would be encouraged to keep his promise to Noah that "While the earth remains, seedtime and harvest, cold and heat, summer and winter, day and night, shall not cease" (Genesis 8.22). Jeremiah 31.35–36 makes the reason for emphasis on the calendar very clear: The alternative is political disintegration:

> Thus says the Lord,
> who gives the sun for light by day
> and the fixed order of the moon
> and the stars for light by night,
> who stirs up the sea so its waves roar—
> the Lord of hosts is his name:
> "If this fixed order departs
> from before me," says the Lord,
> "then shall the descendants of Israel cease
> from being a nation for ever."

Time is the means by which God controls his creation; according to Daniel 2.21, "He changes times and seasons, he removes kings and sets up kings." The famous verses in Ecclesiastes 3.1–8 demonstrate that there is a right time for every action. Beginning, "For everything there is a season, and a time for every matter under heaven, a time to be born, and a time to die"; the passage goes on to specify virtually every conceivable sphere of activity, although the way to determine what may or may not be an appropriate time is not specified.

The division of the land conquered by the Israelites after the Exodus into twelve sections, one for each tribe, was a means of organizing political geography as a mirror of the celestial cosmic state and is directly adapted from the Israelites' camp outlined in Numbers, in which the twelve tribes were arranged in a square of four groups of three. The most important section, was, with the tabernacle and the "tent of meeting," aligned toward the sunrise.[15] Ezekiel converted the Hebrew camp into a sacred city, arranged as a quadrangle aligned to the cardinal points with twelve gates named after the twelve sons of Jacob (Ezekiel 48. 30–35).

The state was organized on cosmic principles embodied in space and time, but astral worship ("of the sun or the moon or any of the host of heaven") was absolutely forbidden in Deuteronomy 17.2: The punishment for conviction on the evidence of two witnesses was stoning (17.5–7). Yet there is evidence of the veneration of celestial deities, notably Solomon's adoration of Ashtoreth, the goddess associated with Venus (I Kings 11.5, 33). In the 6th century BCE Josiah, king of Judah, prohibited worship of the sun, moon, and stars, fair evidence that the practice was widespread (2 Kings 23:5). Such efforts, though, probably had a limited impact, and Ezekiel (8.16–17) condemned the veneration of the rising sun from the Temple:

> And he brought me into the inner court of the house of the Lord; and behold, at the door of the temple of the Lord, between the porch and the altar, were about twenty-five men, with their backs to the temple of the Lord and their faces to the east, worshipping the sun.

To this day, the Amidah, the central prayer of the Jewish liturgy, is recited either facing Jerusalem, or facing east. The distinction between the veneration of the sun, or the direction of the rising sun, in itself, or as a symbol of the divine, is not a clear one. Similar issues affect attitudes to the moon. The prophet Jeremiah (44:15–30) castigated Jewish women for burning offerings to the moon as "queen of heaven" and making cakes with her image. The boundary between such practices and the devout observation of the crescent moon as sign of God's unfolding order is not clear.

Prophetic intolerance generally extended to astrology, which was condemned as either foreign (Jeremiah 10.2–3) or useless when compared with God's power (Isaiah 47.13–14). The problem with such texts, though, is that it is foreign astrology, or its practice by non-Jews, which is condemned. There is no hint of censure when the prophet Daniel was made chief of the Babylonian astrologers (Daniel 5:11). In addition, God himself spoke to his people via celestial omens. Warning of the day when he will come to restore order and inaugurate the next phase of history, God declared, "'And on that day . . .

I will make the sun go down at noon, and darken the earth in broad daylight'" (Amos 8.9).

In spite of the prophetic condemnation of foreign practices, Jewish attitudes toward astrology in general are typically tolerant and are based on the assumption that its practice is acceptable as long as it does not challenge one's devotion to God. In the Rabbinical texts scholars debated whether, for example, it was the *mazzal*—star—of the day or the hour that determined people's fates.[16] The conclusion was that fate could be negotiated by pious behavior, and one who followed the law would never be subject to the dictates of the planets. Above all, according to Rabbi Yohanan, *Ein mazal le'Israel* (there is no star for Israel); only God can directly determine the future of the children of Israel.

Claims were even made that astrology itself was a Jewish invention. According to the *Jewish Antiquities*, written by the 1st-century CE historian Josephus, the children of Seth, the son of Adam, "were the inventors of that peculiar sort of wisdom which is concerned with the heavenly bodies and their order." It was Abraham, Josephus continued, who was the first to publish this idea. It was when he was still resident at Ur that Abraham wrestled with the idea that the irregular motions of the planets "contribute to the happiness of men"; his conclusion was that they do so, but only as agents of the one true God, an idea that he took with him to the Holy Land.[17] Such stories are the origin of the tradition that Abraham himself was an astrologer: There could be no higher approval. Astrological symbolism was central to the core iconography of 1st-century Judaism; Josephus tells us that the menorah, the seven lamps of the sacred candelabra, indicated the seven planets, and the twelve loaves on the table represented the zodiac. The Platonic Jewish writer Philo of Alexandria, also in the 1st century, described the zodiacal imagery on the breastplate worn by the high priest, its purpose being that, when he entered the Holy of Holies, he might become the whole world, which could then enter the inner sanctum with him and share his prayers.[18]

Philo's Jewish Platonism was indicative of the widespread acceptance of a cosmology in which monotheism and astrology were to survive and flourish in both a Jewish and a Christian context. His God was a God of reason, who can be approached through the thirst for knowledge. This thirst, in turn, can be inspired by the heavens, just as the constellation of the Bear enables mariners to discover new lands. But also, Philo claimed, the eye is to the body as the mind to the soul; as the mind receives God so the eye receives the light of the stars, and both can confer wisdom. He continues, in his treatise "On Providence," that all things in heaven, including the stars, exist as a result of

Providence, God's plan, which is why eclipses, revealing divine intentions, are omens of the death of kings or of the destruction of cities.[19]

The most substantial Jewish discussion of astrology remains that of Moses Maimonides (1135–1204), one of the most influential of all medieval Jewish philosophers. He was born in Cordoba, Spain, but seems to have spent most of the latter part of his life in Cairo, where he was head of the Jewish community and physician to the vizier of Saladin.[20] His position on astrology illustrated well the dilemma of the Aristotelian, who both advocated a naturalistic approach to understanding the world and held to a religious faith, whether Islamic, Christian, or, as in his case, Jewish. Maimonides was also profoundly influenced by Platonic notions of the emanation of the material world out of God, rather than its creation by him as an external agent, and hence the interdependence of humanity, the divine, and the celestial spheres. Such problems are no less vital for religious believers now as they were then. Maimonides was a keen advocate of the broad cosmology in which all events on earth were generally related to the celestial spheres, but he rejected any notion whatsoever that this might justify judicial astrology—the casting of horoscopes. In a famous letter to the rabbis of southern France, written in 1194, he set out his objections, beginning with the core question: "It occurred to some of us to ask you about the saying of the old rabbis that 'Israel is not governed by the stars,' and the answer that was given by Rabbi Shrira and Rabbi Haii regarding this matter."[21] What Maimonides clearly objected to in matters of faith was the suggestion that God's power was in any way limited, and he raged against what he saw as the astrologers' stupidity and lies and their "thousands of books of nonsense," which he blamed for the destruction of the Jewish state and the diaspora.[22]

The creative flowering of that introspective strand in medieval Judaism, which responded to the loss of the external space represented in the Jewish kingdom by turning to inner space, was to find its greatest expression in Kabbalah, the traditional or, more important, "received" lore.[23] Kabbalah was, at least in part, an attempt to codify the spontaneous and ecstatic encounters with the celestial realms, such as were recorded in Jacob's dream of the ladder to heaven, or Elijah's ascent to heaven.[24] In the form we know it from the origins of the literary tradition in the 10th century CE, it devised ten points of spiritual power and knowledge, known as *sephirot*, which were placed in ascending order on the three pillars of the tree of life—itself a likely reference to Jacob's ladder. In some accounts the creation of the world begins not with God's movement over the waters but with light, which then permeates and animates the whole of existence.[25] The *sephirot* are the substance of all things, not unlike Platonic archetypes; they are the principles that mediate between God and his creation. Like the archetypes, they emanated, along with the entire material cosmos, out of God. The classic and profoundly enigmatic description of them is found in the *Sefer Yetzirah*, the core text of Kabbalah:

> Ten Sefirot of Nothingness:
> Their measure is ten
> Which have no end
> A depth of beginning
> A depth of end
> A depth of good
> A depth of evil
> A depth of above
> A depth of below
> A depth of east
> A depth of west
> A depth of north
> A depth of south
> The singular Master
> God faithful King
> dominates over them all from his holy dwelling
> until eternity of eternities.[26]

The heart of Kabbalah was an attempt to come closer to God by living a life of spiritual purity, and here the comparison with Platonic, Islam, and Christianity is clear, through using reason as well as faith; scripture was to be interpreted allegorically and metaphorically, drawing out the hidden meaning, and to believe in literal truth was to completely fail to grasp God's true message to humanity. Study, though, was to lead to practice and, as an experiential art, Kabbalah developed a participatory, magical approach to the cosmos. It requires an extensive use of divine names, letter permutations, and similar methods to reach higher states of consciousness in order to influence or alter the natural world. It was absolutely necessary to read the signs God had sent, precisely because his very first act was to engrave the constellations as signs on the heavenly vault.[27] The *Sefer Yetzirah* recorded that, as the creation proceeded, God

> made the letter Heh king over speech
> and He bound a crown to it

And He combined one with another
And with them he formed
Aries in the Universe
Nissan in the Year
And the right foot in the Soul
male and female.[28]

The Kabbalistic cosmos was structured along lines that bear comparison with the Gnostic system, in which a remote creator plays little or no part in the material world, which is presided over by a more immediate power.[29] Kabbalah, though, unlike Gnosticism, which generally assumed that the physical cosmos was inherently evil, tended to take the Platonic view of the cosmos as essentially good, and this lower power is definitely benign. God was too exalted for mortals, and even for angels, to comprehend, so in order to be visible he created a "majesty" or representative, out of the divine fire, which itself is visible to the angels. This power is both God as divine mind envisaged by Plato and Maimonides, and the transcendent anthropomorphic God of scriptural imagery. The Kabbalistic cosmos contains in total four worlds, arranged in a vertical hierarchy: those of the glory (the visible God), the angels, the intellectual soul, and the lowest, the animal soul. It was up to the Kabbalist to control the animal soul, live through the intellectual soul, and so attempt to contact the highest level, the visible God. Closely associated with Kabbalah was the concept of the soul's journey through the seven heavens, the Hekhalot—palaces—inhabited by the planetary powers, an enterprise which could result in profound insight into the nature of the cosmos, and that required personal purity, great discipline, and a detailed knowledge of the correct magical procedures.

The technical astrology that emerged from Kabbalah was partly derived from lunar time. There was considerable attention to the twenty-eight times listed in Ecclesiastes—"a time to be born, a time to plant," and so on.[30] Twenty-eight, of course, is approximately the number of days in the lunar month. These times corresponded to the twenty-eight camps of the divine presence and the zodiacal constellations that, in turn, could refer to the names of God.[31] A true Kabbalistic astrology was therefore concerned less with the use of horoscopes to analyze worldly affairs than with ritual intended to take the initiate on a path to the divine source and transcend the cosmos of celestial influences and planetary diktat. Such ideas found their full expression in the *Sefer HaZohar* (The Book of Splendor). Usually known simply as the *Zohar* (translated as "splendor" or "radiance"),[32] the *Zohar* argued that the act itself of studying the Torah provides divine protection from the heavenly laws of nature, including celestial influences. The milieu, though, in which Kabbalah flourished, encouraged a wide range of astrological practices. The following colophon was found on a 16th-century manuscript: "On the night of Hoshana Rabbah, 53115 am [1556 CE], I saw the shadow of my head in the moonlight; praised be to God, for now I am assured that I shall not die this year."[33] Again, the signs were sent to anyone with the wisdom to understand.

Before the Torah was given to the Jews, all the people in the world were dependent on *mazal*, a word that may be understood as stars, or stellar influence, or destiny. But, after the Torah was given to Moses, the Jews were, potentially, released from the rule of the stars. This is true, though, only for one who studies the Torah. Study, though, needs to be combined with practice, and there were seven stages of initiation on the ascending path, each of which might produce an ecstatic experience. This was an imaginal cosmos in which the soul traveled through inner space, rather than embarking on a literal journey through the seven material spheres. The individual who takes this path will be united with God and shares His existence above the world of celestial influence and natural law. The ignorant, on the other hand, are still subject to the stars, even if they are Jews.

Jewish cosmology remains of vital political importance through the strict adherence of many Jews to the notion of a covenant between God and his people that is located in a specific place, in the state of Israel. On the wider level, modern Judaism parallels its Middle Eastern cousins, Christianity and Islam, in that its adherents can choose whether to treat the scriptures as a set of literal rules to be followed or as a series of analogies to be interpreted. At the heart of it, though, little noticed, lies the discreet, contemplative, quietist practice of Kabbalah, which takes us back to a different form of ancient cosmology, one in which physical space matters far less than the imaginal union of humanity, divinity, and the cosmos.

Jewish cosmogony presents us with the very model of a "cosmic" origin of the world in a deliberate, once-only, purposeful creation. At the margins of Jewish thought we find other ideas such as notions of female deities, multiple gods, and many creations, but the image of the parental, patriarchal sky-god was overwhelmingly dominant as the major sacred texts were composed in the first millennium BCE. A number of interlocking themes run through Jewish cosmology. One is the concept of an order in time, which it is the duty of every individual to observe. Even morality could be considered to be in part a function of time, in that the sacred calendar was absolutely tied to exact moments, as revealed in the cycles of the sun and the moon. Another is the notion of a universe imbued with morality. A third is the belief in obedience to God. A fourth, though, is the understanding that this God can be approached through reason. This last consideration underpins attitudes to astrology, from the use of horoscopes as a source of self-understanding to the practice of Kabbalah as a form of celestial ascent to divine love and wisdom. The prophetic literature is unquivocally hostile to the worship of celestial deities and shows indications of hostility to Babylonian astrology as an alien practice. However, astrology in the form of celestial omens is absolutely central to God's communication with his people via the natural environment. The complex codes of Greek judicial astrology, though, required the same range of responses as we find in Christianity and Islam, chiefly because of the need to preserve God's role as source of all knowledge and the individual's freedom to choose to obey his edicts. The more astrology was seen to ascribe agency to the stars, impinge on God's authority, or deny free will, the more it was likely to be challenged, but if it permitted free choice and acknowledged God's exclusive right to know and plan the future, it could be acceptable.

Classical Greece

Ascent to the Stars

Survey the circling stars as though you yourself were in mid-course with them. . . . Visions of this kind purge away the dross of our earth-bound life.[1]

The civilization of classical Greece was remarkable in its achievements and, in some respects, unique. It has bequeathed us an astonishing legacy of written material in mathematics, astronomy, political thought, and speculative philosophy, as well as a tradition of architecture that still mesmerizes the modern West. However, while we can admire and respect the work of the Greek schools, their nature has been mytholigized and distorted in the service of a particular form of modern Western thought that prides itself on its supposed rationalism. According to this myth, as Greek rationalism emerged, self-contained, from deep within the innate genius of the Greek character and in opposition to the superstitious cultures of Egypt and Babylon, so its descendant, Western rationalism, now exists in a state of inherent purity and antagonism with those forces of superstition that survive in the modern world. This view, borne of a particular form of dualistic cosmology, with its belief in the struggle, and eventual triumph, of light/truth/good against darkness/falsehood/evil, remains remarkably resilient in the popular and academic imagination, although it has been comprehensively demolished by scholars in various specialist areas. David Pingree, for example, criticized the distorting effects of Hellenophilia, love of all things Greek, while Peter Kingsley has demonstrated that the first wave of Greek philosophers were priest-kings; and, even though a skeptical tradition eventually emerged, much Greek philosophy, especially Platonism, retained a profound initiatory, revelatory quality until the close of the Platonic Academy in Athens in 529 CE.[2] Recently, it has been argued in great detail that early Greek cosmology emerged seamlessly out of Near Eastern philosophy and religion.[3]

This is of undoubted importance if we are to understand the pervasive religious significance of one important strand of Greek cosmology: the Platonic.

Until around the 7th century BCE, Greek cosmology appears to have been mainly terrestrial, more concerned with sacred springs and mountains than with stars, while the main gods and goddesses were more likely to be found in the immediate environment than in the sky. By the 5th century BCE Greek cosmology had begun to diversify, following radically different paths. These included four major speculative attempts to create major explanatory or descriptive models. Three of these shared the notion that the cosmos is alive and purposeful, came to dominate the cosmology of the entire classical world, and exerted a huge influence on Islamic and Christian thought. These were the three philosophical schools founded by Plato (428/427–348/347 BCE), Aristotle (384–322 BCE), and Zeno of Citium (334–262 BCE). The fourth school, founded by Leucippus (first half of the 5th century BCE) and his student Democritus (c.460–370 BCE), developed the theory of Atomism, according to which the world is constructed from tiny particles and the cosmos is materialistic and purposeless. In this chapter we focus on the first three and leave Atomism aside on the grounds that it was not concerned with the nature of divinity and had no consequences for astrology. Last, we should consider the vernacular cosmology represented by belief in the pantheon of gods and goddesses and the use of astrology, magic, and ritual to engage with the cosmos. Classical astrology was also diverse in its philosophical context and technical implementation. It could be located within a naturalistic perspective, seeing the planets as sources of physical influence, or as gods and goddesses; might be concerned with daily matters such as wealth and health, or the salvation of the soul; and could allow for different ways of negotiating fate through direct action, magic, or ritual.

The classical period is sometimes narrowly defined as extending from the supposed emergence of the philosophical tradition in the early 6th century BCE until the conquests of Alexander in the 330s BCE. Loosely, though, the classical period extends from the poets Homer and Hesiod in the 8th century BCE, until pagan teaching was prohibited in the Roman empire in the early 6th century CE. The sources on Greek cosmology are extensive, so it becomes necessary to select a few. Many of the primary texts are lost and survive only in fragments, a problem that afflicts many ancient philosophers, from all the pre-Socratic thinkers of the 4th century and earlier, to important later philosophers such as Posidonius, who is credited with making astrology respectable among the Roman intellectual elite in the 1st century BCE. Fortunately the works of Plato and Aristotle survive almost in their entirety, and between them, these two men, master and student, encompassed a substantial range of philosophical positions in later Western culture—in outline if not in detail.

While all Plato's works deal with the question of correct living in the ideal cosmos, two contain explicitly cosmological material: The *Timaeus* includes his cosmogony, and the *Republic* details the soul's origin in, and return to, the stars.[4] Cornford's *Plato's Cosmology* remains the only substantial commentary on Plato's theories.[5] Aristotle's works are far more mechanical and a great deal less inspirational than Plato's, and there is no single passage in which he sets out his theories with clarity; his ideas are spread over four books, *Physics*, *Meteorologica*, *Metaphysics*, and *De Caelo* (On the Heavens).[6]

One result of the interaction of Greek, Babylonian, and Egyptian culture in the Hellenistic period was the creation of a technical astrology that was then disseminated throughout the Roman world and across Asia to India and eventually to China and Japan. The key texts include the *Corpus Hermeticum*, which deals with the soul's relationship with the heavens, and Claudius Ptolemy's 2nd-century CE compilation of rules for reading horoscopes, the *Tetrabiblos*, significant because of the importance it was accorded in the Islamic worlds and in Medieval and Renaissance Europe.[7] Other primary astrological sources are also available, in English translation, ranging from works by the Latin poet Marcus Manilius and the Syrian Dorotheus of Sidon in the 1st century CE to Vettius Valens in the 2nd and, last among the great classical astrological authors, Julius Firmicus Maternus in the 4th.[8]

There are also a number of histories of classical astrology by Tamsyn Barton, Roger Beck, and George Noonan.[9] Wright's book on cosmology is a reasonable introduction, Dreyer's work on astronomy provides a reliable foundation, Kahn's work on the philosopher Anaximander is important, and recent works by Daryn Lehoux and John Steele have provided new insights into the calendar.[10] The first volume of my own *History of Western Astrology* deals in some detail with the development of the zodiac and the framework of technical astrology.[11] There is an extensive literature on Greek religion, but the volumes by Richard Buxton and by Louise Zaidman and Pauline Schmitt Pantel give a sound introduction, emphasising the deep interrelationship between daily ritual and routine life.[12]

Very little is known about Greek attitudes toward the stars before the first millennium, though there is, naturally enough, plenty of speculation. For example, Jane Harrison in the early 20th century identified a pure strain of ethical, archaic celestial-seasonal religion, the worship of the *eniautos daimon*, the god who died and was reborn every year, which she believed predated the degenerate deities of the Olympian pantheon.[13] The familiar cosmology recorded in Greek myths, with its emergence of order out of chaos and generations of capricious, humanlike deities, finds its written form in the 8th century BCE, probably influenced by the similar scheme in the Mesopotamian cosmogony, the *Enuma Elish*. The earliest extant account was given in Hesiod's *Theogony* and, although details were added over the centuries, the basic form remained the same: The cosmos emerged from a primeval chaos—open, unbounded space—which gave birth to three entities; Earth, Eros, and Night. From Night was born Air and Day and from Earth, Ouranos, the "Starry Heaven," which was to be the home of the gods (with their earthly base, Mount Olympus), even though planetary deities themselves were not yet identified.[14] This scheme, dealing in metaphor and imagery, was elaborated upon by generations of later poets and playrights. In the words of the comic writer Aristophanes (ca. 446–ca. 386 BCE), "Firstly, black-winged Night laid a germless egg in the bosom of the infinite deeps of Erebus . . . and thus hatched forth our race, which was the first to see the light."[15]

Two features of Hesiod's creation myth are of interest. One is the notion of an original chaos that is, in its nature, without limit, and the other is a certain naturalism expressed in the generation of Air and Earth. Neither is an unusual characteristic of myth. However, both are used by advocates of Hellenic exceptionalism to argue that Greek philosophy represented a clean break with the past. Two examples are Thales' (624 bc–c. 546 BC) claim that the *arche*, the fundamental substance of which the universe is made, is water, and his student Anaximander's (c. 601–c.546 BCE) argument for the existence of the *apeiron*, the "Unlimited," a boundless reservoir, from which all things come and to which all things return.[16] The former is supposedly the first sign of materialistic inquiry and the latter that of abstract thought. Such claims are fictions, even though they are deeply embedded in the academic literature, and, rather than the clean break with a supposedly superstitious past, classical philosophy emerged very gradually from its religious origins: As the original source of all things, Anaximander's *apeiron* is a development from Hesiod's chaos. In some cases, such as Platonism, classical philosophy continued to serve an overt religious function in that its goal was reconciliation between humanity and the divine.

Hesiod's tract *Works and Days* is also the first surviving literary evidence of a stellar farming calendar in Greece, probably recording practices that date back to the early days of agriculture: "[W]hen Orion and Sirius are come into Midheaven," he wrote, "and rosy fingered Dawn sees Arcturus, then cut off all grape clusters . . . and bring them home."[17] This tradition, we might say, was naturalistic, but then nature was the domain of the divine pantheon, so the distinction between natural and divine worlds is irrelevant. The medical profession, itself frequently temple-based, also saw the movement of the heavenly bodies as integral to the individual's psychic and physical condition. In the 5th century BCE, Hippocrates, whose writings form the foundation of classical medicine, stated unequivocally that "the contribution of astronomy to medicine is not a very small one, but a very great one indeed. For with the seasons man's diseases, like other objective organs, suffer change."[18]

The earliest, most substantial surviving contribution to Greek cosmology was made in the 4th century by Plato, along with Aristotle perhaps the most important philosopher in Western history. Plato borrowed many of his theories from his predecessors, including Heraclitus, who believed that knowledge of the physical world is impossible because the physical world is always changing; Pythagoras, who claimed that the world was constructed from numbers and geometry; and the Orphics, religious reformers who believed that each individual contains a spark of the divine.[19] Plato's cosmology, as set out primarily in the *Timaeus* and the *Republic*, pervaded the religious climate of the classical world, was incorporated into Christianity, with the exception of awkward teachings (such as reincarnation), and has continued to exert a powerful impact in the modern world, from Marxism to New Age culture and abstract art. In the 4th century CE Platonic thought experienced a revival in the hands of a series of philosophers—Plotinus, Iamblichus, Proclus, and Porpyhry—one of whose primary concerns was the return of the soul to the divine, located in or beyond the stars, through virtuous living, scholarship, and magical practices known as theurgy (literally God-work).[20] Collectively these men are now known as Neoplatonists and, after them, it is common to refer to the subsequent strand of Platonism in the Jewish, Christian, and Islamic worlds as Neoplatonic.

In Plato's cosmogony the cosmos emanates out of a single creator, envisaged as a supreme consciousness, more akin to Anaximander's *apeiron* than to a personal God, and therefore permeated by divinity, even when at its most material and corrupt.[21] The entire cosmos is therefore divine, conscious, intelligent, and a single living creature, and all physical form emerges from the soul: Matter is dependent on consciousness. The "world soul" (Latin *anima mundi*) may be considered the organizing principle of the cosmos and is the source of each individual soul. The cosmos is divided into two modes of existence, Being and Becoming. "Being," which is eternal, timeless, and unchanging, contains the "Ideas," later known as archetypes, that were the perfect models of everything in existence. "Becoming," which is where our physical world exists, is characterized by change and the passage of time. True knowledge is available only from Being, the home of eternity, whereas in Becoming, constant change means that, as soon as a truth-claim has been made, circumstances change and what was briefly true is now false. Platonic philosophy is therefore one source of the Western skeptical tradition and is the basis of a view that, even when the principle of astrology is firmly accepted, it can speak in generalized terms, never in exact detail.

Physically, the Platonic cosmos was structured in concentric spheres with the earth at the middle and the planets then orbiting around it on seven spheres beginning with that of the moon, the fastest moving, and then rising to Saturn and beyond that the fixed stars, a model that prevailed in Europe and much of Asia until the 17th century. In spatial terms, the realm of the divine is beyond the stars, even though it also underpins the entire scheme. Platonic cosmology had a number of important consequences for astrology. First, as already noted, all physical phenomena are subject to change and cannot yield truth. Platonism contributed to a significant strand of skepticism which taught that only pure mathematics and abstract thought could assist an understanding of the cosmos, while observing the physical movements of the planets was likely to lead to error. The only useful astrology should therefore be based on abstract principles. Plato himself didn't actually say this, but his successors did. Even though Plato had little to say about astrology, his other statements about the stars were to become the foundation of the Western tradition. First he claimed that the planets "as a consequence of this reasoning and design on the part of God . . . came into existence for the determining and preserving of the numbers of Time. . . ."[22] The clear conclusion, then, is that astrology can be used to peer into the consciousness and intentions of the creator. The creator being best seen as "Mind," though, rather than a personal God, using astrology in this way became a means to develop one's reason, and so draw close to the Reason, with a capital "R," of God. Second, he argued that individual souls originate in the stars and descend to the earth via the planetary spheres as they incarnate, leaving divinity behind, and as they do so the three Moirae, or Fates, spin the web of necessity within which each soul must live out its life.[23] While fate is evident in the repetitive, unavoidable order of celestial motions, choice is still apparent in the legacy of the soul's initial decision to incarnate at a particular moment, and in each person's use of reason in order to alter their lives. Fate itself was then later conceptualized in different forms, such as *heimamene*, a fate that could be negotiated, or *ananke*, inevitable events (such as death) to which all people are subject. Even chance, the unexpected, was considered to be a form of fate. The added feature of the Platonic system was the soul's return to the stars after death, which provided the foundation for theurgic and magical practices, including the mysteries of Mithras, which either used the soul's journey to manipulate the cosmos during life or prepared for its ascent to the stars after death. This single notion, that the soul and stars were inextricably linked, and that it is therefore possible for the individual to connect with the heavenly realms, underpins the whole of classical astrology. The entire Platonic scheme was arranged according to musical harmonies and perfect geometrical forms, and it was both innately good and inherently beautiful: It was the Greeks who gave us the notion of *kosmos* as a perfect, beautiful, order.

One additional feature of Plato's theory of soul that has been largely forgotten but was to be critically important for classical astrology was his division of the individual soul into three functions. In his *Phaedrus* Plato attributed this three-fold structure to Socrates and represented it metaphorically as a charioteer and his two horses.[24] The highest part was the charioteer himself, the rational soul, mind, or intellect that discerns what is true, judges what is real, and makes rational decisions.[25] An astrology that serves these purposes must be, as the word suggests, logical. Next was the spirited soul, the active part, the will, whose function was to carry out what reason has decided. Last, and lowest, was the appetitive soul, the seat of emotion and desire, the source of love and anger, which needs to be restrained by the higher, rational soul if the individual is to be saved from self-destructive behavior. This tripartite division of soul was then adapted by Aristotle, whose definition of "soul" was broadly that it is the animating force in the cosmos, that which enables change, movement, and action. What he actually said was, "Soul is substance in the sense of being the form of a natural body, which potentially has life. And substance in this sense is actuality. The soul, then, is the actuality of the kind of body we have described."[26] He envisaged three stages to the soul: the animal, which governs physical life; the emotional, which enables people to love; and the rational, which enables people to think. The rational soul is then divided into two: The passive is fully embedded in nature and dies with the body, but the active, the true embodiment of reason, enables people to make genuine free choices, and survives death.[27] Combining the Platonic and Aristotelian systems then enabled astrologers to analyze individual destiny in order to understand and amend it. The following is from Claudius Ptolemy, writing in the 2nd century CE:

Of the qualities of the soul, those which concern the reason and the mind are apprehended by means of the condition of Mercury . . . and the qualities of the sensory and irrational part are discovered from the one of the luminaries which is the more corporeal, that is, the moon.[28]

Ptolemy provided a form of simple psychology in which the location of the moon at one's birth indicated a person's physical and emotional drives, while the intellect was represented by Mercury's position in the zodiac and relationship to the other planets.

He added that the Egyptian astrologers would never have forecast the future unless they thought that it could be changed.[29] There was no point in astrology unless destiny could be negotiated, and the precondition for amending it was a proper understanding of the condition of the soul as expressed in the moment of birth. Ptolemy's method became the basis for a system of what we may describe as astronomical psychology, or psychological astronomy, which was widely used until the 17th century.[30]

Aristotle added to classical cosmology a set of mechanisms by which the intentions of the creator might be transmitted to humanity. As far as we know he was the first person ever to do this in a systematic manner, so his work really does mark a break with the past and the beginning of a new way of thinking. He disagreed with those who claimed that the stars might be gods but did say that they are living beings. "The fact is," he wrote, that we are inclined to think of the stars as mere bodies or units, occurring in a certain order but completely lifeless, whereas we ought to think of them as partaking of life and initiative. Once we do this, the events will no longer be "surprising."[31] They were not surprising because the universe ran like clockwork. It was controlled by the prime-mover, the Aristotelian equivalent of God, the character who initiated all motion in the cosmos. Movement then rippled through the planetary spheres, setting up series of influences, including celestial motion (*motus*), which transmitted light and heat; celestial light (*lumen*), which produced day and night; and *influentiae*, intended to explain otherwise inexplicable phenomena, such as magnetism, and the tides. Aristotle presented humanity as embodied in a natural world that was real and solid in itself, not resting in consciousness, as Plato claimed, or subordinate to the celestial deities of vernacular religion. Yet the consequences for religion were profound: For a Jewish, Christian, or Muslim follower of Aristotle, such natural influences could be seen as a means by which God's plan could be implemented. To the matrix of natural influences Aristotle added four kinds of cause that could provide a universal explanatory model.[32] These were the material (the matter from which an object is made), the formal (the essential nature of a thing), the efficient (the object's maker), and the final (the object or purpose). The efficient cause, in which the maker of an object acts in the world, is closest to the modern notion of cause and effect. The other three causes, though, introduce firm concepts of order into Greek cosmology. For example, if the formal cause represents essential nature and the final cause its purpose, then the particular configuration of planets under which one is born represents both who one is and what one might become, embodying a simultaneous subjection to fate and potential escape from fate that lay at the heart of the Platonic paradox: There is no choice, but choice is essential. Aristotle's physics became the foundation of medieval learning and what came to be known as "scholastic" philosophy. Modern Western astrology remains largely "scholastic," in other words purposive, explaining phenomena by their function and nature in terms of Aristotle's causes.

Plato and Aristotle polarized Greek cosmology between one form that gave such a sophisticated expression to the concept of a divinely created and inspired cosmos that it was adopted wholesale by the early church fathers, and another that was effectively atheist. What they shared, though, was an assumption that human beings inhabited an ordered cosmos in which they were directly connected with the stars and planets either psychically, or physically, or both. Elements of the two schools were combined in Zeno of Citium's philosophy, Stoicism, in which God, soul, and nature were identical, the entire cosmos was alive, and human beings, as in the Platonic scheme, were simultaneously subject to an unbending fate and able to alter their lives through a virtuous, clean-living lifestyle, education, and self-awareness.[33] The Stoics were to be among astrology's keenest advocates in the classical world. Like Aristotelians, they could be considered atheist, for they denied the existence of a personal creator God, but they had no problem with the existence of individual gods and goddesses as characters in the natural world.

The distinctions between Platonic spirituality and Aristotelian and Stoic atheism may be substantial when their philosophical writings are compared, but their similarities were such that they were generally blended into a single worldview in which the celestial bodies represented an unfolding order to which all are subject, that might send influences to which people might respond (exactly as they shelter from the noon heat, or go out in the cool of the evening), or that might dispatch omens that act as signs of the times. We add to this the worship of planetary deities, which was introduced from Babylon and Syria in the 4th century BCE, and we have the foundations for an astrology that might be naturalistic or religious, scholarly or simple, and elite or popular.

It appears that, until Plato, the Greeks paid little attention to the planets. In the *Epinomis* (most likely written by his student Philip of Opus), he first addressed the problem that the planets have no names. It is with Plato's work that the pantheon of capricious gods and goddesses begins to be attached to the stars, developing secondary personalities as pure astrological principles rather than as squabbling humanlike figures. Divinity begins to be idealized as something pure and noble, introducing a paradox into the development of the planets as astrological characters. On the one hand they had inherited the capricious personalities of their presiding deities. The planet Venus, for example, was sacred to Aphrodite, goddess of love, and so could be seductive and lustful. Yet we could also see the planet as a principle from which a range of meaning and activities are derived, from erotic love to priestly rites, the playing of sweet music and the wearing of gold.[34] Every planet had its own set of meanings that played out in different ways depending on its location in the zodiac, relationship to the other planets, or position in the twelve "houses" (which governed different areas of life such as wealth, home, or marriage). Predictive techniques of various kinds allowed for a daily assessment of likely events and possible actions.

The encounter between Greek theory; Babylonian astrology, with its twelve zodiac signs and planetary gods and goddesses; and Egyptian astral-theology in Hellenistic Egypt in the 1st and 2nd centuries CE was responsible for the formulation of the kind of complex rules for the calculation and interpretation of horoscopes that were set out by Ptolemy and that could deal with great precision with every area of life. One might, as we have seen, then gain insights into the condition of one's current incarnation. The question raised by Ptolemy is, though, having embarked on a voyage of self-analysis, what does the thinking person do next? One option was to obtain a talisman that relied for its operation on the power of the word, or the manipulation of what the Stoics called *sympatheia*, the inner relationships which connected all things that exist—or might be imagined.[35] Another was to seek advice from a god, perhaps by attending a temple sacred to Serapis, where one's horoscope could be laid out on a board, with appropriate gems representing the planets, and an oracular answer obtained to a question. This account of such an incident gives the flavor:

A voice comes to you speaking. Let the stars be set upon the board in accordance with [their] nature except for the Sun and the Moon. And let the Sun be golden, the Moon silver, Kronos of obsidian, Ares of reddish onyx, Aphrodite lapis lazuli veined with gold, Hermes turquoise: let Zeus be of [whitish?] stone crystalline [?]; and the horoscope, in accordance with [nature?].[36]

Some people went further and joined a mystery cult with the intent of uniting their individual souls with the creator. Such ideas, inspired by Plato, were explained in the *Corpus Hermeticum*, composed in 2nd- and 1st-century BCE Egypt, and the closest, along with some passages in the Gnostic Gospels, that astrology comes to a sacred text, and were institutionalized in the mysteries of Mithras.[37] Mithraism was soteriological—concerned with individual salvation and was a formalized, ritual adaptation of the Hermetic belief that the soul abandoned its earthly vices as it ascended through the planetary spheres at death. Mithraism was essentially practical Platonism, the philosophy's most overtly religious application. The central iconography was the Tauroctony, in which the divine hero Mithras was shown killing a bull, representing Taurus, surrounded by other constellational images, including Canis, the dog; Hydra, the serpent; Crater, the cup; and Corvus, the raven. Last was a scorpion, representing Scorpio, the opposite sign to Taurus, and these two therefore framed the entire celestial mystery. Members of the cult were initiated through a series of levels represented by the planets culminating in the Pater (father), represented by Saturn. We can get an idea of the purpose of the Mithraic ascent from the Hermetic texts, which talk of the soul's return to God via the planetary spheres.[38] As it passes each sphere, the soul discards the vices associated with that planet. As the soul passes the moon, it abandons the natural processes of growth and decay—Mercury trickery, Venus deceit, the sun authority, Mars daring and recklessness, Jupiter greed, and Saturn falsehood. At the eighth sphere, that of the stars, the soul praises God, and having passed beyond it is reunited with God. One could even say it becomes God.

The planets, themselves, were the celestial administrators, conveying a bureaucratic function not unlike that which they exercised in the Chinese state.[39] The Hermetic texts sets out the predicament of humanity, born with an immortal soul but a frail body:

> Man had got from the structure of the heavens the character of the seven Administrators. . . . He is mortal by reason of his body; he is immortal by reason of the Man of eternal substance. He is immortal and has all things in his power; yet he suffers the lot of a mortal, being subject to Destiny (*Heimarmene*). He is exalted above the structure of the heavens; yet he is born a slave of destiny.[40]

It is precisely such a context that allows astrology to be widely interpreted by some classical scholars as a form of divination.[41]

Not all astrology, though, dealt with departure from this world. Most dealt with the here and now, with such brutal matters as life, disease, and death and such profane concerns as one's wealth, marriage, and runaway slaves. The key feature of all classical astrology was the notion of relationship. Each planet and zodiac sign was tied to the rest in a series of relationships that developed as they moved through space and time (Mars liked Aries but not Libra; Libra liked Aquarius but not Capricorn), which extended to everything known in the cosmos, including people. Thus the sun liked Leo, gold, kings, and, according to Ptolemy, Italians, but the moon favored women, watery places, and Mondays (the moon's day). These relationships existed in an ideal state equivalent to the Platonic world of Being, but were constantly shifting so that at any time and place one set of connections and possibilities might be more auspicious than another. The astrological texts set out in great detail the rules for engaging with these shifting spatial and temporal potentialities, enabling kings to found cities, the sick to be healed, and lovers to elope. No detail was too small to be considered and no aspect of human life was not covered. From a 4th-century text we read about the person born when Jupiter and Saturn were separated by three zodiac signs and favorably related to Mercury: Such an individual "will be involved in obscure religious rites, will (often) head a famous legation . . . (will) lose sons and are forced to raise the offspring of others."[42] This might sound trivial, and to classical critics of astrology it was. However, for the majority, this was sacred literature, providing a profound means of establishing the nature of the choices made by the soul before incarnation. On an immediate level the goal was personal advantage, but it was widely known that this was possible only if the gods and goddesses of the sky were respected and life was lived according the harmonies laid out by the creator.

Classical Greek cosmology was not necessarily religious in intent. However, a significant strand—the Platonic, Aristotelian, and Stoic—preserved the notion of the interdependence of all things, psychic and physical, terrestrial and celestial, along with notions of destiny based on a purposeful, unfolding order. It had different functions, from analysis and prediction of individual destinies, arranging auspicious times to conduct important enterprises, managing the state, manipulating the future, and ascending to the stars. We should also remember, in spite of my distinction between the sacred and the profane, that such distinctions blur in a context in which gods and goddesses are ever-present and watching every action, and that divinity is part of the material world, not separate from it. To invoke the supernatural was completely natural.[43] This is why there was no contradiction between using astrology to gain material advantage and using it to save one's soul. And even when questions were asked concerning the location of escaped slaves or the best time to attack one's enemy, a solution was possible only because of the web of psychic relationships that connected people to plants, animals, and stones, as well as to planets, stars, and God.

The distinctive features of Greek cosmology were its variety and its speculative models. It therefore offered a range of solutions to the problems of human existence and change. Previous cultures had explicitly attributed most change to the actions of gods and goddesses, although we can sometimes infer the existence of concepts of fate or time that acted as contexts for human activity. With the Greeks, though, such models became explicit, and human beings were located in a cosmos that could be governed by the Olympian pantheon but was equally subject to the ordered, mathematical unfolding of time; the notion of the cosmos as alive, conscious, and rational; concepts of fate that required different kinds of action; and natural influences transmitted to earth from the planets. Astrology then served a variety of functions, and, even though there were arguments about what it might or might not be able to achieve, everybody was able to accept one of three propositions: that the stars and planets influenced human life; that they were like the hands on a clock, indicating the changing qualities of time; or that they were divine in themselves or served the interests of the gods and goddesses. Greek religion was diverse. It included the formal procedures of the civic cults, the ecstatic rites of the mystery teachings, and the contemplative rationality of the philosophers. Possibly more than in any other culture, this diversity requires the use of the term "worldview." If there is one generalization that we can make about the classical Greek worldview, it is that, whatever of its varieties we are examining, we cannot make sense of it independently of an understanding of theories of the origin of the cosmos and the practical application of the stars to the problems of human existence.

14

Christianity

Influence and Transcendence

The star which they had seen in the East went before them, till it
came to rest over the place where the child was.[1]

Christianity is one of the great trinity of Near Eastern religions,
along with Judaism and Islam. It occurs in many forms, many of which
have historically been mutually antagonistic and some of which don't recognize one another as Christian. Yet there are broad and shared cosmological
themes, such as the belief in Christ's political role as heavenly king.[2] Even
then, there are a range of opinions from the Arian and Unitarian belief that
Christ was solely human, to the Gnostic belief that Christ offered salvation
from a world ruled by the evil God of the Old Testament, and the New Age
belief in the "cosmic Christ" as ruler of the coming Age of Aquarius. Any discussion of Christianity therefore has to recognize diversity both in terms of
origins and cosmology. This is inevitably a difficult task in view of the strong
opinions held by both Christianity's various schools of thought and by their
opponents.

In general, Christian cosmology centers on a creator God who brought the
cosmos into existence out of nothing and exercises supreme political authority, and with whom each individual may have a personal, direct relationship.
I say "in general" because even this apparently fundamental proposition is
not universally accepted. Gnostic Christians, who flourished in the classical
world, regarded the God who created the physical world as fundamentally
evil and posited the existence of a remote Platonic creator who brought the
entire cosmos into existence and was benign but too remote to engage in
personal relationships. Probably the only feature shared by all Christians is
the concept of Christ as savior, and the cosmos as a moral construct, filled
with temptation but equally offering a chance for salvation for those willing
to make the effort. The Persian concept of a perpetual struggle between good

and evil, unknown in Judaism, was adopted from Persian religion, allowing all things in the cosmos to be allocated, potentially, to one or the other. Yet the view which held that the entire cosmos was essentially corrupt, mired in sin since Adam and Eve's expulsion from Eden, was balanced by another opinion, inherited from Plato, in which the universe was essentially good and evil was a mere aberration. There is no essential physical structure to the cosmos, but in the traditional model inherited from classical Greece, heaven, the source of good, as beyond the stars while, in common with many cultures the underworld, which became a venue for endless torment, was somewhere below the surface of the earth. Simply, "up" was good, and "down" was bad. Time, meanwhile, tended to be seen as repetitive and patterned, with events following one another in a purposeful sequence, an example being the expulsion from Eden and the first sin finding redemption in Christ's offer of redemption. Time had a precise beginning in the creation and was to have an equally precise ending when the world, at a future point, was to come to an end, replaced by the eternal Kingdom of God. The Christian world inherited astrology from classical culture, and there were no developments, either technical or philosophical, that were specifically Christian. Rather, Christianity is distinguished by one of two attitudes toward astrology. Either it is regarded with suspicion on the grounds that it detracts from, or challenges, God's authority, or it is seen as a way of studying God's creation and revealing his plan. The arguments for and against astrology that preoccupied theologians in the early centuries of the Christian era have barely changed since and are still reproduced almost verbatim by astrology's critics and apologists.

The primary source for Christianity, of course, is the Bible, consisting of a New Testament that sits in a perpetual and constantly uneasy relationship with the Jewish scriptures, appropriated as the Christian Old Testament. A substantial amount of early sacred literature, though, is not included in the Bible. Montague Rhodes James's *The Apocryphal New Testament* is the authoritative English-language version of the various books excluded from the New Testament, while the *The Nag Hammadi Library in English*, edited by James Robinson, is the standard collection of the Gnostic Gospels, containing heretical cosmologies that were heavily Hermetic and Platonic and were largely, although not entirely, stamped out by the Catholic Church before the 4th century.[3] Alexander Roberts and James Donaldson's edition of *The Ante-Nicene Christian Library* includes the various attacks on astrology by the church fathers, the theologians of the 1st to 4th centuries.[4]

The literature on Christian cosmology in the wide sense of general notions of the relationship between God, space, and time is, naturally, massive, although the only works on astrology tend to be partisan—either for or against, most of which recycle arguments that have remained unchanged for almost 2,000 years.[5] The arguments come down to two fundamental versions: Either the stars obstruct God's relationship with humanity or they enhance it. Both positions rely on *a priori* assumptions, devoid of empirical evidence or personal experience, and contribute little to our understanding of the theological issues. The scholarly work on astrology and Christianity is sparse, although much interesting material is scattered through Lynn Thorndike's encyclopedic *History of Magic and Experimental Science*.[6] Only one recent book is worthy of note—Tim Hegedus's *Early Christianity and Ancient Astrology*, which has shown how the relationship between astrology and Christianity in the classical world (as in the medieval) was complex and nuanced.[7]

To generalize about a phenomenon as diverse as Christianity is risky, but all its forms, peaceful and violent, esoteric and institutional, are united by the belief that Christ, however he is envisaged, is a savior. Most Christianity, but not all, holds to the following principles: There is one God, and Christianity came about as the result of a unique revelation of his relationship with humanity, itself developing out of the unique nature of Judaism, founded on a series of previous unique revelations. All previous belief systems were superseded by Christianity, which inherits from Judaism the notion of absolute truth and absolute falsehood. The cosmos is therefore essentially dualistic, polarized between God and Satan, good and evil, body and spirit, heaven and hell, eternal life and eternal damnation. Humanity was alienated from God as a result of the Fall (Adam and Eve's expulsion from the Garden of Eden), and its purpose is therefore to return to God, worship and obey him, secure personal salvation, and prepare the way for Christ's second coming. Christianity's messianic and apocalyptic qualities mean that it is time-based and predominantly linear, moving from a single creation to a single destruction, in contrast to other systems that may favor neither a beginning to the universe nor an end, or an infinite series of beginnings and endings. There is, though, still a sense of cyclical return in that, at its end, the cosmos returns to its original perfection. Within the single time frame within which the divine plan is played out, God is generally transcendent, moving through the creation but essentially above and separate from it: The classic transcendental model is rooted in the Genesis cosmogony in which God acts as an artisan, external to his creation. As Isaiah (66.1) puts it, "Heaven is my throne and the earth is my footstool."

All these claims are generally true of the Catholic ("universal") Christianity that became dominant in the Roman empire and finds its heirs in both modern Roman Catholicism and the varieties of Orthodoxy and Protestantism that derive from the medieval Catholic Church. However, a feature of Christianity as a whole is its diversity. Nineteenth-century esoteric Christians, ancestors of much New Age thinking on the matter, had no need of a creator God, while the classical Gnostics of the 1st to 4th centuries CE did have a God, but a malevolent one. For New Age Christians such as Alice Bailey and Rudolf Steiner, Christ's role is to ease the transition to the Age of Aquarius, while for Gnostics, his task was to save humanity from God, rather than on behalf of God. Some strains of Christianity supported an emanationist model, often influenced by Platonic theory, in which the cosmos emanates out of the Creator, and he (or she if we prefer) permeates the created world. And, as the entire created world was involved in this process, it incorporated the femaleness that the Catholic Church was later at such pains to exclude. For Gnostics, the Trinity is not necessarily Father, Holy Ghost, and Son but might be Father, Mother, and Son.[8] Some writers find evidence of emanationism (in which the cosmos is not created by God but emanates out of Him) in St. Paul's rhetorical question in I Corinthians 6.19: "Do you not know that your body is a temple of the Holy Spirit within you, which you have from God?" suggesting that God was alive and existent within humanity. The distinction between transcendence and immanence can be a substantial one cosmologically: In a transcendent scheme it becomes possible to see nature as evil and humanity as corrupt and alienated from God, but in an emanationist model, nature has to be essentially good for it contains God, and humanity is connected directly with God and, important for the theme of this book, the stars.

Christian cosmogony is broadly that inherited from the Jewish book of Genesis, and the creation in seven days, although there has always been, and still is, a division between those who prefer to take this account metaphorically and those who believe it literally. However, St. Paul introduced a strong Platonic tone in which the monarchical rule of Christ was extended so that not only did he preside over the cosmos but he *was* the cosmos, in that the church was his body, and all those who were destined to be saved existed in him from the beginning of time.[9] Metaphysically, then, in this version, the cosmos was divine, even if humanity was corrupt. Time was relative, and even though Christ was to return at a fixed moment to inaugurate the kingdom of God, individuals could choose to enter it at any moment and save themselves from evil, a notion popularized in the 18th century and bequeathed to New Age ideology by Emmanuel Swedenborg.[10] In terms of the cosmos's physical structure, by the time Christianity developed, all educated opinion in the eastern Mediterranean accepted the notion of the spherical earth, so belief in the flat earth, promoted briefly by the 6th-century monk Cosmas Indicopleustes, was rarely taken seriously.[11] Christian cosmology in the physical sense is therefore usually the cosmology of the times, and it is only in the Darwinian era that a substantial body of Christians have invoked the literal truth of Genesis in order to reject in its entirety a species of secular cosmology. In the past, even for the strident opponents of judicial astrology, the truth was often nuanced. Even when the Roman Catholic Church turned against Galileo, the "father of modern physics," in the 1600s, its problem was not with his advocacy of the new sun-centered universe but with his public threat to the Vatican's right to guide public discourse on the topic. Some Christian scientists, such as the physicist John Polkinghorne, see no problem with a God operating through the laws of physics, but then the schism is merely redefined as between competing Christians rather than between Christians and scientists.[12]

The Christian calendar provides strong evidence of the incorporation of pagan astrological concepts: that God's plan is played out through time, and the cycles of the sun and moon, which create the divisions of time, therefore designating auspicious moments for sacred rituals. For example, Jesus's birth coincides with the winter solstice, the shortest day. While this critique of Christianity as a variant of pagan astral religion has been popular among atheists since the early 19th century, it is also familiar to those modern evangelicals, such as Jehovah's Witnesses, who prefer not to celebrate Christmas.[13] It is indeed the case that Christianity's principal festivals, Christmas and Easter, are timed by the ancient precepts of astral religion. As Christ was crucified at the Jewish Passover, it follows that Easter, the commemoration of his death and resurrection, the earliest sacred date in the Christian calendar to be fixed, must coincide roughly with Passover. The date of Easter in the Roman Catholic Church, as agreed at the Council of Nicaea, is determined by the Paschal (from the Jewish Pesach, or Passover) Full Moon, the first full moon following the spring equinox, in the tropical sign of Aries, or 14 Nisan in the Jewish calendar, with the celebration of Christ's Resurrection fixed for the first available Sunday.[14] The lineal ancestor of both Passover and Easter is the Babylonian spring equinox festival, the *akitu*, the twelve-day commemoration of death and survival. Christmas Day became significant only later, when the Catholic Church deliberately began to adopt the trappings of the Roman imperial cult. In the Calendar of Filocalus, an illuminated manuscript produced in 354, Christmas was located on 25 December, the feast of Natalis Solis Invicti, sacred to Sol Invictus, the unconquered sun. This was just a few days after the winter solstice, the shortest day and the longest night, and represented the point at which the sun was to embark on its journey back to life from the near-death of midwinter.[15] Christ's birth and the sun's return to life therefore shared a fundamental equivalence. In the east a different tradition emerged; the birth of Christ was celebrated twelve days later, on 6 January, the Epiphany. The boundary between metaphor and the literal truth—between Christ symbolized by the sun and Christ personified as the sun, is a fine one to tread, and the subtlety is easily lost. As Christ had prophesied, in the Kingdom of Heaven "then the righteous will shine like the sun in the kingdom of their Father."[16] The influence of solar monotheism on early Christian conceptions of divinity was reinforced by the monotheistic strand in Greek religion, as evidenced in the widespread reverence for Zeus Hypistos—the highest god.[17] Many pagans had to make only a slight adjustment in order to adapt to the new church.

The most famous example of the appropriation of the imagery of astral omens by Christian apologists is the star of Bethlehem, which supposedly guided the Magi, Persian astrologer-priests, to Christ's birthplace, as described by the author of Matthew's gospel. There have been various attempts over the centuries to locate the origin of the star in a comet, perhaps, or a conjunction of Jupiter and Saturn, none of which are particularly convincing for they do not explain the star's erratic behavior, leading the Magi to Bethlehem and then standing still over the stable.[18] More likely is the theory that the star was a literary device, common in royal hagiographies of the time, to illustrate to an astrologically aware readership that the significance of Christ's birth was revealed in miraculous celestial signs.[19] Christ's transcendent nature was then given celestial confirmation, justifying St. Paul's view, in his letter to the Ephesians (1.20–21), that "he [God] made him [Christ] sit at his right hand in the heavenly places, far above all rule and authority and power and dominion . . . , not only in this age but also in that which is to come."

The New Testament has no expressed clear view on astrology, although references to celestial omens as warnings of the apocalypse offered implicit approval of it. In Mark 13.24–26 we read: "But in those days, after that tribulation, the sun will be darkened, and the moon will not give its light, and the stars will be falling from heaven, and the powers in the heavens will be shaken. And then they will see the Son of man, coming in clouds with great power and glory." Such prophecies became the basis of a sustained tradition of astrological-apocalyptic prophecy down to the 17th century, in which planetary alignments were used to predict Christ's second coming. The celestial significance of such omens was reinforced by passages which implied that Christ's message itself could be understood as a cosmological code. For example, in Mark 8.18–21 Jesus berates his disciples:

> "Having eyes do you not see, and having ears do you not hear? And do you not remember? When I broke the five loaves for the five thousand, how many baskets of broken pieces did you take up?" They said unto him, "Twelve." "And the seven for the four thousand, how many baskets of broken pieces did you take up?" And they said to him, "Seven." And he said to them, "Do you not yet understand?"

The answer to the riddle lies in the numbers seven and twelve, the key ritual numbers in Hebrew tradition, seven being the number of the days of the creation, twelve the number of tribes.[20] Any intelligent audience of the 1st century would have been deeply aware of the cosmological significance of these numbers, there being seven planets and twelve signs of the zodiac. The most overtly cosmological text in the New Testament, though, is the Revelation of St. John, an imaginative work of grand proportions. Its repetition of the number seven—churches in Asia, spirits before the throne of God, the famous seals, and, significantly, stars—ties Christian cosmology to the planets.[21] The woman with a crown of twelve stars is complemented by the tree with twelve kinds of fruit, one for each month for the "healing of the nations" brings in the zodiac:[22]

> Then he showed me the river of the water of life bright as crystal, flowing from the throne of God and of the Lamb through the middle of the city; also on either side of the river, the tree of life with its twelve kinds of fruit, yielding its fruit each month; and the leaves of the tree were for the healing of the nations.

The form of paganism most favored by classical theologians, for it appeared to anticipate monotheism, was Platonism. The most notable of the Platonic Christians was the 2nd- and 3rd-century Alexandrian theologian Origen, who trod the boundaries of heresy when he wrote, "The sun also, and the moon and the rest of the heavenly bodies are living beings."[23] He did not, though, go as far as the Gnostics, who wholeheartedly adopted a Platonic-Hermetic model in which the entire cosmos had emanated out of the creator and was populated by planetary powers, or archons, and a host of other demons.[24] The Gnostics' general cosmology was therefore sympathetic to classical astrology. Human beings retained a direct, interior connection with the creator but existed within a brutal cosmos created by the ignorant and tyrannical god Yaldabaoth, the Yahweh of the Old Testament. Zodiac signs, planets, and the rest of the celestial apparatus were therefore humanity's oppressors rather than its liberators. Only Christ, representing the pure spiritual light of the sun, could save human beings from their awful predicament. This he achieved at his ascension when, passing through the planetary spheres on his way to heaven, he destroyed their power to imprison souls on earth, a story outlined in the Pistis Sophia, one of the Gnostic gospels.[25] At a blow, Christ had defeated the evil powers of the planets. There was, then, no reason for astrology, not even as an aid to salvation. In the balance of debate, then, passages that were used to support astrology, such as Genesis 1.16 ("God made the sun to rule the day and the moon to rule the night"), were trumped by those that were used to attack it, such as Job 25.5 ("the stars are not clean in his sight").

The Christian polemics against astrology were launched in the 2nd century by Justin Martyr, a pagan thinker who converted around 130 and taught for a time in the church at Ephesus before opening a Christian school at Rome; and Tatian the Syrian, who was born around 120 and became a Christian in Rome in around 150–65. Tatian's righteous anger against astrology, which, in his view, was demonic, was uncompromising and, along with Justin's, has set the template for similar Christian rhetoric down to the present day. "Men became the subject of the demons' apostasy," he wrote. "For they showed man a chart of the constellations, and like dice players they introduced the factor of fate. . . . Murderers and their victims, rich and poor, are children of fate, and every nativity gave entertainment as in a theatre to the demons, among whom, like 'the blessed gods' of Homer, 'unquenchable laughter arose.'"[26] There were other objections to astrology, though. One drew on passages such as Matthew 13.32–33 ("But of that day or hour no one knows, not even the angels in heaven, nor the Son, but only the Father. Take heed, watch, for you do not know when the time will come") and Acts 1.6 ("He said to them, 'It is not for you to know times or seasons which the Father has fixed by his own authority'") to challenge humanity's ability to foresee a future that only God knew.

The Bethlehem star remained an apparently obvious pro-astrological statement, although anti-astrology Christians could argue the reverse. For example, St. Ignatius (c. 35–c. 107), who as bishop of Antioch was one of the senior churchmen of his day, argued that the star brought an end to the old beliefs and practices. It was as if the light of God swept away a world of darkness. "This was the reason," he wrote, "why every form of magic began to be destroyed, every malignant spell to be broken, ignorance to be dethroned, and ancient empire to be overthrown."[27] The omen's very existence was turned against those who had seen it, and the Magi were therefore the last of the astrologers to practice their art legitimately. Augustine (354–430), the last and greatest of the classical theologians, also discussed the problem of the Star of Bethlehem, asserting that it was a new star that shone *because* Christ was born and its purpose was to point the way for the Magi to find the Word of God.[28] In venerating Christ, the Magi renounced their former ways; and astrology, which Augustine regarded as demonic, was therefore to be roundly rejected under the new Christian dispensation.[29]

Augustine actually summarized the arguments against astrology that remain, to this day, the core of anti-astrology polemics by both evangelical Christians and skeptical scientists. In the *Confessions*, Augustine's personal renunciation of his previous sinful life, he claimed that to argue that God's authority could be exercised via the stars (a defense that was presumably current among Christian astrologers) caused theological offense, for it both limited God's power to intervene directly in human affairs and implicated him in the stars' less admirable decisions.[30] It also absolved human beings of responsibility for their own actions and, ironically, pushed that guilt onto God, who must, presumably, have instructed the stars to cause men to sin. In his view, then, astrology made God responsible for sin. Augustine also summarized the other arguments against astrology, both religious (that it worshipped the creation rather than the creator) and skeptical (asking how two babies born at the same time could have different lives).[31]

Augustine's attack on astrology was an attempt to de-spiritualize the universe at the same time as he constructed a new moral cosmology. In spite of his respect for Plato, he rejected the notion of the universe as a living creature.[32] Instead, some parts of the world were no longer alive and were distinguished from those that were. But that there was some link between life on earth and the stars could not be challenged, for the sun's relation to the seasons and the moon's to the tides were undeniable. But were these phenomena astrological? Augustine thought not but reluctantly conceded that not just solar and lunar but stellar, including planetary, influences, had to be acknowledged.[33] This concession to the natural world was to be crucial to astrology's revival in Christian Europe in the 12th century, when it was customary to justify the practice as natural philosophy, emphatically not as divination.

However, the Augustinian hypothesis, that astrology-as-divination is demonic and prohibited but that celestial influences were real, is still that held by the Roman Catholic Church. The tension between the two positions was increasingly uneasy until a crisis was reached in the 12th century as a result of the wholesale introduction into the Catholic world of classical astrological texts, mainly from the Islamic world. A resolution was proposed and reached in the 13th century by St. Thomas Aquinas, the most influential of medieval theologians. Having followed Augustine in condemning divination by the stars as unlawful, he wrote, "[A]cts of choice and movements of the will are controlled immediately by God. And human intellectual knowledge is ordered by God through the mediation of the angels. Whereas matters pertinent to bodily things, whether they are internal or external, when they come through the use of man, are governed by God by means of the angels and celestial bodies."[34] The stars affected the body alone, while the soul was free of celestial influence, except via the body. Thus, in a typical example, if a transit of Venus, planet of love, stirred up lustful thoughts, the individual could choose how to respond and, with sufficient prayer and devotion, resist such cosmically derived temptations and transcend the corrupt, material world.

The Catholic Church still follows the Thomist view, and the most recent version of the catechism specifically condemns astrology-as-divination:

> All forms of divination are to be rejected: recourse to Satan or demons, conjuring up the dead or other practices falsely supposed to "unveil" the future. Consulting horoscopes, astrology, palm reading, interpretation of omens and lots, the phenomena of clairvoyance, and recourse to mediums all conceal a desire for power over time, history, and, in the last analysis, other human beings, as well as a wish to conciliate hidden powers. They contradict the honor, respect, and loving fear that we owe to God alone.[35]

Although the catechism was widely regarded as an attack on astrology, Laurence Cassidy, a Jesuit priest and astrologer, pointed out that it was significant for what it didn't say.[36] By arguing that astrology should be condemned as divination, it had omitted the other part of the Thomist formula—that astrology as natural influence is acceptable. The latter position is no longer sustainable in a scientific environment in which such influences are either negligible or confined to the sun and moon, but Cassidy's point was that, regardless of scientific evidence, as long as one was not practicing divination—which, for the catechism, involves communicating to divinities—

astrology is acceptable. A more liberal approach was espoused by the Vatican document on New Age culture "Jesus Christ, Bearer of Living Water: A Christian Reflection on the 'New Age,'" published in 2003.[37] This publication argued that New Age culture, and implicitly astrology, is evidence of a genuine spiritual hunger that is not demonic, merely mistaken. A similarly liberal point of view was adopted by the Church of England report *The Search for Faith and the Witness of the Church* in 1996.[38]

There is, then, no single Christian position on astrology, any more than there is a single Christian cosmology, but each of the different arguments can be positioned within attitudes toward time. In the Thomist view, time, while orderly, can be negotiated, in the sense that its changing qualities, as expressed through shifting planetary influences, can be negotiated. However, the Augustinian position favored the predestination suggested by such passages as Matthew 22.14 ("For many are called, but few are chosen") and Ephesians 1.4–5 ("even as he chose us in him before the foundation of the world, that we should be holy and blameless before him. He destined us in love to be his sons through Jesus"), in which morality and salvation are a matter not of choice but of one's eternal existence. Augustine explained his logic in chapter 11 of the *Confessions*, pointing out that if God was all-powerful and all-knowing, he knew the past, present, and future simultaneously and the whole of time must therefore exist coincidentally. Astrology therefore loses one of its vital functions: It can no longer change the future.

Christianity has always struggled with astrology. The debates are complex and the boundaries between the various positions are often ill defined. The pro-astrology apologists are obliged to negotiate apparently anti-astrology passages in the Old Testament, while the anti-astrology position is fatally undercut by scriptural support for the divine nature of celestial omens and the rhetorical adoption of either naturalistic or devout Christian stances as a defense against allegations that astrology is demonic. Christianity has often proved remarkably adept in incorporating significant features of other religions, and we might point to the appropriation of the Middle Eastern calendar festivals and classical solar monotheism as key examples. The practice of horoscopic astrology itself, though, seems to have become for some a symbol of a line that could not be crossed. Yet other features of classical cosmology were welcomed, in particular the Platonic notion of a cosmos presided over and permeated by the *logos*, the divine reason of John's Gospel, and of a soul that can recognize divinity in the heavens, drawing closer to God as a result. Such philosophical cosmology, encouraged by Jungian psychology, finds a welcome home in such parts of the church as liberal wings of Anglicanism, where one might even find interest in astrology as a source of meaning. Opposition to astrology, though, tends to be strongest among evangelical groups that emphasize the ecstatic experience of being "born again" and/or the literal truth of Old Testament condemnation of astrology. Such people, however, would once have been precisely those who watched the sky for celestial omens of the end in moments of apocalyptic crisis. In this sense, attitudes toward astrology, in a narrow sense, are a weather vane for wider struggles between different kinds of Christianity.

In spite of its diversity, we can draw out certain consistent themes in Christian cosmology. The first is that it locates the individual in time. Possibly more than any other religion, it is concerned with the future and the crucial moment at which the soul is either sent to hell or invited to heaven, entering an eternity of either terrible suffering or of ecstatic bliss. These are concepts that have largely disappeared from most modern Christianity but provided the religious rationale for most of its adherents' behavior for much of the past 2,000 years. This includes attitudes to the stars and astrology, the question always being the extent to which they assist or obstruct one's chances of salvation. At one extreme, astrology in all its forms, including the use of horoscopes, magic, and the ascent through the celestial spheres, is regarded as legitimate. At the other, even a sacred calendar based on sun and moon cycles is regarded with distaste—witness the rejection of Christmas by some evangelicals. The middle ground is occupied by those who regard astrology as acceptable as long as it avoids contact with supernatural agencies. As astrology's status in Western culture, at least among the educated classes, plummeted in the 17th century, it ceased to be a focus of concern for most Christians. The most bitter cosmological arguments these days tend to be reserved (especially in the United States) for the struggle with scientific cosmology, and the battle between creationist fundamentalists, who accept the literal truth of the six-day cosmogony in Genesis, and Darwinian evolutionists.

15

Islam

Faith and Reason

To Him belongs the dominion of the heavens and the earth.[1]

The term "Islamic cosmology" carries with it a certain ambiguity and a question that nobody has yet answered satisfactorily: Are we to consider Islamic cosmology in the sense of theories of the cosmos that arise out of Islamic teachings, or should we consider the cosmologies that have flourished in the Islamic world? To an extent we have to do both, just as long as we are aware of the difference, as well as of the frequent difficulties in distinguishing among them. The astrologers and astronomers of the medieval Islamic world might themselves be Jews or Christians as much as Muslims. What is considered Islamic thought is therefore often best seen as a conversation between members of all three faiths, writing in Arabic. The same problem occurs wherever we have a language of widespread intellectual discourse, whether Greek in the Hellenistic period or English in the 21st century.

Additionally, the Islamic world eventually extended from West Africa to the Philippines, and from Spain to Indonesia, encompassing huge variations in culture. The problem is solved, to an extent, by focusing on the cosmology of the so-called Golden Age of Islam, the Abbasid period from 750 to 1258, an era of almost 500 years of intense creativity and deep scholarship, when Islamic learning was expressed through the Arabic-speaking world and the new religion first encountered, and then appropriated, the worldviews of antiquity—of Greece, the Near East, Persia, and India. As in all cultures that practice a complex astrology and possess a rich, theoretical cosmology, there is a gap between the world of scholarship and that of the mass of the population who follow practices and adhere to beliefs that may have little to do with the elite. It is therefore also common to talk of Arabic folk-astronomy as a separate genre from the speculative cosmology of the philosophers and theologians. In dealing with the classical period of the Abbasid dynasty, I am inevitably excluding the range of Islamic reactions to modern scientific cosmology, but I am dealing with attitudes toward astrology and the foundations of religious cosmology that are still current. However, there is a lack of scholarly studies of the modern world regarding the continuity of popular astrological traditions. Scholarly treatments of modern vernacular cosmology are rare, with exceptions such as a study of the legacy of Arabic astrology in Madagascar and an ethnography of Bedouin in the Negev.[2]

For primary sources, the English translation of the Koran by Abdullah Yusuf Ali is regarded as reliable.[3] There are many general sources on medieval Islamic philosophy. Henry Corbin's *History of Islamic Philosophy*, *Spiritual Body and Celestial Earth*, and *Cyclical Time and Ismaili Gnosis* and Majid Fakhry's *A History of Islamic Philosophy* are fine introductions that contain much of relevance to this chapter.[4] George Saliba's *A History of Arabic Astronomy* and John Steele's *A Brief Introduction to Astronomy in the Middle East* are excellent introductions to scientific astronomy, while David King's *Astronomy in the Service of Islam* examines astronomy's cultural context.[5] Edith Jachimowicz's brief chapter on "Islamic Cosmology" in Blacker Loewe's *Ancient Cosmologies* is a sound introduction to the topic, drawing on religious sources.[6] Seyyed Hossein Nasr's *An Introduction to Islamic Cosmological Doctrines* is the only authoritative English-language work to deal adequately with philosophical cosmology.[7] There is little scholarly commentary on Islamic astrology aside from works by David Pingree and Edward Kennedy dealing with astrological views of history.[8] There is, though, an increasing number of primary astrological texts in English translation, particularly works by Abu Ma'shar (787–886), Al-Qabisi (fl. 10th century), and Masha'allah (c. 740–815).[9]

Persian culture had a profound impact on the astrology of the Islamic Golden Age, through its transmission of Hellenistic astrology. The Zoroastrian religion, which preceded Islam in Persia, lacked the tensions between monotheistic purity and astrological plurality from which its cousins, Judaism, Christianity, and Islam, suffered. However, the sources are sparse and we have almost no direct knowledge of any distinctive features of Persian astrology beyond the apparent invention of a system of historiography based on Jupiter-Saturn cycles, which we will consider below, and astrological interpretations of the sacred text, the Bundahishn, that survive only from after the Islamic conquests.[10] As the caliphs turned to astrology, they therefore encountered a worldview and cosmic-political theory that could easily be adapted to an Islamic context. This is how one Persian, Zoroastrian text described the chain of command in the political cosmos: "And the creator Ohrmazd entrusted all the good things which are in this creation to Mithr [Mithra] and the Moon and the twelve Signs of the Zodiac which are called by the Religion the twelve commanders."[11]

The first wave of Islamic rulers, those responsible for conquering the vast empire that stretched from the Pyrenees in the west to the Hindu Kush in the east, regarded their religion as primarily for Arabs alone and had little interest in the wisdom of the cultures they now ruled. It was the Abbasid caliphs, who took power in 750, who broke with this purist introspection, revived the previous Persian dynasty's high regard for ancient learning, and were responsible for the wholesale introduction of astrological lore, from Greece through Persia to India, into Arabic. A succession of rulers established the conditions for this renaissance, beginning with al-Mansur (754–75). His successors included al-Mahdi (775–785), who founded schools and patronized the arts; Harun al-Rashid (786–809), who signaled his respect for pagan learning by ordering a collection of original Greek manuscripts; and al-Mamun (813–33), who set up the Bait al-Hikma (House of Wisdom) in Baghdad, as a deliberate attempt to bring scholars together to translate Greek, Syriac, Persian, and Sanskrit works into Arabic and, among other areas, to exchange ideas about the nature of the cosmos.

Islamic cosmology, strictly, is based on the primacy of God, the single creator, a fact from which all other theological notions follow. The single fact of God's omnipotence leads to similar debates concerning determinism to those we find in Judaism and Christianity. The question is this: If God is all-knowing, does he know the future, and, if he knows the future, is it already fixed or does he have the power to amend it? Is the cosmos on a trajectory that cannot be changed, or is it open to negotiation? And if it is open to negotiation, can this be legitimately accomplished only through prayer and religious devotion, or can it be achieved through a knowledge of nature, an understanding of cosmology, and the practice of astrology? The other main feature of Islamic cosmology is a reverence for order as expressed in time through the appearance of the new crescent moon and the precise observation of the lunar calendar, as well as daily times for prayer, and in space through the obligation to pray facing Mecca.

The primary sources for Islamic cosmology are the Koran, God's revelation to Mohammed; the *hadith*, accounts of Mohammed's sayings and actions; and the Pentateuch, the first five books of the Hebrew Torah (the Christian Old Testament). The Koran, of course, is the most important of all primary sources and contains the foundations of Islamic cosmology, including a concept of seven Firmaments suggestive of the classical seven-fold structure of the universe, or of seven regions of the spiritual heaven. The world's political allegiance to the one God is also spelled out. In Surah 65.12, God's messenger, Jibril, the archangel Gabriel in Jewish-Christian mythology, announces:

> God is He Who
> Created seven Firmaments
> And of the earth,
> A similar number
> Through the midst
> Of them all descends
> His command: that ye may
> Know that all things, and that
> God comprehends all things
> In (His) Knowledge.

Furthermore, Surah 65.3 argues that God's universe is based on a mathematically regulated order ("Verily for all things has God appointed a due proportion") and Surah 65.11 points to the notion of the natural world as a series of conversations with God, offered as encouragement for the faithful:

> An apostle who rehearses
> To you the Signs of God
> Containing clear explanations,
> That he may lead forth
> Those who believe
> And do righteous deeds.

The unrighteous, meanwhile, are likely to be attacked by meteors and comets originating from constellations in the "lower heaven," closest to earth (Surah 37.6–10).

The notion of a world characterized by both a fundamental order and the communication of signs through natural phenomena leads inexorably, through a process of what we might call cognitive drift, to an astrology either in which life evolves through a series of stages measured by astronomical motions or in which the astrologer reads and translates celestial omens. However, strict Islam, exactly like Christianity, tends to reject astrology both as a distraction from the purity of knowledge derived from God and scripture and as likely to lead to falsehood by elevating the creation over the creator. The counter-argument, proposed by apologists for astrology, is that the creation is itself a representative of God's plan and, therefore, necessarily a path to truth. The theologically safe position for any Islamic astrologer was to explore the unfolding of God's divine plan, while avoiding any interference in it that might second-guess his right to control the future. Surah 113.1–4, for example, warns against the dark arts:

> Seek refuge With the Lord of the Dawn,
> from the mischief of created things;
> from the mischief of darkness as it overspreads;
> from the mischief of those who practise secret arts.

Simply, only God can know the future. Like the Christian and Jewish Gods, though, their Islamic counterpart undercut injunctions against divination by himself speaking in signs; the Arabic for the entire cosmos, including the earth, 'âlam, shares a root with 'alâma (sign, mark) and a connection with 'ilm (knowledge), in the sense that the cosmos is everything about which one can have knowledge. Cosmos can therefore be understood as the vehicle by which one obtains knowledge of the external world (al-'alam al-khaariji), as opposed to the inner world within each person (al-'alam al-daakhili). Astrology itself was known as Ahkam al-Nudium, literally, "the decrees of the stars," suggesting a role for the celestial bodies as messengers of the divine. The world, by which we mean everything other than God, is therefore a means for God to speak to humanity, and all natural phenomena are therefore signs, âyât, of the divine. Additionally, everything that happens in this world is a manifestation of God's plan, carrying a message and a meaning for anyone who cares to listen. Even human actions may be read as divine omens. As Surah 11.82 warned, "And we turned (the Cities) upside down, and rained down on them brimstones hard as baked clay. Behold! In this are signs for those who by tokens do understand. . . . Behold! In this is a sign for those who believe." The political message, of course, is that God cannot be resisted, and those who mistakenly try to do so will be destroyed by his armies. Surah 16.49, reinforcing similar texts in the Old Testament, warns all living things, including the angels, to bow down before God. For those Islamic Platonists who were to come later, the stars and planets, being alive, were also subject to this command. Surah 10.101 does seem to promise wisdom from the stars, but only for the true believers. Of course, it would be a matter of individual judgment whether this wisdom could, or should, be derived from the casting of horoscopes, rather than the simple contemplation of God's splendor. Even Surah 85, which is titled *Al-Burüj*, the Zodiac, has nothing explicit to offer astrologers who might be looking for divine approval, being concerned more with the wonder of God's creation than with any technical means of reading his signs. For the devout, then, astrology, with all its complexities, was essentially redundant. As the preamble to Surah 45 reads, "The Signs of God are everywhere: His power, wisdom and goodness are shown through all Creation and in Revelation." In other words, the pious believer has no need of anything other than simple faith. The tensions opened by the Islamic encounter with astrology were therefore very similar to those faced earlier by Christianity: There can be no other source of authority but God, and the development of learning as a whole, including astrology, was thus faced with the constant dilemma that any search of natural causes can seem to detract from God's ability to intervene spontaneously in any level of existence as, and when, he wishes.

A typical statement of the anti-astrology case was provided by Ibn Khaldun's 14th-century work the *Muqaddimah*, a comprehensive history of the world based upon a Platonic cyclical scheme in which empires and societies were destined to rise and fall in line with underlying patterns. Like Plato, Ibn Khaldun argued that the historical process might benefit from sensible life-style choices, including religious faith, but suffer from stupid behavior, under which he included astrology.[12]

The astrology of the Islamic world drew on two major sources: the textual corpus of the judicial astrological texts derived from the Hellenistic, Near Eastern, and Indian worlds, and the "folk astronomy" inherited in part from the calendrical and progonistic practices of pre-Islamic Arabia. These practices included weather prediction (especially the prediction of rain) based on the periodic appearance of the *anwā*, or rain stars, and the use of the twenty eight *manāzil*, or lunar stations (often known in English translation as mansions), which appear to have been adapted from India, although opinions differ, probably during the Islamic period and also occur in Chinese astrology.[13] The meanings of the stations were transmitted orally, sometimes as rhyming verses, and developed over time.[14] Typical was the interpretation attached to the rising of the mansion *butayn* in early May:

> When *butayn* rose
> Debts were paid,
> Finery appeared,
> The perfumer and the smith were pursued.[15]

Anthropological work by Clinton Bailey in the early 1970s indicated that such ideas had survived in part but were rapidly dying out under the impact of modernization.[16] In an Islamic context, folk-astronomy has three primary functions: regulation of the lunar calendar, the organization of the five daily prayer times, and the determination of the sacred direction of Mecca.[17] These three functions remain as important in the 21st century as they were in the 7th. Observation of the moon itself was vital, because the month, and therefore the entire religious calendar, was based on the first observation of the rising crescent new moon. Being completely lunar, the twelve months of the Islamic calendar shift gradually in relation to the solar year by eleven or twelve days a year, coming back into alignment every thirty-three years. The consequence is that the holy month, Ramadan, slips progressively through the seasons. The daily prayer cycle was tied to the sun with five critical moments: sunset, nightfall, daybreak (to be completed by sunrise), shortly after midday, and the time when the shadow of any object has increased beyond its midday minimum by the length of the object. The notion of correct orientation in space, important in all religious traditions, also became much more complex because of the significance of the *qibla*, the direction from any location in the world to the Kaaba, the massive granite cube that sits at the center of the mosque in Mecca. Prayer, ritual sacrifice, and burial were all to be conducted facing the *qibla* while other acts, such as performing bodily functions, should, the rules stated, be perpendicular to it. Knowledge of where, exactly, the *qibla* lies is therefore of crucial importance for the pious Muslim. On a spherical planet, though, the *qibla* is exceptionally difficult to locate and the rising and setting of the sun and stars and the direction of the winds might all be used for calculation. The Kaaba itself, which was a pagan shrine before being appropriated by Mohammed, may have been constructed to align with the rising of the fixed star Canopus, the summer sunrise, midwinter sunset, and the southernmost midwinter moonset.[18] It has also been suggested that the whole of pre-Islamic Mecca was aligned, following the Kaaba, with the spring equinox.[19] Islamic cosmology was unambiguously heir to an ancient tradition in which human life was designed to correspond to the celestial realms. It also borrowed heavily from the classical philosophical schools founded by Plato, Aristotle, and Zeno, three schools of thought that were to allow scholars to adapt the framework offered by the Koran to different cosmological models.

The significant discussions in Islamic cosmology, though, went way beyond arguments, such as Ibn Khaldun's, about whether there was any practical use in astrology. It was the theoretical argument that mattered, especially the continuing need to reconcile Neoplatonic thought with the Koran. This problem was taken up by Ibn Sina (980–1037), known in Latin Europe as Avicenna. Facing the problem of how classical pagan teachings could be reconciled with Koranic wisdom, Avicenna developed a form of the "cosmological argument" which states that all things need a cause, in this case, ultimately God. In the hierarchy of influences, he reasoned, all things must be sustained by necessary causes. In other words, all layers of reality are contingent, or dependent, on the one above, going up to the top one that is necessary and self-existent. In its essence this is a restatement, in an Islamic context, of the Aristotelian notion of descending causes, in which causes come down to earth from the mind of God via the stars and successive planetary spheres. Therefore, any pagan notion of the planets as independent agents, which was objectionable to Islamic theologians, was contained within a structure in which the planets could function as secondary causes, without challenging God's absolute sway over the entire cosmos. More explicitly, Neoplatonic influences surfaced in Avicenna's advocacy of the origin of the world in emanation out of God rather than creation by him, and his argument that celestial substances are kinds of intelligences—in other words that the cosmos is alive. Avicenna himself adhered to the position held by many leading Platonists in which predictive judicial astrology was roundly rejected while Hermetic cosmology, with all its overtones of both spiritual and physical planetary influence, was valued.

Avicenna's work encouraged the development of groups that continued the practice of Hermeticism as a religion, of which the most notable was the Ikhwan al-Safa, or Brethren of Purity. Their encyclopedia, the *Rasa'il*, probably composed in the 9th century, was a synthesis of Neoplatonic and Hermetic teachings presented, for political reasons, within an Islamic context.[20] The strand of thought represented by such groups was substantial, has been credited with the tolerant religious policies pursued by Shiite rulers, and was developed by Sufi teachings and among the Ismailis. Such tendencies were also emphasized in the Sufi emphasis on *kashf*, or unveiling, through which the initiate might gain direct knowledge of the divine source of cosmic truths. And, in tangible terms, such concepts, expressed through geometry, were embodied in the harmonious patterns that are characteristic of Islamic art.[21] To gaze on such a geometrical design in a mosque or on a tile is therefore to absorb an image of the cosmos as alive and rational.

Islamic Neoplatonism provided a tidy justification for both astrology and magic, but Avicenna's view was to be substantially challenged in the 12th century by the Andalusian philosopher Ibn Rushd (1126–98), better known under his Latinized name, Averroës. Averroës set out to rescue Aristotle from what he saw as Neoplatonic, Hermetic, and other religious impurities. He wanted to understand the cosmos as it was, not as it should be. He attacked the cosmological argument—that as all things must be caused by something else, there must be a supreme cause, a creator—and argued that only physical arguments can explain physical things. However, and this was to be his significance in the history of astrology, he adopted the Aristotelian notion of a universal, agent intellect that provides what is common and immortal in human beings.

Averroës may have purified Aristotle, but some of his ideas were no more Islamic than Avicenna's. In fact, so pervasive was Neoplatonism that he could never free himself from its legacy. Aristotle's belief in an eternal world, for example, that was never created and can never be destroyed, is fundamentally at odds with the entire Judaeo-Christian-Islamic notion of a world that was created out of nothing and will eventually be destroyed.

The last major proponent of the synthesis of Islam with the mystery teachings of the classical world was Ibn 'Arabi (1165–1240), whose honorific title, *al-Shaykh al-Akbar*, "the greatest master," is the best evidence of the respect he commanded in his lifetime.[22] Born into a family of government officials in Andalucia, Ibn 'Arabi experienced as a teenager a profound gnostic revelation of the invisible world. He left Andalucia on a quest for spiritual wisdom, pursuing his vision, eventually settling in Damascus, where he wrote more than 700 books and treatises, of which about 500 survive. Whereas the influence of such philosophers as Avicenna and Averroës was generally confined to intellectuals, Ibn 'Arabi spoke to the masses, perhaps because he remained close to the language of the Koran and the *hadith*. The essence of Ibn 'Arabi's teaching, widely quoted in later cosmological writings, was the oneness of being, in which a single reality, *wujûd*, equivalent to the eternal, intangible, world of Platonic being, both underlies all existence and is identical to God himself. Everything else that we can see, touch, and feel exists in the phenomenal world, the Platonic realm of "Becoming," which, though, real to us, is a mirror of the true reality embedded in Being. The concept of the archetypal perfect man, who has a simultaneously human, cosmic, and divine nature and embodied everything that human beings should strive to achieve, proved especially appealing. On the cosmic level, the macrocosm, the perfect man, as an archetype, existed in the mind of God. As the microcosm, and as an intelligent being, the individual man is made in the image of God, and, through realizing God in himself, he can rule the macrocosm, the cosmos itself. This ideology encouraged a sort of popular religious magic in which the harmony of the cosmos was maintained through the pursuit of divine wisdom, and it was to find its most powerful and enduring expression in Sufism. For the whirling Dervishes, the most famous Sufis, astrology is practiced not through the casting of horoscopes but through the imitation of the spinning of the planets around the earth. This is more than imitation, though; it is participation, and through it, cosmic harmony is maintained.

The technical judicial astrology of the Hellenistic, Near Eastern, and Indian worlds, with its dependence on complex rules for the interpretation of horoscopes designed to evaluate individual destiny, arrange auspicious moments to conduct various enterprises, answer questions, and analyze world history, was translated into the Arabic language and became part of high Islamic culture from the latter part of the 8th century even if, as we have seen, some theologians and philosophers retained theological and skeptical objections. Such rarefied concerns, though, rarely trouble the mass of people. The adoption of judicial astrology into popular culture is not well understood. On the one hand, it was some time before knowledge of the lunar stations reached the religious scholars.[23] On the other hand, horoscopic astrology itself originated in the Near Eastern and Hellenistic worlds a millennium prior to the Islamic conquests and was a part of the prevailing culture of the region.

One of the most distinctive contributions of the Islamic astrologers to the discipline was their adaptation of the Persian theory of astrological historiography, which was to become one of the most important means of tracking God's unfolding plan and of anticipating apocalyptic cataclysms. This scheme was derived from the coincidence of timing between the apocalyptic teachings of Zoroastrian religion and the combined cycle of Jupiter and Saturn, the two slowest-moving planets.[24] According to the Zoroastrians, world history was driven forward by a dialectical process characterized by 12 phases of 1,000 years each. As one millennium came to an end and another began, a crucial phase was initiated in the bitter struggle for supremacy between Ahura Mazda, or Ormazd, the god of light, and Ahriman, his dark counterpart. At some point, perhaps after the Persian occupation of Babylon in 539 BCE, most likely following the spread of Hellenistic astrology after the 2nd century BCE, it was noticed that the conjunctions between the two slow-moving planets, Jupiter and Saturn, which take place every 20 years, progress through the signs of the zodiac in an orderly sequence that repeats itself after 960 years.[25]

We need to emphasize the religious significance of Persian conjunctional theory: It allowed nothing less than a full description and analysis of God's unfolding plan. It was the application of astrology to the religious concerns of humanity *par excellence*, and its consequences were to reverberate through the apocalyptic upheavals of the Christian world down to the 17th century. The practice survives in a secular form among a tiny number of modern astrologers, while the concept of an astrological mechanism for religious development survives in such millenarian beliefs as the coming Age of Aquarius or Maya calendar prophecies. There is a further heresy evident in such thinking, and that is a kind of religious relativism which teaches that, while God's Truth may be absolute, the truths that any prophet, including Mohammed, teaches are provisional and likely to be superseded by his successor.

The fundamental premise was that the nature of any Jupiter-Saturn conjunction, on which was based its use as a forecasting mechanism, was indicated by the horoscope cast for the preceding spring equinox, the date every year when the sun entered Aries. The logic was that, at this moment, a new cycle of time began, within which all possibilities for that cycle were contained. Masha'allah included the horoscopes for the spring equinoxes (the sun's annual entry into Aries on 21 March) preceding the Jupiter-Saturn conjunctions prior to the great deluge (it was believed that the rains which caused the flood began at midnight precisely, on 18 February 3101 BCE, with a conjunction of planets in Pisces, appropriately the last of the "water" signs) and the births of both Christ and Mohammed. These were, naturally, fortunate horoscopes; they could hardly be anything else. However, both were saturnine, and Saturn, Masah'allah reminds us, indicated "general misery and violence."[26] In Scorpio, the sign of the Arabs, this pointed to Mohammed's death in the East, but the chart was saved by an exalted, benevolent Venus in Pisces, a counter-indication that revealed the Arabs' essential strength. Masha'allah's work was potentially dangerously heretical, suggesting that God's plan was subject in some way to mathematically regulated planetary cycles. His God, though Jewish, was also the supreme mind of the Neoplatonic philosophers, whose divinity was revealed in his devotion to a somewhat mathematical, bureaucratic cosmic order. Political changes are permitted a quarter way through the cycle, around every 240 years while great prophets appear when the cycle is complete; every 960 years a new prophet appears.

Every planetary combination could bring its own set of warnings. When Jupiter is in the seventh house (about to set over the western horizon) when the sun enters Aries and is moving closer to Saturn but is still about 60^0 or 120^0 away from it, there will be lawsuits among the ordinary people, and "plenty of terrors"; a conjunction of Mars and Saturn indicates skin diseases, a harmonious relationship trine (meaning there are three complete zodiac signs between them) from Mars to Saturn points to fraud among pious people and kings and, when the sun is involved in such a pattern in the appropriate manner, he expected "the annulment of evil."[27] He then became more specific: When Aries is rising at the Aries ingress, which would occur in years when the sun itself enters Aries at around dawn, we can expect tyranny, war, high pressure in the spring, and intense cold in winter. And, in a possible echo of Assyrian texts, we are told that the Babylonian king may go on a journey and defeat his enemies while Armenia might suffer drought and starvation and the king of India may die.[28]

Such work is part prophecy, part proto-sociology, and entirely a matter of political management. We need to understand that, even though Abu Ma'shar's rationale is clearly Aristotelian (he talks of "generation and corruption," the "influences" and "mixtures" of the celestial bodies[29]), the naturalistic, physical model of influences descending from the stars, and planets acting as natural causes, had little effect on his astrology. The actual structure of Abu Ma'shar's astrology is precisely mathematical, derived from the Pythagorean strand within Platonism. Everything in the historical process can be reduced to numerical formulae: When Jupiter is moving toward Saturn but still has 120° to travel, prophecies will appear; when it has 90° to go, religious and political leaders' affairs will alter; and, when there are 60° left, conditions will prevail similar to those that prevailed when the 120° situation took place. The whole situation is mathematically regulated: Social, political, and religious developments unfold with an unerring regularity.

While it was prediction that aroused criticism of astrology from religious conservatives, forecasting the future was only a part of the astrological project. Astrology's most important function was to manage the present and change the future, a goal that could be achieved through magic, by which we mean the manipulation of the sympathies, rays, and correspondences recognized by the Islamic Neoplatonists Al Kindi and Avicenna. These theoretical models found their practical expression in a work known as the *Ghayat al-Hakim* (the Aim of the Wise), composed in Andalucia around the year 1000. Translated into Latin in 1256 by the Castilian monarch Alfonso the Wise, it was known in medieval Europe as the *Picatrix* and was to be the key text of magical astrology until the 17th century. The *Picatrix* included direct extracts from the *Rasa-il* and therefore provided a direct line of transition for Islamic Hermeticism, and hence for Babylonian celestial deities, straight into the 13th-century Christian West. Once the required invocation of God had been completed, the text began with a standard formulation of Neoplatonic cosmology: All things derive from the One, the most important human attribute is wisdom, and wisdom lies in knowing the reasons for the existence of things that derive from the One. Also, all things being derived from the One, they exist in relation to one another, and those relations may be close or distant, sympathetic or hostile. Magic is defined simply as "everything that absolutely fascinates minds and attracts souls by means of words and deeds."[30] It is an attempt to change the world by actively engaging with the sympathies that link everything, including words, thoughts, objects, plants, animals, planets, angels—literally everything. These aims can be achieved through sound, through music and incantations, through words and images written down or inscribed. The central tool of such magic was the talisman, defined as a "spirit within a body."[31] The astrological talisman was a physical object designed to possess the sympathy, or even the life force of a star, planet, or zodiac sign. The astrological component enters the picture because the qualities of time are represented by the zodiac and planets. An effective talisman should take into account the planet most relevant to the sympathies or correspondences that need manipulating and should be constructed when that planet is strong, at its hour, on its day, and out of a substance it rules. A Venusian talisman, which might be made to enhance a love affair or soothe a fever, would have been made out of copper, Venus's metal, on Friday (Venus's day) after dawn (the first hour on Friday was ruled by Venus), when Venus was in a sympathetic part of the zodiac, such as Taurus or Libra (the signs it ruled) and making good aspects to other planets. One talisman was made to ensure permanent love according to the following instructions:

> [M]ake two talismans in an ascendant of good luck when the moon and Venus are in Taurus. In the first picture draw 220 numbers of thousands or zeros and draw in the second picture 284 numbers also of thousands or zeroes. Then make them embrace once another and bury them in the location of one of them and permanent love and strong affection will ensue.[32]

As far as mechanisms for astrology are concerned, the complete range of possibilities inherited from the Hellenistic world was open to the astrologers of the Islamic world with the exception, of course, of autonomous planetary deities. At one end of the spectrum was the notion of heaven and earth as symbiotic reflections of each other. Among those texts from the Islamic world that were to form the centerpiece of later astrological thought, the shortest, and perhaps most influential, was known in the West as the *Tabula*

Smaragdina, or Emerald Tablet.[33] It was this text which established unambiguously the concept that earth and heaven mirror each other and that change in one is complemented by change in the other.

The sack of Baghdad by the Mongols in 1258 is often regarded as a symbolic end to the Islamic golden age. This may be true as far as Mesopotamia is concerned, but not the rest of the Islamic world. The construction of the magnificent observatory at Samarkand in 1420 by Ulugh Beg, grandson of the great conqueror Tamurlane, is evidence of a flourishing tradition of scientific learning in central Asia, while the Ottoman rulers of Turkey were often patrons of learning. However, the half-millennium during which Baghdad was a center of learning of the highest quality, the focal point of a network of scholarship that extended from Andalucia to northern India, was a distinct phenomenon that was never to be repeated. As a consequence, Islamic astrology from the 13th century onward is almost entirely neglected by Western scholars. There are just a few examples of studies up to modern times.[34] The notion of an Islamic golden age of learning that came to an end in the 11th century suited the vanity of European historians in the 20th century who saw intellectual vigor moving to Catholic Europe. Other evidence suggests continuity, or even that astronomy in the region boomed in the period following the Mongol conquest: In the early 15th century, Samarkand, home to the observatory of Ulugh Beg, Tamurlane's grandson, and around sixty or seventy astronomers, had a claim to being the astronomical capital of the world.[35] The demand for astrology remained, as witnessed by a Persian study of world history, using Abu Ma'shar's theories and Jupiter-Saturn conjunctions, that was written in 1691.[36]

The golden age of classical Islam came to an end more than 700 years ago, around the same time as the translation of Arabic texts into Latin was having an electrifying effect on the Christian world. The legacy of this intellectual earthquake was still felt in Europe in the 17th century. However, since the 19th century the Islamic world in general and the Arabic world in particular has been coping with its encounter with colonialism and modernity. The scholarly appreciation of cosmology invariably loses out to the study of more immediate political, economic, and social concerns: the place of women, the role of oil, and the nature of fundamentalism. However, it is precisely this lack of attention which indicates that there is work to be done.

Islamic cosmology, as we have seen, can be defined in one of two ways. First is the cosmology derived from the Koran. Second is the wider cosmology of the Islamic, chiefly Arabic-speaking, world, which was influenced both by vernacular traditions and imported philosophies, such as Platonic and Aristotelian thought from classical Greece. There were often tensions between Koranic cosmology, which asserted the exclusive primacy of God, and broader cosmological ideas. The latter posed a range of possibilities that were seen to dilute God's authority, such as natural influences emerging from the planets, or the horoscope, with its mathematically regulated concepts of destiny. Both the cosmology and astrology of the Islamic, Arabic-speaking world should be described as "cosmic," the former in the sense that there was a single act of intentional creation, the latter because it was highly codified. Islamic cosmology experienced a creative period in the so-called golden age from around 700 to 1200 CE, when the wider cosmology inherited from the classical world was exported to Latin Europe. Even though cosmological inquiry and astronomical thought continued to flourish in individual centers for many centuries, the notion of a secular cosmology, as developed in the Christian world following the "scientific revolution," remained unknown.

Theosophical, New Age, and Pagan Cosmologies

Nature and Transformation

> We could be on the verge of a true Golden Age, for the Water Bearer [i.e., Aquarius] is the Grail Carrier who has found the vessel of rebirth and brought it into the world that its redeeming waters may be poured out for all in need.[1]

The religious culture of the modern West is distinguished by the institutional decline of the Christian church in all its forms. Only the United States bucks the trend, with high levels of regular churchgoing and vigorous participation by Christian groups in politics. Even in the United States, though, the religious climate outside established organized Christian groups is distinguished by a plurality of voices.

This phenomenon is explained by secularization theory, which assumes that the fall in church attendance is evidence of a drop in religiosity as a whole. This conclusion is challenged by advocates of privatization, who argue that, far from declining, religiosity is being diverted into a range of private spiritualities, a shift in the zeitgeist that some commentators refer to as a spiritual revolution.[2] Privatized spirituality comes in a variety of forms, but the two most frequently used labels are New Age and Pagan. In their modern form, both can be traced to the 19th century, though naturally with earlier roots, and have flourished since the 1970s. Insiders in both New Age and Pagan groups frequently claim an ancient lineage, rejecting notions of modern invention. I emphasize New Age thought in this chapter mainly because it has more to say about astrology than paganism and has had more of an impact on it, especially in the development of the concept that the world is about to enter the Age of Aquarius, my major theme.

To bracket New Age and Paganism together is controversial among both some academics and many practitioners, who regard them as entirely distinct: There may indeed be substantial differences between the pure forms, or ideal types, of each. Some versions of New Age rhetoric, for example are strongly Christian, which is anathema to many pagans, while paganism tends to emphasize engagement with the natural world, in contrast to a common New Age concern with transcendence. However, aside from the most ardent advocates of particular New Age prophecies, or Pagan activities (which are themselves very diverse), most individuals whom we might identify as either New Age or Pagan are difficult to classify as belonging to one group or the other. Conversations with Pagans who believe the New Age is coming and that reality is transcendent, and with apparent New Agers, for whom engagement with nature and pagan rituals is an important step toward the Age of Aquarius, the coming astrological epoch, indicate that, in practice, the boundary between Pagan and New Age cultures is fluid and porous. My research suggests that most people who might be engaged in such practices are unaware of the distinction.

The primary sources in modern New Age and Pagan culture are many and varied. The closest New Age culture comes to sacred texts are the works of H. P. Blavatsky, the charismatic, eccentric, founder, in 1875, of the Theosophical Society: *Isis Unveiled* and *The Secret Doctrine*.[3] Paganism, being diverse, has no foundational texts, although the works of Gerald Gardner, the founder of Wicca, are important: Gardner's first books were fiction: in 1939 *A Goddess Arrives* and, in 1949, *High Magic's Aid*.[4] He then laid the foundations for Wicca in two nonfiction books: in 1954 *Witchcraft Today* and, in 1959, *The Meaning of Witchcraft*.[5] The quantity of post-Blavatskyan and post-Gardnerian primary texts is immense and has multiplied exponentially with the coming of the World Wide Web. Increasingly pagans are turning to modern editions of medieval works as sources for their practices and beliefs.

There are, though, excellent scholarly works in both New Age and Pagan studies. For New Age, Antoine Faivre's work provides the best historical background, while Wouter Hanegraaff, Paul Heelas, and Michael York produced three very different books in the mid-1990s.[6] The academic literature on paganism includes works by Margot Adler and Graham Harvey, anthropological studies by Tanya Luhrmann and Susan Greenwood, and comprehensive histories of British paganism by Ronald Hutton.[7]

Both New Age and Paganism (in its modern forms) are difficult to define. As the sociologist Michael York wrote of New Age culture, "Even the concept of a New Age is vague: on the one hand, there is the formal initiation; and on the other, is someone who attends a t'ai chi ch'uan workshop or a talk by Peter Russell on creative management automatically a New Ager?"[8] York went on, though, to suggest a single core feature of New Age culture, the need for personal transformation as necessary to an inexorable process of spiritual cosmic evolution:

> What unites all New Agers, however, is the vision of radical mystical trans-formation on both the personal and collective levels. In fact, the awaken-ing to the potential abilities of the human self—one's individual psychic powers and the capability for physical and/or psychological healing—is the New Age springboard for the quantum leap of collective consciousness which is to bring about and constitute the New Age itself.[9]

At the heart of New Age cosmology, then, lies the proposition, inherited from Platonism and encouraged by modern contacts between Westerners and Indian religion, that the cosmos is essentially spiritual in nature and that the material world is illusory. This is combined with a modern evolutionary perspective in which the cosmos is thought to be moving toward a "higher," more spiritual condition that it will achieve in the New Age. It is therefore necessary for every individual to undergo a personal transformation in order to serve this cosmic purpose. The individual self-development that lies at the heart of all New Age activities is therefore actually designed to lead to the dissolution of individuality within the cosmic whole.

Paganism is also subject to competing definitions. Again, according to Michael York, paganism is "A religious option that reveres physical spiritual-ity either as the exclusive parameter of the divine or as the initial source of evolutionary progress"; he adds that "Paganism holds that there is nothing beyond nature: nature is all that there is."[10] Implicitly this excludes Neopla-tonism and Hinduism, which regard reality as spiritual and transcendent, and nature, sometimes, as a mask for this higher reality, or even as an "illu-sion." The historian Prudence Jones offered an alternative view. She wrote: "A Pagan religion has three characteristics. It is polytheistic, recognising a plurality of divine beings who may or may not be reducable to an underlying One—or Two, or Three, etc. It sees the material world and its laws . . . as a theophany, a manifestation of divinity. . . . Finally Pagan religions recognise the female face of divinity, called by modern Pagans the Goddess."[11] As with religion in general, then, we can adopt a more exclusive position or a more inclusive one: Each may have advantages and disadvantages when it comes to discussing the material. To apply a classical Greek model, Michael York's emphasis on immanence of the divine as nature tends to the Stoic, while the space Prudence Jones allows for transcendence is more Platonic.

The one core feature of New Age cosmology that is not central to Pagan cosmology (even though individual pagans may share it) is its millenarian expectation of a coming global upheaval, followed by a new spiritual era, the Age of Aquarius in astrological terminology.[12] The Aquarian Age will begin when the sun is in Aquarius at the spring equinox, 21 March. Unfortunately nobody can agree when this event takes place. Some think it has already happened; others put it hundreds of years in the future. The New Age is, in spite of the adjective "new," part of a matrix of ideas which depend on the notion that the world, or even the entire cosmos, is about to experience a cataclysmic transformation and that can be traced back to the first millennium BCE. The distinction between New Age and Paganism as "ideal types" (rather than actually practiced by individuals), then, lies in competing attitudes toward time. New Age prioritizes the future liberation as a one-off event, while Paganism emphasizes the repetitive condition of the here and now. In celestial terms, New Age looks forward to the single and once-only shift of the equinoctial sun into Aquarius, while Paganism celebrates the endless round of new and full moons and calendar festivals. Pagan ideologies have no need of the belief in the coming historical transformation that is central to New Age prophecy. Even then, individual pagans may look forward to the coming of the Aquarian Age.

New Age culture itself is best understood if divided into two.[13] On the one hand, the narrow New Age *sensu stricto* depends on the belief that the entire world is passing into a new, more spiritual, historical phase. On the other hand, we can identify a wider culture, the New Age *sensu lato*, in which there is little concern with historical transformation but an engagement with the range of practices considered important by those who believe in the coming historical transformation, from aromatherapy, astrology, and acupuncture to yoga.[14] The same principle of a strict adherence on the one hand, and a loose affiliation on the other, can be applied to many movements and ideologies. In the Pagan world, for example, we may distinguish a devoted member of a Heathen group, or a leader of a Wiccan coven, or a practitioner of the magical rituals of the Golden Dawn, from the individual who may generally believe that there is a goddess, or that nature is the source of divinity, or who has attended a summer solstice celebration but has no commitment to the truth of any particular dogma.

Paganism is diverse, but the main internal distinction lies between those who draw their inspiration from the "northern tradition"—Norse and Scandinavian mythologies and deities—and those who are wholly or partly influenced by the transcendent and magical ideologies of the eastern Mediterranean and Near East, among whom we can include Wiccans, Druids, followers of Isis and Ishtar, and members of Hermetic and Gnostic groups.[15] All these groups share with New Age thought a common origin in the Western esoteric tradition, extending back to classical Platonism and the Egyptian mysteries.[16]

On a personal level there is a distinction between individuals who may be regarded as, respectively, New Age or Pagan *sensu stricto*. While some New Agers' esoteric Christianity renders pagan beliefs unpalatable, some Pagans are contemptuous of what they see as the shallowness of New Age activities, asserting their own superiority by virtue of their supposed deeper commitment to their path. However, in the *sensu lato*, the distinctions disappear. For example, while, as we have noted, one possible difference between New Age and Pagan cosmologies lies in attitudes toward historical time, individual testimony tells a different story, and many Pagans believe in the coming Age of Aquarius. For example, two influential Wiccan writers, Janet and Stewart Farrar, regarded what they saw as the current "reintegration of the Ego and the Unconscious, on a new and higher level" as the prelude to a "new and unimaginable fruitful evolutionary phase; call it, if you will, the Aquarian Age."[17] Yet another prominent Wiccan, Vivianne Crowley, identified the New Age and Age of Aquarius, which she regarded as synonymous, as particularly favorable to the spread of Wicca, on the grounds that one of the Aquarian/New Age's manifestations is the awakening of the goddess in human consciousness: Culturally it is the Age's pluralism that provides a sympathetic environment for Wicca; theologically it is its emphasis on the inner divinity that, being so sympathetic to Wiccan cosmology, will enable the new religion "to serve the religious needs of many in the Aquarian Age."[18] Some prominent Pagans among those who favor the notion that nature is underpinned transcendent or imminent have become influential in New Age circles, a key example being Starhawk, the American eco-feminist and environmental activist.[19]

The catalyst for the modern emergence of New Age thought as a popular and intellectual force was H. P. Blavatsky's founding of the Theosophical Society in New York in 1875.[20] Blavatsky set herself two goals. The first was to recover what she considered to be the lost wisdom of a once-universal human civilization by bringing together its surviving fragments from Indian, Platonic, Hermetic, and Kabbalistic thought. The second was to form a body of people who, by studying and practicing ancient wisdom, could prepare the world for the imminent shift into a new historical era. Influenced by the German idealist philosopher George Friedrich Hegel (1770–1831), whose theories of history, she argued, had "their application in the teachings of Occult science," Blavatsky set out her theory of cyclical history, in which complex patterns of cycles regulate a cosmos in which physical evolution is dependent on spiritual evolution. In her own words:

> The revolution of the physical world, according to the ancient doctrine, is attended by a like revolution in the world of intellect—the spiritual evolution of the world proceeding in cycles, like the physical one.[21]

Blavatsky's synthesis of Indian and Platonic theories of history was based on the simple idea that the cosmos moves through an infinite series of cycles of creation and destruction and that in each one its pure spiritual nature was gradually concealed behind a mask—"veil" was her preferred word—of matter. At a crucial point, which she thought was imminent, the return to pure spirit would begin and matter would begin to lose its power. Eventually the entire cosmos would return to pure spirit before the process was repeated. No individual is immune, and each is obliged to prepare for the coming age (Blavatsky herself didn't use the term "New Age") by undertaking whatever steps are necessary to awaken their spiritual awareness. These might include studying astrology or practicing yoga or any of the other practices since added to the list, from aromatherapy through crystal healing to channeling and meditation. A number of paradoxes underpinned her system, though, and these are familiar from ancient astrological systems: The coming of the future age is inevitable, but all individuals must work to ensure that it arrives, and while the first goal of the developmental process is to reach individual self-awareness—to "individuate" in Jungian terms—the second is to open up to benign higher intelligences and to submit to possession and direction by them to serve the goal of eventual reintegration of all things into a single great whole. What we may call "self-spirituality," the elevation of the self to the position of spiritual authority, is actually just the first stage in a process that hopes for the elimination of self.[22]

Although Blavatsky had little sympathy for Christianity, a great many esoteric Christians (who respect Christ as a spiritual teacher but reject the mainstream, institutional churches) joined the Theosophical Society, resulting in a tension between what Joscelyn Godwin has designated the Western and Eastern Theosophists.[23] The latter were drawn to Eastern cosmologies and are represented by all those who later followed Indian gurus. The former were subdivided into two groups: on the one hand, those who favored the European magical tradition and who subsequently gathered in groups such as the

Hermetic Order of the Golden Dawn (which had a decisive influence) and, on the other hand, a group of nondogmatic, anti-church, esoteric Christians, of whom Rudolf Steiner and Alice Bailey were to be the most influential. It was the esoteric Christians who developed the dominant, Christian strand of rhetoric in Aquarian Age rhetoric, which Blavatsky labeled "Christism" rather than Christianity.[24] Steiner and Bailey adapted the Gnostic Christian belief that God is within each human being and predicted that the coming of the Age of Aquarius would be marked by a rise in "Christ-consciousness" in each receptive individual. The cosmology of the Western Theosophists emphasizes the progression of the cosmos through disjointed epochs—astrological ages—with a hope that the coming age will see the beginning of the cosmos's resolution into pure spirit, whereas Eastern Theosophical cosmology tends to rely on the endless repetition of time that is fundamental to Hindu religion.

The theosophist Max Heindel (1865–1919) gave what may have been the first relatively detailed version of the astrological ages in his *Message of the Stars*, first published in the 1900s. Heindel joined the Theosophical Society after moving to Los Angeles in 1903 and formed the Rosicrucian Fellowship after 1907, and his teaching, writing, and publishing activities made him an important figure in the spread of astrology in the early 20th century.[25] The Aquarian Age, he announced, "will be illuminated and vivified by the solar precession, for the upliftment of the Son of Man (Aquarius), by the Christ within, the Lion of Judah (Leo), to the estate of Superman," adding that the Age will bring Christ's second coming, the "wedding feast of the Higher Self to the lower."[26]

Heindel's work was paralleled by that of Rudolf Steiner, who achieved prominence as the leader of the German Theosophical Society until 1912, after which he left to found his Anthroposophical Society.[27] Anthroposophy is perhaps the most vibrant of New Age movements, standing at the heart of a network of organizations such as the Waldorf Schools; the Camphill Trusts, which assist disabled people; and biodynamic farms, which apply Steiner's astrological theories to agriculture. Steiner developed a historical cosmology that postulated a major shift into a new spiritual age known by later advocates, including Robert Powell, as the New Age.[28] Humanity, in short, was to be transformed. In 1910 Steiner commented:

> There is much talk about periods of transition. We are indeed living just at the time when the Dark Age has run its course and a new epoch is just beginning, in which human beings will slowly and gradually develop new faculties and in which human souls will gradually undergo a change. . . .

What is beginning at this time will slowly prepare humanity for new soul faculties.[29]

The key event of the beginning of the age of light is Christ's second coming, but not in physical form. Steiner insists that Christ will never again take on a material body but will exist only in the atmosphere, as he did after his crucifixion. "Christ is always present," he wrote, "but He is in the spiritual world; we can reach Him if we raise ourselves into that world."[30] In Steiner's astrology the shift into the Age of Aquarius is regarded as an essential guide to the universe's spiritual evolution and hence to the individual's relationship with the cosmic whole.[31]

While never a member of the Theosophical Society, the psychologist C. G. Jung, erstwhile colleague of Sigmund Freud and the founder of analytical psychology, was certainly a theosophist in that he believed in the underlying truths revealed by all religions and followed previous ideas that the beginning of the astrological Age of Pisces around 2,000 years ago coincided with the origins of Christianity. He set out a historical philosophy in which cultural change follows shifts in the collective unconscious that, in turn, are revealed by psychic projections on to the cosmos, arguing that,

> If, as seems probable, the aeon of the fishes is ruled by the archetypal motif of the hostile brothers, then the approach of the next Platonic month, namely Aquarius, will constellate the problem of the union of opposites. It will then no longer be possible to write off evil as the mere privation of good; its real existence will have to be recognised. This problem can be recognised neither by philosophy, nor by economics, nor by politics, but only by the individual being, via his experience of the loving spirit, whose fire descended upon Joachim, one of many, and, despite all contemporary misunderstandings, was handed onward into the culture.[32]

There is no ambiguity here, but a clear statement that the development of analytical psychology was intended to serve a cosmic goal, the realization of a true Christianity, an inner one, replacing the institutional externalities of the previous two millennia, of rigid hierarchies and fixed dogma. The Heindel-Steiner-Jung view was shared by Alice Bailey and disseminated in her many books and still influential. In 1948, Bailey wrote,

> In the age into which we are now emerging, the Aquarian Age, this mode of group work will reach a very high point of development, and the world

will be saved and reconstructed *by groups* far more than by individuals. . . .
In them is vested a spirit of construction; they are the builders of the new
age. . . . They are disciples of the Christ, working consciously and frequently unconsciously for His reappearance.[33]

The notion of collective action and a utopian future continues, and, in
2003 Steve Nobel, a director of the influential group "Alternatives," based at
St. James's Church, Piccadilly, in London, eloquently paraphrased Bailey's
call for collective action to encourage the coming of the New Age.[34]

It's abundantly clear that active participation in the cosmic process is
absolutely central to New Age cosmology, and groups such as Alice Bailey's
New World Servers perform a parallel function to that of the Marxist revolutionary vanguards of the 20th century. The political implications of Esoteric
Christian New Age thought are radical, for it is assumed that the state, capi-
talist economics, and the entire fabric of modern society will pass away, or
wither in communist terminology. When this is couched in secular terms, as
it was by Cyril Fagan, a prominent Irish astrologer in the mid–20th century,
it becomes more acceptable to Eastern Theosophists and Pagans by rejecting
Christian rhetoric.[35] Fagan gave the Aquarian Age a revolutionary-utopian
quality but retained the centrality of the inner process, rather than outer
struggle. Fagan's New Age was a non-Christian version to which Pagans
could and do subscribe: In 1962, the foundation of the Wiccan Church of
Tzaddi in California was deliberately associated with the dawn of the Aquarian Age.[36]

One of the key tools for implementing the rise in self-awareness required
by the current times is astrology, which Michael York referred to as the lingua
franca of the New Age.[37] However, the astrology of the 19th century was thought
to be inadequate to the task and was in urgent need of reform. Blavatsky herself
set the tone for theosophical attitudes to astrology when she stated:

Astrology is a science *as infallible* as astronomy itself, with the condition,
however, that its interpreters must be equally infallible; and it is this condition, however, *sine qua non*, so very difficult of realization, that has always
proved a stumbling block to both. Astrology is to exact astronomy what
psychology is to exact physiology. In astrology one has to step beyond the
visible world of matter, and enter into the domain of transcendent spirit.[38]

In two sentences Blavatsky had set out a manifesto for what was to become
New Age astrology. The core argument was that astrology, as what Annie

Besant, later president of the Theosophical Society, called a "Department of the Divine Wisdom," is infallible but that astrologers, being only human, are all too fallible.[39] However, by moving beyond the realm of the visible into the transcendent, they can become, in effect, infallible. Blavatsky thus established a requirement for those astrologers with a deep commitment to the theosophical vision of New Age to condemn the fallible astrologers they saw all around them and instead set out to create an astrology that would be, as she hoped, infallible. Infallibility, though, was to lie not in prediction but in the revelation of spiritual truths.

The chief engineer of Blavatsky's new astrology was the English Eastern Theosophist Alan Leo (1860–1917). Leo concluded that astrology should abandon its predictive pretensions and focus instead on spiritual awareness. Enthused by Indian philosophy, he proclaimed that astrology makes no sense outside of the moral framework provided by the doctrines of karma and reincarnation.[40] Leo's insistence that the soul was central to astrology was to become orthodoxy among some of the most influential astrologers of the 20th century. Charles Carter, who was president of the Astrological Lodge of the Theosophical Society from 1920 to 1952 and wrote a series of standard works on the subject, gave the following statement of his views on astrology, phrased deliberately as an article of faith: "i believe, and many believe with me, that the Zodiac portrays the pathway of the soul of man and humanity."[41]

The astrology that developed in order to serve the entry into the New Age eschews all talk of prediction and instead concentrates on psychological and spiritual analysis, the assumption being that self-aware individuals alter their behavior and so change the future. The result was a shift toward relative technical simplicity but rich interpretation. Alan Oken, a follower of Alice Bailey, wrote a series of books published in the 1970s that converted theosophical precepts into precise guidelines for astrological interpretation. This is how he described the astrological sun: It represents "an individual's sense of self-integration and the structure of one's inner motivations."[42] Prepared with knowledge of one's motivations, one may then find it possible to join those who are readying for the New Age. Such an approach has proved highly popular, although most astrologers ignore the second stage, strongly advocated by Dane Rudhyar, possibly the most influential American astrologer of the 20th century, that individuation should be a prelude to submergence of the self in the cosmic whole.[43]

The pagan world also provided a means for disseminating the news of the coming of the Aquarian Age. A core text on witchcraft in the 1980s by Marian Green, whose series of books on magic have done much to spread popular paganism, considered the prospects of an improvement in the human condition, as the Piscean Age gives way to the Aquarian.[44] Later she wrote:

> A lot is happening, even in the political world. . . . This is only the start of the many changes the next couple of hundred years will bring. We could be on the verge of a true Golden Age, for the Water Bearer [i.e. Aquarius] is the Grail Carrier who has found the vessel of rebirth and brought it into the world that its redeeming waters may be poured out for all in need.[45]

To distinguish a New Age from a Pagan astrology is to talk in terms of pure types, rather than the individual preferences of those who might identify themselves as having one affiliation or the other. However, if an ideal New Age astrology deals with self-awareness and inner transformation, an ideal pagan one deals with magical ritual, intended to heal the self, or the community, through the use of astrological principles, calendar festivals, and auspicious timing.[46] Starhawk takes such notions into inner spaces, using creative visualization. Her "Moon Meditation for Facing Death" begins with advice to "imagine the dark sphere of the new moon filling your belly" and concludes with an instruction to "thank the moon in all her aspects."[47] In general, Pagan cosmology tends to emphasize ritual activity, and the concern tends to be less what zodiac sign the Moon occupies than with "drawing down the moon," the invocation of benign lunar power.[48] Ceremonial activity is focused on the eight calendar festivals that were worked into a single system in the 1950s, incorporating the summer and winter solstices, spring and autumn equinoxes, together with the Celtic quarter festivals Imbolc (2 February), Beltane (1 May), Lughnasadh (1 August), and Samhain (1 November).[49]

While the celebration of the eight festivals of the so-called Wheel of the Year is common to all pagan traditions, pagan groups tend to divide into two, depending on their source of inspiration. One group, including Druids and Wiccans, has emerged from the Western magical tradition and can trace its beliefs and practices via theosophy and Neoplatonism to the ancient Near East, in particular to Egypt.[50] The other finds its inspiration in "northern"—that is, Scandinavian and Germanic—traditions and therefore tends to emphasize Norse mythology and lay less stress on the transcendentalism of the theosophical and Platonic traditions.[51] Instead, the greater emphasis on nature may lead to an engagement, say, with ecology, and activities such as tree planting as an exercise in practical terrestrial cosmology.

While New Age cosmologies tend to emphasize the self and its reunion with the cosmos, an event that, whether individual or collective, tends to lie in the future, the pagan worldview focuses on engagement with the natural world: Cosmological concepts tend to feature World Trees, rather than communication with distant galaxies, and collective life is based on rituals that preferably occur in the outdoors. However, once we remove the key ideologists from the picture—Christian-oriented New Age millenarians on the one hand, and the leaders of certain nature-based pagan groups on the other— the differences between the two begin to disappear. Even in the case of some prominent figures, such as Starhawk, the distinctions between New Age and Pagan as emblems are negligible. Individuals may self-identify as pagan or New Age, but both are part of a single phenomenon, the privatization of spirituality in the modern West.

New Age and Pagan are both part of the same phenomenon in modern Western culture—the fragmentation of religious affiliation and privatization of spirituality. Both are emblems that describe families of spiritual practice that may be described separately in terms of their rhetoric and some leading protagonists but overlap for the majority of adherents or practitioners. We may therefore identify core features of New Age spirituality as transcendent, concerned with a future apocalypse and requiring personal transformation. Paganism, by contrast, tends to focus on nature, the present, and being true to one's self. However, as we have noted, New Agers can be concerned with nature and Pagans can emphasize transcendental realities and the coming of the New Age. It makes more sense, then, to consider the similarities between them. First, they share a rejection of mainstream, institutional Western religion and place a high value on ancient and non-Western spiritualities. Second, all New Agers and Pagans emphasize the interconnectedness of all things, including the integration of the divine with nature. There is no specifically Pagan attitude toward astrology, although certain groups, such as Wiccans, may be more predisposed to its use than others, such as Heathens, for whom most astrology, as of Near Eastern origin, is part of an alien tradition. However, all Pagans tend to share a calendrical astrology in the sense that the phases of the moon and the stages of the solar year are the cue for significant rituals. New Agers, on the other hand, have developed a distinctive astrology that rejects certain traditional activities, such as prediction, and instead prioritizes self-awareness and spiritual growth.

Notes

CHAPTER 1

1. Emile Durkheim, *The Elementary Forms of Religious Life*, trans. Karen E. Fields (New York: Free Press, 1995 [1st ed., *Les Formes élémentaires de la vie religieuse*, Paris: F. Alcan 1912]), 8.

2. Carl Sagan, "Who Speaks for Planet Earth," transcript for the final program in the "Cosmos" series, PBS (1980). http://www.cooperativeindividualism.org/sagan_cosmos_who_speaks_for_earth.html.

3. Nancy Ellen Abrams and Joel R. Primack, "Views from the Center of the Universe," in José Alberto Rubiño-Martín, Juan Antonio Belmonte, Francisco Prada, and Anxton Alberdi (eds.), *Cosmologies Across Cultures* (San Francisco: Astronomical Society of the Pacific, 2009), 13.

4. Nicholas Campion, *A History of Western Astrology*, 2 vols. (London: Continuum, 2009), vol. 1, ch. 3, 6, 16; vol. 2, ch. 12, 13.

5. Seneca, *Naturales Questiones*, trans. T. H. Corcoran, 2 2 vols. (Cambridge, MA: Harvard University Press, 1971), III.xxvii.4, 46.

6. Xiaochun Sun, "Crossing the Boundaries between Heaven and Man: Astronomy in Ancient China," in Helaine Selin (ed.), *Astronomy Across Cultures: The History of Non-Western Astronomy* (Dordrecht: Kluwer Academic Publishers, 2000), 425.

7. David Friedel, Linda Schele, and Joy Parker, *Maya Cosmos: Three Thousand Years on the Shaman's Path* (New York: Morrow, 1993), 112.

8. Anthony Aveni, *Empires of Time: Calendars, Clocks, and Cultures* (London: Tauris Parkes Paperbacks, 2000), 260.

9. Norris D. Hetherington, *The Encyclopedia of Cosmology: Historical, Philosophical and Scientific Foundations of Modern Cosmology* (New York: Garland, 1993), 116.

10. Pliny, *Natural History*, vol. 1, book 2, III, trans. H. Rackham (London: Harvard University Press, 1929), 8.

11. Hans Jonas, *The Gnostic Religion: The Message of the Alien God and the Beginnings of Christianity*, 2nd ed. (Boston: Beacon Press, 1963), 241.

12. André Jean Festugière, *Personal Religion among the Greeks* (London: Cambridge University Press, 1954).

13. See Diogenes Laertius, "Zeno" in *Lives of Eminent Philosophers*, vol. 2, trans. R. D. Hicks (London: William Heinemann, 1925), 243.

14. Denise Arnold, "Kinship as Cosmology: Potatoes as Offspring among the Aymara of Highland Bolivia," in Don McCaskill (ed.), "Amerindian Cosmology," *Canadian Journal of Native Studies and the Traditional Cosmology Society* (1988): 323.

15. William K. Powers, "Cosmology and the Reinvention of Culture: The Lakota Case," in Don McCaskill (ed.), "Amerindian Cosmology," *Canadian Journal of Native Studies and the Traditional Cosmology Society* (1988): 165.

16. Nathan Sivin, "State, Cosmos, and Body in the Last Three Centuries B.C.," *Harvard Journal of Asiatic Studies* 55, no. 1 (June 1995): 5.

17. Freya Mathews, *The Ecological Self* (Abingdon: Routledge, 1991), 109.

18. Nicholas Campion, *The Great Year: Astrology, Millenarianism and History in the Western Tradition* (London: Penguin, 1994).

19. Stephen McCluskey, "Native American Cosmologies," in Norris Hetherington (ed.), *Encyclopedia of Cosmology* (New York: Garland, 1993), 427.

20. Sivin, "State, Cosmos, and Body in the Last Three Centuries B.C.," 5–37.

21. Deborah Kaspin, "A Chewa Cosmology of the Body," *American Ethnologist* 23, no. 3 (August 1996): 561–78.

22. Mircea Eliade, *The Sacred and the Profane: The Nature of Religion* (New York: Harcourt Brace Jovanovich, 1959), 29–32.

23. Claude Lévi-Strauss, *The Raw and the Cooked: Introduction to a Science of Mythology* (London: Harper & Row, 1969), 168.

24. Claude Lévi-Strauss, *The Raw and the Cooked: Introduction to a Science of Mythology* (New York: Harper & Row, 1969).

25. C. G. Jung, *The Archetypes and the Collective Unconscious,* trans. R. F. C. Hull (London: Routledge & Kegan Paul, 1968), vol. 9, part 1 of *Collected Works.*

26. John Polkinghorne, *Faith, Science and Understanding* (London: Society for Promoting Christian Knowledge, 2000).

27. Joel Primack, "Cosmology and Culture," http://physics.ucsc.edu/cosmo/primack_abrams/COSMO.HTM, accessed 10 October 2010.

28. Jonathan Z. Smith, *Imagining Religion: From Babylon to Jonestown* (Chicago: University of Chicago Press, 1982).

29. J. G. Frazer, *The Golden Bough: A Study in Magic and Religion*, abridged edition (London: Macmillan, 1971 [1922]), I, I: 221–22.

30. Durkheim, *The Elementary Forms of Religious Life*, 41.

31. J. Milton Yinger, "A Structural Examination of Religion," *Journal for the Scientific Study of Religion* 8 (Spring 1969): 91.

32. Ninian Smart, *Dimensions of the Sacred: An Anatomy of the World's Beliefs* (Berkeley: University of California Press, 1996), 10–12.

33. Bronislaw Malinowski, *Argonauts of the Western Pacific* (New York: Dutton, 1922), 517.

34. Robert Redfield, "The Primitive World View," *Proceedings of the American Philosophical Society* 96 (1952): 30.

35. Robert Redfield, *The Primitive World and Its Transformation* (Ithaca, NY: Cornell University Press, 1953), 85.

CHAPTER 2

1. C. G. Jung, "Richard Wilhelm: In Memoriam," in *The Spirit in Man, Art, And Literature*, Collected Works, vol. 15, trans. R. F. C. Hull (London: Routledge & Kegan Paul, 1971), 53–62; see the frontispiece of Margaret Hone's influential *Modern Textbook of Astrology* (London: L. N. Fowler, 4th ed. reprinted 1973 [1951]) for an example of the use of Jung's phrase.

2. Edmund Husserl, *Ideas: General Introduction to Pure Phenomenology* (London: Collier-Macmillan, 1972) [1913, Eng. trans. 1931], 91–100.

3. Roy Willis and Patrick Curry, *Astrology, Science and Culture: Pulling Down the Moon* (Oxford: Berg, 2004).

4. Nicholas Campion, *Astrology and Popular Religion in the Modern West: Prophecy, Cosmology and the New Age Movement* (Abingdon: Ashgate, 2012).

5. Lynn Thorndike, *History of Magic and Experimental Science*, 8 vols. (New York: Columbia University Press, 1923–58); Nicholas Campion, *A History of Western Astrology*, 2 vols. (London: Continuum, 2008–9).

6. Hone, *The Modern Textbook of Astrology.*

7. Derek Walters, *Chinese Astrology: Interpreting the Revelations of the Celestial Messages* (Wellingborough: Aquarian Press, 1987).

8. Xiaochun Sun, "Crossing the Boundaries between Heaven and Man: Astronomy in Ancient China," in Helaine Selin (ed.), *Astronomy Across Cultures: The History of Non-Western Astronomy* (Dordrecht: Kluwer Academic Publishers, 2000), 425.

9. Trudy Griffin-Pierce, *Earth Is My Mother, Sky Is My Father: Space, Time and Astronomy in Navajo Sandpainting* (Albuquerque: University of New Mexico Press, 1995), 63.

10. Alexander Roob, *Alchemy and Mysticism* (London: Taschen, 1997), 8–9.

11. Alan Oken, *As Above, So Below: A Primary Guide to Astrological Awareness* (New York: Bantam Books, 1973).

12. Mircea Eliade, *The Sacred and the Profane*, 29–32.

13. Arthur O. Lovejoy, *The Great Chain of Being* (Cambridge, MA: Harvard University Press, 1936).

14. Nicholas Campion, *A History of Western Astrology*, vol. 1: *The Ancient World* (London: Continuum, 2009), esp. chaps. 4, 13.

15. C. G. Jung, "Synchronicity: An Acausal Connecting Principle," *Collected Works*, vol. 8, trans. R. F. C. Hull (London: Routledge and Kegan Paul, 1963), 417–531.

16. Henry Corbin, *Spiritual Body and Celestial Earth from Mazdean Iran to Shi'ite Iran* (Princeton, NJ: Princeton University Press, 1977); *Mundus Imaginalis, or the Imaginary and the Imaginal* (1964), http://www.hermetic.com/bey/mundus_imaginalis.htm (accessed 13 June 2011).

17. Lucien Lévi-Bruhl, *How Natives Think* (Princeton, NJ: Princeton University Press, 1985).

18. Roger Beck, *The Religion of the Mithras Cult in the Roman Empire: Mysteries of the Unconquered Sun* (Oxford: Oxford University Press, 2006), esp. chap. 8; Edgar Laird, "Christine de Pizan and Controversy Concerning Star Study in the Court of Charles V," *Culture and Cosmos*. 1, no. 2 (Winter/Autumn 1997): 35–48.

19. E. C. Krupp, "Sky Tales and Why We Tell Them," in Helaine Selin (ed.), *Astronomy Across Cultures*, 1–30.

20. Dane Rudhyar, *The Astrology of Personality* (Garden City, NY: Doubleday, 1970 [1936]), 48.

21. Claude Lévi-Strauss, *The Savage Mind* (London: Weidenfeld & Nicolson, 1972), 36; see also 42.

22. C. G. Jung, *The Archetypes and the Collective Unconscious*, *Collected Works*, vol. 9.1, trans. R. F. C. Hull (Princeton, NJ: Princeton University Press, 1959), paras. 87–110, 115.

23. C. G. Jung, "Richard Wilhelm: In Memoriam," in *The Spirit in Man, Art, and Literature*, *Collected Works*, vol. 15, trans. R. F. C. Hull (London: Routledge and Kegan Paul,

1971), 53–62. See the frontispiece of Hone's influential *Modern Textbook of Astrology* for an example of the use of Jung's phrase.

24. Anthony Aveni, "Introduction: Making Time," in Aveni (ed.), *The Sky in Mayan Literature* (Oxford: Oxford University Press, 1992), 5.

25. Nicholas Campion, *Astrology and Popular Religion*, ch. 8.

26. Krupp, "Sky Tales and Why We Tell Them," in Selin (ed.), *Astronomy Across Cultures*, 5.

27. Stephen McCluskey, "Native American Cosmologies," in Norris Hetherington (ed.), *Encyclopedia of Cosmology* (New York: Garland, 1993), 429.

28. Anthony Aveni, "Introduction: Making Time," Aveni (ed.), *The Sky in Mayan Literature* (Oxford: Oxford University Press, 1992), 4.

29. Roslynn D. Haynes, "Astronomy and the Dreaming: The Astronomy of the Aboriginal Australians," in Selin (ed.), *Astronomy Across Cultures*, 53. See also p. 56.

30. Haynes, "Astronomy and the Dreaming," 60.

31. Keith Thomas, *Religion and the Decline of Magic* (Harmondsworth: Peregrine Books, 1980 [1971]), 386–87.

32. Michael Rowlands, "The Role of Memory in the Transmission of Culture," *World Archaeology* 25, no. 2 (October 1993): 141–51.

33. Brian S. Bauer and David S.P. Dearbon, *Astronomy and Empire in the Ancient Andes* (Austin: University of Texas Press, 1995), 56, 137.

34. Michael D. Coe, *The Maya* (London: Thames and Hudson, 1984), 43–44.

35. Aveni, "Introduction: Making Time," 5.

36. Liz Greene and Howard Sasportas, *The Development of the Personality: Seminars in Psychological Astrology* (London: Arkana, 1987), xii.

37. Bartel Van der Waerden, *Science Awakening*, 2 vols., II: *The Birth of Astronomy* (Leyden: Oxford University Press, 1974), 9.

38. Bernulf Kanitscheider, "A Philosopher Looks at Astrology," *Interdisciplinary Science Reviews* 16, no. 3 (1991): 259.

39. Joseph Needham, *Science and Civilisation in China*, vol. 3: *Mathematics and the Sciences of the Heavens and Earth* (Cambridge: Cambridge University Press, 1959), 171.

40. Rodney Stark and William Simms Bainbridge, *The Future of Religion: Secularization, Revival, and Cult Formation* (Berkeley: University of California Press, 1985), 34.

41. Julius R. Bennett, "The Aquarian Age, and the Evidence of Its Inception," *Astrology* 1, no. 5 (Winter 1927): 39, 43.

42. Pamela Crane, *The Birth of Christ* (Faversham: Shoestring Publications, 1994), 24.

43. Brian Warner, "Traditional Astronomical Knowledge in Africa," in Christopher Walker (ed.), *Astronomy Before the Telescope* (London; British Museum Press, 1996), 306.

44. Steven Kemper, "Time, Person, and Gender in Sinhalese Astrology," *American Ethnologist* 7, no. 4 (November 1980): 744–58.

45. Nicholas Campion, *Astrology and Popular Religion in the Modern West*, ch. 14.

46. Emile Durkheim, *The Elementary Forms of Religious Life*, trans. Karen E. Fields (New York: The Free Press, 1995 [1912]), 41.

47. J. G. Frazer, *The Golden Bough: A Study in Magic and Relgion*, abridged edition (London: Macmillan, 1971 [1922]), I, I: 221–22.

48. J. Milton Yinger, "A Structural Examination of Religion," *Journal for the Scientific Study of Religion* 8 (Spring 1969): 91.

CHAPTER 3

1. Jane Goodale, *Tiwi Wives: A Study of the Women of Melville Island, Seattle and London* (Seattle: University of Washington Press, 1971), 146, cited in Chris Knight, *Blood Relations: Menstruation and the Origins of Culture* (New Haven, CT: Yale University Press, 1991), 358.

2. Raymond Haynes, Roslynn Haynes, David Malin, and Richard McGee, *Explorers of the Southern Sky: A History of Australian Astronomy* (Cambridge: Cambridge University Press, 1996), 7; Roslynn D. Haynes, "Astronomy and the Dreaming: The Astronomy of the Aboriginal Australians," in Helaine Selin (ed.), *Astronomy Across Cultures: The History of Non-Western Astronomy* (Dordrecht: Kluwer Academic Publishers, 2000), 53.

3. Hugh Cairns, "Aboriginal Sky-Mapping? Possible Astronomical Interpretation of Australian Aboriginal Ethnographic and Archaeological Material," in Clive Ruggles (ed.), *Archaeoastronomy in the 1990s* (Loughborough: Group D Publications, 1993), 143.

4. Haynes, "Astronomy and the Dreaming," 53.

5. See for example Hugh Cairns, *Dark Sparklers, Yidumduma's Wardaman Aboriginal Astrology, North Australia, 2003* (Merimbula: C. C. Cairns, 2003). See also the Australian Aboriginal Astronomy Project at Macquarie University at http://www.atnf.csiro.au/research/AboriginalAstronomy/index.html (accessed 4 July 2011).

6. Isobel White, "Sexual Conquest and Submission in the Myths of Central Australia," in L. R. Hiatt (ed.), *Australian Aboriginal Mythology* (Canberra: Australian Institute of Aboriginal Studies, 1975), 126.

7. Douglass Price-Williams and Rosslyn Gaines, "The Dreamtime and Dreams of Northern Australian Aboriginal Artists," *Ethos* 22, no. 3 (September, 1994), 383.

8. Bruce Chatwin, *The Songlines* (London: Picador, 1988), 2.

9. Price-Williams and Gaines, "The Dreamtime and Dreams of Northern Australian Aboriginal Artists," 373–88.

10. Patrick Wolfe, "On Being Woken Up: The Dreamtime in Anthropology and in Australian Settler Culture," *Comparative Studies in Society and History* 33, no. 2 (1991): 197–224.

11. Peter MacPherson, "Astronomy of the Australian Aborigines," *Journal and Proceedings of the Royal Society of New South Wales* 15: 71–72.

12. Haynes, "Astronomy and the Dreaming," 56.

13. R. D. Haynes, "Aboriginal Astronomy," *Australian Journal of Astronomy* 4, no. 3 (1992): 134.

14. Ibid., 133–34.

15. Ibid., 135–38.

16. Dianne Johnson, "Interpretations of the Pleiades in Australian Aboriginal Astronomies," in *Building Bridges Between Cultures*, Ninth "Oxford" International Symposium on Archaeoastronomy, Lima, January 2011 (Cambridge: Cambridge University Press, 2011), forthcoming.

17. Haynes, "Aboriginal Astronomy," 130.

18. Haynes, "Astronomy and the Dreaming," 56.

19. Duane Hamacher and Ray Norris, "Australian Aboriginal Astronomy: Transient Celestial Phenomena," in *Building Bridges Between Cultures*, Ninth 'Oxford' International Symposium on Archaeoastronomy, Lima, January 2011 (Cambridge: Cambridge University Press, 2011), forthcoming.

20. Goodale, *Tiwi Wives*, 146, cited in Knight, *Blood Relations*, 358.

21. Cairns, "Aboriginal Sky-Mapping?," 149.

CHAPTER 4

1. Martha Beckwith, *Hawaiian Mythology* (Honolulu: University of Hawaii Press, 1970), 44.

2. Patrick Vinton Kirch, *On the Road of the Winds: An Archaeological History of the Pacific Islands before European Contact* (Berkeley: University of California Press, 2000).

3. D. Lewis, "Voyaging Stars: Aspects of Polynesian and Micronesian Astronomy," *Philosophical Transactions of the Royal Society of London. Series A, Mathematical and Physical Sciences* 276, no. 1257: *The Place of Astronomy in the Ancient World* (May 2, 1974): 133–48.

4. Ben R. Finney, *Pacific Navigation and Voyaging* (Honolulu: Bishop Museum Press, 2003); David Lewis, *The Voyaging Stars: Secrets of the Pacific Island Navigators* (Sydney: William L. Collins Publishers, 1978), and *We, the Navigators: The Ancient Art of Landfinding in the Pacific* (Honolulu: University of Hawaii Press, 1994).

5. Clive Ruggles, "Cosmology, Calendar and Temple Orientations in Ancient Hawai'i," in Clive Ruggles and Gary Urton (eds.), *Skywatching in the Ancient World: New Perspectives in Cultural Astronomy* (Boulder: University Press of Colorado, 2007), 293.

6. W. Bruce Masse, "The Celestial Engine at the Heart of Traditional Hawaiian Culture," in Nicholas Campion, Barbara Rappenglück, and Michael Rappenglück (eds.), *Astronomy and Power: How Worlds Are Structured* (with Barbara Rappenglück and Michael Rappenglück) (Oxford: British Archaeology Reports, 2011, forthcoming).

7. Robert Williamson, *Religious and Cosmic Beliefs of Central Polynesia*, 2 vols. (Cambridge: Cambridge University Press, 1933); Maud Worcester Makemson, *The Morning Star Rises: An Account of Polynesian Astronomy* (New Haven, CT: Yale University Press, 1941); Rubellite Kawena Johnson and John Kaipo Mahelona, *Na Inoa Hoku: A Catalogue of Hawaiian and Pacific Star Names* (Honolulu: Topgallant Publishing Co., 1975).

8. Martha Beckwith, *Hawaiian Mythology* (Honolulu: University of Hawaii Press, 1970); W. Bruce Masse, Rubellite Kawena Johnson, and H. David Tuggle, *Islands in the Sky: Traditional Astronomy and the Role of Celestial Phenomena in Hawaiian Myth, Language, Religion and Chiefly Power* (Honolulu: University of Hawaii Press, forthcoming).

9. Elsdon Best, *The Astronomical Knowledge of the Maori, Genuine and Empirical, Including Data Concerning Their Systems of Astrogeny, Astrolatory and Natural Astrology, with Notes on Certain Other Natural Phenomena* (Wellington: Dominion Museum, 1955 [1922]).

10. Beckwith, *Hawaiian Mythology*, 43.

11. W. Bruce Masse, Elizabeth Wayland Barber, Luigi Piccardi, and Paul T. Barber, *Exploring the Nature of Myth and Its Role in Science*, in Luigi Piccardi and W. Bruce Masse (eds.), *Myth and Geology*, no. 273 (London: The Geological Society, 2007).

12. Beckwith, *Hawaiian Mythology*, 42–43.

13. Ibid., 44.

14. Williamson, *Religious and Cosmic Beliefs*, vol. 1, 155.

15. Lewis, "Voyaging Stars": 133–48.

16. See the summary in Michael E. Chauvin, "Useful and Conceptual Astronomy in Ancient Hawaii," in Helaine Selin (ed.), *Astronomy Across Cultures: The History of Non-*

Western Astronomy (Dordrecht: Kluwer Academic Publishers, 2000), 117–22. See also William Liller, "Celestial Happenings on Easter Island: AD 760–837," *Archaeoastronomy: The Journal of the Centre for Archaeoastronomy* 9, nos. 1–4 (1986): 52–58, and "The Megalithic Astronomy of Easter Island: Orientations of Ahu and Moai," *Archaeoastronomy: Supplement to the Journal for the History of Astronomy*, no. 13 (1989): S21–S48.

17. Ruggles, "Cosmology, Calendar and Temple Orientations," 310.

18. Edmundo Edwards, "The 'Megalithic' Astronomy of Easter Island: A Reassessment," *Journal of the History of Astronomy* 38, no. 5 (2005): xxx; Edmundo Edwards, "The Polynesian Ritual Cycle of Activities and Their Archaeological Markers in Eastern Polynesia," in Clive Ruggles (ed.), *Proceedings of the Oxford IX International Symposium on Archaeoastronomy* (Cambridge: Cambridge University Press, 2011, forthcoming).

19. See W. Bruce Masse, "The Celestial Engine at the Heart of Traditional Hawaiian Culture."

20. Chauvin, "Useful and Conceptual Astronomy," 98.

21. Best, *The Astronomical Knowledge of the Maori*, 68.

22. Chauvin, "Useful and Conceptual Astronomy," 116.

23. Malcolm Clark, "Sun, Moon and Volcanoes on Easter Island," *Second International Congress on Easter Island and East Polynesia* (Santiago: University of Chile Press, 1998).

24. Best, *The Astronomical Knowledge of the Maori*, 6.

25. Ibid., 19.

26. Ibid., 68.

27. Cited in Wayne Orchiston, "A Polynesian Astronomical Perspective: The Maori of New Zealand," in Selin (ed.), *Astronomy Across Cultures*, 175.

28. Best, *The Astronomical Knowledge of the Maori*, 6.

29. John White, *The Ancient History of the Maori, His Mythology and Traditions*, vol. 1 (Wellington: Government Printer, 1887), 115.

CHAPTER 5

1. Von Del Chamberlain, "The Algonquin Song of the Stars," http://www.clarkfoundation.org/astro-utah/vondel/songofstars.html (accessed 11 September 2010).

2. For doubt on the supposed difference between Native American and English concepts of time, for example, see Thomas McElwain, "Seneca Iroquois Concepts of Time," in Don McCaskill, "Amerindian Cosmology," *Canadian Journal of Native Studies and the Traditional Cosmology Society* (1988): 265–77.

3. Anthony Aveni (ed.), *Native American Astronomy* (Austin: University of Texas Press, 1975); Von Del Chamberlain, *When Stars Came Down to Earth: Cosmology of the Skidi Pawnee Indians of North America* (Los Altos, CA: Ballena Press, 1982); Jerry H. Gill, *Native American Worldviews: An Introduction* (Amherst, NY: Humanity Books, 2002); Trudy Griffin-Pierce, *Earth Is My Mother, Sky Is My Father: Space, Time and Astronomy in Navajo Sandpainting* (Albuquerque: University of New Mexico Press, 1995); Dennis Tedlock and Barbara Tedlock (eds.), *Teachings from the American Earth: Indian Religion and Philosophy* (New York: Liveright, 1975); Ray A. Williamson, *Living the Sky: The Cosmos of the American Indian* (Norman: University of Oklahoma Press, 1987); and Ray A. Williamson and Claire R. Farrer (eds.), *Earth and Sky: Visions of the Cosmos in Native American Folklore* (Albuquerque: University of New Mexico Press, 1992).

4. J. McKim Malville, *Guide to Prehistoric Astronomy in the Southwest* (Boulder, CO: Johnson Books, 2008).

5. Stephen McCluskey, "Native American Cosmologies," in Norris Hetherington (ed.), *Encyclopedia of Cosmology* (New York: Garland, 1993), 427.

6. Ibid., 427.

7. Alice C. Fletcher, "Pawnee Star Lore," *The Journal of American Folklore* 16, no. 60 (January–March 1903): 10–15.

8. Peter Nabakov, *A Forest of Time: American Indian Ways of History* (Cambridge: Cambridge University Press, 2002), 43.

9. William B. Gibbon, "Asiatic Parallels in North American Star Lore: Ursa Major," *Journal of American Folklore* 77 (1964): 236–50; Owen Gingerich, *The Great Copernicus Chase and Other Adventures in Astronomical History* (Cambridge: Cambridge University Press, 1992), 10.

10. Roslyn Frank, "Hunting the European Sky Bears: A Proto-European Vision Quest to the End of the Earth," in John W. Fountain and Rolf M. Sinclair (eds.), *Current Studies in Archaeoastronomy: Conversations Across Time and Space* (Durham, NC: Carolina Academic Press, 2005), 455–74.

11. Gibbon, "Asiatic Parallels in North American Star Lore," 237.

12. Charles G. Leland, *The Algonquin Legends of New England or Myths and Folklore of the Micmac, Passmaquoddy, and Penobscot Tribes* (Boston: Houghton Mifflin Harcourt, 1884).

13. Chamberlain, "The Algonquin Song of the Stars."

14. Gibbon, "Asiatic Parallels," 236–37.

15. Chamberlain, *When Stars Came Down to Earth*, 129.

16. For insight into the issues see William K. Powers, "Cosmology and the Reinvention of Culture: The Lakota Case," in McCaskill, "Amerindian Cosmology," 165–80, esp. 177, and the discussion in Benjamin Lee Whorf, "An American Model of the Universe," in Tedlock and Tedlock (eds.), *Teachings from the American Earth*, 121–29.

17. Harold Courlander, *The Fourth World of the Hopis* (Albuquerque: University of New Mexico Press, 1971), 17.

18. Griffin-Pierce, *Earth Is My Mother, Sky Is My Father*, 63.

19. Chamberlain, *When Stars Came Down to Earth*.

20. Fletcher, "Pawnee Star Lore"; see also Alice C. Fletcher, "Star Cult among the Pawnee—A Preliminary Report," *American Anthropologist*, New Series 4, no. 4 (October–December 1902): 730–36.

21. M. Jane Young, *Signs from the Ancestors: Zuni Cultural Symbolism and Perceptions of Rock Art* (Albuquerque: University of New Mexico Press, 1988), 95–103.

22. Fletcher, "Pawnee Star Lore," 11.

23. Melburn D. Thurman, "The Timing of the Skidi-Pawnee Morning Star Sacrifice," *Ethnohistory* 30, no. 3 (Summer 1983): 155–63.

24. R. Campbell Thompson, *The Reports of the Magicians and Astrologers of Nineveh and Babylon in the British Museum*, 2 vols. (London: Luzac and Co., 1900), 176.

25. Fletcher, "Pawnee Star Lore," 11.

26. Joseph Brown and Emily Cousins, *Teaching Spirits: Understanding Native American Religious Traditions* (Oxford: Oxford University Press, 2001), 11.

27. Tedlock and Tedlock (eds.), *Teachings from the American Earth*, 215–16.

28. Ingrid van Dooren, "Navajo Hohgan and Navajo Cosmos," in McCaskill, "Amerindian Cosmology," 260–62.

29. Julian H. Steward, "Notes on Hopi Ceremonies in their Initiatory Form in 1927–8," *American Anthropologist*, New Series, 33, no. 1 (January–March 1931): 56–79.

30. Steward, "Hopi Ceremonies," 59.

31. Ibid., 60.

32. Claire Farrer, "Star Clocks: Mescalero Apache Ceremonial Timing," in McCaskill, "Amerindian Cosmology," 235.

33. Gill, *Native American Worldviews*, 17.

34. Ralph N. Buckstaff, "Stars and Constellations of a Pawnee Sky Map," *American Anthropologist*, New Series, 29, no. 2 (April 1927): 279–85; Patricia O'Brien, "Prehistoric Evidence for Pawnee Cosmology," *American Anthropologist*, New Series, 88, no. 4 (December 1986): 939–46.

35. John A. Eddy, "Medicine Wheels and Plains Indians Astronomy," in Anthony Aveni (ed.), *Native American Astronomy* (Austin: University of Texas Press, 1975), 149–53.

36. Malville, *Prehistoric Astronomy in the Southwest*, 60–64.

CHAPTER 6

1. Description of an Inca sun-ceremony in Sabine MacCormack, *Religion in the Andes: Vision and Imagination in Early Colonial Peru* (Princeton, NJ: Princeton University Press, 1991), 75–76.

2. Anthony Aveni, *Skywatchers of Ancient Mexico* (Austin: University of Texas Press, 1980); Aveni, *The Sky in Mayan Literature* (Oxford: Oxford University Press, 1992); Aveni, *Empires of Time: Calendars, Clocks, and Cultures* (London: Tauris Parkes Paperbacks, 2000); David Friedel, Linda Schele, and Joy Parker, *Maya Cosmos: Three Thousand Years on the Shaman's Path* (New York: Morrow, 1993); Susan Milbrath, *Star Gods of the Maya: Astronomy in Art, Folklore, and Calendars* (Austin: University of Texas Press, 1994); Don McCaskill (ed.), "Amerindian Cosmology," *Canadian Journal of Native Studies and the Traditional Cosmology Society* (1988); Brian S. Bauer and David S.P. Dearbon, *Astronomy and Empire in the Ancient Andes* (Austin: University of Texas Press, 1995); Gary Urton, *At the Crossroads of the Earth and the Sky: An Andean Cosmology*, Latin American Monographs, no. 55 (Austin: University of Texas Press, 1981); Gerardo Reichel-Dolmatoff, *Amazonian Cosmos: The Sexual and Religious Symbolism of the Tukano Indians* (Chicago: University of Chicago Press, 1971).

3. Martti Pärssinen, Denise Schaan, and Alceu Ranzi, "Pre-Columbian Geometric Earthworks in the Upper Purús: A Complex Society in Western Amazonia," *Antiquity* 83, no. 322 (December 2009): 1084–96.

4. D. Stuart and S. Houston, "Maya Writing," *Scientific American* (August 1989): 82–89.

5. Dennis Tedlock (trans.), *Popul Vuh* (London: Simon and Schuster, 1996), 64.

6. Barbara Tedlock, *Time and Highland Maya* (Albuquerque: University of New Mexico Press, 1992), 173–78.

7. Tedlock (trans.), *Popul Vuh*, 63–64.

8. Ibid.

9. For Maya astronomy see Friedel, Schele, and Parker, *Maya Cosmos*, 75–112.

10. David Carrasco, *Quetzalcoatl and the Irony of Empire: Myths and Prophecies in the Aztec Tradition* (Chicago: University of Chicago Press, 1982).

11. Aveni, *Skywatchers of Ancient Mexico*, 364–65.

12. Urton, *At the Crossroads of the Earth and the Sky*, 119.

13. Bauer and Dearbon, *Astronomy and Empire*, 138–39.

14. Reichel-Dolmatoff, *Amazonian Cosmos*, 73.

15. Elizabeth Reichel, "The Eco-Politics of Yakuna and Tanimuka Cosmology (Northwest Amazon, Colombia)" (PhD Thesis, Cornell University, 1997).

16. John Bierhorst, *The Mythology of South America* (New York: Morrow, 1988), 32–33.

17. Stephen McCluskey, "Native American Cosmologies," in Norris Hetherington (ed.), *Encyclopedia of Cosmology* (New York: Garland, 1993), 427.

18. Anthony Aveni, "Introduction: Making Time," in Aveni (ed.), *The Sky in Mayan Literature* (Oxford: Oxford University Press, 1992), 4.

19. Michael Coe, *The Maya*, 3rd edition (London: Thames and Hudson, 1984), 154.

20. Aveni, *Empires of Time*, 219.

21. Aveni, "Introduction: Making Time," 5.

22. Miguel León-Portilla (ed.), *The Broken Spears: The Aztec Account of the Conquest of Mexico* (Boston: Beacon Press, 1992), 7.

23. Aveni, "Introduction: Making Time," 4.

24. Ibid., 4–5.

25. Ibid., 7.

26. Bauer and Dearbon, *Astronomy and Empire*, 54–56.

27. Eric Thompson, *A Commentary on the Dresden Codex* (Philadelphia: American Philosophical Society, 1972), 62–71.

28. Coe, *The Maya*, 43; Vincent H. Malmstrom, "Origin of the Mesoamerican 260-Day Calendar," *Science* 181 (1973): 939–41.

29. See Mary Miller and Karl Taube, *The Gods and Symbols of Ancient Mexico and the Maya: An Illustrated Dictionary of the Mesoamerican Religion* (London: Thames and Hudson, 1993), for a list of the Aztec and Maya names. See also Aveni, *Empires of Time*, 191–203; Sharon L. Gibbs, "Mesoamerican Calendrics as Evidence of Astronomical Activity," in Aveni (ed.), *Native American Astronomy*, 21–35; Sylvanus Morley, *An Introduction to the Study of Maya Hieroglyphics* (New York: Dover Publications, 1975), 37–51; and Tedlock (trans.), *Popul Vuh*, 205–6.

30. Coe, *The Maya*, 43–44; for a Western adaptation see Ariel Spilsbury and Michael Bryner, *The Mayan Oracle: Return Path to the Stars* (Rochester, VT: Bear and Company, 1992).

31. José Arguelles, *The Mayan Factor: Path Beyond Technology* (Santa Fe: Bear and Company, 1987).

32. John W. Hoopes, "Mayanism Comes of (New) Age," in Joseph Gelfer (ed.), *2012: Decoding the Counterculture Apocalypse* (London: Equinox Publishing, 2011); Mark Van Stone, *2012: Science and Prophecy of the Ancient Maya* (San Diego: Tlacaélel Press, 2010).

33. John B. Carlson, "Venus-Regulated Warfare and Ritual Sacrifice in Mesoamerica," in Clive L.N. Ruggles and Nicholas J. Saunders (eds.), *Astronomies and Cultures* (Niwot: University Press of Colorado, 1993), 202–52.

34. For the Aztec ritual year see Aveni, *Empires of Time*, 255–73; and Richard Townsend, *The Aztecs* (London: Thames and Hudson, 1992), 212–15.

35. Sabine MacCormack, *Religion in the Andes: Vision and Imagination in Early Colonial Peru* (Princeton, NJ: Princeton University Press, 1991), 75–76.

36. Ivan Šprajc, "The Venus-Rain-Maize Complex in the Mesoamerican World View," *Journal for the History of Astronomy* 24 (1993): 17–70.

37. For sacred space in Aztec culture see Townsend, *The Aztecs*, 129–54.

38. See Ivan Šprajc, "More on Mesoamerican Cosmology and City Plans," *Latin American Antiquity*, vol. 16, no. 2 (Jun. 2005): 209–16. For criticism of the astronomical hypothesis, see Michael E. Smith, "Did the Maya Build Architectural Cosmograms?," *Latin American Antiquity* 16, no. 2 (June 2005): 217–24.

39. Ivan Šprajc, "Astronomical Alignments at Teotihuacan, Mexico," *Latin American Antiquity* 11, no. 4 (June 2005): 403–15; Saburo Sugiyama, "Teotihuacan City Layout as a Cosmogram: Preliminary Results of the 2007 Measurement Unity Study," in Iain Morley and Colin Renfrew (eds.), *The Archaeology of Measurement: Comprehending Heaven, Earth and Time in Ancient Societies* (Cambridge: Cambridge University Press, 2010), 111–49.

40. Bauer and Dearbon, *Astronomy and Empire in the Ancient Andes*, 67–100.

41. Brian Bauer, *The Sacred Landscape of the Inca: The Cusco Ceque System* (Austin: University of Texas Press, 1998).

CHAPTER 7

1. Basuto prayer displaying possible Christian influence, cited in Dominique Zahan, *The Religion, Spirituality and Thought of Traditional Africa* (Chicago: University of Chicago Press, 1979), 49.

2. Ibid., 87–89.

3. James Denbow, "Heart and Soul: Glimpses of Ideology and Cosmology in the Iconography of Tombstones from the Loango Coast of Central Africa," *The Journal of American Folklore*, vol. 112, no. 445: "Theorizing the Hybrid" (Summer 1999): 404–23.

4. Keith Snedegar, "Astronomical Practices in Africa South of the Sahara," in Helaine Selin (ed.), *Astronomy Across Cultures: The History of Non-Western Astronomy* (Dordrecht: Kluwer Academic Publishers, 2000), 455. See also Maxwell Owusu, "Ethnography of Africa: The Usefulness of the Useless," *American Anthropologist*, New Series, 80, no. 2 (June 1978), 310–34.

5. Denbow, "Heart and Soul," 404.

6. Clive Ruggles, "The Borana Calendar: Some Observations," *Archaeoastronomy, Supplement to the Journal for the History of Astronomy*, no. 11 (1987): S50–51.

7. Jarita Holbrook, Rodney Medupe, and Johnson Urama (eds.), *African Cultural Astronomy: Current Archaoeastronomy and Ethnoastronomy Research in Africa* (Amsterdam: Springer Verlag, Astrophysics and Space Science Proceedings, 2008).

8. http://www.saao.ac.za/~wgssa/archive/as11/as11_web.pdf, accessed 4 March 2011.

9. John S. Mbiti, *African Religions and Philosophy*, 2nd edition, revised (London: Heinemann, 2008).

10. Allen F. Roberts, "'Comets Importing Change of Times and States': Ephemerae and Process among the Tabwa of Zaire," *American Ethnologist* 9, no. 4: Symbolism and Cognition LL (November 1982): 712.

11. Owusu, "Ethnography of Africa," 312.

12. Jacquetta Hawkes, *Man and the Sun* (London: Cresset Press, 1962), 47–48.

13. Alexander Marshak, "Lunar Notation on Upper Palaeolithic Remains," *Science* 146 (1964): 743–45.

14. Zahan, *The Religion, Spirituality and Thought of Traditional Africa*, 3.

15. Lucien Lévi-Bruhl, *How Natives Think* (Princeton, NJ: Princeton University Press, 1985).

16. Mbiti, *African Religions and Philosophy*, 19.

17. Ibid.

18. Michael Dietler and Ingrid Herbich, "Living on Luo Time: Reckoning Sequence, Duration, History and Biography in a Rural African Society," *World Archaeology* 25, no. 2: Conceptions of Time and Ancient Society (October 1993): 250.

19. Dietler and Herbich, "Living on Luo Time," 254.

20. Brian Warner, "Traditional Astronomical Knowledge in Africa," in Christopher Walker (ed.), *Astronomy Before the Telescope* (London: British Museum Press, 1996), 306.

21. Mbiti, *African Religions and Philosophy*, 20.

22. Dafon Aimé Ségla, "The Cosmological Vision of the Yoruba-Idaacha of Benin Republic (West Africa): A Light on Yoruba History and Culture," in Holbrook, Medupe, and Urama (eds.), *African Cultural Astronomy*, 189–207.

23. Asmarom Legesse, *Gada: Three Approaches to the Study of African Society* (London: Collier-Macmillan, 1973).

24. Marco Bassi, "On the Borana Calendrical System: A Preliminary Field Report," *Current Anthropology* 29, no. 4 (August–October 1988): 619–24; Laurance R. Doyle, "The Borana Calendar Reinterpreted," *Current Anthropology* 27, no. 3 (June 1986): 286–87; Dietrick Thomsen, "What Mean These African Stones?," *Science News* 126, no. 11 (September 15, 1984): 168–69, 174.

25. Ruggles, "The Borana Calendar," S35–S53; David Turton et al., "Agreeing to Disagree: The Measurement of Duration in a Southwestern Ethiopian Community [and Comments and Reply]," *Current Anthropology* 19, no. 3 (September 1987): 585–600.

26. Robert Temple, *The Sirius Mystery* (London: Sidgwick and Jackson, 1976).

27. Walter E.A. van Beek, "Haunting Griaule: Experiences from the Restudy of the Dogon," *History in Africa* 31 (2004): 43–68.

28. Deborah Kaspin, "A Chewa Cosmology of the Body," *American Ethnologist* 23, no. 3 (August 1996): 566.

29. Lorna A. Marshall, "Kung Bushman Religious Beliefs," *Africa: Journal of the International African Institute* 32, no. 3 (July 1962): 148.

30. Barth Chukwuezi, "The Relationship Between Human Destiny and the Cosmic Forces—A Study of the IGBO Worldview," in Holbrook, Medupe, and Urama (eds.), *African Cultural Astronomy*, 211.

31. R. J. McIntosh, *Ancient Middle Niger: Urbanism and the Self-Organizing Landscape* (Cambridge: Cambridge University Press, 2005).

32. Damian U. Opata, "Cultural Astronomy in the Lore and Literature of Africa," in Holbrook, Medupe, and Urama (eds.), *African Cultural Astronomy*, 218–19.

33. Dafon Aimé Ségla, "The Cosmological Vision of the Yoruba-Idaacha of Benin Republic (West Africa): A Light on Yoruba History and Culture," in Holbrook, Medupe, and Urama (eds.), *African Cultural Astronomy*, 193.

34. Chukwuezi, "The Relationship Between Human Destiny and the Cosmic Forces," 211.

35. Peter Morton-Williams, "An Outline of the Cosmology and Cult Organisation of the Oyo Yoruba," *Africa: Journal of the International African Institute* 34, no. 3 (July 1964): 243–61.

36. J. C. Hollmann, "'The Sky's Things': |xam Bushman '*Astrological Mythology*' as recorded in the Bleek and Lloyd Manuscripts', in African Skies, Proceedings of the African Astronomical History Symposium held in Cape Town on 8 & 9 November 2005, 7–12.

37. Marshall, "Kung Bushman Religious Beliefs," 221.

38. Snedegar, "Astronomical Practices in Africa South of the Sahara," 460.

39. J. McKim Malville, Fred Wendorf, A. A. Mazaar, and Romauld Schild, "Megaliths and Neolithic Astronomy in Southern Egypt," *Nature* 392 (1988): 488–91.

40. Suzanne Blier, *The Anatomy of Architecture: Ontology and Metaphor in Batammaliba Architectural Expression* (Cambridge: Cambridge University Press, 1987). See also the summary in Snedegar, "Astronomical Practices in Africa South of the Sahara," 455–74.

41. Chukwuezi, "The Relationship Between Human Destiny and the Cosmic Forces," 214.

42. Eric Ten Raa, "The Moon as a Symbol of Life and Fertility in Sandawe Thought," *Africa: Journal of the International African Institute* 39, no. 1 (January 1969): 24.

43. Warner, "Traditional Astronomical Knowledge in Africa," 312–13; Allen F. Roberts, "Comets Importing Change of Times and States," 712–29.

44. John Anenechukwu, *After God Is Dibia: Igbo Cosmology, Healing, Divination of Sacred Science in Nigeria*, 2 vols. (London: Karnak, 1999), 43, cited in Damian Opata, "Cultural Astronomy in the Lore and Literature of Africa," in Holbrook, Medupe, and Urama (eds.), *African Cultural Astronomy*, 217–29.

45. Dietler and Herbich, "Living on Luo Time," 250.

46. Snedegar, "Astronomical Practices in Africa South of the Sahara," 469.

47. Peter Morton-Williams, William Bascom, and E. M. McClelland, "Two Studies of Ifa Divination. Introduction: The Mode of Divination," *Africa: Journal of the International African Institute* 36, no. 4 (October 1966): 406–31.

48. Christel Mattheeuws, "Towards an Anthropology in Life: The Astrological Archiecture of Zanandroandrea Land in West Bezanozano, Madagascar" (PhD Thesis, University of Aberdeen, 2008), 70.

49. Wim Binsbergen, "Regional and Historical Connections of Four-Tablet Divination in Southern Africa," *Africa: Journal of Religion in Africa* 26, fasc. 1 (February 1996): 19.

50. Muusa H.I. Galaal, *Stars, Seasons and Weather in Somali Pastoral Tradition* (Niamey: Celhto, 1992), 10.

51. Snedegar, "Astronomical Practices in Africa South of the Sahara," 455–74.

52. Galaal, *Stars, Seasons and Weather in Somali Pastoral Tradition*, 25.

53. Warner, "Traditional Astronomical Knowledge in Africa," 313.

54. Deborah Kaspin, "A Chewa Cosmology of the Body," *American Ethnologist* 23, no. 3 (August 1996): 561–78.

55. Christopher C. Fennell, *Crossroads and Cosmologies: Diasporas and Ethnogenesis in the New World* (Gainsville: University Press of Florida, 2007), esp. 68–95.

56. Zahan, *The Religion, Spirituality and Thought of Traditional Africa*, 87–89.

CHAPTER 8

1. Samuel Mercer, *The Pyramid Texts* (New York: Longmans Green, 1952), utterance 44.

2. Erik Hornung, *The Secret Lore of Egypt: Its Impact on the West*, trans. David Lorton (Ithaca, NY: Cornell University Press, 2001).

3. Otto Neugebauer and R. A. Parker, *Egyptian Astronomical Texts* (Providence, RI: Brown University Press, 1960).

4. E. A. Wallis Budge, *The Book of the Dead* (London: Kegan Paul, 1899); O. R. Faulkner, *The Book of the Dead* (London: British Museum Publications, 1985) and *The Ancient Egyptian Coffin Texts*, Vol. 1, spells 1–354, Vol. 2, spells 355–787, vol. 3, spells 788–1186 (Warminster: Aris and Phillips, 1973); Thomas G. Urban, *The Egyptian Book of the Dead: Documents in the Oriental Institute Museum at the University of Chicago* (Chicago: University of Chicago Press, 1960); Mercer, *The Pyramid Texts*.

5. Marshall Clagett, *Ancient Egyptian Science: A Sourcebook, Vol. 2: Calendars, Clocks and Astronomy* (Philadelphia: American Philosophical Society, 1995).

6. R. A. Parker, "Egyptian Astronomy, Astrology and Calendrical Reckoning," in Charles Coulston (ed.), *Dictionary of Scientific Biography* (New York: Charles Scribner's Sons, 1970), 706–27, and "Ancient Egyptian Astronomy," *Philosophical Transactions of the Royal Society of London*, Series A, Mathematical and Physical Sciences, vol. 276, no. 1257: The Place of Astronomy in the Ancient World" (May 2, 1974): 51–65.

7. Otto Neugebauer, *A History of Ancient Mathematical Astronomy* (Berlin: Springer Verlag, 1975), II, 559–66; Gregg de Young, "Astronomy in Ancient Egypt" in Helaine Selin (ed.), *Astronomy Across Cultures: The History of Non-Western Astronomy* (Dordrecht: Kluwer Academic Publishers, 2000), 480–82; Kurt Locher, "Egyptian Cosmology," in Norris Hetherington (ed.), *Encyclopedia of Cosmology* (New York: Garland, 1993), 189–94; Ronald A. Wells, "Astronomy in Egypt," in Christopher Walker (ed.), *Astronomy Before the Telescope* (London: British Museum Press, 1996), 34.

8. Juan Antonio Belmonte and Mosalem Shaltout (eds.), *In Search of Cosmic Order: Selected Essays on Egyptian Archaeoastronomy* (Cairo: Supreme Council of Antiquities Press, 2009).

9. Jan Assmann, *The Mind of Egypt: History and Meaning in the Time of the Pharaohs*, trans. Andrew Jenkins (New York: Metropolitan Books, 2002); Stephen Quirke, *The Cult of Ra: Sun-worship in Ancient Egypt* (London: Thames and Hudson, 2001); Siegfried Morenz, *Egyptian Religion* (Ithaca, NY: Cornell University Press, 1992); Byron Shafer (ed.), *Religion in Ancient Egypt* (Ithaca, NY: Cornell University Press, 1991); Louis Žabkar, *A Study of the Ba Concept in Ancient Egyptian Texts*, Studies in Ancient Oriental Civilization 34 (Chicago: University of Chicago Press, 1968).

10. Jeremy Naydler, *Temple of the Cosmos: The Ancient Egyptian Experience of the Sacred* (Rochester, VT: Inner Traditions, 1996) and *Shamanic Wisdom in the Pyramid Texts: The Mystical Tradition of Ancient Egypt* (Rochester, VT: Inner Traditions, 2005).

11. Assmann, *The Mind of Egypt*, esp. 204–7.

12. Plutarch, "Isis and Osiris," *Moralia*, Vol. 5, trans. F. C. Babbit (Cambridge, MA: Harvard University Press, 1936).

13. Leonard H. Lesko, "Ancient Egyptian Cosmogonies and Cosmology" in Shafer (ed.), *Religion in Ancient Egypt*, 88–122; Morenz, *Egyptian Religion*, 159–82, J. M. Plumley, "The Cosmology of Ancient Egypt," in Carmen Blacker and Michael Loewe, *Ancient Cosmologies* (London: George Allen and Unwin Ltd., 1975), 17–41.

14. Mark S. Smith, "Democratization of the Afterlife," in Jacco Dieleman and Willeke Wendrich (eds.), *UCLA Encyclopedia of Egyptology* (Los Angeles, 2009), 1–16.

15. Herodotus, *The Histories*, trans. Aubrey de Sélincourt (Harmondsworth: Penguin, 1972), II.123.

16. Eliade, *The Sacred and the Profane*, 29–32.

17. Faulkner, *Pyramid Texts*, utterance 600.

18. Plumley, "The Cosmology of Ancient Egypt," 36–37.

19. Parker, "Ancient Egyptian Astronomy," 52.

20. Parker, "Egyptian Astronomy, Astrology and Calendrical Reckoning," chapters 1, 3.

21. De Young, "Astronomy in Ancient Egypt," 481.

22. J. Viau, "Egyptian Mythology," in Felix Guirand (ed.), *Larousse Encyclopaedia of Mythology*, trans. Richard Aldington and Delano Ames (London: Paul Hamlyn, 1959), 19. See also Campion, *The Great Year*, 144–45, 150–51.

23. Faulkner, *The Book of the Dead*, Spells 15, 41.

24. I. E. S. Edwards, *The Pyramids of Egypt* (London: Penguin, revised 1988), 278; Paul Jordan, *Riddles of the Sphinx* (Stroud: Sutton Publishing, 1998), 139; E. C. Krupp, *Skywatchers, Shamans and Kings: Astronomy and the Archaeology of Power* (New York: Wiley, 1997), 288.

25. Richard W. Wilkinson, *Symbol and Magic in Egyptian Art* (London: Thames and Hudson, 1994); Edwards, *The Pyramids*, 277.

26. Neugebauer and Parker, *Egyptian Astronomical Texts*, 175–82, plate 1.

27. José Lull and Juan Antonio Belmonte, "The Constellations of Ancient Egypt" in Juan Antonio Belmonte and Mosalem Shaltout (eds.), *In Search of Cosmic Order: Selected Essays on Egyptian Archaeoastronomy* (Cairo: Supreme Council of Antiquities Press, 2009), 155–94.

28. Parker, "Ancient Egyptian Astronomy," 53–56;

29. Ibid., 51.

30. Steven C. Haack, "The Astronomical Orientation of the Egyptian Pyramids," *Archaeoastronomy: Supplement to Journal for the History of Astronomy* 7 (1984): S119–S125; Kate Spence, "Ancient Egyptian Chronology and the Astronomical Orientation of Pyramids," *Nature* 408 (16 November 2000), 320–24; Hugh Thurston, "Aligning Giza: Astronomical Orentation of the Great Pyramid," *Griffith Observer* 65, no. 9 (September 2001): 11–17; Juan Antonio Belmonte, "On the Orientation of Old Egyptian Pyramids," *Archaeoastronomy, Supplement to the Journal for History of Astronomy*, no. 26 (2001): S1–S20.

31. Edwards, *The Pyramids*, 278.

32. Virginia Trimble, "Astronomical Investigation Concerning the So-Called Air-Shafts of Cheops' Pyramid," *Mitteilungen des deutsches Akademie Berlin* 10 (1964): 183–87; Alexander Badawy, "The Stellar Destiny of Pharoah and the So-Called Air Shafts of Cheops' Pyramid," in *Mitteilungen des deutsches Akademie Berlin*, Band 10 (1964), 198–206. See also I. E. S. Edwards, "The Air Channels of Chephren's Pyramid," in *Studies in Honor of Dows Dunham* (Boston: Museum of Fine Arts, 1981), 55–57.

33. Faulkner, *The Pyramid Texts*, 250, utterance 606.1688–89, 196, utterance 523.1231.

34. Mark Lehner, *The Complete Pyramids* (London: Thames and Hudson, 1997), 28–29.

35. Lehner, *The Complete Pyramids*, 33.

36. Krupp, *Skywatchers, Shamans and Kings*, 289.

37. Richard H. Wilkinson, *The Complete Temples of Ancient Egypt* (London: Thames and Hudson, 2000), 79. See also Richard W. Wilkinson, *Symbol and Magic in Egyptian Art* (London: Thames and Hudson, 1994), 60, 66, 69–71, 76.

38. Juan Antonio Belmonte, Mosalem Shaltout, and Magdi Fekri, "Astronomy, Landscape and Symbolism: A Study of the Orientation of Ancient Egyptian Temples," in Juan

Antonio Belmonte and Mosalem Shaltout (eds.), *In Search of Cosmic Order: Selected Essays on Egyptian Archaeoastronomy* (Cairo: Supreme Council of Antiquities Press, 2009), 213–83.

39. De Young, "Astronomy in Ancient Egypt," 492.

40. Parker, "Ancient Egyptian Astronomy," 51–52.

41. Campion, *A History of Western Astrology*, vol. 1, 106–7.

42. Parker, "Egyptian Astronomy, Astrology and Calendrical Reckoning," 721–23.

43. Libellus I.25, in Walter Scott (trans.), *Hermetica*, Vol. 1, 129.

44. Text A, System IV, 26–27, in R. A. Parker, "Egyptian Astronomy, Astrology and Calendrical Reckoning," 723.

45. Hans Dieter Betz, *The Greek Magical Papyri in Translation, Including the Demotic Spells* (Chicago: University of Chicago Press, 1992), PGM VII.284–99, 124.

46. J. M. Plumley, "The Cosmology of Ancient Egypt," in Carmen Blacker and Michael Loewe, *Ancient Cosmologies* (London: George Allen and Unwin Ltd., 1975), 38.

CHAPTER 9

1. The purpose of cosmology according to Sima Qian, 90 BCE, cited in Xiaochun Sun, "Crossing the Boundaries between Heaven and Man: Astronomy in Ancient China," Helaine Selin (ed.), *Astronomy Across Cultures: The History of Non-Western Astronomy* (Dordrecht: Kluwer Academic Publishers, 2000), 425.

2. Shigeru Nakayama, "Characteristics of Chinese Astrology," *Isis* 57, no. 4 (Winter 1966): 442.

3. Sun, "Crossing the Boundaries," 452.

4. Nathan Sivin, "State, Cosmos, and Body in the Last Three Centuries B.C.," *Harvard Journal of Asiatic Studies* 55, no. 1 (June 1995): 6.

5. Chao Wei-Pang, "Chinese Fate Calculation" http://nirc.nanzan-u.ac.jp/publications/afs/pdf/a40.pdf (accessed 13 June 2011).

6. Nathan Sivin, *Granting the Seasons: The Chinese Astronomical Reform of 1280, with a Study of Its Many Dimensions and Annotated Translation of Its Records* (New York: Springer, 2009).

7. For Japanese astrology see Lucia Dolce, *The Worship of Stars in Japanese Religious Practice*, Proceedings of the Conference on "The Worship of Stars in Japanese Religious Practice," School of Oriental and African Studies (September 2004), *Culture and Cosmos*, Vol. 10, Nos. 1 and 2 (Spring and Summer, Autumn and Winter 2006); Steven L. Renshaw and Saori Ihara, "A Cultural History of Astronomy in Japan," in Selin (ed.), *Astronomy Across Cultures*, 385–407; the Web site run by Steven Renshaw and Saori Ihara at http://www2.gol.com/users/stever/jastro.html; and Shigeru Nakayama, *A History of Japanese Astronomy: Chinese Background and Western Impact* (Cambridge, MA: Harvard University Press, 1969).

8. Karyn L. Lai, *An Introduction to Chinese Philosophy* (Cambridge: Cambridge University Press, 2008), 199–234.

9. Walters, *Chinese* Astrology, 194–249.

10. John S. Major, *Heaven and Earth in Early Han Thought* (Albany: State University of New York Press, 1993), 55–139.

11. Derek Walters, *Chinese Astrology: Interpreting the Revelations of the Celestial Messages* (Wellingborough: Aquarian Press, 1987).

12. David N. Keightley, "Shang Divination and Metaphysics," *Philosophy East and West* 38, No. 4 (October 1988): 367–97.

13. Joseph Needham, *Science and Civilisation in China*, Vol. 3: "Mathematics and the Sciences of the Heavens and Earth" (Cambridge: Cambridge University Press, 1959), 399; Shigeru Nakayama, "Characteristics of Chinese Astrology," *Isis* 57, No. 4 (Winter 1966): 442; Xiaochun Sun, "Crossing the Boundaries," 425; Walters, *Chinese Astrology*.

14. Anne Birrell, *Chinese Mythology: An Introduction* (Baltimore: Johns Hopkins University Press, 1993), 27.

15. Needham, *Science and Civilisation*, 210–28.

16. Têng Mu, *Po Ya Chhin*, cited in Needham, *Science and Civilisation*, 221.

17. Cited in Needham, *Science and Civilisation*, 217.

18. Lai, *Chinese Philosophy*, 209.

19. Richard Wilhelm, *The I Ching or Book of Changes* (London: Routledge and Kegan Paul, 1951, 3rd edition 1968), 280.

20. For both the Five Phases and Yin-Yang, see A. C. Graham, *Yin-Yang and the Nature of Correlative Thinking* (Singapore: Institute of East Asian Philosophies, 1986).

21. Lao Tzu, *Tao Te Ching*, I.I–3a, trans. D. C. Lau (Harmondsworth: Penguin, 1972). See also David W. Pankenier, "A Brief History of Beiji (Northern Culmen), with an Excursus on the Origin of the Character di," *Journal of the American Oriental Society* 124, No. 2 (April–June 2004), 218–20.

22. Lai, *Chinese Philosophy*, 35–54; Mary Evelyn Tucker, "Religious Dimensions of Confucianism: Cosmology and Cultivation," *Philosophy East and West* 48, No. 1: "The Religious Dimension of Confucianism in Japan" (January 1998): 5–45.

23. Sun, "Crossing the Boundaries," 425.

24. Needham, *Science and Civilisation*, 171.

25. David Pankenier, "The Cosmo-political Background of Heaven's Mandate," *Early China*, No. 20 (1995):121n2.

26. Xiaochun Sun and Jacob Kistemaker, *The Chinese Sky during the Han—Constellating Stars and Society* (Leiden: Brill, 1997), 15–18.

27. Mark Edward Lewis, "Evolution of the Calendar in Shang China," in Iain Morley and Colin Renfrew (eds.), *The Archaeology of Measurement: Comprehending Heaven, Earth and Time in Ancient Societies* (Cambridge: Cambridge University Press, 2010), 198.

28. Needham, *Science and Civilisation*, 242–59.

29. Needham, *Science and Civilisation*, 175, 202, 204–5, 273, 321; Derek Walters, *Chinese Astrology: Interpreting the Revelations of the Celestial Messages* (Wellingborough: Aquarian Press, 1987), 283–86.

30. David Pankenier, "The Planetary Portent of 1524 in Europe and China," *The Journal of World History* 20, No. 3 (September 2009): 339–75.

31. Walters, *Chinese Astrology*, 283–86, 291–325.

32. Johannes Thomann, "Square Horoscope Diagrams in Middle Eastern Astrology and Chinese Cosmological Diagrams: Were These Designs Transmitted Through the Silk Road?," in Philippe Forêt and Andreas Kaplony (eds.), *The Journey of Maps and Images on the Silk Road* (Leiden: Brill, 2008), 97–117.

33. For a detailed discussion of the problems of mathematical calendar construction, see Christopher Cullen, *Astronomy and Mathematics in Ancient China: The Zhou bi suan jing* (Cambridge: Cambridge University Press, 1996).

34. Edward H. Schafer, *Pacing the Void: T'ang Approaches to the Stars* (Berkely: University of California Press, 1977), 55.

35. Wilhelm, *The I Ching or Book of Changes*, 280.

36. Ibid.

37. Needham, *Science and Civilisation*, 188.

38. See Needham, *Science and Civilisation*, 303–5, and the detailed instructions for use in Walters, *Chinese Astrology*, 255–82; Mark Edward Lewis, *The Construction of Space in Early China* (Albany: State University of New York Press, 2006), 273–83.

39. Needham, *Science and Civilisation*, 419, 422–23.

40. Pankenier, "A Brief History of Beiji," 211–36.

41. Julia Ching, *Mysticism and Kingship in China: The Heart of Chinese Wisdom* (Cambridge: Cambridge University Press, 1997).

42. Bruce E. Brooks and A. Taeko Brooks, *The Original Analects: Sayings of Confucius and His Successors* (New York: Columbia University Press, 1998), 109.

43. Paul Wheatley, *The Pivot of the Four Quarters: A Preliminary Enquiry into the Origin and Character of the Ancient Chinese City* (Edinburgh: Edinburgh University Press, 1971); Lewis, *Space in Early China*, 260–72; Jeffrey F. Meyer, "'Feng-Shui' of the Chinese City," *History of Religions* 18, No. 2 (November 1978): 138–55.

44. David W. Pankenier, "Cosmic Capitals and Numinous Precincts in Early China," *Journal of Cosmology* 9 (2010): 2030–40.

45. David W. Pankenier, "Characteristics of Field Allocation (*fenye*) Astrology in Early China," in J. W. Fountain and R. M. Sinclair (eds.), *Current Studies in Archaeoastronomy: Conversations across Time and Space* (Durham, NC: Carolina Academic Press, 2005), 499–513; and "Applied Field-Allocation Astrology in Zhou China: Duke Wen of Jin and the Battle of Chengpu (632 B.C.)," *Journal of the American Oriental Society* 119, No. 2 (April–June 1999): 261–79. For Beijing see E. C. Krupp, "The Cosmic Temples of Old Beijing," in Anthony F. Aveni, *World Archaeoastronomy* (Cambridge: Cambridge University Press, 1989), 65–75; J. F. Meyer, "Feng-Shui of the Chinese City," *History of Religions* 18, No. 2 (1978): 138–45.

46. Needham, *Science and Civilisation*, 251.

47. Ibid., 398.

48. Zhenoao Xu, David W. Pankenier, and Yaotiao Jiang, *East Asian Archaeoastronomy: Historical Records of Astronomical Observations of China, Japan, and Korea* (Amsterdam: Gordon and Breach Science Publishers, 2000), 237.

49. Cited in Shigeru Nakayama, "Characteristics of Chinese Astrology," *Isis* 57, no. 4 (Winter 1966): 442.

50. Needham, *Science and Civilisation*, 423.

51. Walters, *Chinese Astrology*, 231.

52. Sun, "Crossing the Boundaries," 448–49.

53. Needham, *Science and Civilisation*, 424–27.

54. Ibid., 402–6.

55. Walters, *Chinese Astrology*, 69.

56. See chapter 16.

57. Needham, *Science and Civilisation*, 405.

58. Walters, *Chinese Astrology*, 301.

59. Ibid., 307.

CHAPTER 10

1. The creation of the cosmos in the *Rig Veda*, in Wendy Donniger O'Flaherty (trans.), *The Rig Veda: An Anthology* (London: Penguin, 1981), 10.90.13–14, 31.

2. Thomas McEvilley, *The Shape of Ancient Thought* (New York: Allsworth Press, 2002); R. Baine Harris (ed.), *Neoplatonism and Indian Thought* (Norfolk: International Society for Neoplatonic Studies, 1982).

3. Haribhai Pandya, Somdutt Dikshit, and N. M. Kansara, *Issues in Vedic Astronomy and Astrology* (Delhi: Motilal Banarsidass Publishers, 1992).

4. S. N. Sen and K. S. Shukla, *History of Astronomy in India* (New Delhi: Indian National Science Academy, 1985); Richard L. Thompson, *Vedic Cosmography and Astronomy* (Delhi: Motilal Banarsidass Publishers Private Ltd., 2004); S. S. Lishk, *Jaina Astronomy* (Delhi: Oriental and Scientific Researdh Publication Centre, 1987).

5. Hari Shankar Prasad (ed.), *Time in Indian Philosophy* (Delhi: Sri Satguru Publications, 1992); R. F. Gombrich, "Ancient Indian Cosmology," in Carmen Blacker and Michael Loewe (eds.), *Ancient Cosmologies* (London: George Allen and Unwin Ltd., 1975), 110–42; F. B. J. Kuiper, *Ancient Indian Cosmogony* (New Delhi: Vikas, 1983).

6. Rana P.B. Singh, *Cosmic Order and Cultural Astronomy: Sacred Cities of India* (Newcastle: Cambridge Scholars Publishing, 2009).

7. David Pingree, *From Astral Omens to Astrology: From Babylon to Bikaner* (Rome: Istituto Italiano Per L'Africa E L'Oriente, 1997). For three important papers see David Pingree, "Astronomy and Astrology in India and Iran," *Isis* 54, no. 2 (June 1963): 229–46; "Indian Astronomy," *Proceedings of the American Philosophical Society* 122, no. 6 (December 18, 1978): 361–64; and "Indian Planetary Images and the Tradition of Astral Magic," *Journal of the Warburg and Courtauld Institutes* 52 (1989): 1–13.

8. Steven Kemper, "Time, Person, and Gender in Sinhalese Astrology," *American Ethnologist* 7, No. 4 (November 1980): 744–58; Martin Gansten, "Patterns of Destiny: Hindu Nadi Astrology" (PhD Thesis, Lund University, 2003), published as *Patterns of Destiny: Hindu Nadi Astrology, Lund Studies in History of Religions*, Vol. 17 (Stockholm: Almqvist and Wiksell International, 2003).

9. Lagadha, *Vedanga Jyotisa* (New Delhi: Indian National Science Academy, 1984).

10. David Pingree, *The Yavanajataka of Sphujidhvaja*, 2 vols., Harvard Oriental Series 48 (Cambridge, MA: Harvard University Press, 1978).

11. M. Ramakrishna Bhat, *Varahamihira's Brhat Samhita*, 2 vols. (Delhi: Motilal Banarsidass Publishers, 1993); B. V. Raman, *A Manual of Hindu Astrology* (Bangalore: P. N. Kamat, 1979); David Frawley, *The Astrology of the Seers: A Guide to Vedic (Hindu) Astrology* (Salt Lake City: Passage Press, 1990); Komilla Sutton, *The Essentials of Vedic Astrology* (Bournemouth: Wessex Astrologer, 1999).

12. Denise Cush, Catherine Robinson, and Lynn Foulston (eds.), *The Encyclopaedia of Hinduism* (London: Routledge, 2007).

13. K. M. Sen, *Hinduism* (London: Penguin, 1991).

14. Thompson, *Vedic Cosmography and Astronomy*.

15. K. V. Sarma (trans.) and with notes by T. S. K. Sastry, *Vedanga Jyotisa of Lagadha* (New Delhi: Indian National Science Academy, 1985); O'Flaherty, *Rig Veda*, 1.164.3, 11.

16. T. N. Dharmadhikari, "Nakshatras and Vedic Astrology," in Haribhai Pandya, Somdutt Dikshit and N. M. Kansara (eds.), *Issues in Vedic Astronomy and Astrology* (Delhi: Motilal Banarsidass Publishers, 1992), 249–53.

17. Dharmadhikari, "Vedic Astrology," 249–53.

18. O'Flaherty, *Rig Veda*, 10.129.1–4, 25

19. Ibid., 10.190.1–2, 34.

20. Ibid., 10.129.7, 25.

21. Ibid., 10.90.1, 30.

22. Ibid., 10.90.13–14, 31.

23. R. F. Gombrich, "Ancient Indian Cosmology," in Blacker and Loewe, *Ancient Cosmologies*, 111.

24. Max Müller, trans., *Hymns of the Atharva Veda*, The Sacred Books of the East, Vol. 42 (Delhi: Low Cost Publications, 1996 [1880]), IV, I.11.2, 99.

25. Gombrich, "Ancient Indian Cosmology," in Blacker and Loewe, 120–24.

26. Nicholas Campion, *The Great Year: Astrology, Millenarianism and History in the Western Tradition* (London: Penguin, 1994).

27. Wendy Donniger O'Flaherty (trans.), *The Rig Veda: An Anthology* (London: Penguin, 1981), 10.90.12, 31; Brian K. Smith, *Classifying the Universe: The Ancient Indian Varna System and the Origins of Caste* (Oxford: Oxford University Press, 1994).

28. John McKim Malville, "Foreword to Rana P.B. Singh," *Cosmic Order and Cultural Astronomy: Sacred Cities of India* (Newcastle: Cambridge Scholars Publishing, 2009), 1.

29. Sashikala Ananth, *Vaastu: The Classical Indian Science of Architecture and Design* (London: Penguin 1999).

30. S. K. Chatterjee and Apurba Kumar Chakravarty, "Indian Calendar from Post-Vedic Period to AD 1900," in S. N. Sen and K. S. Shukla, *History of Astronomy in India* (New Delhi: Indian National Science Academy, 1985), 252–307.

31. Subas Rai, *Kumbha Mela: History and Religion, Astronomy and Cosmobiology* (Varanasi: Ganga Kaveri Pub. House, 1993).

32. Steven Kemper, "Sinhalese Astrology, South Asian Caste Systems, and the Notion of Individuality," *Journal of South Asian Studies* 38, No. 3 (May 1979): 477–97.

33. Jyanat V. Narlikar, "Vedic Astrology or Jyotirvigyan: Neither Vedic nor Vigyan," *Economic and Political Weekly* 36, No. 24 (June 16, 2001): 2113–15.

34. Kemper, "Time, Person, and Gender," 750.

35. Komilla Sutton, *The Essentials of Vedic Astrology* (Bournemouth: Wessex Astrologer, 1999), 74.

36. B. V. Raman, *A Manual of Hindu Astrology* (Bangalore: P.N. Kamat, 1979), 130–33.

37. Frawley, *The Astrology of the Seers*, 192.

38. Sutton, *Vedic Astrology*, 253.

39. Gansten, "Patterns of Destiny."

40. David Pingree, *The Yavanajataka of Sphujidhvaja*, 2 vols., Harvard Oriental Series 48 (Cambridge, MA: Harvard University Press, 1978), 43.4.6.

41. Peter Holt, *Stars of India: Travels in Search of Astrologers and Fortune-Tellers* (Edinburgh: Mainstream Publishing, 1998), 22.

42. M. Ramakrishna Bhat, *Varahamihira's Brhat Samhita*, 2 vols. (Delhi: Motilal Banarsidass Publishers, 1993), 16.

43. Paramahansa Yogananda, *Autobiography of a Yogi* (Los Angeles: Self-Realisation Fellowship, 11th edition, 1988), 187.

44. Max Müller (trans.), *Hymns of the Atharva Veda*, The Sacred Books of the East, Vol. 42 (Delhi: Low Cost Publications, 1996 [1880]), X.XIX.53.2–5, 224.

45. Eric Bellman, "When the Stars Align, Indians Say, It's a Good Time to Have a C-Section: Moms-to-Be Consult Their Astrologers, Request the Operation on Auspicious Days," *Wall Street Journal*, 5 October 2010, 1, http://online.wsj.com/article/SB10001424052 748704394704575495413840008880.html?KEYWORDS=when+the+stars+align (accessed 4 July 2011).

CHAPTER 11

1. A. Leo Oppenheim, "A Babylonian Diviner's Manual," *Journal of Near Eastern Studies* 33 (January–October 1974): 204.

2. H. Frankfort, H. A. Frankfort, William A. Irwin, Thorkild Jacobsen, and John A. Wilson, *The Intellectual Adventure of Ancient Man: An Essay on Speculative Thought in the Ancient Near East* (Chicago: University of Chicago Press, 1946); Henri Frankfort, *Kingship and the Gods: A Study of Near Eastern Religion as the Integration of Society and Nature* (Chicago: University of Chicago Press, 1978 [1948]); Thorkild Jacobsen, *The Treasures of Darkness: A History of Mesopotamian Religion* (New Haven, CT: Yale University Press, 1976).

3. Samuel Noah Kramer, *Sumerian Mythology: A Study of Spiritual and Literary Achievement in the Third Millennium BC* (Philadephia: University of Pennsylvania Press, 1972 [1944]).

4. Hermann Hunger, *Astrological Reports to Assyrian Kings* (Helsinki: Helsinki University Press, 1992); Hermann Hunger and David Pingree, "Mul Apin: An Astronomical Compendium in Cuneiform," *Archiv für Orientforschung* 24 (1989), 1–163; Simo Parpola, *Letters from Assyrian and Babylonian Scholars* (Helsinki: Helsinki University Press, 1993); David Pingree and Erica Reiner, *Babylonian Planetary Omens, Part 2: Enuma Anu Enlil, Tablets 50–51* (Malibu, CA: Undena Publications, 1981); Erica Reiner with David Pingree, *Babylonian Planetary Omens, Part 1: The Venus Tablet of Ammisaduqa, Enuma Anu Enlil, tablet 63* (Malibu, CA: Undena Publications, 1975).

5. Alexander Heidel, *The Babylonian Genesis* (Chicago: University of Chicago Press, 1963). Also see the modern translation in Benjamin Foster, *Before the Muses: An Anthology of Akkadian Literature* (Bethesda, MD: CDL Press, 2005).

6. David Brown, *Mesopotamian Planetary Astronomy-Astrology* (Groningen: Styx Publications, 2000); Hermann Hunger and David Pingree, *Astral Sciences in Mesopotamia* (Leiden, Boston, Koln: Brill, 1999); David Pingree, *From Astral Omens to Astrology: From Babylon to Bikaner* (Rome: Istituto Italiano Per L'Africa E L'Oriente, 1997); Francesca Rochberg, *The Heavenly Writing: Divination, Horoscopy, and Astronomy in Mesopotamian Culture* (Cambridge: Cambridge University Press, 2004) and *In the Path of the Moon: Babylonian Celestial Divination and Its Legacy* (Leiden: Brill, 2010); Erica Reiner, *Astral Magic in Babylonia* (Philadelphia: American Philosophical Society, 1995).

7. Michael Baigent, *From the Omens of Babylon: Astrology and Ancient Mesopotamia* (London: Penguin, 1994).

8. Alexander Heidel, *The Babylonian Genesis* (Chicago: University of Chicago Press, 1963). Also see the modern translation in Foster, *Before the Muses*.

9. Heidel, *The Babylonian Genesis*, I.1–2, 9, 18.

10. Ibid., I.8, 18.

11. Rochberg, *The Heavenly Writing*, 127.

12. Wayne Horowitz, *Mesopotamian Cosmic Geography* (Winona Lake: Eisenbrauns, 1998), 4. Also see W. G. Lambert, "The Cosmology of Sumer and Babylon," in Carmen Blacker and Michael Loewe (eds.), *Ancient Cosmologies* (London: George Allen and Unwin Ltd., 1975), 42–65.

13. Reiner, *Astral Magic,* 9. See also C. J. Gadd, *Ideas of Divine Rule in the Ancient East*, Schweich Lectures of the British Academy, 1945 (Munich: Kraus Reprint, 1980), 57.

14. Mul Apin: Gap A 1–7, in Hermann Hunger and David Pingree, "Mul Apin: An Astronomical Compendium in Cuneiform," *Archiv für Orientforschung* 24 (1989), 88–89.

15. Hunger and Pingree, "Mul Apin: An Astronomical Compendium in Cuneiform," I.iv, 33–39, 68–69.

16. Simo Parpola, *Letters from Assyrian Scholars to the Kings Esarhaddon and Assurbanipal*, part 1, texts (Neukirchen-Vluyn: Verlag Butzon & Bercker Kevelaer, 1970), LXXIV; John Van Seters, *In Search of History: Historiography in the Ancient World and the Origins of Biblical History* (New Haven, CT: Yale University Press, 1983), 96–97.

17. Reiner, *Astral Magic*, 16. Also see Scott Noegel (ed.), *Prayer, Magic, and the Stars in the Ancient and Late Antique World* (Philadelphia: Pennsylvania State University Press, 2003).

18. A. Leo Oppenheim, "A Babylonian Diviner's Manual," *Journal of Near Eastern Studies* 33 (January–October 1974): 204.

19. Cited in Reiner, *Astral* Magic, 98.

20. From the Hittite "Removal of the Threat Implied in an Evil Omen" in James B. Pritchard (ed.), *Ancient Near Eastern Texts Relating to the Old Testament* (Princeton, NJ: Princeton University Press, 1969), 355.

21. Parpola, *Letters from Assyrian and Babylonian Scholars*, 217, 278.

22. Betty De Shong Meador (trans.), *Inanna, Lady of Largest Heart: Poems of the Sumerian High Pristess Enheduanna* (Austin: University of Texas Press, 2001).

23. Samuel Noah Kramer and Diane Wolkstein, *Inanna, Queen of Heaven and Earth: Her Stories and Hymns from Sumer* (New York: Harper & Row, 1983), 52–89.

24. Jacobsen, *The Treasures of Darkness*, 122.

25. Ibid., 135.

26. Francesca Rochberg, *Babylonian Horoscopes* (Philadelphia: American Philosophical Society, 1998); A. J. Sachs, "Babylonian Horoscopes," *Journal of Cuneiform Studies* 6 (1952): 49–75.

27. Sachs, "Babylonian Horoscopes," 68.

28. Margaret Hone, *The Modern Textbook of Astrology* (London: L. N. Fowler, fourth edition reprinted 1973, [1951]), 27–31.

29. Bartel van der Waerden, *Science Awakening*, Vol. II: The Birth of Astronomy (Leyden: Oxford University Press, 1974), chap. 5.

30. A. J. Sachs, "The Lastest Datable Cuneiform Texts," in Barry L. Eichler (ed.), *Kramer Anniversary Volume: Studies in Honor of Samuel Noah Kramer, Alter Orient und Altes Testament* 25 (1976), 379–98.

CHAPTER 12

1. Psalms 19.1.
2. Thomas L. Thompson, *The Mythic Past: Biblical Archaeology and the Myth of Israel* (London: Jonathan Cape, 1992).
3. Nicholas Campion, *The Great Year: Astrology, Millenarianism and History in the Western Tradition* (London: Penguin, 1994), chapters 4 and 5.
4. I have used the English translation by the Jewish Publication Society (*Tanakh: the Holy Scriptures*, Philadelphia and Jerusalem, 1985).
5. James H. Charlesworth (ed.), *The Old Testament Pseudepigrapha*, 2 vols. (New York: Doubleday, 1983); H. F. D. Sparks (ed.), *The Apocryphal Old Testament* (Oxford: Clarendon Press, 1984); Florentino Garcia Martinez, *The Dead Sea Scrolls Translated: The Qumran Texts in English* (Leiden: E. J. Brill, 1994).
6. Roger T. Beckwith, *Calendar and Chronology, Jewish and Christian* (Leiden: Brill, 2001); J. Edward Wright, *The Early History of Heaven* (Oxford: Oxford University Press, 2000); J. W. McKay, *Religion in Judah under the Assyrians* (London: SCM Press Ltd., 1973); Lester Ness, *Written in the Stars: Ancient Zodiac Mosaics* (Warren Center, PA: Shangri La Publications, 1999).
7. Gershom Scholem (ed.), *Zohar: The Book of Splendor* (New York: Schocken Books, 1963); Aryeh Kaplan, *Sefer Yetzirah: The Book of Creation in Theory and Practice* (York Beach: Weiser Books, 1997); Gershom Scholem, *On the Kabbalah and Its Symbolism* (New York: Schocken Books, 1965).
8. Gideon Bohak, *Ancient Jewish Magic: A History* (Cambridge: Cambridge University Press, 2008); Frederick H. Cryer, *Divination in Ancient Israel and Its Near Eastern Environment: A Socio-Historical Investigation* (Sheffield: Sheffield Academic Press, 1994); Ann Jeffers, *Divination and Prophecy in Israel and Palestine* (Leiden: Brill, 1996); Howard Schwartz, *Tree of Souls: The Mythology of Judaism* (Oxford: Oxford University Press, 2004); Dov Schwartz, *Studies in Astral Magic in Medieval Jewish Thought* (Leiden: Brill, 2004).
9. Louis Jacobs, "Jewish Cosmology," in Carmen Blacker and Michael Loewe (eds.), *Ancient Cosmologies* (London: George Allen and Unwin Ltd., 1975), 66–67.
10. For a recent analysis see Mark S. Smith, *The Priestly Vision of Genesis 1* (Minneapolis: Fortress Press, 2010).
11. For a good contemporary account of the Jewish Festival year see Hayyim Schauss, *The Jewish Festivals: A Guide to Their History and Observance* (New York: Schocken Books, 1996, 1st ed. 1938).
12. Exodus 12.6–20. See also Leviticus 23.5, Ezekiel 45.21, Numbers 9.11.
13. See Millar Burrows, "Ancient Israel," in Robert C. Dentan (ed.), *The Idea of History in the Ancient Near East* (New Haven, CT: Yale University Press, 1983), 99–131, esp. 112, 122.
14. The Community Rule X in G. Vermes, *The Dead Sea Scrolls in English* (Harmondsworth: Pelican, 1962); Also see Ezra 3.5 for new moon observances.
15. Numbers 2, 1–31. See also the discussion in Burrows, "Ancient Israel," 129.
16. See the discussion in Kocku von Stuckrad, "Jewish and Christian Astrology in Late Antiquity—A New Approach," *Numen* XLVII, no. 1 (2000): 25–28.
17. Josephus, "The Antiquities of the Jews" I.2.3 in *Works*, trans. William Whiston (Peabody, MA: Hendrickson Publishers, 1987).

18. Philo, "On the Life of Moses," II.133–35, in *The Works of Philo*, trans. C. D. Yonge (Peabody, MA: Hendrickson, 1993), 502.

19. Philo, "On Providence," fr. II, 48–54, *Works*, 753–54.

20. For background to Maimonides see Lynn Thorndike, *History of Magic and Experimental Science*, 8 vols. (New York: Columbia University Press, 1923–58), Vol. 2, 205–13, esp. 211–12 on astrology.

21. Meira B. Epstein, *The Correspondence between the Rabbis of Southern France and Maimonides about Astrology* (Reston: ARHAT Publications, 1998), 6, para. 2.

22. Epstein, *Correspondence*, 13–14, para. 6–7.

23. For Kabbalah see J. H. Laenes, *Jewish Mysticism: An Introduction* (London: Westminster John Knox Press, 2001); Gershom Scholem, *Origins of the Kabbalah*, trans. Allan Arkush (Princeton, NJ: Princeton University Press, 1987); Alan Unterman, *The Jews: Their Religious Beliefs and Practices* (Brighton: Sussex Academic Press, 1999), esp. chapter 6; Perle Epstein, *Kabbalah: The Way of the Jewish Mystic* (London: Shambhala, 2001).

24. Genesis 28.11–19, 2 Kings 2:12.

25. Howard Schwartz, *Tree of Souls: The Mythology of Judaism* (Oxford: Oxford University Press, 2004), 89.

26. Kaplan, *Sefer Yetzirah*, 1:5, 44.

27. Scholem (ed.), *Zohar*, 27.

28. Kaplan, *Sefer Yetzirah*, 5:7, 215.

29. Hans Jonas, *The Gnostic Religion: The Message of the Alien God and the Beginnings of Christianity*, 2nd ed. (Boston: Beacon Press, 1963); Nicholas Campion, *A History of Western Astrology*, Vol. 1: The Ancient World (London: Continuum, 2009), chap. 17.

30. Ecclesiastes 3:2–8.

31. Kaplan, *Sefer Yetzirah*, 221–26.

32. Harry Sperling and Maurice Simon (eds.), *The Zohar*, 5 vols. (London: Soncino Press, 1949). For extracts, see Isaiah Tishby (ed.), *The Wisdom of the Zohar: An Anthology of Texts*, trans. David Goldstein, 3 vols. (Oxford: Oxford University Press, 1989); Daniel C. Matt, *Zohar: Annotated and Explained* (Woodstock: SkyLights Paths Publishing Co., 2002); Gershom Scholem (ed.), *Zohar: The Book of Splendor* (New York: Schocken Books, 1963).

33. Joshua Trachtenberg, *Jewish Magic and Superstition* (Philadelphia: University of Pennsylvania Press, 2004), 215.

CHAPTER 13

1. Marcus Aurelius, *Meditations*, trans. Maxwell Staniforth (Harmondsworth: Penguin, 1964), 112, V.47; see also 114, IX.29. See Plato, *Republic*, 2 vols., trans. Paul Shorey (Cambridge, MA: Harvard University Press, 1937), 516B.

2. David Pingree, "Hellenophilia versus the History of Science," *Isis* 83 (1991): 554–63; Peter Kingsley, *Ancient Philosophy, Mystery and Magic: Empedocles and Pythagorean Tradition* (Oxford: Clarendon Press, 1995), and *In the Dark Places of Wisdom* (Inverness: Golden Sufi Center, 1999).

3. Carolina Lopez-Ruis, *When the Gods Were Born: Greek Cosmogonies and the Near East* (Cambridge, MA: Harvard University Press, 2010).

4. Plato, *Timaeus*, trans. R. G. Bury (Cambridge, MA: Harvard University Press, 1931), and *Republic*, 2 vols., trans. Paul Shorey (Cambridge, MA: Harvard University Press, 1937).

5. F. M. Cornford, *Plato's Cosmology: The Timaeus* (London: Routledge, 1937).

6. Aristotle, *On the Heavens* (De Caelo), trans. W. K. C. Guthrie (Cambridge, MA: Harvard University Press, 1921); *Physics*, 2 vols., trans. F. M. Cornford and P. H. Wickstead (Cambridge, MA: Harvard University Press, 1930); *Metaphysics*, 2 vols., Vol. 1 trans. Hugh Tredennick, Vol. 2 trans. Hugh Tredennick and G. Cyril Armstrong (Cambridge, MA: Harvard University Press, 1933); *Meterologica*, trans. H. D. P. Lee (Cambridge, MA: Harvard University Press, 1937).

7. Clement Salaman, Dorine van Ovin, William D. Wharton, and Jean-Pierre Mahé, *The Way of Hermes: New Translations of the Corpus Hermeticum and the Definitions of Hermes Trismegistus to Asclepius* (Rochester, VT: Inner Traditions, 2000); Walter Scott (trans.), *Hermetica: The Ancient Greek and Latin Writings Which Contain Religious or Philosophic Teachings Ascribed to Hermes Trismegistus*, 4 vols. (Boulder, CO: Shambala, 1982); Claudius Ptolemy, *Tetrabiblos*, trans. F. E. Robbins (Cambridge, MA: Harvard University Press, 1940).

8. Marcus Manilius, *Astronomica*, trans. G. P. Goold (Cambridge, MA: Harvard University Press, 1977); Dorotheus of Sidon, *Carmen Astrologicum*, ed. and trans. David Pingree (Leipzig: BSG B.G. Teubner Verlagsgesellschaft, 1976); Vettius Valens, *The Anthology*, books 1–5, trans. Robert Schmidt (Berkeley Springs, WV: Golden Hind Press, 1993–96); Julius Firmicus Maternus, *Mathesis*, trans. Jean Rhys Bram, as *Ancient Astrology: Theory and Practice* (Park Ridge, NJ: Noyes Press, 1975).

9. Tamsyn Barton, *Ancient Astrology* (London: Routledge, 1994); Roger Beck, *A Brief History of Ancient Astrology* (Oxford: Blackwell, 2007); George C. Noonan, *Classical Scientific Astrology* (Tempe, AZ: American Federation of Astrologers, 1984).

10. M. R. Wright, *Cosmology in Antiquity* (London: Routledge, 1995); J. L. E. Dreyer, *A History of the Planetary Systems from Thales to Kepler* (New York: Dover, 1953 [1906]); Charles H. Kahn, *Anaximander and the Origins of Greek Cosmology* (New York: Hacket, 1960); Daryn Lehoux, *Astronomy, Weather, and Calendars in the Ancient World: Parapegmata and Related Texts in Classical and Near-Eastern Societies* (Cambridge: Cambridge University Press, 2007); John M. Steele, *Calendars and Years: Astronomy and Time in the Ancient Near East* (Oxford: Oxbow Books, 2007).

11. Nicholas Campion, *A History of Western Astrology*, Vol. 1: The Ancient World (London: Continuum, 2009), chs. 9–13.

12. Richard Buxton (ed.), *Oxford Readings in Greek Religion* (Oxford: Oxford University Press, 2000); Louise Bruit Zaidman and Pauline Schmidt Pantel, *Religion in the Ancient Greek City*, trans. Paul Cartledge (Cambridge: Cambridge University Press, 1994).

13. Jane Harrison, *Themis: A Study of the Origins of Greek Religion* (London: Merlin Press, 1963).

14. Hesiod, *The Homeric Hymns and Homerica, including "Works and Days" and "Theogonis,"* trans. Hugh G. Evelyn-White (Cambridge, MA: Harvard University Press, 1917).

15. Aristophanes, *The Birds* (The Internet Classics Archive, 1994), http://classics.mit.edu/Aristophanes/birds.html (accessed 26 March 2010).

16. For Thales see the discussion in G. S. Kirk, J. E. Raven, and M. Schofield, *The Presocratic Philosophers*, 2nd edition (Cambridge: Cambridge University Press, 1983), 92. For Anaximander's surviving fragments see Kirk, Raven, and Schofield, *The Presocratic Philosophers*, 100–42. See also Charles H. Kahn, *Anaximander and the Origins of Greek Cosmology* (New York: Hackett, 1960).

17. Hesiod, *Works and Days*, trans. Evelyn-White, lines 609–13.

18. Hippocrates, *Airs, Waters, Places* II, in Hippocrates, *Works,* 4 vols., trans. W. Jones and E. Withington (Cambridge, MA: Harvard University Press, 1923).

19. Heracleitus, *Fragments*, 4 vols., trans. W. Jones and E. Withington (Cambridge, MA: Harvard University Press, 1923); Kenneth Guthrie, *The Pythagorean Sourcebook and Library* (Grand Rapids, MI: Phanes Press, 1987), 137–40; William Guthrie, *Orpheus and Greek Religion: A Study of the Orphic Movement* (Princeton, NJ: Princeton University Press, 1993 [London 1935, 2nd (revised) edition London 1952]).

20. R. T. Wallis, *Neoplatonism* (London: Duckworth, 1995).

21. Plato, *Timaeus*, trans. R. G. Bury (Cambridge, MA: Harvard University Press, 1931), 28–40.

22. Plato, *Timaeus*, 38C; see also 42A and D.

23. Plato, *Epinomis*, trans. W. R. M. Lamb (Cambridge, MA: Harvard University Press 1929), Book X.

24. Plato, *Phaedrus*, 246A, 253 C–D.

25. See Plato, *Timaeus*, 28A.

26. Aristotle, *On the Soul*, trans. W. S. Hett (Cambridge, MA: Harvard University Press, 1936), II.1 (412a).

27. Aristotle, *On the Soul*, III.V.430a.

28. Claudius Ptolemy, *Tetrabiblos*, trans. F. E. Robbins (Cambridge, MA: Harvard University Press, 1940), III.13.

29. Ptolemy, *Tetrabiblos*, trans. F. E. Robbins, 32–33, I.3.

30. Nicholas Campion, "Astronomy and Psyche in the Classical World: Plato, Aristotle, Zeno, Ptolemy," *Journal of Cosmology* 9 (2010): 2179–86

31. Aristotle, *On the Heavens*, II.xii.292a. (For denial that the stars and planets are gods see *Metaphysics*, XII.1074b.)

32. Aristotle, *Metaphysics*, 995b–996a and *Physics*, 194b–195a.

33. Diogenes Laertius, "Zeno," in *Lives of Eminent Philosophers*, trans. R. D. Hicks, Vol. 2 (London: William Heinemann, 1925), 110–263.

34. Vettius Valens, *The Anthology*, I.1

35. Diogenes Laertius, "Zeno," in *Lives of Eminent Philosophers*, trans. R.D. Hicks (London: William Heinemann, 1925), VII.140.

36. Hans Dieter Betz, *The Greek Magical Papyri in Translation, including the Demotic Spells* (Chicago: University of Chicago Press, 1992), 312.

37. Roger Beck, *The Religion of the Mithras Cult in the Roman Empire: Mysteries of the Unconquered Sun* (Oxford: Oxford University Press, 2006); Manfred Clauss, *The Roman Cult of Mithras*, trans. Richard Gordon (Edinburgh: Edinburgh University Press, 2000); David Ulansey, *The Origins of the Mithraic Mysteries: Cosmology and Salvation in the Ancient World* (New York: Oxford University Press, 1989).

38. Libellus I.25, in Scott, *Hermetica*, vol. 1, 129.

39. Libellus I. 13a, in Scott, *Hermetica*, vol. 1, 121.

40. Libellus I.15–16, in Scott, *Hermetica*, vol. 1, 123. See also "Excerpt 14: Hermes to Tat," 1–2, in Scott, *Hermetica*, vol. 1, 437.

41. Michael Flower, *The Seer in Ancient Greece* (Berkeley: University of California Press, 2008), 127; Sarah Iles Johnston, *Ancient Greek Divination* (Oxford: Blackwell, 2008), 2, 22.

42. Julius Firmicus Maternus, *Mathesis*, trans. Jean Rhys Bram, as *Ancient Astrology: Theory and Practice* (Park Ridge, NJ: Noyes Press, 1975), VI.III.5–6.

43. Robert Fowler, "Greek Magic, Greek Religion," in Buxton (ed.), *Greek Religion*, 317.

CHAPTER 14

1. Matthew 2.9.

2. Ephesians 1.20–23.

3. Montague Rhodes James (ed.), *The Apocryphal New Testament* (Oxford: Clarendon Press, 1924); James M. Robinson (ed.), *The Nag Hammadi Library in English* (Leiden: Brill, 1988).

4. Alexander Roberts and James Donaldson (eds.), *The Ante-Nicene Christian Library* (Edinburgh: Y and T Clark, 1847).

5. For anti-astrology polemics, see Peter Anderson, *Satan's Snare: The Influence of the Occult* (Welwyn: Evangelical Press, 1988); Doug Harris, *Occult Overviews and New Age Agendas: A Comprehensive Examination of Major Occult and New Age Groups* (Richmond, U.K.: Reachout Trust, 1999); Robert A. Morey, *Horoscopes and the Christian: Does Astrology Accurately Predict the Future? Is It Compatible with Christianity?* (Minneapolis: Bethany House Publishers, 1981). For pro-astrology works, see Pamela Crane, *The Birth of Christ* (Faversham: Shoestring Publications, 1994); Don Jacobs, *"MobyDick," Astrology's Pew in Church* (The Joshua Foundation, 1995); and Gordon Strachan, *Christ and the Cosmos* (Dunbar: Labarum Publications, 1985).

6. Lynn Thorndike, *History of Magic and Experimental Science*, 8 vols. (New York: Columbia University Press), 1923–58.

7. Tim Hegedus, *Early Christianity and Ancient Astrology* (New York: Peter Lang, 2007).

8. Apocryphon of John 2.

9. Ephesians 1.4, 22–23.

10. Galatians 6.15; Emanuel Swedenborg, *The New Jerusalem*, trans. John Chadwick (London: The Swedenborg Society, 1990).

11. Cosmas Indicopleustes, *The Christian Topography of Cosmas Indicopleustes*, in J. W. McCrindle (ed.) (Cambridge: Cambridge Library Series–Hakluyt Society, 2010).

12. John Polkinghorne, *Faith, Science and Understanding* (London: Society for Promoting Christian Knowledge, 2000).

13. JW Info Line, "Is Christmas Pagan," http://www.jwinfoline.com/Documents/Christmas/Is_Christmas_pagan.htm (accessed 5 October 2010).

14. Frankfort, *Kingship and the Gods*, 313–33.

15. Gaston H. Halsberghe, *The Cult of Sol Invictus* (Leiden: E. J. Brill, 1972).

16. Matthew 13.43.

17. Polymnia Athanassiadi-Fowden and Michael Frede, *Pagan Monotheism in Late Antiquity* (Oxford: Oxford University Press, 2001).

18. For recent studies see David Hughes, *The Star of Bethlehem Mystery* (London: J. M. Dent and Sons, 1979); Mark Kidger, *The Star of Bethlehem: An Astronomer's View* (Princeton, NJ: Princeton University Press, 1999); Michael R. Molnar, *The Star of Bethlehem: The Legacy of the Magi* (New Brunswick, NJ: Rutgers University Press, 1999); Percy Seymour, *The Birth of Christ: Exploding the Myth* (London: Virgin Publishing Ltd., 1998); William

Barclay, *The Gospel of Matthew*, The Daily Study Bible (Edinburgh: St. Andrew Press, 1975).

19. Martin Wells, "The Messianic Star: A Critical Examination of Matthew 2 in Light of Astrological Astronomical Interpretations of the Star of Bethlehem" (PhD Thesis, University of Wales, Lampeter, 2009).

20. See for example Genesis 37.9, Numbers 2.1–31, 3.38; Campion, *The Great Year*, 142–46.

21. For seven stars see Revelation 1.17 and 3.1.

22. Revelation 12.1, 22.2.

23. Origen, *Works*, G. W. Butterworth (ed.) (Cambridge, MA: Harvard University Press, 1936), bk. 1, ch. 7.

24. "The Apocryphon of John," x–xi, 110–11; Robinson (ed.), *The Nag Hammadi Library in English*, 384–86.

25. Pistis Sophia, *Book one*, trans. Carl Schmidt and Violet Mcdermott, http://www.gnosis.org/library/psoph1.htm. See Alexandra von Lieven, "Gnosis and Astrology: 'Book IV' of the Pistis Sophia," in John M. Steele and Annette Imhausen, *Under One Sky: Astronomy and Mathematics in the Ancient Near East*, Alter Oient und Altes Testament Bsnd 297 (Munster: Ugarit Verlag, 2002), 223–36.

26. Tatian, *Oratio ad Graecos*, trans. Molly Whittaker (Oxford: Clarendon Press, 1982), 8.

27. Ignatius of Antioch, "To the Ephesians" in James A. Kleist (trans.), *The Epistles of St. Clement of Rome and St. Ignatius of Antioch* (New York: Newman Press, 1946), 67.

28. Augustine, *Contra Faustum Manichaeum* 2.5 (PL 42: cols 212–13) cited in Tester, *History*, 111–12.

29. Augustine, *Confessions* 4.3, *City of God* V.7.

30. Augustine, *Confessions*, 4.3, 7.6, trans. R. S. Pine-Coffin (Harmondsworth: Penguin, 1961).

31. Augustine, *Confessions*, 3.6, *City of God* V.1–7.30.

32. Augustine, *City of God*, trans. Henry Bettenson (Harmondsworth: Penguin, 1972), 2.4.

33. Ibid., Book 5, 6.

34. Thomas Aquinas, *Summa Contra Gentiles*, 3.91.2, in *Summa Contra Gentiles*, 4 vols., trans. Vernon J. Bourke (Notre Dame: University of Notre Dame Press, 1975), book III, part 2, 40.

35. The Roman Catholic Church, *Catechism of the Catholic Church 1994*, Divination and magic, para. 2116, http://www.christusrex.org/www1/CDHN/ccc.html (accessed 5 October 2010).

36. Rev. Lawrence Cassidy, "The Believing Christian as a Dedicated Astrologer," *Astrology Quarterly* 64, No. 3 (Summer 1994): 3–13.

37. Pontifical Council for Culture, Pontifical Council for Interreligious Dialogue, *JESUS CHRIST THE BEARER OF THE WATER OF LIFE: A Christian reflection on the "New Age,"* (2003), http://www.vatican.va/roman_curia/pontifical_councils/interelg/documents/rc_pc_interelg_doc_20030203_new-age_en.html (accessed 5 October 2010).

38. Anon., *The Search for Faith and the Witness of the Church: An Exploration by the Mission Theological Advisory Group* (London: Church House Publishing, 1996), 3.22–23.

CHAPTER 15

1. Surah 57.5, Abdullah Yusuf Ali, *The Holy Qur'an* (Ware: Wordsworth Editions Limited, 2000).

2. Christel Mattheeuws, "Towards an Anthropology in Life: The Astrological Architecture of Zanandroandrea Land in West Bezanozano, Madagascar" (PhD Thesis, University of Aberdeen, 2008); Clinton Bailey, "Bedouin Star-Lore in Sinai and the Negev," *Bulletin of the School of Oriental and African Studies, University of London* 37, no. 3 (1974): 580–96.

3. Abdullah Yusuf Ali, *The Holy Qur'an*.

4. Henry Corbin, *History of Islamic Philosophy*, trans. Liadain Sherrard and Philip Sherrard (London: Kegan Paul International in association with Islamic Publications for The Institute of Ismaili Studies, 1993), *Cyclical Time and Ismaili Gnosis* (London: Kegan Paul, 1983), and *Spiritual Body and Celestial Earth from Mazdean Iran to Shi'ite Iran* (Princeton, NJ: Princeton University Press, 1977); Majid Fakhry, *A History of Islamic Philosophy* (New York: Columbia University Press, 1983).

5. George Saliba, *A History of Arabic Astronomy: Planetary Theories During the Golden Age of Islam* (New York: New York University Press, 1994); John M. Steele, *A Brief Introduction to Astronomy in the Middle East* (London: Saqi Books, 2008); David A. King, *Astronomy in the Service of Islam* (Aldershot: Variorum, 1993).

6. Edith Jachimowicz, "Islamic Cosmology," in Carmen Blacker and Michael Loewe (eds.), *Ancient Cosmologies* (London: George Allen and Unwin Ltd., 1975), 143–71.

7. Seyyed Hossein Nasr, *An Introduction to Islamic Cosmological Doctrines* (New York: State University of New York Press, 1993).

8. E. S. Kennedy and David Pingree, *The Astrological History of Masha'Allah* (Cambridge, MA: Harvard University Press, 1971); David Pingree, *The Thousands of Abu Ma'shar* (London: Warburg Institute, 1968).

9. Abu Ma'shar, *The Abbreviation of the Introduction to Astrology, Together with the Medieval Latin Translation of Adelard of Bath*, ed. and trans. Charles Burnett, Keiji Yamamoto, and Michio Yano (Leiden: E. J. Brill, 1994), and *On Historical Astrology: The Book of Religions and Dynasties (On the Great Conjunctions)*, ed. and trans. Keiji Yamamoto and Charles Burnett, 2 vols. (Leiden: Brill, 2000); Al-Qabisi (Alcabitius), *The Introduction to Astrology*, ed. and trans. Charles Burnett, Keiji Yamamoto, and Michio Yano (London: The Warburg Institute, 2004); Masha'allah, *Book of Nativities*, trans. Robert Hand (Berkeley Springs, WV: Golden Hind Press, 1994), and Masha'allah, *On Reception*, trans. Robert Hand (Reston: ARHAT, 1998); Benjamin Dykes (ed. and trans.), *Works of Sahl and Masha'allah* (Minneapolis: Cazimi Press, 2008), and *Persian Nativities*, Vol. 1: *Masah'allah and Abu'Ali* (Minneapolis, Cazimi Press, 2009).

10. E. S. Kennedy and B. L. van der Waerden, "The World-Year of the Persians," *Journal of the American Oriental Society* 83, No. 3 (August–September 1963): 315–27; D. N. MacKenzie, "Zoroastrian Astrology in the 'Bundahisn,'" *Bulletin of the School of Oriental and African Studies, University of London* 27, No. 3 (1964): 511–29; David Pingree, "Astronomy and Astrology in India and Iran," *Isis* 54, no. 2 (June 1963): 229–46; and David Pingree, "Classical and Byzantine Astrology in Sassanian Persia," *Dumbarton Oaks Papers* 43 (1989): 227–39.

11. Extract from chapter 12 of the Zoroastrian text, the *Mēnōk I Xrat*, in Richard Charles Zaehner, *Zurvan: a Zoroastrian Dilemma* (Oxford: Clarendon Press, 1955), 400.

12. See the discussion in Al-Azmeh, *Ibn Khaldun* (London: Routledge, 1990).

13. Daniel Martin Varisco, "The Origin of the anwā' in Arab Tradition," *Studia Islamica*, no. 74 (1991): 5–28.

14. Ben Adams, "From Rain Stars to Lunar Stations: The Restructuring of Early Islamic Cosmology in Qur'anic Commentaries," in Nicholas Campion, *Astronomy and Power: How Worlds Are Structured* (with Barbara Rappenglück and Michael Rappenglück), (Oxford: British Archaeology Reports, 2011), forthcoming.

15. Daniel Martin Varisco, "Islamic Folk Astronomy," in Helaine Selin (ed.), *Astronomy Across Cultures: The History of Non-Western Astronomy* (Dordrecht: Kluwer Academic Publishers, 2000), 624.

16. Clinton Bailey, "Bedouin Star-Lore in Sinai and the Negev," *Bulletin of the School of Oriental and African Studies*, University of London 37, No. 3 (1974): 580–96.

17. David King, "Folk-Astronomy in the Service of Religion: The Case of Islam," in Clive Ruggles and Nicholas Saunders (eds.), *Astronomies and Cultures* (Niwot: University Press of Colorado, 1993), 125.

18. David King, "On the Astronomical Orientation of the Kaaba" (with Gerald S. Hawkins), *Journal for the History of Astronomy* 13 (1982): 102–9.

19. Ibrahim Allawi, "Some Evolutionary and Cosmological Aspects to Early Islamic Town Planning," in Margaret Bentley Sevcenko (ed.), *Theories and Principles of Design in the Architecture of Islamic Societies* (Cambridge: Aga Khan Program for Islamic Architecture 1988), 58.

20. Nasr, *Islamic Cosmological Doctrines*, 25–104.

21. Keith Critchlow, *Islamic Patterns: An Analytical and Cosmological Approach* (London: Thames and Hudson, 1983).

22. Titus Burckhardt, *Mystical Astrology According to Ibn'Arabi*, trans. Bulent Rauf (Abingdon: Beshara Publications, 1977).

23. Ben Adams, "From Rain Stars to Lunar Stations: The Restructuring of Early Islamic Cosmology in Qur'anic Commentaries," in Nicholas Campion, *Astronomy and Power: How Worlds Are Structured* (with Barbara Rappenglück and Michael Rappenglück) (Oxford: British Archaeology Reports, 2011), forthcoming.

24. Pingree, *From Astral Omens to Astrology*, 49; Robert Hand (ed.) and Robert Schmidt (trans.), *The Astrological Records of the Early Sages in Greek* (Berkeley Springs, WV: Golden Hind Press, 1995), xiv.

25. Abu Ma'shar, *On Historical Astrology*, I.16, 11–13.

26. Kennedy and Pingree, *The Astrological History of Masha'Allah*, 51–52, see also 45; David Pingree, "Masha'allah's Zoroastrian Historical Astrology," in Günther Oestmann, H. K. von Stuckrad, G. Oestmann, and D. Rutkin (eds.), *Horoscopes and History* (Berlin: Walter de Gruyter, 2005), 95–100.

27. Abu Ma'shar, *On Historical Astrology*, 3.7–10.

28. Ibid., 4.1.4.

29. Ibid., 1.1.3.

30. Anon., *Ghayat Al-Hakim.Picatrix: The Goal of the Wise*, trans. Hashem Atallah (Seattle: Ouroboros Press, 2002), I.2, 7.

31. Ibid., I.2, 11.

32. Ibid., I.5, 39.

33. E. J. Holmyard, *Alchemy* (Harmondsworth: Penguin Books, 1957).

34. See, for example, L. P. Elwell-Sutton, *The Horoscope of Asadullah Mirzā: A Specimen of Nineteenth-Century Persian Astrology* (Leiden: Brill, 1977).

35. See "The Heritage of Ulugh Beg" in Edward S. Kennedy, *Astronomy and Astrology in the Medieval Islamic World* (Aldershot: Ashgate, 1998), chap. XI.

36. Edward S. Kennedy, "An Astrological History Based on the Career of Ghenghis Khan," in Edward S. Kennedy, *Astronomy and Astrology in the Medieval Islamic World* (Aldershot: Ashgate, 1998), chap. XVII.

CHAPTER 16

1. Marian Green, *Magic for the Aquarian Age: A Contemporary Textbook of Practical Magical Techniques* (Wellingborough: Aquarian Press, 1983), 211–12.

2. Bryan Wilson, *Religion in Secular Society: A Sociological Comment* (Harmondsworth: Pelican, 1969); Paul Heelas, Linda Woodhead, Benjamin Seel, Karin Tusting, and Bron Szerszynski, *The Spiritual Revolution: Why Religion Is Giving Way to Spirituality* (Oxford: Blackwell, 2005).

3. H. P. Blavatsky, *Isis Unveiled*, 2 vols. (Pasadena: Theosophical University Press, 1976, facsimile of 1877 edition); *The Secret Doctrine*, 2 vols. (Los Angeles: The Theosophy Company, 1982, facsimile of 1888 edition).

4. Gerald Gardner, *A Goddess Arrives* (London: Stockwell, 1939), and *High Magic's Aid* (London: Michael Houghton, 1949).

5. Gerald Gardner, *Witchcraft Today* (London: Rider, 1954), and *The Meaning of Witchcraft* (London: Aquarian Press, 1959)

6. Antoine Faivre, *Theosophy, Imagination, Tradition: Studies in Western Esotericism* (New York: State University of New York Press, 2000); Wouter J. Hanegraaff, *New Age Religion and Western Culture* (Leiden: E. J. Brill, 1996); Paul Heelas, *The New Age Movement* (Oxford: Blackwell, 1996); Michael York, *The Emerging Network: A Sociology of the New Age and Neo-Pagan Movements* (London: Rowman and Littlefield, 1995).

7. M. Adler, *Drawing Down the Moon: Witches, Druids, Goddess Worshippers and Other Pagans in America Today* (Boston: Beacon Press, 1986); Harvey Graham, *Listening People, Speaking Earth: Contemporary Paganism* (London: Hurst, 1997); G. Harvey and C. Hardman, *Pagan Pathways: A Guide to the Ancient Earth Traditions* (London: Thorsons, 1995); Jenny Blain, Douglas Ezzy, and Graham Harvey (eds.), *Researching Paganisms* (Walnut Creek: Altamira Press, 2004); T. Luhrmann, *Persuasions of the Witch's Craft: Ritual Magic in Contemporary England* (Cambridge, MA: Harvard University Press, 1989); Susan Greenwood, *Magic, Witchcraft and the Otherworld: An Anthropology* (Oxford: Berg, 2000); Ronald Hutton, *The Triumph of the Moon: A History of Modern Pagan Witchcraft* (Oxford: Oxford University Press, 1999).

8. York, *The Emerging Network*, 22.

9. Ibid., 39.

10. Michael York, *Historical Dictionary of New Age Movements* (Lanham: Scarecrow, 2003), 142.

11. Prudence Jones, "Pagan Theologies," in Harvey and Hardman, *Pagan Pathways*, 34.

12. Hanegraaff, *New Age Religion*, chaps. 5–8.

13. Ibid., 97, 521.

14. Ibid.

15. See Harvey, *Contemporary Paganism: Listening People, Speaking Earth*; Harvey and Hardman, *Pagan Pathways*.

16. Ronald Hutton, "Astral Magic: The Acceptable Face of Paganism," in Nicholas Campion, Patrick Curry, and Michael York (eds.), *Astrology and the Academy*, papers from the inaugural conference of the Sophia Centre, Bath Spa University College, 13–14 June 2003 (Bristol: Cinnabar Books, 2004), 10–24.

17. Janet Farrar and Stewart Farrar, *The Witches' Way: Principles, Rituals and Beliefs of Modern Witchcraft* (London: Robert Hale, 1984), 159–60.

18. Vivianne Crowley, *Wicca: The Old Religion in the New Age* (Wellingborough: Aquarian Press, 1989), 242. See also 49, 162.

19. Hanegraaff, *New Age Religion*, 218.

20. See Bruce H. Campbell, *Ancient Wisdom Revived: A History of the Theosophical Movement* (Berkeley: University of California Press, 1980).

21. Blavatsky, *The Secret Doctrine*, Vol. 1, 641.

22. Heelas, *The New Age Movement*, 18, 23

23. Joscelyn Godwin, *The Theosophical Enlightenment* (New York: State University of New York Press, 1994), 338, 340, 344.

24. Blavatsky, *Isis Unveiled*, Vol. 2, 272.

25. James H. Holden and Robert A. Hughes, *Astrological Pioneers of America* (Tempe: American Federation of Astrologers, 1988), 75.

26. Max Heindel, *The Rosicrucian Cosmo-Conception* (London: Fowler, 1929 [1909]), 12–13.

27. Rudolf Steiner, *An Autobiography* (New York: Steiner Books, 1980); Geoffrey Ahern, *Sun at Midnight: The Rudolf Steiner Movement and the Western Esoteric Tradition* (Wellingborough: Aquarian Press, 1984).

28. Robert Powell, *The Christ Mystery: Reflections on the Second Coming* (Fair Oaks, CA: Rudolf Steiner College Press, 1999), 1, 9, 14, 29, 54; Rudolf Steiner, *The Reappearance of Christ in the Etheric* (Spring Valley, NY: Anthroposophic Press, 1983), 15.

30. Steiner, *The Reappearance of Christ*, 19.

31. Elisabeth Vreede, *Anthroposophy and Astrology* (Great Barrington: Anthroposophic Press, 2001), 101.

32. C. G. Jung, "The Sign of the Fishes" in *Aion*, Collected Works, Vol. 9, Part 2, trans. R. F. C. Hull (London: Routledge and Kegan Paul, 1959), 87.

33. Alice A. Bailey, *The Reappearance of the Christ* (New York: Lucis Publishing Company, 1948), 182–83.

34. Steve Nobel, "Hope Springs Eternal," *Alternatives* (Winter/Spring 2003), 1.

35. Cyril Fagan, "Interpretation of the Zodiac of Constellations," *Spica* 1, No. 1 (October 1951): 24.

36. James R. Lewis, *Witchcraft Today: An Encyclopedia of Wiccan and Neopagan Traditions* (Santa Barbara: ABC-CLIO, 1990), 332.

37. York, *Historical Dictionary of New Age Movements*, 25–26.

38. Blavatsky, *Isis Unveiled*, Vol 1.259.

39. Annie Besant, "An Appreciation," in Bessie Leo (ed.), *The Life and Work of Alan Leo* (London: Modern Astrology, 1919), 8.

40. Alan Leo, *Esoteric Astrology: A Study in Human Nature* (London: Modern Astrology, 1925 [1913]), vii.

41. Charles Carter, *The Zodiac and the Soul* (London: Theosophical Publishing House, 1948), 13.

42. Alan Oken, *The Horoscope, the Road and Its Traveler: A Manual of Consciousness Expansion through Astrology* (New York: Bantam, 1974), 10.

43. Dane Rudhyar, *The Astrology of Transformation: A Multilevel Approach* (Wheaton: Theosophical Publishing House, 1984 [1980]), 136.

44. Green, *Magic for the Aquarian Age*, 32–33.

45. Ibid., 211–12.

46. Vivianne Crowley, *Wicca: The Old Religion in the New Age* (Wellingborough: Aquarian Press, 1989).

47. Starhawk, *The Pagan Book of Living and Dying* (San Francisco: HarperCollins, 1997), 37, 39.

48. Wren Side, "Drawing Down the Moon and Candlemas Ritual Cake," in Chas. Clifton and Graham Harvey (eds.), *The Paganism Reader* (London: Routledge, 2004), 330–34.

49. Ronald Hutton, *The Pagan Religions of the Ancient British Isles: Their Nature and Legacy* (London: BCA, 1991), 227–341.

50. Hutton, *Triumph of the Moon*.

51. Harvey, *Contemporary Paganism*.

Bibliography

Abram, David. *The Spell of the Sensuous*. New York: Vintage, 1997.

Abu Ma'shar. *On Historical Astrology: The Book of Religions and Dynasties (On the Great Conjunctions)*, ed. and trans. Keiji Yamamoto and Charles Burnett, 2 vols. Leiden: Brill, 2000.
————. *The Abbreviation of the Introduction to Astrology, Together with the Medieval Latin Translation of Adelard of Bath*, ed. and trans. Charles Burnett, Keiji Yamamoto, and Michio Yano. Leiden: E. J. Brill, 1994.

Adams, Ben. "From Rain Stars to Lunar Stations: The Restructuring of Early Islamic Cosmology in Qur'anic Commentaries," in Nicholas Campion, *Astronomy and Power: How Worlds Are Structured* (with Barbara Rappenglück and Michael Rappenglück). Oxford: British Archaeology Reports, forthcoming 2012.

Adler, M. *Drawing Down the Moon: Witches, Druids, Goddess Worshippers and Other Pagans in America Today*. Boston: Beacon Press, 1980.

Ahern, Geoffrey. *Sun at Midnight: The Rudolf Steiner Movement and the Western Esoteric Tradition*. Wellingborough: Aquarian Press, 1984.

Al-Azmeh. *Ibn Khaldun*. London: Routledge, 1990.

Al-Biruni. *The Book of Instruction in the Elements of the Art of Astrology*, trans. R. Ramsay Wright. London: Luzac and Co., 1934.

Al Kindi. *On the Stellar Rays*, trans. Robert Zoller. Berkeley Springs, WV: Project Hindsight, The Golden Hind Press, 1993.

Allawi, Ibrahim. "Some Evolutionary and Cosmological Aspects to Early Islamic Town Planning" in Margaret Bentley Sevcenko (ed.), *Theories and Principles of Design in the Architecture of Islamic Societies*. Cambridge: Aga Khan Program for Islamic Architecture 1988, 57–72.

Al-Qabisi (Alcabitius). *The Introduction to Astrology*, ed. and trans. Charles Burnett, Keiji Yamamoto, and Michio Yano. London: The Warburg Institute and Nino Arangho Editore, 2004.

Ali, Abdullah Yusuf. *The Holy Qur'an*. Ware: Wordsworth Editions Limited, 2000.

Ananth, Sashikala. *Vaastu: The Classical Indian Science of Architecture and Design*. London: Penguin, 1999.

Anderson, Peter. *Satan's Snare: The Influence of the Occult*. Welwyn: Evangelical Press, 1988.

Anenechukwu, John. *After God Is Dibia: Igbo Cosmology, Healing, Divination of Sacred Science in Nigeria*, 2 vols. London: Karnak, 1999.

Anon. *Ghayat Al-Hakim. Picatrix: The Goal of the Wise*, trans. Hashem Atallah. Seattle: Ouroboros Press, 2002.

Anon. *The Search for Faith and the Witness of the Church: An Exploration by the Mission Theological Advisory Group*. London: Church House Publishing, 1996.

Aquinas, Thomas. *Summa Contra Gentiles*, 3.91.2, in *Summa Contra Gentiles*, 4 vols., trans. Vernon J. Bourke. Notre Dame: University of Notre Dame Press, 1975.

Arguelles, José. *The Mayan Factor: Path Beyond Technology*. Santa Fe: Bear and Company, 1987.

Aristophanes. *The Birds*. The Internet Classics Archive, 1994, http://classics.mit.edu/Aristophanes/birds.html (accessed 26 March 2010).

Aristotle. *Metaphysics*, 2 vols., Vol. 1 trans. Hugh Tredennick, Vol. 2 trans. Hugh Tredennick and G. Cyril Armstrong. Cambridge, MA: Harvard University Press, 1933.

———. *Meterologica*, trans. H. D. P. Lee. Cambridge, MA: Harvard University Press, 1937.

——— *On the Heavens* (De Caelo), trans. W. K. C. Guthrie. Cambridge, MA: Harvard University Press, 1921.

———. *On the Soul*, trans. W. S. Hett. Cambridge, MA: Harvard University Press, 1936.

———. *Physics*, 2 vols., trans. F. M. Cornford and P. H. Wickstead. Cambridge, MA: Harvard University Press, 1930.

———. *Secreta Secretorum*. New York: Da Capo, 1970.

Arnold, Denise. "Kinship as Cosmology: Potatoes as Offspring among the Aymara of Highland Bolivia," in Don McCaskill, "Amerindian Cosmology." *Canadian Journal of Native Studies and the Traditional Cosmology Society*, 1988.

Assmann, Jan. *The Mind of Egypt: History and Meaning in the Time of the Pharaohs*, trans. Andrew Jenkins. New York: Metropolitan Books, 2002.

Athanassiadi-Fowden, Polymnia, and Michael Frede. *Pagan Monotheism in Late Antiquity*. Oxford: Oxford University Press, 2001.

Augustine. *City of God*, trans. Henry Bettenson. Harmondsworth: Penguin, 1972.

———. *Confessions*, trans. R. S. Pine-Coffin. Harmondsworth: Penguin, 1961.

Aveni, Anthony. *Empires of Time: Calendars, Clocks, and Cultures*. London: Tauris Parkes Paperbacks, 2000.

———. "Introduction: Making Time," in *The Sky in Mayan Literature*. Oxford: Oxford University Press, 1992, pp. 3–17.

———. *Skywatchers of Ancient Mexico*. Austin: University of Texas Press, 1980.

Aveni, Anthony, ed. *Native American Astronomy*. Austin: University of Texas Press, 1975.

Badawy, Alexander. "The Stellar Destiny of Pharoah and the So-Called Air Shafts of Cheops' Pyramid," in *Mitteilungen des deutsches Akademie Berlin*, band 10, 1964, pp 198–206.

Baigent, Michael. *From the Omens of Babylon: Astrology and Ancient Mesopotamia*. London: Penguin, 1994.

Bailey, Alice A. *The Reappearance of the Christ*. New York: Lucis Publishing Company, 1948.

Bailey, Clinton. "Bedouin Star-Lore in Sinai and the Negev," *Bulletin of the School of Oriental and African Studies, University of London* 37, No. 3 (1974): 580–96.

Barclay, William. *The Gospel of Matthew*, The Daily Study Bible. Edinburgh: St. Andrew Press, 1975.

Barton, Tamsyn. *Ancient Astrology*. London: Routledge, 1994.

Bassi, Marco. "On the Borana Calendrical System: A Preliminary Field Report," *Current Anthropology* 29, No. 4 (August–October 1988): 619–24.

Bauer, Brian. *The Sacred Landscape of the Inca: The Cusco Ceque System*. Austin: University of Texas Press, 1998.

Bauer, Brian S., and David S.P. Dearbon. *Astronomy and Empire in the Ancient Andes.* Austin: University of Texas Press, 1995.

Beck, Roger. *A Brief History of Ancient Astrology.* Oxford: Blackwell, 2007.

———. *The Religion of the Mithras Cult in the Roman Empire: Mysteries of the Unconquered Sun.* Oxford: Oxford University Press, 2006.

Beckwith, Roger T. *Calendar and Chronology, Jewish and Christian.* Leiden: Brill, 2001.

Beckwith, Martha. *Hawaiian Mythology.* Honolulu: University of Hawaii Press, 1970.

Beek, Walter E.A. van. "Haunting Griaule: Experiences from the Restudy of the Dogon," *History in Africa* 31 (2004): 43–68.

Bellman, Eric. "When the Stars Align, Indians Say, It's a Good Time to Have a C-Section: Moms-to-Be Consult Their Astrologers, Request the Operation on Auspicious Days," *Wall Street Journal,* 5 October 2010, p. 1, http://online.wsj.com/article/SB1000142405274 8704394704575495413840008880.html?KEYWORDS=when+the+stars+align.

Belmonte, Juan Antonio. "On the Orientation of Old Egyptian Pyramids," *Archaeoastronomy, Supplement to the Journal for History of Astronomy,* No. 26 (2001), pp. S1–S20.

Belmonte, Juan Antonio, and Mosalem Shaltout, eds. *In Search of Cosmic Order: Selected Essays on Egyptian Archaeoastronomy.* Cairo: Supreme Council of Antiquities Press, 2009.

Belmonte, Juan Antonio, Mosalem Shaltout, and Magdi Fekri. "Astronomy, Landscape and Symbolism: A Study of the Orientation of Ancient Egyptian Temples," in Juan Antonio Belmonte and Mosalem Shaltout, eds., *In Search of Cosmic Order: Selected Essays on Egyptian Archaeoastronomy.* Cairo: Supreme Council of Antiquities Press, 2009.

Bennett, Julius R. "The Aquarian Age, and the Evidence of Its Inception," *Astrology* 1, No. 5 (Winter 1927): 38–44.

Besant, Annie. "An Appreciation," in Bessie Leo, *The Life and Work of Alan Leo.* London: Modern Astrology, 1919.

Best, Elsdon. *The Astronomical Knowledge of the Maori, Genuine and Empirical, including Data Concerning Their Systems of Astrogeny, Astrolatory and Natural Astrology, with Notes on Certain Other Natural Phenomena.* Wellington: Dominion Museum, 1955 [1922].

Betz, Hans Dieter. *The Greek Magical Papyri in Translation, including the Demotic Spells.* Chicago: University of Chicago Press, 1992.

Bhat, M. Ramakrishna. *Varahamihira's Brhat Samhita,* 2 vols. Delhi: Motilal Banarsidass Publishers, 1993.

Bierhorst, John. *The Mythology of South America.* New York: Morrow, 1988.

Biler, Suzanne. *The Anatomy of Architecture: Ontology and Metaphor in Batammaliba Architectural Expression.* Cambridge: Cambridge University Press, 1987.

Binsbergen, Wim. "Regional and Historical Connections of Four-Tablet Divination in Southern Africa," *Africa: Journal of Religion in Africa* 26, fasc. 1 (February 1996): 2–29.

Birrell, Anne. *Chinese Mythology: An Introduction.* Baltimore: Johns Hopkins University Press, 1993.

Blain, Jenny, Souglas Ezzy, and Graham Harvey, eds. *Researching Paganisms.* Walnut Ceek: Altamira Press, 2004.

Blavatsky, H. P. *Isis Unveiled.* Pasadena: Theosophical University Press, 1976, 2 vols., facsimile of 1877 edition.

———. *The Secret Doctrine,* 2 vols. Los Angeles: The Theosophy Company, 1982, facsimile of 1888 edition.

Bohak, Gideon. *Ancient Jewish Magic: A History*. Cambridge: Cambridge University Press, 2008.

Brooks, Bruce E., and A. Taeko Brooks. *The Original Analects: Sayings of Confucius and His Successors*. New York: Columbia University Press, 1998.

Brown, David. *Mesopotamian Planetary Astronomy-Astrology*. Groningen: Styx Publications, 2000.

Brown, Joseph, and Emily Cousins. *Teaching Spirits: Understanding Native American Religious Traditions*. Oxford: Oxford University Press, 2001.

Buckstaff, Ralph N. "Stars and Constellations of a Pawnee Sky Map," *American Anthropologist*, New Series 29, No. 2 (April 1927): 279–85.

Budge, E. A. Wallis. *The Book of the Dead*. London: Kegan Paul, 1899.

Burckhardt, Titus. *Mystical Astrology According to Ibn' Arabi*, trans. Bulent Rauf. Abingdon: Beshara Publications, 1977.

Burrows, Millar. "Ancient Israel," in Robert C. Dentan (ed.), *The Idea of History in the Ancient Near East*. New Haven, CT: Yale University Press, 1983, pp. 99–131.

Buxton, Richard, ed. *Oxford Readings in Greek Religion*. Oxford: Oxford University Press, 2000.

Cairns, Hugh. "Aboriginal Sky-Mapping? Possible Astronomical Interpretation of Australian Aboriginal Ethnographic and Archaeological Material," in Clive Ruggles (ed.), *Archaeoastronomy in the 1990s*. Loughborough: Group D Publications, 1993, pp. 136–52.

———. *Dark Sparklers, Yidumduma's Wardaman Aboriginal Astrology, North Australia, 2003*. Merimbula: C. C Cairns, 2003.

Campbell, Bruce H. *Ancient Wisdom Revived: A History of the Theosophical Movement*. Berkeley: University of California Press, 1980.

Campion, Nicholas. "Astronomy and Psyche in the Classical World: Plato, Aristotle, Zeno, Ptolemy," *Journal of Cosmology* 9 (2010): 2179–86, http://journalofcosmology.com/AncientAstronomy118.html.

———. *The Great Year: Astrology, Millenarianism and History in the Western Tradition*. London: Penguin, 1994.

———. *A History of Western Astrology*, 2 vols. London: Continuum, 2009.

———. "Prophecy, Cosmology and the New Age Movement: The Extent and Nature of Contemporary Belief in Astrology," PhD thesis, University of the West of England, 2004.

———. *Astrology and Popular Religion in the Modern West: Prophecy, Cosmology and the New Age Movement*. Abingdon: Ashgate, 2012.

Carlson, John B. "Venus-Regulated Warfare and Ritual Sacrifice in Mesoamerica," in Clive Ruggles and Nicholas Saunders (eds.), *Astronomies and Cultures*. Niwot: University of Colorado Press, 1993, 202–52.

Carrasco, David. *Quetzalcoatl and the Irony of Empire: Myths and Prophecies in the Aztec Tradition*. Chicago: University of Chicago Press, 1982.

Carter, Charles. *The Zodiac and The Soul*. London: Theosophical Publishing House, 1948.

Cassidy, Rev. Lawrence. "The Believing Christian as a Dedicated Astrologer," *Astrology Quarterly* 64, No. 3 (Summer 1994): 3–13.

Chamberlain, Von Del. "The Algonquin Song of the Stars," http://www.clarkfoundation.org/astro-utah/vondel/songofstars.html (accessed 11 September 2010).

———. *When Stars Came Down to Earth: Cosmology of the Skidi Pawnee Indians of North America*. Los Altos, CA: Ballena Press, 1982.

Charlesworth, James H., ed. *The Old Testament Pseudepigrapha*, 2 vols. New York: Doubleday, 1983.

Charlesworth, Max. "Introduction," in Max Charlesworth, Françoise Dussart, and Howard Morphy (eds.), *Aboriginal Religions in Australia*. Farnham: Ashgate, 2005, pp. 1–27.

Chatterjee, S. K., and Apurba Kumar Chakravarty. "Indian Calendar from Post-Vedic Period to AD 1900," in S. N. Sen and K. S. Shukla (eds.), *History of Astronomy in India*. New Delhi: Indian National Science Academy, 1985, pp. 252–307.

Chatwin, Bruce. *The Songlines*. London: Picador, 1988.

Cosmas Indicopleustes. *The Christian Topography of Cosmas Indicopleustes*, J. W. McCrindle, ed. Cambridge: Cambridge Library Series—Hakluyt Society, 2010.

Chauvin, Michael E. "Useful and Conceptual Astronomy in Ancient Hawaii," in Helaine Selin (ed.), *Astronomy Across Cultures: The History of Non-Western Astronomy*. Dordrecht: Kluwer Academic Publishers, 2000, pp. 91–125.

Ching, Julia. *Mysticism and Kingship in China: The Heart of Chinese Wisdom*. Cambridge: Cambridge University Press, 1997.

Chukwuezi, Barth. "The Relationship Between Human Destiny and the Cosmic Forces— A Study of the IGBO Worldview," in Jarita Holbrook, Rodney Medupe, and Johnson Urama (eds.), *African Cultural Astronomy: Current Archaoeastronomy and Ethnoastronomy Research in Africa*. Amsterdam: Springer Verlag, Astrophysics and Space Science Proceedings, 2008, pp. 209–15.

Cicero. *De Divinatione*, trans. W. A. Falconer. Cambridge, MA: Harvard University Press, 1929.

Clagett, Marshall. *Ancient Egyptian Science: A Sourcebook*, Vol. 2: Calendars, Clocks and Astronomy. Philadelphia: American Philosophical Society, 1995.

Clark, Malcolm. "Sun, Moon and Volcanoes on Easter Island," *Second International Congress on Easter Island and East Polynesia*. Santiago: University of Chile Press, 1998.

Clauss, Manfred. *The Roman Cult of Mithras*, trans. Richard Gordon. Edinburgh: Edinburgh University Press, 2000.

Cleomedes. "On the Heavens," in *Cleomedes' Lectures on Astronomy*, trans. Alan C. Bowen and Robert B. Todd. Berkeley: University of California Press, 2004.

Coe, Michael. *The Maya*, 3rd edition. London: Thames and Hudson, 1984.

Corbin, Henry. *Cyclical Time and Ismaili Gnosis*. London: Kegan Paul, 1983.

———. *History of Islamic Philosophy*, trans. Liadain Sherrard and Philip Sherrard. London: Kegan Paul International in association with Islamic Publications for The Institute of Ismaili Studies, 1993.

———. *Mundus Imaginalis, or the Imaginary and the Imaginal* (1964), http://www.hermetic. com/bey/mundus_imaginalis.htm (accessed 13 June 2011).

———. *Spiritual Body and Celestial Earth from Mazdean Iran to Shi'ite Iran*. Princeton, NJ: Princeton University Press, 1977.

Cornford, F. M. *Plato's Cosmology: The Timaeus*. London: Routledge, 1937.

Courlander, Harold. *The Fourth World of the Hopis* (Albuquerque: University of New Mexico Press, 1971).

Crane, Pamela. *The Birth of Christ*. Faversham: Shoestring Publications, 1994.

Critchlow, Keith. *Islamic Patterns: An Analytical and Cosmological Approach*. London: Thames and Hudson, 1983.

Crowley, Vivianne. *Wicca: The Old Religion in the New Age*. Wellingborough: Aquarian Press, 1989.

Cryer, Frederick H. *Divination in Ancient Israel and Its Near Eastern Environment: A Socio-Historical Investigation*. Sheffield: Sheffield Academic Press, 1994.

Cullen, Christopher. *Astronomy and Mathematics in Ancient China: The Zhou bi suan jing*. Cambridge: Cambridge University Press, 1996.

Curry, Patrick. "Astrology on Trial, and Its Historians: Reflections on the Historiography of 'Superstition,'" *Culture and Cosmos* 4, No. 2 (2000): 47–56.

Cush, Denise, Catherine Robinson, and Lynn Foulston, eds. *The Encyclopaedia of Hinduism*. London: Routledge, 2007.

Davis, Virginia Lee. "Identifying Ancient Egyptian Constellations," *Archaeoastronomy: Supplement to the Journal for the History of Astronomy*, No. 9 (1985), pp. S103–4.

De Young, Gregg. "Astronomy in Ancient Egypt," in Helaine Selin (ed.), *Astronomy Across Cultures: The History of Non-Western Astronomy*. Dordrecht: Kluwer Academic Publishers, 2000, pp. 475–508.

Denbow, James. "Heart and Soul: Glimpses of Ideology and Cosmology in the Iconography of Tombstones from the Loango Coast of Central Africa," *The Journal of American Folklore* 112, No. 445 "Theorizing the Hybrid" (Summer 1999): 404–23.

Dharmadhikari, T. N. "Nakshatras and Vedic Astrology," in Haribhai Pandya, Somdutt Dikshit, and N. M. Kansara (eds.), *Issues in Vedic Astronomy and Astrology*. Delhi: Motilal Banarsidass Publishers, 1992, 249–53.

Dietler, Michael, and Ingrid Herbich. "Living on Luo Time: Reckoning Sequence, Duration, History and Biography in a Rural African Society," *World Archaeology* 25, No. 2: Conceptions of Time and Ancient Society (October 1993): 248–60.

Diogenes Laertius. "Zeno," in *Lives of Eminent Philosophers*, Vol. 2, trans. R. D. Hicks. London: William Heinemann, 1925, 110–263.

Dolce, Lucia. *The Worship of Stars in Japanese Religious Practice*, proceedings of the conference on "The Worship of Stars in Japanese Religious Practice," School of Oriental and African Studies, September 2004, *Culture and Cosmos*. 10, Nos. 1 and 2 (Spring and Summer, Autumn and Winter 2006).

Dooren, Ingrid van. "Navajo Hohgan and Navajo Cosmos," in Don McCaskill, "Amerindian Cosmology." *Canadian Journal of Native Studies and the Traditional Cosmology Society*, 1988, 259–66.

Dorotheus of Sidon. *Carmen Astrologicum*, ed. and trans. David Pingree. Leipzig: BSG B.G. Teubner Verlagsgesellschaft, 1976.

Doyle, Laurance R. "The Borana Calendar Reinterpreted," *Current Anthropology* 27, No. 3 (June 1986): 286–87.

Dreyer, J. L. E. *A History of the Planetary Systems from Thales to Kepler*. New York: Dover, 1953 [1906].

Durkheim, Emile. *The Elementary Forms of Religious Life*, trans. Karen E. Fields. New York: Free Press, 1995 [1st edn., *Les Formes élémentaires de la vie religieuse*, Paris; F. Alcan 1912].

Dykes, Benjamin (ed. and trans.). *Persian Nativities*, Vol. 1: Masah'allah and Abu'Ali. Minneapolis: Cazimi Press, 2009.

———. *Works of Sahl and Masha'allah*. Minneapolis: Cazimi Press, 2008.

Eddy, John A., "Medicine Wheels and Plains Indians Astronomy," in Anthony Aveni, ed., *Native American Astronomy*. Austin: University of Texas Press, 1975, 147–69.

Edwards, Edmundo. "The 'Megalithic' Astronomy of Easter Island: A Reassessment," *Journal of the History of Astronomy* 38, No. 5 (2005): 421–33.

———. "The Polynesian Ritual Cycle of Activities and Their Archaeological Markers in Eastern Polynesia," paper presented at the Oxford IX International Symposium on Archaeoastronomy, Lima, Peru, 5–9 January 2011.

———. "The Polynesian Ritual Cycle of Activities and Their Archaeological Markers in Eastern Polynesia," in Clive Ruggles (ed.), *Proceedings of the Oxford IX International Symposium on Archaeoastronomy*, Lima, Peru, 5–9 January 2011. Cambridge: Cambridge University Press, 2011, forthcoming.

Edwards, I. E. S. "The Air Channels of Chephren's Pyramid," in *Studies in Ancient Egypt, the Aegean and the Sudan: Essays in Honor of Dows Dunham on the Occasion of his 90th Birthday, June 1, 1980*, ed. William Kelly Simpson and Whitney M. Davies. Boston: Museum of Fine Arts, 1981, pp. 55–57.

———. *The Pyramids of Egypt*. London: Penguin, revised 1988.

Eliade, Mircea. *The Sacred and the Profane: The Nature of Relgion*. New York: Harcourt Brace Jovanovich, 1959.

Elwell-Sutton, L. P. *The Horoscope of Asadullah Mirzā: A Specimen of Nineteenth-Century Persian Astrology*. Leiden: Brill, 1977.

Epstein, Meira B. *The Correspondence between the Rabbis of Southern France and Maimonides about Astrology*. Reston: ARHAT Publications, 1998.

Epstein, Perle. *Kabbalah: The Way of the Jewish Mystic*. London: Shambhala, 2001.

Evans, James. *The History and Practice of Ancient Astronomy*. Oxford: Oxford University Press, 1998.

Faivre, Antoine. *Theosophy, Imagination, Tradition: Studies in Western Esotericism*. New York: State University of New York Press, 2000.

Fakhry, Majid. *A History of Islamic Philosophy*. New York: Columbia University Press, 1983.

Farrar, Janet, and Stewart Farrar. *The Witches' Way: Principles, Rituals and Beliefs of Modern Wichcraft*. London: Robert Hale, 1984.

Farrer, Claire. "Star Clocks: Mescalero Apache Ceremonial Timing," in Don McCaskill, "Amerindian Cosmology." *Canadian Journal of Native Studies and the Traditional Cosmology Society* (1988): 223–36.

Faulkner, O. R. *The Ancient Egyptian Coffin Texts*, Vol. 1, spells 1–354, Vol. 2, spells 355–787, Vol. 3., spells 788–1186. Warminster: Aris and Phillips, 1973, 1977, 1978.

———. *The Ancient Egyptian Pyramid Texts*, 2 vols. Oxford: Oxford University Press 1969; 2nd ed., Warminster: Aris and Philips 1993.

———. *The Book of the Dead*. London: British Museum Publications, 1985.

Fennell, Christopher C. *Crossroads and Cosmologies: Diasporas and Ethnogenesis in the New World*. Gainesville: University Press of Florida, 2007.

Festugière, André Jean. *Personal Religion among the Greeks*. London: Cambridge University Press, 1954.

Finney, Ben R. *Pacific Navigation and Voyaging*. Honolulu: Bishop Museum Press, 2003.

Fletcher, Alice C. "Pawnee Star Lore," *The Journal of American Folklore* 16, No. 60 (January–March 1903): 10–15.

———. "Star Cult among the Pawnee—a Preliminary Report," *American Anthropologist*, New Series 4, No. 4 (October–December 1902): 730–36.

Flower, Michael Attyah. *The Seer in Ancient Greece*. Berkeley: University of California Press, 2008.

Foster, Benjamin. *Before the Muses: An Anthology of Akkadian Literature.* Bethesda, MD: CDL Press, 2005.

Fowler, Robert, "Greek Magic, Greek Religion," in Richard Buxton, ed., *Oxford Readings in Greek Religion.* Oxford: Oxford University Press, 2000, 317–43.

Frank, Roslyn. "Hunting the European Sky Beers: A Proto-European Vision Quest to the End of the Earth," in John W. Fountain and Rolf M. Sinclair, eds., *Current Studies in Archaeoastronomy: Conversations Across Time and Space.* Durham, NC: Carolina Academic Press, 2005, pp. 455–74.

Frankfort, H., and H. A. Frankfort, William A. Irwin, Thorkild Jacobsen, and John A. Wilson, *The Intellectual Adventure of Ancient Man: An Essay on Speculative Thought in the Ancient Near East.* Chicago: University of Chicago Press, 1946.

Frankfort, Henri. *Kingship and the Gods: A Study of Near Eastern Religion as the Integration of Society and Nature.* Chicago: University of Chicago Press, 1978.

Frawley, David. *The Astrology of the Seers: A Guide to Vedic (Hindu) Astrology.* Salt Lake City: Passage Press, 1990.

Frazer, J. G. *The Golden Bough: A Study in Magic and Religion,* abridged ed. London: Macmillan, 1971 [1922].

Friedel, David, Linda Schele, and Joy Parker. *Maya Cosmos: Three Thousand Years on the Shaman's Path.* New York: Morrow, 1993.

Gadd, C. J. *Ideas of Divine Rule in the Ancient East,* Schweich Lectures of the British Academy, 1945. Munich: Kraus Reprint, 1980.

Galaal, Muusa H. I. *Stars, Seasons and Weather in Somali Pastoral Tradition.* Niamey: Celhto, 1992.

Gansten, Martin. *Patterns of Destiny: Hindu Nadi Astrology, Lund Studies in History of Religions,* Vol. 17. Stockholm: Almqvist and Wiksell International, 2003.

———. "Patterns of Destiny: Hindu Nadi Astrology," PhD Thesis, Lund University, 2003.

Gardner, Gerald. *A Goddess Arrives.* London: Stockwell, 1939.

———. *High Magic's Aid.* London: Michael Houghton, 1949.

———. *Witchcraft Today.* London: Rider, 1954.

———. *The Meaning of Witchcraft.* London: Aquarian Press, 1959.

Gibbon, William B. "Asiatic Parallels in North American Star Lore: Milky Way, Pleaides, Orion," *Journal of American Folklore* 85, No. 337 (1972): 236–47.

———. "Asiatic Parallels in North American Star Lore: Ursa Major," *Journal of American Folklore* LXXVII (1964): 236–50.

Gibbs, Sharon L. "Mesoamerican Calendrics as Evidence of Astronomical Activity," in Anthony Aveni, ed., *Native American Astronomy.* Austin: University of Texas Press, 1975, 21–35.

Gill, Jerry H. *Native American Worldviews: An Introduction.* Amhurst: Humanity Books, 2002.

Gingerich, Owen. "The Origin of the Zodiac," in *The Great Copernicus Chase and Other Adventures in Astronomical History.* Cambridge: Sky Publishing Corporation, 1992, pp. 7–12.

Godwin, Joscelyn. *The Theosophical Enlightenment.* New York: State University of New York Press, 1994.

Gombrich, R. F. "Ancient Indian Cosmology," in Carmen Blacker and Michael Loewe (eds.), *Ancient Cosmologies.* London: George Allen and Unwin Ltd., 1975, pp. 110–42.

Goodale, Jane. *Tiwi Wives: A Study of the Women of Melville Island*. Seattle: University of Washington Press, 1971.

Graham, A. C. *Yin-Yang and the Nature of Correlative Thinking*. Singapore: Institute of East Asian Philosophies, 1986.

Green, Marian. *Magic for the Aquarian Age: A Contemporary Textbook of Practical Magical Techniques*. Wellingborough: Aquarian Press, 1983.

Greene, Liz, and Howard Sasportas. *The Development of the Personality: Seminars in Psychological Astrology*. London: Arkana, 1987.

Greenwood, Susan. *Magic, Witchcraft and the Otherworld: An Anthropology*. Oxford: Berg, 2000.

Griffin-Pierce, Trudy. *Earth Is My Mother, Sky Is My Father: Space, Time and Astronomy in Navajo Sandpainting*. Albuquerque: University of New Mexico Press, 1995.

Guthrie, Kenneth. *The Pythagorean Sourcebook and Library*. Grand Rapids: Phanes Press, 1987.

Guthrie, William. *Orpheus and Greek Religion: A Study of the Orphic Movement*. Princeton, NJ: Princeton University Press, 1993 [London 1935, 2nd (revised) ed. London, 1952].

Haack, Steven C. "The Astronomical Orientation of the Egyptian Pyramids," *Archaeoastronomy: Supplement to the Journal for the History of Astronomy* 7 (1984): S119–S125.

Hakim, Mohammed, and Ansar Zahid Zhan. *Al-Biruni: His Times, Life and Works*. Delhi: Renaissance Publishing House, 1990.

Halsberghe, Gaston H. *The Cult of Sol Invictus*. Leiden: E. J. Brill, 1972.

Hand, Robert, ed. and Robert Schmidt, trans. *The Astrological Records of the Early Sages in Greek*. Berkeley Springs, WV: Golden Hind Press, 1995.

Hanegraaff, Wouter J. *New Age Religion and Western Culture: Esotericism in the Mirror of Secular Thought*. Leiden: E. J. Brill, 1996.

Harris, Doug. *Occult Overviews and New Age Agendas: A Comprehensive Examination of Major Occult and New Age Groups*. Richmond: Reachout Trust, 1999.

Harris, R. Baine, ed. *Neoplatonism and Indian Thought*. Norfolk: International Society for Neoplatonic Studies, 1982.

Harrison, Jane. *Themis: A Study of the Origins of Greek Religion*. London: Merlin Press, 1963.

Harvey, G. *Listening People, Speaking Earth: Contemporary Paganism*. London: Hurst, 1997.

Harvey, G., and C. Hardman. *Pagan Pathways: A Guide to the Ancient Earth Traditions*. London: Thorsons, 1995.

Hawkes, Jacquetta. *Man and the Sun*. London: The Cresset Press, 1962.

Haynes, R. D. "Aboriginal Astronomy," *Australian Journal of Astronomy* 4, No. 3 (1992): 127–41.

Haynes, Raymond, Roslynn Haynes, David Malin, and Richard McGee. *Explorers of the Southern Sky: A History of Australian Astronomy*. Cambridge: Cambridge University Press, 1996.

Haynes, Roslynn D. "Astronomy and the Dreaming: The Astronomy of the Aboriginal Australians," in Helaine Selin (ed.), *Astronomy Across Cultures: The History of Non-Western Astronomy*. Dordrecht: Kluwer Academic Publishers, 2000, 53–90.

Heelas, Paul. *The New Age Movement*. Oxford: Blackwell, 1996.

Heelas, Paul, Linda Woodhead, Benjamin Seel, Karin Tusting, and Bron Szerszynski. *The Spiritual Revolution: Why Religion Is Giving Way to Spirituality*. Oxford: Blackwell, 2005.

Hegedus, Tim. *Early Christianity and Ancient Astrology*. New York: Peter Lang, 2007.

Heidel, Alexander. *The Babylonian Genesis*. Chicago: University of Chicago Press, 1963.

Heindel, Max. *The Rosicrucian Cosmo-Conception*. London: Fowler, 1929 [1909].

Heracleitus. *Fragments*, 4 vols., trans. W. Jones and E. Withington. Cambridge, MA: Harvard University Press, 1923.

Herodotus. *The Histories*, trans. Aubrey de Sélincourt. Harmondsworth: Penguin, 1972.

Hesiod. *The Homeric Hymns and Homerica, including "Works and Days" and "Theogonis,"* trans. Hugh G. Evelyn-White. Cambridge, MA: Harvard University Press, 1917.

Hetherington, Norris D. *The Encyclopaedia of Cosmology: Historical, Philosophical and Scientific Foundations of Modern Cosmology*. New York: Garland, 1993.

Hippocrates. *Works*, 4 vols., trans. W. Jones and E. Withington. Cambridge, MA: Harvard University Press, 1923.

Holbrook, Jarita, Rodney Medupe, and Johnson Urama, eds. *African Cultural Astronomy: Current Archaoeastronomy and Ethnoastronomy Research in Africa*. Amsterdam: Springer Verlag, Astrophysics and Space Science Proceedings, 2008.

Holden, James H., and Robert A. Hughes. *Astrological Pioneers of America*. Tempe: American Federation of Astrologers, 1988.

Hollmann, J. C. "The Sky's Things: |xam Bushman '*Astrological Mythology*'" as recorded in the Bleek and Lloyd Manuscripts, in African Skies, Proceedings of the African Astronomical History Symposium held in Cape Town on 8 & 9 November 2005, pp. 7–12. http://www.saao.ac.za/~wgssa/archive/as11/as11_web.pdf (accessed 4 July 2011).

Holmyard, E. J. *Alchemy*. Harmondsworth: Penguin, 1957.

Holt, Peter. *Stars of India: Travels in Search of Astrologers and Fortune-Tellers*. Edinburgh: Mainstream Publishing, 1998.

Hone, Margaret. *The Modern Textbook of Astrology*. London: L. N. Fowler, 4th edition reprinted 1973 [1951].

Hoopes, John W. "Mayanism Comes of (New) Age," in Joseph Gelfer (ed.), *2012: Decoding the Counterculture Apocalypse*. London: Equinox Publishing, 2011.

Hornung, Erik. *The Secret Lore of Egypt: Its Impact on the West*, trans. David Lorton. Ithaca, NY: Cornell University Press, 2001.

Horowitz, Wayne. *Mesopotamian Cosmic Geography*. Winona Lake: Eisenbrauns, 1998.

Hughes, David. *The Star of Bethlehem Mystery*. London: J. M. Dent and Sons, 1979.

Hunger, Hermann. *Astrological Reports to Assyrian Kings*. Helsinki: Helsinki University Press, 1992.

Hunger, Hermann, and David Pingree. *Astral Sciences in Mesopotamia*. Leiden: Brill, 1999.

———. "Mul Apin: An Astronomical Compendium in Cuneiform," *Archiv für Orientforschung* 24 (1989): 1–163.

Husserl, Edmund. *Ideas: General Introduction to Pure Phenomenology*. London: Collier-Macmillan, 1972 [1913, Eng. trns.1931], 91–100.

Hutton, Ronald. "Astral Magic: The Acceptable Face of Paganism," in Nicholas Campion, Patrick Curry, and Michael York (eds.), *Astrology and the Academy*, papers from the inaugural conference of the Sophia Centre, Bath Spa University College, 13–14 June 2003. Bristol: Cinnabar Books, 2004, 10–24.

———. *The Pagan Religions of the Ancient British Isles: Their Nature and Legacy*. London: BCA, 1991.

———. *The Triumph of the Moon: A History of Modern Pagan Witchcraft*. Oxford: Oxford University Press, 1999.

Ibn-Khaldun. *The Muqaddimah: An Introduction to History*, trans. Franz Rosenthal. London: Routledge and Kegan Paul, 1987.

Ignatius of Antioch. "To the Ephesians," in James A. Kleist (trans.), *The Epistles of St. Clement of Rome and St Ignatius of Antioch*. New York: Newman Press, 1946.

Jachimowicz, Edith. "Islamic Cosmology," in Carmen Blacker and Michael Loewe (eds.), *Ancient Cosmologies*. London: George Allen and Unwin Ltd., 1975, pp. 143–71.

Jacobs, Don. "*Moby Dick*," *Astrology's Pew in Church*. The Joshua Foundation, 1995.

Jacobs, Louis. "Jewish Cosmology," in Carmen Blacker and Michael Loewe (eds.), *Ancient Cosmologies*. London: George Allen and Unwin Ltd., 1975, pp. 66–86.

Jacobsen, Thorkild. *The Treasures of Darkness: A History of Mesopotamian Religion*. New Haven, CT: Yale University Press, 1976.

James, Montague Rhodes, ed. *The Apocryphal New Testament*. Oxford: Clarendon Press, 1924.

Jeffers, Ann. *Divination and Prophecy in Israel and Palestine*. Leiden: Brill, 1996.

Johnson, Rubellite Kawena, and John Kaipo Mahelona. *Na Inoa Hoku: A Catalogue of Hawaiian and Pacific Star Names*. Honolulu: Topgallant Publishing Co., 1975.

Johnston, Sarah Iles. *Ancient Greek Divination*. Oxford: Blackwell, 2008.

Jonas, Hans. *The Gnostic Religion: The Message of the Alien God and the Beginnings of Christianity*, 2nd ed. Boston: Beacon Press, 1963.

Jones, Prudence. "Pagan Theologies," in G. Harvey and C. Hardman (eds.), *Pagan Pathways: A Guide to the Ancient Earth Traditions*. London: Thorsons, 1995.

Jordan, Paul. *Riddles of the Sphinx*. Stroud: Sutton Publishing, 1998.

Josephus, "The Antiquities of the Jews," I.2.3 in *Works*, trans. William Whiston, 1736. Hendrickson Publishers, 1987.

Jung, C. G. *The Archetypes and the Collective Unconscious*, Collected Works, Vol. 9.1, trans. R. F. C. Hull. Princeton, NJ: Princeton University Press, 1959.

———. *The Archetypes and the Collective Unconscious*, trans. R. F. C. Hull. London: Routledge and Kegan Paul, 1968.

———. "Richard Wilhelm: In Memoriam," in *The Spirit in Man, Art, And Literature*, Collected Works, Vol. 15, trans. R. F. C. Hull. London: Routledge and Kegan Paul, 1971, 53–62.

———. "The Sign of the Fishes," in *Aion*, Collected Works, Vol. 9, part 2, trans. R. F. C. Hull. London: Routledge and Kegan Paul, 1959, 72–102.

———. "Synchronicity: An Acausal Connecting Principle," Collected Works, Vol. 8: trans. R. F. C. Hull. London: Routledge and Kegan Paul, 1963, 417–531.

JW Info Line. "Is Christmas Pagan," http://www.jwinfoline.com/Documents/Christmas/Is_Christmas_pagan.htm (accessed 5 October 2010).

Kahn, Charles H. *Anaximander and the Origins of Greek Cosmology*. New York: Hacket Publishing Co, 1960.

Kanitscheider, Bernulf. "A Philosopher Looks at Astrology," *Interdisciplinary Science Reviews* 16, No. 3 (1991): 258–66.

Kaplan, Aryeh. *Sefer Yetzirah: The Book of Creation in Theory and Practice*. York Beach: Weiser Books, 1997.

Kaspin, Deborah. "A Chewa Cosmology of the Body," *American Ethnologist* 23, No. 3 (August 1996): 561–78.

Keightley, David N. "Shang Divination and Metaphysics," *Philosophy East and West* 38, No. 4 (October 1988): 367–97.

Kelly, David, and Eugene F. Milone. *Exploring Ancient Skies: An Encyclopedic Survey of Archaeoastronomy*. New York: Spring, 2005, ch. 11.

Kemper, Steven. "Sinhalese Astrology, South Asian Caste Systems, and the Notion of Individuality," *Journal of South Asian Studies* 38, No. 3 (May 1979): 477–97.

———. "Time, Person, and Gender in Sinhalese Astrology," *American Ethnologist* 7, No. 4 (November 1980): 744–58.

Kennedy, Edward .S. "An Astrological History Based on the Career of Genghis Khan," in S. Seikaly, R. Baalbaki, and P. Dodd (eds.), *Quest for Understanding: Arabic and Islamic Studies in Memory of Malcolm Kerr*. Beirut: American University of Beirut Press, 1991, 223–31.

———. *Astronomy and Astrology in the Medieval Islamic World*. Aldershot: Ashgate, 1998.

Kennedy, E. S., and B. L. van der Waerden. "The World-Year of the Persians," *Journal of the American Oriental Society* 83, No. 3 (August–September 1963): 315–27.

Kennedy, E. S., and David Pingree. *The Astrological History of Masha'Allah*. Cambridge, MA: Harvard University Press, 1971.

Kidger, Mark. *The Star of Bethlehem: An Astronomer's View*. Princeton, NJ: Princeton University Press, 1999.

King, David. "Folk-Astronomy in the Service of Religion: The Case of Islam," in Clive Ruggles and Nicholas Saunders (eds.), *Astronomies and Cultures*. Niwot: University Press of Colorado, 1993, 124–38.

———. "On the Astronomical Orientation of the Kaaba" (with Gerald S. Hawkins), *Journal for the History of Astronomy* 13 (1982): 102–9.

King, David A. *Astronomy in the Service of Islam*. Aldershot: Variorum, 1993.

Kingsley, Peter. *Ancient Philosophy, Mystery and Magic: Empedocles and Pythagorean Tradition*. Oxford: Clarendon Press, 1995.

———. *In the Dark Places of Wisdom*. Inverness: Golden Sufi Center, 1999.

Kirch, Patrick Vinton. *On the Road of the Winds: An Archaeological History of the Pacific Islands before European Contact*. Berkeley: University of California Press, 2000.

Kirk, G. S., J. E. Raven, and M. Schofield, *The Presocratic Philosophers*, 2nd ed. Cambridge: Cambridge University Press, 1983.

Knight, Chris. *Blood Relations: Menstruation and the Origins of Culture*. New Haven, CT: Yale University Press, 1991.

Kogan, Barry S. *Averroës and the Metaphysics of Causation*. Albany: State University of New York Press, 1985.

Kramer, Samuel Noah, *Sumerian Mythology: A Study of Spiritual and Literary Achievement in the Third Millennium BC*. Philadephia: University of Pennsylvania Press, 1972 [1944].

Kramer, Samuel Noah, and Diane Wolkstein. *Inanna, Queen of Heaven and Earth: Her Stories and Hymns from Sumer*. New York: Harper & Row, 1983.

Krupp, E. C. *Beyond the Blue Horizon: Myths and Legends of the Sun, Moon and Stars and Planets*. Oxford: Oxford University Press, 1991.

———. "The Cosmic Temples of Old Beijing," in Anthony F. Aveni (ed.), *World Archaeoastronomy*. Cambridge: Cambridge University Press, 1989, 65–75.

———. "Sky Tales and Why We Tell Them," in Helaine Selin (ed.), *Astronomy Across Cultures: The History of Non-Western Astronomy*. Dordrecht: Kluwer Academic Publishers, 2000, 1–30.

———. *Skywatchers, Shamans and Kings: Astronomy and the Archaeology of Power.* New York: John Wiley, 1997.

Kuiper, F. B. J. *Ancient Indian Cosmogony.* New Delhi: Vikas, 1983.

Laenes, J. H. *Jewish Mysticism: An Introduction.* London: Westminster John Knox Press, 2001.

Lagadha. *Vedanga Jyotisa.* New Delhi: Indian National Science Academy, 1984.

Lai, Karyn L. *An Introduction to Chinese Philosophy.* Cambridge: Cambridge University Press, 2008.

Laird, Edgar. "Christine de Pizan and Controversy Concerning Star Study in the Court of Charles V," *Culture and Cosmos* 1, no. 2 (Winter/Autumn 1997): 35–48.

Lambert, W. G. "The Cosmology of Sumer and Babylon," in Carmen Blacker and Michael Loewe (eds.), *Ancient Cosmologies.* London: George Allen and Unwin Ltd., 1975. pp. 42–65.

Lao Tzu. *Tao Te Ching,* trans. D. C. Lau. Harmondsworth: Penguin, 1972.

Larsen, Mogens Trolle. "The Mesopotamian Lukewarm Mind: Reflections on Science, Divination and Literacy," in Francesca Rochberg-Halton (ed.), *Language, Literature and History.* New Haven, CT: American Oriental Society, 1987.

Leaman, Olivier. *Averroës and His Philosophy.* London: Routledge, 1997.

Legesse, Asmarom. *Gada: Three Approaches to the Study of African Society.* London: Collier-Macmillan, 1973.

Lehner, Mark. *The Complete Pyramids.* London: Thames and Hudson, 1997.

Lehoux, Daryn. *Astronomy, Weather, and Calendars in the Ancient World: Parapegmata and Related Texts in Classical and Near-Eastern Societies.* Cambridge: Cambridge University Press, 2007.

Leland, Charles G. *The Algonquin Legends of New England or Myths and Folklore of the Micmac, Passmaquoddy, and Penobscot Tribes.* Boston: Houghton-Mifflin, 1884.

Leo, Alan. *Esoteric Astrology: A Study in Human Nature.* London: Modern Astrology, 1925 [1913].

Léon-Portilla, Miguel, ed. *The Broken Spears: The Aztec Account of the Conquest of Mexico.* Boston: Beacon Press, 1992.

Lesko, Leonard H. "Ancient Egyptian Cosmogonies and Cosmology" in Byron Shafer (ed). *Religion in Ancient Egypt.* Ithaca, NY: Cornell University Press, 1991, 88–122.

Lévi-Bruhl, Lucien. *How Natives Think.* Princeton, NJ: Princeton University Press, 1985.

Lévi-Strauss, Claude. *The Raw and the Cooked: Introduction to a Science of Mythology.* London: Harper & Row and Jonathan Cape, 1969.

———. *The Savage Mind.* London: Weidenfeld and Nicolson, 1972.

Lewis, D. "Voyaging Stars: Aspects of Polynesian and Micronesian Astronomy," *Philosophical Transactions of the Royal Society of London. Series A, Mathematical and Physical Sciences* 276, No. 1257: The Place of Astronomy in the Ancient World (May 2, 1974): 133–48.

Lewis, David. *The Voyaging Stars: Secrets of the Pacific Island Navigators.* Sydney: William L. Collins Publishers, 1978.

———. *We, the Navigators: The Ancient Art of Landfinding in the Pacific.* Honolulu: University of Hawaii Press, 1994.

Lewis, James R. *Witchcraft Today: An Encyclopedia of Wiccan and Neopagan Traditions.* Santa Barbara: ABC-CLIO, 1990.

Lewis, Mark Edward. "Evolution of the Calendar in Shang China," in Iain Morley and Colin Renfrew (eds.), *The Archaeology of Measurement: Comprehending Heaven, Earth and Time in Ancient Societies*. Cambridge: Cambridge University Press, 2010, 195–202.

———. *The Construction of Space in Early China*. Albany: State University of New York Press, 2006.

Lieven, Alexandra von. "Gnosis and Astrology: 'Book IV' of the Pistis Sophia," in John M. Steele and Annette Imhausen (eds.), *Under One Sky: Astronomy and Mathematics in the Ancient Near East*, Alter Oient und Altes Testament Bsnd 297. Munster: Ugarit Verlag, 2002.

Liller, William. "Celestial Happenings on Easter Island: AD 760–837," *Archaeoastronomy: the Journal of the Centre for Archaeoastronomy* IX, Nos. 1–4 (1986): 52–58.

———. "The Megalithic Astronomy of Easter Island: Orientations of Ahu and Moai," *Archaeoastronomy: Supplement to the Journal for the History of Astronomy*, No. 13 (1989): S21–S48.

Lishk, S. S. *Jaina Astronomy*. Delhi: Oriental and Scientific Research Publication Centre, 1987.

Locher, Kurt. "Egyptian Cosmology," in Norris Hetherington (ed.), *Encyclopedia of Cosmology*. New York: Garland, 1993, 189–94.

———. "Probable Identification of the Ancient Egyptian Circumpolar Constellations," *Archaeoastronomy: Supplement to the Journal for the History of Astronomy*, No. 9, 1 (1985): S152–53.

Lopez-Ruis, Carolina. *When the Gods Were Born: Greek Cosmogonies and the Near East*. Cambridge, MA: Harvard University Press, 2010.

Lovejoy, Arthur O. *The Great Chain of Being*. Cambridge, MA: Harvard University Press, 1936.

Luhrmann, T. M. *Persuasions of the Witch's Craft: Ritual Magic in Contemporary England*. Cambridge, MA: Harvard University Press, 1989.

MacCormack, Sabine. *Religion in the Andes: Vision and Imagination in Early Colonial Peru*. Princeton, NJ: Princeton University Press, 1991.

MacKenzie, D. N. "Zoroastrian Astrology in the 'Bundahisn,'" *Bulletin of the School of Oriental and African Studies, University of London* 27, No. 3 (1964): 511–29.

Major, John S. *Heaven and Earth in Early Han Thought*. Albany: State University of New York Press, 1993.

Makemson, Maud Worcester. *The Morning Star Rises: An Account of Polynesian Astronomy*. New Haven, CT: Yale University Press, 1941.

Malinowski, Bronislaw. *Argonauts of the Western Pacific*. New York: Dutton, 1922.

———. *Magic, Science and Religion*, New York: Doubleday, 1954.

Malmstrom, Vincent H. "Origin of the Mesoamerican 260-Day Calendar," *Science* 181 (1973): 939–41.

Malville, J. McKim. *Guide to Prehistoric Astronomy in the Southwest*. Boulder, CO: Johnson Books, 2008.

Malville, John McKim. "Foreword to Rana P. B. Singh," *Cosmic Order and Cultural Astronomy: Sacred Cities of India*. Newcastle: Cambridge Scholars Publishing, 2009, 1–7.

Malville, J. McKim, Fred Wendorf, A. A. Mazaar, and Romauld Schild. "Megaliths and Neolithic astronomy in southern Egypt," *Nature* 392 (1988): 488–91.

Manilius, Marcus. *Astronomica*, trans. G. P. Goold. Cambridge, MA: Harvard University Press, 1977.

Marshak, Alexander. "Lunar Notation on Upper Palaeolithic Remains," *Science* 146 (1964): 743–45.

Marshall, Lorna A. "Kung Bushman Religious Beliefs," *Africa: Journal of the International African Institute* 32, No. 3 (July 1962): 221–52.

Martinez, Florentino Garcia. *The Dead Sea Scrolls Translated: The Qumran Texts in English.* Leiden: E. J. Brill, 1994.

Masha'allah. *Book of Nativities*, trans. Robert Hand. Berkeley Springs, WV: Golden Hind Press, 1994.

———. *On Reception*, trans. Robert Hand. Reston: ARHAT, 1998.

Masse, W. Bruce. "The Celestial Engine at the Heart of Traditional Hawaiian Culture," in Nicholas Campion, Barbara Rappenglück, and Michael Rappenglück (eds.), *Astronomy and Power: How Worlds Are Structured.* Oxford: British Archaeology Reports, 2011 forthcoming.

Masse, W. Bruce, Elizabeth Wayland Barber, Luigi Piccardi, and Paul T. Barber. *Exploring the Nature of Myth and Its Role in Science*, in Luigi Piccardi and W. Bruce Masse (eds.), *Myth and Geology*, Geological Society of London Special Publication 273. London: The Geological Society, 2007.

Masse, W. Bruce, Rubellite Kawena Johnson, and H. David Tuggle. *Islands in the Sky: Traditional Astronomy and the Role of Celestial Phenomena in Hawaiian Myth, Language, Religion and Chiefly Power.* Honolulu: University of Hawaii Press, forthcoming.

Maternus, Julius Firmicus. *Mathesis*, trans. as *Ancient Astrology: Theory and Practice*, Jean Rhys Bram (ed). Park Ridge, NJ: Noyes Press, 1975.

Mathews, Freya. *The Ecological Self.* Savage: Barnes and Noble, 1991.

Matt, Daniel C. *Zohar: Annotated and Explained.* Woodstock: SkyLights Paths Publishing, 2002.

Mattheeuws, Christel. "Towards an Anthropology in Life: The Astrological Archiecture of Zanandroandrea Land in West Bezanozano, Madagascar," PhD Thesis, University of Aberdeen, 2008.

Mbiti, John S. *African Religions and Philosophy*, 2nd edition, revised. London: Heinemann, 2008.

McCaskill, Don, ed. "Amerindian Cosmology." *Canadian Journal of Native Studies and the Traditional Cosmology Society*, 1988.

McCluskey, Stephen. "Native American Cosmologies," in Norris Hetherington (ed.), *Encyclopedia of Cosmology.* New York: Garland, 1993, 427–36.

McElwain, Thomas. "Seneca Iroquois Concepts of Time," in Don McCaskill, "Amerindian Cosmology." *Canadian Journal of Native Studies and the Traditional Cosmology Society*, 1988, 265–77.

McEvilley, Thomas. *The Shape of Ancient Thought.* New York: Allsworth Press, 2002.

McIntosh, R. J. *Ancient Middle Niger: Urbanism and the Self-Organizing Landscape.* Cambridge: Cambridge University Press, 2005.

MacPherson, Peter. "Astronomy of the Australian Aborigines," *Journal and Proceedings of the Royal Society of New South Wales* 15: 71–80.

Meador, Betty De Shong, trans. *Inanna, Lady of Largest Heart: Poems of the Sumerian High Pristess Enheduanna.* Austin: University of Texas Press, 2001.

Melton, Gordon, Jerome Clarke, and Aidan A. Kelly. *New Age Almanac.* London: Visible Ink Press, 1991.

Mercer, Samuel. *The Pyramid Texts*. New York: Longmans Green, 1952.

Meyer, Jeffrey F. "'Feng-Shui' of the Chinese City," *History of Religions* 18, No. 2 (November 1978): 138–55.

Midgley, Mary. *Evolution as Religion*. London: Routledge, 2002 [1985].

Milbrath, Susan. *Star Gods of the Maya: Astronomy in Art, Folklore, and Calendars*. Austin: University of Texas Press, 1994.

Miller, Mary, and Karl Taube. *The Gods and Symbols of Ancient Mexico and the Maya: An Illustrated Dictionary of the Mesoamerican Religion*. London: Thames and Hudson, 1993.

Molnar, Michael R. *The Star of Bethlehem: The Legacy of the Magi*. New Brunswick, NJ: Rutgers University Press, 1999.

Morenz, Siegfried. *Egyptian Religion*. Ithaca, NY: Cornell University Press, 1992.

Morey, Robert A. *Horoscopes and the Christian: Does Astrology Accurately Predict the Future? Is It Compatible with Christianity?* Minneapolis: Bethany House Publishers, 1981.

Morley, Sylvanus. *An Introduction to the Study of Maya Hieroglyphics*. New York: Dover Publications, 1975.

Morton-Williams, Peter. "An Outline of the Cosmology and Cult Organisation of the Oyo Yoruba," *Africa: Journal of the International African Institute* 34, No. 3 (July 1964): 243–61.

Morton-Williams, Peter, William Bascom, and E. M. McClelland. "Two Studies of Ifa Divination. Introduction: The Mode of Divination," *Africa: Journal of the International African Institute* 36, No. 4 (October 1966): 406–31.

Müller, Max, trans. *Hymns of the Atharva Veda*, The Sacred Books of the East, Vol. 42. Delhi: Low Cost Publications, 1996 [1880].

Nabakov, Peter. *A Forest of Time: American Indian Ways of History*. Cambridge: Cambridge University Press, 2002.

Nakayama, Shigeru. "Characteristics of Chinese Astrology," *Isis* 57, No. 4 (Winter 1966): 442–54.

———. *A History of Japanese Astronomy: Chinese Background and Western Impact* (Cambridge, MA, Harvard University Press, 1969).

Narlikar, Jyanat V. "Vedic Astrology or Jyotirvigyan: Neither Vedic nor Vigyan," *Economic and Political Weekly* 36, No. 24 (June 16–11, 2001): 2113–15.

Nasr, Seyyed Hossein. *An Introduction to Islamic Cosmological Doctrines*. New York: State University of New York Press, 1993.

Naydler, Jeremy. *Shamanic Wisdom in the Pyramid Texts: The Mystical Tradition of Ancient Egypt*. Rochester: Inner Traditions, 2005.

———. *Temple of the Cosmos: The Ancient Egyptian Experience of the Sacred*. Rochester: Inner Traditions, 1996.

Needham, Joseph. *Science and Civilisation in China*, Vol. 3: "Mathematics and the Sciences of the Heavens and Earth." Cambridge: Cambridge University Press, 1959.

Ness, Lester. *Written in the Stars: Ancient Zodiac Mosaics*. Warren Center: Shangri La Publications 1999.

Neugebauer, Otto. *A History of Ancient Mathematical Astronomy*. Berlin: Springer Verlag, 1975.

Neugebauer, Otto, and R. A. Parker. *Egyptian Astronomical Texts*. Providence, RI: Brown University Press, 1960.

Nobel, Steve. "Hope Springs Eternal," *Alternatives* (Winter/Spring 2003): 1.

Noegel, Scott, ed. *Prayer, Magic, and the Stars in the Ancient and Late Antique World*. University Park: Pennsylvania State University Press, 2003.

Noonan, George C. *Classical Scientific Astrology*. Tempe: American Federation of Astrologers, 1984.

O'Brien, Patricia. "Prehistoric Evidence for Pawnee Cosmology," *American Anthropologist*, New Series 88, No. 4 (December 1986): 939–46.

O'Flaherty, Wendy Donniger, trans. *The Rig Veda: An Anthology*. London: Penguin, 1981.

Oken, Alan. *As Above, So Below: A Primary Guide to Astrological Awareness*. New York: Bantam Books, 1973.

———. *The Horoscope, the Road and Its Traveller: A Manual of Consciousness Expansion through Astrology*. New York: Bantam, 1974.

Opata, Damian U. "Cultural Astronomy in the Lore and Literature of Africa," in Jarita Holbrook, Rodney Medupe, and Johnson Urama (eds.), *African Cultural Astronomy: Current Archaoeastronomy and Ethnoastronomy Research in Africa*. Amsterdam: Springer Verlag, Astrophysics and Space Science Proceedings, 2008, 217–29.

Oppenheim, A. Leo. "A Babylonian Diviner's Manual," *Journal of Near Eastern Studies* 33 (January–October 1974): 197–220.

Orchiston, Wayne. "A Polynesian Astronomical Perspective: The Maori of New Zealand," in Helaine Selin (ed.), *Astronomy across Cultures: The History of Non-Western Astronomy*. Dordrecht: Kluwer Academic Publishers, 2000, 161–96.

Origen. *Works*, G. W. Butterworth, ed. Cambridge, MA: Harvard University Press, 1936.

Owusu, Maxwell. "Ethnography of Africa: The Usefulness of the Useless," *American Anthropologist*, New Series 80, No. 2 (June 1987): 310–34.

Pandya, Haribhai, Somdutt Dikshit, and N. M. Kansara. *Issues in Vedic Astronomy and Astrology*. Delhi: Motilal Banarsidass Publishers, 1992.

Pankenier, David W. "A Brief History of Beiji (Northern Culmen), with an Excursus on the Origin of the Character di," *Journal of the American Oriental Society* 124, No. 2 (April–June 2004): 211–36.

———. "Applied Field-Allocation Astrology in Zhou China: Duke Wen of Jin and the Battle of Chengpu (632 B.C.)," *Journal of the American Oriental Society* 119, No. 2 (April–June 1999): 261–79.

———. *Bringing Heaven Down to Earth in Ancient China*. Cambridge University Press, 2012.

———. "Characteristics of Field Allocation (*fenye*) Astrology in Early China," in J. W. Fountain and R. M. Sinclair (eds.), *Current Studies in Archaeoastronomy: Conversations across Time and Space*. Durham, NC: Carolina Academic Press, 2005, 499–513.

———. "Cosmic Capitals and Numinous Precincts in Early China," *Journal of Cosmology* 9 (2010): 2030–40.

———. "The Cosmo-political Background of Heaven's Mandate," *Early China* 20 (1995): 121–76.

———. "The Planetary Portent of 1524 in Europe and China," *The Journal of World History* 20, No. 3 (September 2009): 339–75.

Parker, R. A. "Ancient Egyptian Astronomy," *Philosophical Transactions of the Royal Society of London*, Series A, Mathematical and Physical Sciences 276, No. 1257: The Place of Astronomy in the Ancient World (May 2, 1974): 51–65.

———. *The Calendars of Ancient Egypt*. Chicago: Oriental Institute of Chicago, Studies in Ancient Oriental Civilization, No. 26, University of Chicago Press, 1950.

———. "Egyptian Astronomy, Astrology and Calendrical Reckoning," in Charles Coulston (ed.), *Dictionary of Scientific Biography.* New York: Charles Scribner's Sons, 1970, 706–27.

Parpola, Simo. *Letters from Assyrian and Babylonian Scholars.* Helsinki: Helsinki University Press, 1993.

———. *Letters from Assyrian Scholars to the Kings Esarhaddon and Assurbanipal,* part 1, texts. Neukirchen-Vluyn: Verlag Butzon & Bercker Kevelaer, 1970.

Pärssinen, Martti, Denise Schaan, and Alceu Ranzi. "Pre-Columbian Geometric Earthworks in the Upper Purús: A Complex Society in Western Amazonia," *Antiquity* 83, No. 322 (December 2009): 1084–96.

Philo. "On the Life of Moses," II.133–5, in *The Works of Philo*, trans. C. D. Yonge. Peabody: Hendrickson, 1993.

———. "On Providence," fr II, 48–54, in *The Works of Philo*, trans. C. D. Yonge. Peabody: Hendrickson, 1993.

Pingree, David. "Astronomy and Astrology in India and Iran," *Isis* 54, No. 2 (June 1963): 229–46.

———. "Classical and Byzantine Astrology in Sassanian Persia," *Dumbarton Oaks Papers* 43 (1989): 227–39.

———. *From Astral Omens to Astrology: From Babylon to Bikaner.* Rome: Istituto Italiano Per L'Africa E L'Oriente, 1997.

———. "Hellenophilia versus the History of Science," *Isis* 83 (1991): 554–63.

———. "Indian Astronomy," *Proceedings of the American Philosophical Society* 122, No. 6 (December 18, 1978): 361–64.

———. "Indian Planetary Images and the Tradition of Astral Magic," *Journal of the Warburg and Courtauld Institutes* 52 (1989): 1–13.

———. "Masha'allah's Zoroastrian Historical Astrology," in Gűnther Oestmann, H. K. von Stuckrad, G. Oestmann, and D. Rutkin (eds.), *Horoscopes and History.* Berlin: Walter de Gruyter, 2005, 95–100.

———. *The Thousands of Abu Ma'shar.* London: Warburg Institute, 1968.

———. *The Yavanajataka of Sphujidhvaja,* 2 vols., Harvard Oriental Series 48. Cambridge, MA: Harvard University Press, 1978.

Pingree, David, and Erica Reiner. *Babylonian Planetary Omens, Part 2, Enuma Anu Enlil, Tablets 50–51.* Malibu: Undena Publications, 1981.

Pistis Sophia. *Book One,* trans. Carl Schmidt and Violet Mcdermott, http://www.gnosis. org/library/psoph1.htm (accessed 14 May 2010).

Plato. *Epinomis,* trans. W. R. M. Lamb. Cambridge, MA: Harvard University Press, 1929.

———. *Phaedrus,* trans. H. N. Fowler. Cambridge, MA: Harvard University Press, 1914.

———. *Republic,* 2 vols., trans. Paul Shorey. Cambridge, MA: Harvard University Press, 1937.

———. *Timaeus,* trans. R. G. Bury. Cambridge, MA: Harvard University Press, 1931.

Pliny. *Natural History,* Vol. 1, book II, trans. H. Rackham. Cambridge, MA: Harvard University Press, 1929.

Plumley, J. M. "The Cosmology of Ancient Egypt," in Carmen Blacker and Michael Loewe (eds.), *Ancient Cosmologies.* London: George Allen and Unwin Ltd., 1975, 17–41.

Plutarch. "Isis and Osiris," *Moralia,* Vol. 5, trans. F. C. Babbit. Cambridge, MA: Harvard University Press, 1936.

Polkinghorne, John. *Faith, Science and Understanding.* London: Society for Promoting Christian Knowledge, 2000.

Pontifical Council for Culture, Pontifical Council for Interreligious Dialogue, *JESUS CHRIST THE BEARER OF THE WATER OF LIFE: A Christian reflection on the "New Age,"* (2003), http://www.vatican.va/roman_curia/pontifical_councils/interelg/documents/rc_pc_interelg_doc_20030203_new-age_en.html (accessed 18 April 2010).

Powell, Robert. *The Christ Mystery: Reflections on the Second Coming.* Fair Oaks, CA: Rudolf Steiner College Press, 1999.

Powers, William K. "Cosmology and the Reinvention of Culture: The Lakota Case," in Don McCaskill, "Amerindian Cosmology." *Canadian Journal of Native Studies and the Traditional Cosmology Society,* 1988, 161–80.

Prasad, Hari Shankar, ed. *Time in Indian Philosophy.* Delhi: Sri Satguru Publications, 1992.

Price-Williams, Douglass, and Rosslyn Gaines. "The Dreamtime and Dreams of Northern Australian Aboriginal Artists," *Ethos* 22, No. 3 (September 1994): 373–88.

Primack, Joel. "Cosmology and Culture," http://physics.ucsc.edu/cosmo/primack_abrams/COSMO.HTM (accessed 10 October 2010).

Pritchard, James B., ed. *Ancient Near Eastern Texts Relating to the Old Testament.* Princeton, NJ: Princeton University Press, 1969.

Ptolemy, Claudius. *Tetrabiblos,* trans. F. E. Robbins. Cambridge, MA: Harvard University Press, 1940.

Quirke, Stephen. *The Cult of Ra: Sun-worship in Ancient Egypt.* London: Thames and Hudson, 2001.

Raa, Eric Ten. "'The Moon as a Symbol of Life and Fertility in Sandawe Thought," *Africa: Journal of the International African Institute* 39, No. 1 (January 1969): 24–53.

Rai, Subas. *Kumbha Mela: History and Religion, Astronomy and Cosmobiology.* La Jolla: Entourage Publishing, 1993.

Raman, B. V. *A Manual of Hindu Astrology.* Bangalore: P. N. Kamat, 1979.

Redfield, Robert. "The Primitive World View," *Proceedings of the American Philosophical Society* 96 (1952): 30–36.

———. "Primitive World View and Civilizations," in *The Primitive World and Its Transformation.* Ithaca, NY: Cornell University Press, 1953.

Reichel, Elizabeth. "The Eco-Politics of Yakuna and Tanimuka Cosmology (Northwest Amazon, Colombia)," PhD Thesis, Cornell University, 1997.

Reichel-Dolmatoff, Gerardo. *Amazonian Cosmos: The Sexual and Religious Symbolism of the Tukano Indians.* Chicago: University of Chicago Press, 1971.

Reiner, Erica, *Astral Magic in Babylonia.* Philadelphia: American Philosophical Society, 1995.

Reiner, Erica, with David Pingree. *Babylonian Planetary Omens,* part 1: The Venus Tablet of Ammisaduqa, Enuma Anu Enlil, tablet 63. Malibu: Undena Publications, 1975.

Renshaw, Steven. On Japan, http://www2.gol.com/users/stever/jastro.html (accessed 21 August 2009).

Renshaw, Steven L., and Saori Ihara. "A Cultural History of Astronomy in Japan," in Helaine Selin (ed.), *Astronomy Across Cultures: The History of Non-Western Astronomy.* Dordrecht: Kluwer Academic Publishers, 2000, 385–407.

Roberts, Alexander, and James Donaldson, eds. *The Ante-Nicene Christian Library.* Edinburgh: Y and T Clark, 1847.

Roberts, Allen F. "'Comets Importing Change of Times and States': Ephemerae and Process among the Tabwa of Zaire," *American Ethnologist* 9, No. 4: Symbolism and Cognition LL (November 1982): 712–29.

Robinson, James M., ed. *The Nag Hammadi Library in English*. Leiden: Brill, 1988.

Rochberg, Francesca. *Babylonian Horoscopes*. Philadelphia: American Philosophical Society, 1998.

———. *The Heavenly Writing: Divination and Horoscopy, and Astronomy in Mesopotamian Culture*. Cambridge: Cambridge University Press, 2004.

———. *In the Path of the Moon: Babylonian Celestial Divination and Its Legacy*. Leiden: Brill, 2010.

The Roman Catholic Church, *Catechism of the Catholic Church 1994, Divination and magic, para. 2116*, http://www.christusrex.org/www1/CDHN/ccc.html.

Roob, Alexander. *Alchemy and Mysticism*. London: Taschen, 1997.

Rowlands, Michael, "The Role of Memory in the Transmission of Culture," *World Archaeology* 25, No. 2: Conceptions of Time and Ancient Society (October 1993): 141–51.

Rudhyar, Dane. *The Astrology of Personality*. Garden City, NY: Doubleday, 1970 [1936].

———. *The Astrology of Transformation: A Multilevel Approach*. Wheaton: Theosophical Publishing House, 1984 [1980].

Ruggles, Clive. "The Borana Calendar: Some Observations," *Archaeoastronomy, Supplement to the Journal for the History of Astronomy* 11 (1987): S35–S53.

———. "Cosmology, Calendar and Temple Orientations in Ancient Hawai'i," in Clive Ruggles and Gary Urton (eds.), *Skywatching in the Ancient World: New Perspectives in Cultural Astronomy*. Boulder: University Press of Colorado, 2007, 287–329.

Sachs, A. J. "Babylonian Horoscopes," *Journal of Cuneiform Studies* 6 (1952): 49–75.

———. "The Latest Datable Cuneiform Texts," in Barry L. Eichler (ed.), *Kramer Anniversary Volume: Studies in Honor of Samuel Noah Kramer, Alter Orient und Altes Testament* 25 (1976): 379–98.

Sagan, Carl. "Who Speaks for Planet Earth," Transcript for the final program in the "Cosmos" series, PBS (1980), http://www.cooperativeindividualism.org/sagan_cosmos_who_speaks_for_earth.html (accessed 4 March 2011).

Salaman, Clement, Dorine van Ovin, William D. Wharton, and Jean-Pierre Mahé. *The Way of Hermes: New Translations of the Corpus Hermeticum and the Definitions of Hermes Trismegistus to Asclepius*. Rochester: Inner Traditions, 2000.

Saliba, George. *A History of Arabic Astronomy: Planetary Theories during the Golden Age of Islam*. New York: New York University Press, 1994.

Sarma, K. V., trans., and with notes by T. S. K. Sastry. *Vedanga Jyotisa of Lagadha*. New Delhi: Indian National Science Academy, 1985.

Schafer, Edward H. *Pacing the Void: T'ang Approaches to the Stars*. Berkeley: University of California Press, 1977.

Schauss, Hayyim. *The Jewish Festivals: A Guide to Their History and Observance*. New York: Schocken Books, 1996.

Schwartz, Dov. *Studies in Astral Magic in Medieval Jewish Thought*. Leiden: Brill, 2004.

Schwartz, Howard. *Tree of Souls: The Mythology of Judaism*. Oxford: Oxford University Press, 2004.

Scott, Walter, trans. *Hermetica: The Ancient Greek and Latin Writings which contain Religious or Philosophic Teachings ascribed to Hermes Trismegistus*, 4 vols. Boulder, CO: Shambala, 1982.

Ségla, Dafon Aimeé. "The Cosmological Vision of the Yuruba-Idaaca of Benin Republic (West Africa): A Light on Yoruba History and Culture," in Jarita Holbrook, Rodney Medupe, and Johnson Urama (eds.), *African Cultural Astronomy: Current Archaoeastronomy and Ethnoastronomy Research in Africa.* Amsterdam: Springer Verlag, Astrophysics and Space Science Proceedings, 2008, 189–207.

Sen, S. N., *Hinduism.* London: Penguin, 1991.

Sen, S. N., and K. S. Shukla. *History of Astronomy in India.* New Delhi: Indian National Science Academy, 1985.

Seneca. *Naturales Questiones,* trans. T. H. Corcoran, 2 vols. Cambridge, MA: Harvard University Press 1971.

Seymour, Percy. *The Birth of Christ: Exploding the Myth.* London: Virgin Publishing Ltd., 1998.

Side, Wren. "Drawing Down the Moon and Candlemas Ritual Cake," in Chas. Clifton and Graham Harvey (eds.), *The Paganism Reader.* London: Routledge, 2004, 330–34.

Singh, Rana P.B. *Cosmic Order and Cultural Astronomy: Sacred Cities of India,* with a Foreword by John McKim Malville. Newcastle: Cambridge Scholars Publishing, 2009.

Sivin, Nathan. "State, Cosmos, and Body in the Last Three Centuries B.C.," *Harvard Journal of Asiatic Studies* 55, No. 1 (June 1995): 5–37.

———. *Granting the Seasons: The Chinese Astronomical Reform of 1280, With a Study of Its Many Dimensions and Annotated Translation of Its Records.* New York: Springer, 2009.

Smart, Ninian. *Dimensions of the Sacred: An Anatomy of the World's Beliefs.* Berkeley: University of California Press, 1996.

———. *The Science of Religion and the Sociology of Knowledge: Some Methodological Questions.* Princeton, NJ: Princeton University Press, 1973.

Smith, Brian K. *Classifying the Universe: The Ancient Indian Varna System and the Origins of Caste.* Oxford: Oxford University Press, 1994.

Smith, Jonathan Z. *Imagining Religion: From Babylon to Jonestown* Chicago: University of Chicago Press, 1982.

Smith, Mark S. "Democratization of the Afterlife," in Jacco Dieleman and Willeke Wendrich (eds.), *UCLA Encyclopedia of Egyptology.* Los Angeles, 2009, 1–16.

———. *The Priestly Vision of Genesis 1.* Minneapolis: Fortress Press, 2010.

Smith, Michael E. "Did the Maya Build Architectural Cosmograms?," *Latin American Antiquity* 16, No. 2 (June 2005): 217–24.

Snedegar, Keith. "Astronomical Practices in Africa South of the Sahara," in Helaine Selin(ed.), *Astronomy Across Cultures: The History of Non-Western Astronomy.* Dordrecht: Kluwer Academic Publishers, 2000, 455–74.

Sparks, H. F. D., ed. *The Apocryphal Old Testament.* Oxford: Clarendon Press, 1984.

Speiser, E. A. "The Creation Epic," in J. B. Pritchard (ed.), *Ancient Near Eastern Texts Relating to the Old Testament.* Princeton, NJ: Princeton University Press, 1969, 60–72.

Spence, Kate. "Ancient Egyptian Chronology and the Astronomical Orientation of Pyramids," *Nature* 408 (16 November 2000): 320–24.

Sperling, Harry, and Maurice Simon, eds. *The Zohar,* 5 vols. London: Soncino Press, 1949.

Spilsbury, Ariel, and Michael Bryner. *The Mayan Oracle: Return Path to the Stars.* Rochester: Bear and Company, 1992.

Šprajc, Ivan. "Astronomical Alignments at Teotihuacan, Mexico," *Latin American Antiquity* 11, No. 4 (June 2005): 403–15.

———. "More on Mesoamerican Cosmology and City Plans," *Latin American Antiquity* 16, No. 2 (June 2005): 209–16.

———. "The Venus-Rain-Maize Complex in the Mesoamerican World View," *Journal for the History of Astronomy* 24 (1993): 17–70.

Starhawk. *The Pagan Book of Living and Dying*. San Francisco: HarperCollins, 1997.

Stark, Rodney, and William Simms Bainbridge. *The Future of Religion: Secularization, Revival, and Cult Formation*. Berkeley: University of California Press, 1985.

Steele, John M. *A Brief Introduction to Astronomy in the Middle East*. London: Saqi Books, 2008.

———. *Calendars and Years: Astronomy and Time in the Ancient Near East*. Oxford: Oxbow Books, 2007.

Steiner, Rudolf. *An Autobiography*. New York: Steiner Books, 1980.

———. *The Reappearance of Christ in the Etheric*. Spring Valley, NY: Anthroposophic Press, 1983.

Steward, Julian H. "Notes on Hopi Ceremonies in their Initiatory Form in 1927–8," *American Anthropologist*, New Series 33, No. 1 (January–March 1931): 56–79.

Stone, Mark Van. *2012: Science and Prophecy of the Ancient Maya*. San Diego: Tlacaélel Press, 2010.

Strachan, Gordon. *Christ and the Cosmos*. Dunbar: Labarum Publications, 1985.

Stuart, D., and S. Houston. "Maya Writing," *Scientific American* (August 1989): 82–89.

Stuckrad, Kocku von. "Jewish and Christian Astrology in Late Antiquity—A New Approach," *Numen* XLVII, No. 1 (2000): 1–40.

Sugiyama, Saburo. "Teotihuacan City Layout As a Cosmogram: Preliminary Results of the 2007 Measurement Unity Study," in Iain Morley and Colin Renfrew (eds.), *The Archaeology of Measurement: Comprehending Heaven, Earth and Time in Ancient Societies*. Cambridge: Cambridge University Press, 2010, 111–49.

Sun, Xiaochun. "Crossing the Boundaries between Heaven and Man: Astronomy in Ancient China," in Helaine Selin (ed.), *Astronomy Across Cultures: The History of Non-Western Astronomy*. Dordrecht: Kluwer Academic Publishers, 2000, 423–54.

Sun, Xiaochun, and Jacob Kistemaker. *The Chinese Sky during the Han—Constellating Stars and Society*. Leiden: Brill, 1997.

Sutton, Komilla. *The Essentials of Vedic Astrology*. Bournemouth: Wessex Astrologer, 1999.

Swedenborg, Emanuel, *The New Jerusalem*, trans. John Chadwick. London: The Swedenborg Society, 1990.

Tacitus. *Histories and Annales*, trans. Clifford H. Moore. Cambridge, MA: Harvard University Press, 1925.

Tanakh: The Holy Scriptures. Philadelphia: Jewish Publication Society, 1985.

Tatian. *Oratio ad Graecos*, trans. Molly Whittaker. Oxford: Clarendon Press, 1982.

Tedlock, Barbara. *Time and Highland Maya*. Albuquerque: University of New Mexico Press, 1992.

Tedlock, Dennis, trans. *Popul Vuh*. London: Simon and Schuster, 1996.

Tedlock, Dennis, and Barbara Tedlock, eds. *Teachings from the American Earth: Indian Religion and Philosophy*. New York: Liveright, 1975.

Temple, Robert. *The Sirius Mystery*. London: Sidgwick and Jackson, 1976.

Tester, Jim. *A History of Western Astrology*. Woodbridge: Boydell Press 1987.

Thomas, Keith, *Religion and the Decline of Magic*. Harmondsworth: Peregrine Books, 1980 [1971].

Thompson, Eric. *A Commentary on the Dresden Codex*. Philadelphia: American Philosophical Society, 1972.

Thompson, R. Campbell. *The Reports of the Magicians and Astrologers of Nineveh and Babylon in the British Museum*, 2 vols. London: Luzac and Co., 1900.

Thompson, Richard L., *Vedic Cosmography and Astronomy*. Delhi: Motilal Banarsidass Publishers Private Ltd., 2004.

Thompson, Thomas L. *The Mythic Past: Biblical Archaeology and the Myth of Israel*. London: Jonathan Cape, 1992.

Thomsen, Dietrick. "What Mean These African Stones?," *Science News* 126, No. 11 (September 15, 1984):168–69, 174.

Thorndike, Lynn. *History of Magic and Experimental Science*, 8 vols. New York: Columbia University Press, 1923–58.

———. *The Sphere of Sacrobosco and Its Commentators*. Chicago: University of Chicago Press, 1949.

Thurman, Melburn D. "The Timing of the Skidi-Pawnee Morning Star Sacrifice," *Ethnohistory* 30, No. 3 (Summer 1983): 155–63.

Thurston, Hugh. "Aligning Giza: Astronomical Orientation of the Great Pyramid," *Griffith Observer* 65, No. 9 (September 2001): 11–17.

Tishby, Isaiah, ed. *The Wisdom of the Zohar: An Anthology of Texts*, trans. David Goldstein, 3 vols. Oxford: Oxford University Press, 1989.

Townsend, Richard. *The Aztecs*. London: Thames and Hudson, 1992.

Trachtenberg, Joshua. *Jewish Magic and Superstition*. Philadelphia: University of Pennsylvania Press, 2004.

The Traditional Cosmology Society, http://www.tradcos.co.uk/ (accessed 4 February 2010).

Trimble, Virginia. "Astronomical Investigation Concerning the So-Called Air-Shafts of Cheops' Pyramid," *Mitteilungen des deutsches Akademie Berlin*, Band 10 (1964): 183–87.

Tucker, Mary Evelyn. "Religious Dimensions of Confucianism: Cosmology and Cultivation," *Philosophy East and West* 48, No. 1: The Religious Dimension of Confucianism in Japan (January 1998): 5–45.

Turton, David, et al. "Agreeing to Disagree: The Measurement of Duration in a Southwestern Ethiopian Community [and Comments and Reply]," *Current Anthropology* 19, No. 3 (September 1978): 585–600.

Ulansey, David. *The Origins of the Mithraic Mysteries: Cosmology and Salvation in the Ancient World*. Oxford: Oxford University Press, 1989.

Unterman, Alan. *The Jews: Their Religious Beliefs and Practices*. Brighton: Sussex Academic Press, 1999.

Urban, Thomas G., *The Egyptian Book of the Dead: Documents in the Oriental Institute Museum at the University of Chicago*. Chicago: University of Chicago Press, 1960.

Urton, Gary. *At the Crossroads of the Earth and the Sky: An Andean Cosmology*, Latin American Monographs, no. 55. Austin: University of Texas Press, 1981.

Valens, Vettius. *The Anthology*, Books 1–5, trans. Robert Schmidt. Berkeley Springs, WV: Golden Hind Press, 1993–96.

Van der Waerden, Bartel. *Science Awakening*, II: The Birth of Astronomy. Leyden: Oxford University Press, 1974.

Van Seters, John. *In Search of History: Historiography in the Ancient World and the Origins of Biblical History*. New Haven, CT: Yale University Press, 1983.

Varisco, Daniel Martin. "Islamic Folk Astronomy," in Helaine Selin (ed.), *Astronomy Across Cultures: The History of Non-Western Astronomy*. Dordrecht: Kluwer Academic Publishers, 2000, 615–50.

———. "The Origin of the anwā' in Arab Tradition," *Studia Islamica*, No. 74 (1991): 5–28.

Vermes, G. *The Dead Sea Scrolls in English*. Harmondsworth: Pelican, 1962.

Viau, J. "Egyptian Mythology," in Felix Guirand, *Larousse Encyclopaedia of Mythology*, trans. Richard Aldington and Delano Ames. London: Paul Hamlyn, 1959, 8–48.

Vreede, Elisabeth. *Anthroposophy and Astrology*. Great Barrington: Anthroposophic Press, 2001.

Wallis, R. T. *Neoplatonism*. London: Duckworth, 1995.

Walters, Derek. *Chinese Astrology: Interpreting the Revelations of the Celestial Messages*. Wellingborough: Aquarian Press, 1987.

Warner, Brian. "Traditional Astronomical Knowledge in Africa," in Christopher Walker (ed.), *Astronomy before the Telescope*. London: British Museum Press, 1996, 304–17.

Wei Pang, Chao. "The Chinese Science of Fate Calculation," http://nirc.nanzan-u.ac.jp/publications/afs/pdf/a40.pdf (accessed 4 July 2011).

Wells, Martin. "The Messianic Star: A Critical Examination of Matthew 2 in Light of Astrological Astronomical Interpretations of the Star of Bethlehem," PhD diss., University of Wales, Lampeter, 2009.

Wells, Ronald A. "Astronomy in Egypt," in Christopher Walker (ed.), *Astronomy before the Telescope*. London: British Museum Press, 1996, 28–41.

Wheatley, Paul. *The Pivot of the Four Quarters: A Preliminary Enquiry into the Origin and Character of the Ancient Chinese City*. Edinburgh: Edinburgh University Press, 1971.

White, Isobel. "Sexual Conquest and Submission in the Myths of Central Australia," in L. R. Hiatt (ed.), *Australian Aboriginal Mythology*. Canberra: Australian Institute of Aboriginal Studies, 1975, 123–42.

White, John. *The Ancient History of the Maori, His Mythology and Traditions*, Vol. 1. Wellington: Government Printer, 1887.

Wilhelm, Richard. *The I Ching or Book of Changes*, 3rd ed. London: Routledge and Kegan Paul, 1968.

Wilkinson, Richard H. *The Complete Temples of Ancient Egypt*. London: Thames and Hudson, 2000.

———. *Symbol and Magic in Egyptian Art*. London: Thames and Hudson, 1994.

Williamson, Ray A. *Living the Sky: The Cosmos of the American Indian*. Norman: University of Oklahoma Press, 1987.

Williamson, Ray A., and Claire R. Farrer, eds. *Earth and Sky: Visions of the Cosmos in Native American Folklore*. Albuquerque: University of New Mexico Press, 1992.

Williamson, Robert. *Religious and Cosmic Beliefs of Central Polynesia*, 2 vols. Cambridge: Cambridge University Press, 1933.

Willis, Roy, and Patrick Curry. *Astrology, Science and Culture: Pulling Down the Moon*. Oxford: Berg, 2004.

Wilson, Bryan. *Religion in Secular Society: A Sociological Comment*. Harmondsworth: Pelican, 1969.

Wolfe, Patrick. "On Being Woken Up: The Dreamtime in Anthropology and in Australian Settler Culture," *Comparative Studies in Society and History* 33, No. 2 (1991): 197–224.

Wolfson, Elliot R. *Through a Speculum That Shines: Vision and Imagination in Medieval Jewish Mysticism*. Princeton, NJ: Princeton University Press, 1994.

Wright, J. Edward. *The Early History of Heaven*. Oxford: Oxford University Press, 2000.

Wright, M. R. *Cosmology in Antiquity*. London: Routledge, 1995.

Xu, Zhenoao, David W. Pankenier, and Yaotiao Jiang. *East Asian Archaeoastronomy: Historical Records of Astronomical Observations of China, Japan, and Korea*. Amsterdam: Gordon and Breach Science Publishers, 2000.

Yinger, J. Milton. "A Structural Examination of Religion." *Journal for the Scientific Study of Religion* 8 (Spring 1969): 88–99.

Yogananda, Paramahansa. *Autobiography of a Yogi*. Los Angeles: Self-Realization Fellowship, 1988.

York, Michael. *Historical Dictionary of New Age Movements*. Lanham, MD: Scarecrow, 2003.

———. *The Emerging Network: A Sociology of the New Age and Neo-Pagan Movements*. London: Rowman and Littlefield, 1995.

Young, M. Jane. *Signs from the Ancestors; Zuni Cultural Symbolism and Perceptions of Rock Art*. Albuquerque: University of New Mexico Press, 1988.

Zaehner, Richard Charles. *Zurvan: A Zoroastrian Dilemma*. Oxford: Clarendon Press, 1955.

Žabkar, Louis. *A Study of the Ba Concept in Ancient Egyptian Texts*, Studies in Ancient Oriental Civilization 34. Chicago: University of Chicago Press, 1968.

Zahan, Dominique. *The Religion, Spirituality and Thought of Traditional Africa*. Chicago: University of Chicago Press, 1979.

Zaidman, Louise Bruit, and Pauline Schmidt Pantel. *Religion in the Ancient Greek City*, trans. Paul Cartledge. Cambridge: Cambridge University Press, 1994.

Index

Abbasid dynasty, 174, 175
Aboriginal culture and cosmology: astrology of, 30; astronomy, 19, 28–29; collapse of culture, 25; emergent and chaotic cosmology, 24–25, 31; gendered cosmos of, 29; rock art, 30–31
Abraham, 137, 142
Abu Ma'shar, 174, 184, 186
Acausal synchronicity, Jung's, 15
Africa and Sub-Saharan Africa, 24, 69–81; Arabic influences on, 80; bodily markings in, 80; calendars of, 74–75, 78; cosmology defined in pre-modern, 6; deities in, 77; Dogon controversy and, 70, 75–76; human evolution beginning in, 71–72; humanist cosmology of, 73; Islamic influences in, 69, 72–73, 74, 80, 81; limited knowledge concerns for, 70; major characteristics of cosmology, 72–73; Muslims in, 70; regional divisions of, 69–70; religion in, 72, 77, 81; scholarship on, 71–72; sources on, 71; timekeeping in, 73–75; Western influence, 70, 80–81
Age of Aquarius. See Aquarian Age
Ah Kin (Mayan priest), 62
Ahül (Sun kachina), 50–51
Alexander the Great, 133
Algonquin, sky poem of, 44–45
Alternatives (group), 196
Amazon, monumental remains recently found in, 55
Amenope, 90
Amidah (Jewish prayer), 141
Andean culture, 54–68; astrology of, 54–55, 61–62, 68; chaotic astrology in, 68; four-fold cosmos of, 57–58
Animal symbols, in Chinese Jupiter cycle, 107–8
Anthroposophical Society, 194

Apache rituals, 51
Apocalyptic prophecies, alleged Mayan calendar, 64
Aquarian Age, 188, 191, 194–98; Bailey on, 195–96; esoteric Christians and, 193–94, 196
Aquinas, Thomas (saint), 170, 171
Arabic astrology, 80, 101, 174
Arabic-speaking world, 175, 177, 182, 186–87; folk-astronomy and, 173–74
Arguelles, Jose, 64
Aristotle, 155–56, 159, 179, 181; survival and nature of works by Plato and, 149–50
Assyrian period, 125, 126, 129, 130
Astrology: astronomy as interchangeable with, 11; classical, 15–16, 162; cosmology context for defining, 1–2; cultural assumptions for, 12; definitions of, 11–23; diversity in, 15–16, 23; as divination, 158–59; evangelical opposition to, 165, 169, 172; as instrument of state, 94, 95, 121; interpretive, 91, 92, 93; meaning construction in, 15, 37; New Age, 196–97, 198; pagan calendrical, 199; rationale for, 13–14; reflective, 13–14, 96; relationship premise of, 14; as religion, 20–23; scholarship on, 12–13; sociology and, 19–20; symbolic language of, 17–18; technical and interpretive treatises on, 13; Thomas on Western, 19–20; as universal and culture-specific, 17–18; use of term, 11; Western types of, 16; word derivation, 11. See also Chaotic astrology; Cosmic astrology; Judicial astrology; Natural astrology; specific cultures; specific regions
Astrology, Science and Culture (Curry and Willis), 12
Astrology and Popular Religion in the Modern West (Campion), 12
Astron, 11

Astronomy: astrology as interchangeable with, 11; cosmology branch of, 3–4; cultural and ethno-, 2; McCluskey on predictive, 62; Newtonian view, 2; phenomena types in pre-modern, 14–15; use of term, 11. *See also specific cultures*

Atharva Veda, time personified in, 122

Atheism, Newtonians and, 2

Atomism, 149

Augustine (saint), 169–70, 171

Australia, 24–32; artifacts indicating antiquity of astronomy in, 24; religious concerns in, 32; sources on, 25–26, 31. *See also* Aboriginal culture and cosmology

Aveni, Anthony, 18–19; on calendrical shamans, 62–63; on Mayan astronomy as astrological, 62, 63–64; Quetzalcoatl story told by, 60

Averroës (Ibn Rushd), 180–81

Avicenna (Ibn Sina), 180, 181

Aztec culture, 3, 64; deities and cosmogony of, 57–60, 65, 67; four worlds of, 58; warning signs seen by, 63

Babylon, 15, 124–34, 139, 156; deities of, 127–34; Egypt's zodiac from, 92; empires, 126; Greece and, 157; interpretive astrology as imported from, 91, 93; Judah conquest by, 137; naturalistic cosmology of, 127; temples of, 133; van der Waerden on astrology in, 20–21

Bailey, Alice, 164, 194, 195–96

Bailey, Clinton, 179

Barasana people, 62

Barrumbir (Aboriginal), 28–29

Bath Spa University, 9

Being and Becoming, Plato's, 152, 181

Bennett, Julius, 21

Besant, Annie, 196–97

Best, Elsdon, 34, 35, 38, 39

Bethlehem star, 166, 168, 169

Bible: Christian literature not included in, 162; sections of (as *Tanakh*), 136

Big Dipper, in Apache ritual, 51

Bird-Milky Way analogy, 45

Blavatsky, H. P., 189, 192–93, 196–97

Book of Splendor (*Zohar*), 145–46

The Book of the Dead, 88

Boorong people, 29

Borana calendar, 74–75

Brhat Samhita (Varahamihira), 111, 121

Buddhism: Indian astrology and, 121–22; temples, 120

Bushmen (San), 76, 77–78

Calendars: African, 74–75, 78; Chinese, 95, 101–2; Christian festivals and, 165–66; Egypt's pre-dynastic, 86–88, 90, 93; Hebrew, 139–40; Incan rituals associated with, 65–66; Indian festivals based on, 115–16; Islamic, 175; Jewish festivals and, 139–40, 146; Maya, 64; Mesoamerican 260 day-count, 64; Mesopotamian, 128–29, 131; Native American ritual importance of, 43; pagan, 199

Calendrical shamans, 20, 54, 62–63

Campion, Nicholas, 12, 13

Carter, Charles, 197

Cassidy, Laurence, 170

Caste system, 115

Catholic Church, 162, 164; astrology-as-divination in current catechism, 170; Roman, 163–64, 165, 170

Central America. *See* South and Central America

Chaco Canyon, New Mexico, 52

Chamberlain, Von Del, 41, 45

Chaotic astrology, 23, 62; Andean culture, 68; in Australia, 24–25, 31; cosmic astrology distinguished from, 81; Mesopotamia's, 124–25. *See also* Cosmic astrology

Chaotic cosmogonies, 54, 93, 109, 126–27, 133; Native American cosmic and, 53

Chaotic cosmology, 40, 76, 123

China and Chinese cosmology, 3, 94–109; astronomy, 99–100; calendars, 95, 101–2; celestial deities in, 99; communism and, 108–9; constellations of, 104; cosmogony of, 97, 109; cosmology defined in pre-modern, 6; deities of, 99, 104; divinatory oracle bones in, 100; influence on other cultures, 95; nature-based cosmology,

99; physical and medical applications of, 109; planets and planetary cycles in, 105–6; religion of, 99–100, 109; sacred building orientation in, 109; scholarship on, 96–97; supernovas recorded in, 100; symbolism in, 102; Warring States period, 102

Chinese astrology, 101–2; as arm of state, 94, 95; crucial concept in, 102; Fate-Calculation in, 94, 95, 109; Field Allocation in, 105; Five Phases in, 98, 105, 107, 108; fourness theme in, 104; horoscopes in, 101, 108; *Hsiu* lunar zodiac, 101, 104, 107; If-then formula in, 106; Jupiter cycle and animal symbols in, 107–8; local weather influencing, 106–7; official astrologer incident in 1300s, 103–4; political use of, 104–5; precision and exactitude in, 94–95; tradition, 94–95

Chinese Astrology (Walters), 13

Christ: Bailey on New Age and, 196; cosmic, 161; Steiner on second coming of, 195

Christianity and Christian cosmology, 161–72; astrology-as-divination objection, 170; astrology objections and support in, 162, 163, 165–72; Augustine's attack on astrology, 169–70, 171; Bethlehem star omen, 166, 168, 169; calendar and festivals in, 165–66; Christmas and, 165–66, 172; classical Greek astrology inherited by, 162; cosmogony of, 163, 164, 172; cosmological literature, 162–63; diversity of, 161, 163, 164, 172; dualistic cosmology of, 163; emanationism and transcendence conflict, 164; Gnosticism, 161, 162, 167–68; Hawaiian cosmogony similarity to, 34–35; Kabbalah and, 144; metaphorical-literal opposition in, 164–65, 166; Piscean Age and, 195; Platonism and, 152, 162, 164, 167; principles of, 163; scholarship on astrology and, 163; seven and twelve in, 167; sources on, 162–63; Theosophical Society's esoteric, 193–94; trinity of, 161; zodiac in, 167

Christianization, 34–35, 70, 80–81

Christmas, 165–66, 172

Classical astrology, 15–16, 162

Classical Gnosticism, 4–5

Comets, in Oceanian astrology, 38

Comparative religion, 2

Confucius, 96, 99, 104

Conjunctional theory, Persian, 182–83

Cosmic astrology: chaotic distinguished from, 81; China's astrology as, 109; India's, 123; Islamic cosmology and, 187; Mayan astrology as, 54, 68. *See also* Chaotic astrology

Cosmic piety, Festugière's, 5

Cosmic State, 2

Cosmogonies: Aztec deities and, 57–60, 65, 67; chaotic, 53, 54, 93, 109, 126–27, 133; Chinese, 97; Christian, 163, 164, 172; Egyptian, 85, 93; Greek, 151, 152–53; Indian, 113, 114; Jewish, 138; Kaballah, 145; Mayan, 56–57, 58; Mesopotamian, 124, 126–27, 133–34; Native American, 46–47; Platonic, 152–53; Polynesian, 34–36; South and Central America, 54

Cosmology: astronomy branch of, 3–4; definitions of, 1–8, 10; Gnostic view of, 4–5, 168; modern, 7–8; New Age, 190, 191, 192; New Age and pagan, 192; pagan, 192, 198; Plato's works dealing with, 150; political ideology and, 2, 40, 54, 103, 104, 146; pre-modern cultural definitions of, 6–7; Steiner's historical, 194–95. *See also specific cultures; specific regions*

Cosmotheism: Chinese, 109; Egyptian, 83

Council of Nicaea, 165

Crane, Pam, 21

Creation stories. See Cosmogonies

Crowley, Vivianne, 192

Cultures: astrology as both universal and specific to, 17–18; astrology assumptions in various, 12; cosmic astrological, 81; cosmology defined by pre-modern, 6–7; cultural astronomy, 2; modern Western religious, 188; sky viewed by, 3; star myths common to most, 30. *See also* New Age culture; *specific cultures*

Curry, Patrick, 12

India and Indian cosmology, 95–96; architecture, 115; astronomical alignment of sacred sites, 115; calendar and calendar festivals, 115–16; caste system, 115; chaotic cosmology with cosmic astrology, 123; Chinese contact with, 101, 108; cosmogony of, 113, 114; earliest known civilization, 112–13; Egyptian influence on, 82; Greek contact with, 110; Mesopotamian influence on, 124; scholarship on, 110–11; snycretic cosmology, 114. *See also* Hinduism

Indian astrology, 110–23; Buddhism and, 121–22; calendar festivals in, 115–16; classic texts on, 119; as cosmic, 123; horoscope in, 110, 116–19; interpretive functions, 120; *jyotish* as astronomy and, 110; *Nakshatras* and zodiac of, 113, 117–18; planets in, 117, 119; *prasna* question in, 117; predictions in, 121; reincarnation and, 118; relational nature of, 113; religion central to, 123; ritual use in, 120; scholarship on, 110–11; secondary horoscope (*navamsha*), 118; sources on, 111; time and, 111, 119–20, 122; tradition of technical, 110; zodiac in, 116, 117

Indus Valley, 112

Influentiae, 155

Initiatory knowledge, 43

Iroquois people, 46

Islam and Islamic cosmology, 173–87; Abbasid dynasty and, 174, 175; Africa influenced by, 69, 72–73, 74, 80, 81; astrological talismans in, 185; astrology and anti-astrology in, 176–82; basis of cosmology, 175; calendar of, 175; contribution of Islamic astrologers, 182; cosmology and astrology as cosmic, 187; folk-astronomy and, 179; geographical boundaries of, 173; Golden Age of, 173, 174, 186; horoscopes, 183–84; influences on, 174–75; "Islamic cosmology" ambiguity, 173; Jupiter-Saturn cycles and, 174; Koran, 174, 175–81; Koranic vs. Arabic-speaking broader context for, 186–87; magic defined in, 185; main features of,

175; Neoplatonism and, 180–81, 183; Persian conjunctional theory significance to, 182–84; planetary combinations and warnings, 183–84; Plato and, 144, 177, 179; scholarship on, 173–74; sources on, 174, 175–76, 178; South Africa influenced by, 79; sun in daily prayer cycle, 179; *Tabula Smaragdina*, 13, 186; three faiths converged in, 173; two cosmology definitions in, 186–87. *See also* Koran

Israel, split into two sections, 137

Israelites, 140–41

Jacobs, Louis, 137

Japan, 101

Jewish astrology: context for practice of, 142; Kabbalistic practices of, 146; Moses Maimonides exemplifying, 143; prophetic condemnation of foreign astrology, 141–42; sanctioned and forbidden, 137–38, 141, 147; symbolism, 142; technical astrology of Kaballah, 145–46. *See also* Judaism and Jewish cosmology

Jonas, Hans, 4

Jones, Prudence, 190

Josephus (Jewish historian), 142

Judah, Babylon conquest of, 137

Judaism and Jewish cosmology, 135–47; Amidah as central prayer in, 141; Aristotelian dilemma in, 143; astral religion through ritual calendar, 140; astrology as invented in, 142; calendar and festivals, 139–40, 146; celestial omens of God, 141–42, 147; cosmogony of, 146; early and later forms of God in, 137–38; Exodus, 137, 140–41; female deities in, 146; historicity to ultra-revisionist views of, 135; horoscopes opposed in, 143; Jewish religion emergence, 135; judicial astrology rejected by, 137–38, 143; Kabbalah, 137, 143–46, 147; literary sources on, 136–37; modern, 146; Philo's Jewish Platonism, 142–43; planet worship dilemma in, 136; politics of ritual in, 140; pre-modern history, 137–38; prophetic distinguished from vernacular traditions, 136; Rabbinic period, 138; royal phase of, 137; sun and moon in, 139, 141, 146; time as God's control of creation, 140; Torah/Genesis, 138

Judicial astrology, 16; Greek, 147; Judaism and, 137–38, 143. *See also* Natural astrology

Jung, C. G., 7, 171; acausal synchronicity, 15; as astrologer, 18; on Piscean and Aquarian Ages, 195

Jupiter: Chinese animal symbols in cycle of, 107–8; in Chinese cosmology, 100; in Indian astrology, 119; in Mesopotamian cosmology, 128

Jupiter-Saturn conjunctions, in Islamic astrology, 182–84, 186

Jupiter-Saturn cycles, Persian astrology's, 174, 182

Juwuku (Australian), 30

Jyotish (Indian astronomy and astrology), 110

Kaaba, 179

Kabbalah, 137, 143–46, 147; core text of, 144; cosmogony, 145; *sephirot* of, 143–44; technical astrology of, 145–46

Kachina, 50–51

Kane (Polynesian creator), 35–36

Kemper, Stephen, 21–22, 111

Kepelino, 35

Khumba Mela, 116

King Lear, 11

Kingsley, Peter, 148

Kinship systems, 5

Kivas, 47

Koran, 174, 175–76, 178, 179, 180, 181

Kosmos, 2–3, 5

Krupp, Ed, 17

Kublai Khan, 95

Lakota people, 5, 50

Language: African divisions by, 69; cosmology definitions and, 2–3; Mesopotamian cosmology and, 131; symbolic, 17–18. See also Arabic-speaking world

Lao Tzu, 98–99

Latuka people, 74

Lau, Theodora, 108

Legresse, Asmaron, 75

Leland, Charles G., 44–45

Leo, Alan, 197

Leucippus, 149

Lévi-Strauss, Claude, 18

Lévy-Bruhl, Lucien, 62; participation mystique, 16, 72

Lewis, David, 33

Life-world, 12

Llama constellation, 61

Logos, 11

Lovejoy, Arthur, 14

Lunar counters, Australian, 24

Lunar zodiac: *Hsiu* as Chinese, 101, 104, 107; India's, 113; Mesopotamia's, 128

Luo people, 74, 79

Ma'at (Egyptian personified order), 86, 88, 90, 93

Machina mundi, 68, 86, 119–20

MacPherson, Peter, 28

MacQuarie University, 26

Magic, 92–93, 185

Maimonides, Moses, 143

Malville, Kim, 115

Maori culture, 34, 38–39

Marduk (Babylonian deity), 127, 128, 131–32

Martyr, Justin, 168

Marxism, 8

Masah'allah, 174, 183

Mathew, Freya, 5–6

Mayan culture, 3, 54–68; astrology, 54, 62, 63, 68; astronomy as astrological in function, 62, 63–64; calendar, 64; cosmogony, 56–57, 58; deciphering of Maya script, 56; four worlds of, 58; religious-cosmic structure of state in, 67–68

Mbiti, John S., 71, 73

McCluskey, Stephen, 6, 19, 42, 62

McIntosh, R. J., 77

Mecca, alignment of, 179

Medicine wheels, 52

Medupe, Thebe, 70

Melanesia, 33
Mercury-Venus conjunction, 106
Mescalero Apache, 51
Mesoamerican culture and cosmology, 54–68; astrology in, 54–55, 61–64; calendar, 64; Cuzo pillar system, 68; deities in, 59–60; Maya script deciphering, 56; monotheism and polytheism in, 58–59; pyramids in, 67–68; resurrection themes in, 60; sacred architecture of, 66–67; sacrifice in, 65
Mesopotamian astrology: birth charts and planetary personalities in, 132; constellations and zodiac, 128; cosmological rationale for, 130; growth from chaotic to meaning-infused, 124–25; religion and, 129, 132–33; surviving texts on, 126
Mesopotamian culture and cosmology, 124–34; calendar and festivals, 128–29, 131; cosmogony of, 124, 126–27, 133–34; Greece influenced by cosmogony of, 124; overview of systems and influences of, 124; paradox in, 133–34; political and social organization, 125–26; scholarship on, 125; time in, 130
Meteors, 30, 38
Micronesia, 33
Milky Way-bird analogy, 45
Mithraism, 158
Modern cosmology, 7–8
Modern Text Book of Astrology (Hone), 13, 132
Mohammed, 175, 179, 183
Monarchy, 99
Mongols, Baghdad sacked by, 186
Monotheism, 45–46, 58–59; solar, 171
Moon: Babylonian omens of, 130; blemishes on surface of, 58, 62; in Egyptian cosmology, 89; fertility and, 30; in Islamic cosmology, 175, 179; in Jewish cosmology, 139, 141, 146; Pyramid of, 67; stories of hare and, 76
Morning star ceremony, 28
Muqaddimah (Ibn Khaldun), 178
Muslims, in Sub-Saharan Africa, 70

Nadi astrology (Palm-leaf horoscopes), 118–19
Nakshatras (in Indian astrology), 113, 117–18
Na Reau (Polynesian creator), 36
Native American cosmologies, 13, 41–53; astrology, 48–49, 51, 53; astronomical tales of, 44–45; astronomy links with Europe, Asia and, 44; calendrical ritual importance in, 43; common patterns across, 43; cosmogony and, 46–47; diversity of, 42; electional astrology of, 53; four-fold cosmos of, 49–50; geographical boundaries of North America, 42; McCluskey on, 6; monument-building practices, 52–53; orientation of dwellings, 51–52; politics of studying, 41; possible Christianization as difficulty in studying, 42–43; religion in, 53; scholarship on, 41–42; secrecy of knowledge, 43; sources on, 42–43; sun worship in, 45, 50, 51. See also specific tribes
The Native Tribes of Central Australia (Gillen and Spencer), 26
Natural astrology, 16, 34, 38, 39, 79. See also Judicial astrology
Naturalistic cosmology, Babylonian, 127
Navamsha (secondary horoscope), 118
Needham, Joseph, 96, 97, 107; Chinese astronomy and religion viewed by, 100; skepticism on Greek astronomy in China, 101
Neoplatonism, 152, 190; Islamic, 180–81, 183
New Age and Paganism, 188–99; astrology distinctions between, 198; astrology's role in, 196–97; collective action required for New Age, 196; common and diverse origins of, 191–92; controversial combining of, 188–89; cosmological differences between, 192; New Age cosmology, 190, 191, 192; politics of Esoteric Christian New Age, 196; privatized spirituality in, 188, 199; roots of, 188; scholarship on, 189; sources on, 189; time viewed by, 191, 192; transcendence

and, 189, 190, 199. *See also* Blavatsky, H. P.; Paganism

New Age culture: Aquarian Age and, 188, 191; Christianity in, 164; Egyptian cosmology in, 93; globalizing tendencies of, 25; Maya calendar misunderstanding in, 64; Native American lore in, 43; personal transformation central to, 190; privatized spirituality of, 188; *sensu stricto* and *sensu lato*, 191; Vatican document on, 171; York on, 189–90, 196

New Testament: astrology and, 166–67; books excluded from, 162

Newtonian view, astronomical theory in, 2

New Zealand, 33; Maori culture of, 34, 38–39

Nile River, 86, 87

Nobel, Steve, 196

North America. *See* Native American cosmologies

Oceania, 33–40; astrology in, 37–40; astronomy's importance to travelers in, 37; calendar of, 36, 37; geography of, 33; Pleiades in, 33; Polynesian zones of, 33. *See also* New Zealand; Polynesia

Ohrmazd (Persian creator), 175

Oken, Alan, 197

Old Testament, 138–39, 171, 177

Oracle bones, 100

Orange Free State. *See* Free State, South Africa

Paganism, 167–68; astrology and, 165; calendrical astrology, 199; competing definitions of, 190; cosmology of, 192, 198; Kaaba, 179; northern and Near East distinction in, 191–92, 198; roots of New Age and, 188. *See also* New Age and Paganism

Palace of the Governor, Mesoamerican, 66

Palm-leaf horoscopes, 118–19

participation mystique, Lévy-Bruhl's, 16, 72

Pascal, Blaise, 5

Passover, 139, 165

Persian culture and astrology, 108, 126, 175; conjunctional theory of, 182–84; Islamic astrology influenced by, 174–75; Jupiter-Saturn cycles, 174, 182; religion and, 161–62, 182–83

Peru, 56

Philo of Alexandria, 142–43

Physics, 7–8, 116, 120, 150, 156, 165

Picatrix, 184

Piety, cosmic, 5

Pingree, David, 148, 174

Piscean Age, 195

Plato and Platonism, 7, 142–43, 148–57; Aristotle's works compared to, 149–50; Being and Becoming, 152, 181; Christianity influenced by, 152, 162, 164, 167; cosmogony of, 152–53; fate and choice in system of, 153–54, 156; Islam influenced by, 177; Judaism and, 144; Kabbalah and, 143–44; Mithraism as religious application of, 158; Neoplatonism, 152, 180–81, 183, 190; New Age transcendence and, 190; physical cosmos of, 153; planetary personalities contribution of, 157; predecessors, 152; revelatory quality of, 148–49; surviving works of Aristotle and, 149–50; tripartite soul concept of, 154

Pleiades: in Aboriginal astronomy, 28–29; Incan view of, 60; MacPherson's Stanbridge on, 28; Mesoamerican view of, 60–61; Native American cosmologies and, 44; in Oceania, 33; in Polynesian astronomy, 37

Pliny, 4

Plumed Serpent, 57, 59–60

Plumley, J. M., 86

Political ideology: Chinese astrology and, 103, 104–5; cosmologies and, 2, 40, 54, 140, 146

Polkinghorne, John, 7, 165

Polynesia, 34–40; astrology of, 38–39; chief celestial bodies in, 36–37; Christianization and, 34–35; cosmogony, 34–36; cosmology as chaotic, 40; lost sky lore of, 40; myth of Na Reau, 36;

Stanbridge, W. E., 28
Star clocks, Egyptian, 90
Starhawk, 192, 198, 199
Star myths: Imperishable Stars of Egyptian cosmology, 88–89; meteor collisions in, 30
Star Stories, 17, 19, 77
Steiner, Rudolf, 164, 194–95
Steward, Julian H., 50
Stoicism (Greek), 14, 133, 156, 157, 159, 190
Structuralism, Lévi-Strauss's, 18
Sub-Saharan Africa. See Africa and Sub-Saharan Africa
Sufism, 182
Sun, 91; African calendars marked by, 78; Aquarian Age, 191; in Chinese cosmology, 103, 105; in Egyptian cosmology, 82, 85–86, 87, 88–89; Incan rituals involving, 66; in Islamic prayer, 179; in Jewish cosmology, 139, 141, 146; in Mesoamerican cultures, 59; in Native American cosmologies, 45, 50, 51; Pyramid of, 67; solar monotheism, 171; solar zodiac of Mesopotamia, 128; Venus at war with, 60; Venus conjunction with, 64–65; watcher, 50–51
Supernovas, China's recording of, 100

Tabula Smaragdina (Islamic Emerald Tablet), 13, 185–86
Tanakh (Bible), three sections of, 136
Tang dynasty, 101
Tao Te Ching (Lao Tzu), 98–99
Tatian the Syrian, 168
Tecuciztecatl (Aztec creator), 58
Temple, Robert, 75
Temples, 120, 133
Têng Mu, 97
Teotihuacan, Pyramid of the Sun in, 67
Thailand, 95
Theosophical Society, 192; esoteric Christians in, 193–94
Thomas, Keith, 19–20
Thorndike, Lynn, 12–13, 163
Thoth (Egyptian deity), 89
Tiamat (Babylonian goddess), 127

Timaeus (Plato), 150, 152
Time: African approach to, 73–75; deification of, 18; early Christianity view of, 162; Egyptian attitude towards, 93; four-fold division of space and, 49–50; Indian astrology and, 111, 119–20, 122; Indian yugas, 114; Jewish God's control through, 140; Mesoamerican management of, 65; Mesopotamian principle of, 130; New Age distinguished from pagan attitudes toward, 191, 192
Tiwi people, 29–30
Tohunga kokorangi (Maori), 38–39
Tonalpohualli. See Tzolkin/Tonalpohualli
Torah: complexities of Genesis, 138; cosmology in, 138–39. See also Old Testament
Transcendence: emanationism and, 164; New Age and, 189, 190, 199
Tyon (Lakota wise man), 50
Tzolkin/Tonalpohualli (Mesoamerican 260 day-count), 64

Universus, 2–3
Unus verto, 3
Ursa Major. See Great Bear

Vaastu (Indian architecture), 115
Van der Waerden, Bartel, 20–21, 132–33
Varahamihira, 111, 121
Vatican document, on New Age culture, 171
Vedas (Indian sacred texts), 110, 112–13, 122
Venus: in Aboriginal astronomy, 29; Chinese text on, 107; conjunction with Mercury, 106; conjunction with sun, 64–65; in Indian astrology, 119; in Mesoamerican cosmologies, 59–60, 66–67; morning star ceremony, 28; at war with sun, 60
Vernacular religion, astrology as, 22

Walking the songlines, 32
Walters, Derek, 13, 96
Warring States period, China, 102
Washington Post, 122–23

About the Author

NICHOLAS CAMPION is Senior Lecturer in Archaeology and Anthropology and Director of the Sophia Centre for the Study of Cosmology in Culture at the University of Wales, Lampeter. His books include *History of Western Astrology Volume I: The Ancient and Classical Worlds* and *History of Western Astrology Volume II: The Medieval and Modern Worlds.*

Lightning Source UK Ltd.
Milton Keynes UK
UKHW010727280619

345201UK00001B/147/P